I0760148

HITLER'S WAR AGAINST POLAND'S PARTISANS

HITLER'S WAR AGAINST POLAND'S PARTISANS

THE BATTLE BEHIND THE EASTERN FRONT 1939–1945

DR ANTONIO J. MUÑOZ

FRONTLINE BOOKS

HITLER'S WAR AGAINST POLAND'S PARTISANS
The Battle Behind the Eastern Front 1939–1945

First published in Great Britain in 2025
by Frontline Books
An imprint of
Pen & Sword Books Ltd
Yorkshire - Philadelphia

ISBN 978 1 03613 346 7

A CIP catalogue record for this book is available from the British Library

Typeset by Lapiz Digital
Printed and bound in the UK by CPI Group (UK) Ltd,
Croydon, CR0 4YY.

Printed on paper from a sustainable source by
CPI Group (UK) Ltd, Croydon, CR0 4YY

The Publisher's authorised representative in the EU for product safety is Authorised Rep Compliance Ltd., Ground Floor, 71 Lower Baggot Street, Dublin D02 P593, Ireland.
www.arccompliance.com

For a complete list of Pen & Sword titles please contact
PEN & SWORD BOOKS LTD
47 Church Street, Barnsley, South Yorkshire, S70 2AS, England
E-mail: enquiries@pen-and-sword.co.uk
Website: www.pen-and-sword.co.uk
or
PEN & SWORD BOOKS
1950 Lawrence Rd, Havertown, PA 19083, USA
E-mail: uspen-and-sword@casematepublishers.com

This book is dedicated to the brave Polish people who, time and again, have had to endure foreign occupation.

CONTENTS

AUTHOR'S NOTE

A regime, of whatever kind, collapses only under the weight of defeat.

Benito Mussolini

History is cyclical

John Gray was one of only a few academics in the world who anticipated, and warned of, the coming economic collapse of 2008. He claims that economic boom periods in the market can be deceptive, given that history is cyclical. The key word we should take note of is 'cyclical', meaning that history is never progressive but recurring. In simple terms, history repeats itself. With regard to history repeating itself, I have observed numerous parallels between Adolf Hitler and Vladimir Putin, proving Dr Gray's analysis of repeating cycles. Back in the 1930s and 1940s it was expansionist dictatorships that threatened the world. Although Benito Mussolini and the Empire of Japan were a threat to peace, it was Adolf Hitler and Nazism who were the greater dangers. Today Xi Jinping is pushing communist China into a more aggressive stance with regard to the South China Sea and the issue of Taiwan.

Yet, it is Vladimir Putin of the Russian Federation who is now the larger danger to world peace. During the past ten years, our world has seen the rise of autocrats all over the planet. Many nations are now run by authoritarian regimes. Examples that immediately come to mind are Kim Jong-un of North Korea, Viktor Orbán of Hungary, Recep Tayyip Erdoğan of Turkey, Daniel Ortega of Nicaragua, Nicolas Maduro of Venezuela, Miguel Diaz-Canel of Cuba, Aleksander Lukashenko of Belarus and Ramzan Kadirov of Chechnya. The list of autocrats is much longer. In fact, in the past seventeen years, there has been a decline in democracy around the world. Only twenty-five nations have seen improvements in human rights and advances in liberal reforms, while a whopping sixty nations have slipped into authoritarianism.[1]

That is more than double the number of nations who have come closer to democracy. If our twentieth-century history is our guidepost, and if this trend continues, then the twenty-first century will likely see more conflicts brought on by men calling themselves 'General Secretary', 'Chairman', 'Supreme Leader', or even 'President for Life'. While most authoritarian leaders today are content with oppressing their own people, Putin has begun 'exporting' his dictatorship to other nations. That is what sets him apart from other despots. Of course, I'm referring to the current invasion of Ukraine. The parallels between Hitler and Putin, as we shall see, are there for anyone to observe if they care to notice.

Waiting in the wings, much like Benito Mussolini did from 1939 to 1940, Xi Jinping of China is looking to see if Putin gets away with carving up Ukraine. Like Putin, Xi Jinping has an eye on conquering land outside the current borders of mainland China. In addition to building artificial islands in the South China Sea, then claiming 'territorial waters' around them, the Chinese communist government in Beijing has always claimed that Taiwan is a breakaway province that rightfully belongs to mainland China. Taiwan was established on the island of Formosa after General Chiang Kai-shek and the Nationalist forces lost the Chinese civil war in 1949. If Putin succeeds in taking Ukraine, the Chinese communist leader may feel emboldened to make a similar attempt to grab Taiwan by force, sooner rather than later.

Poland and the long Russian authoritarian winter

In 1960 Gerald Reitlinger published a groundbreaking study titled *The House built on Sand: The Conflicts of German Policy in Russia, 1941–1945*. Dr Reitlinger explained how the German attempt at empire building in the East failed, given the absurd and counterproductive Nazi policies towards the very people that they wished to rule. This work was released around the height of the Cold War. It was timely then because it showed, among other things, that many of the people who inhabited the Soviet Union had been and continued to be unhappy with the communist system. The establishment of the 'Iron Curtain', as Winston Churchill described it in 1946, imprisoned not only those peoples living within the borders of the USSR, but all of Eastern Europe as well. The population in these areas chafed at the lack of freedom and inaccessibility to even basic consumer goods that were needed for everyday life. The Soviet system stifled individuality and only offered repression, deprivations and harshness to its citizens.

Throughout history, Poland in particular has always been subject to the imperial and expansionist designs of its neighbouring kingdoms.

Over hundreds of years Poland has suffered military aggression from Prussia, Lithuania, Sweden, Austria, Imperial Russia, Nazi Germany, Axis Slovakia, and the Soviet Union. It is unfortunate for Poland's history that, topographically speaking, most of the country is made up of open plains. It has been through those flat fields that, traditionally, invading armies have moved either east, west or south. Aside from the mountainous regions where Poland borders its southern neighbours, the rest of the country has always been open to attack. The Polish people have persevered, bravely, and have suffered greatly on account of their nation's geographic location. Defending Poland is a difficult task. This is why Poland, after it gained its independence from communism in 1989, has been careful to spend a sufficient amount of funds on making sure that their defence forces are properly armed and supplied. The current attempts by Vladimir Putin to recreate a Russian empire in the image of the USSR has caused serious concern in Warsaw. Poles realise that Putin will not stop if he takes Ukraine. The next step might be a move on either Poland or the Baltic States.

Solidarność, Pope John Paul II and Mikhail Gorbachev

The beginnings of the Polish labour union *Solidarność* (Solidarity) can be traced back to the summer of 1980, in the context of a deteriorating political and economic situation in Poland under communist rule. At the time, Poland was experiencing significant unrest due to economic hardships, such as high inflation, food shortages, and low wages, all of which fuelled growing dissatisfaction with the government. The rise of the union and its effect on bringing democracy to Poland can be attributed to the following significant events:

1. The Gdańsk Shipyard Strike (August 1980): The immediate catalyst for the formation of *Solidarność* was a strike that began at the Lenin Shipyard in Gdańsk on 14 August 1980. The workers were protesting against the dismissal of a popular activist, Anna Walentynowicz, and demanding better working conditions, higher wages, and the right to form independent trade unions.
2. Lech Wałęsa and the Leadership of the Strike: Lech Wałęsa, an electrician at the Gdańsk Shipyard, became a central figure in the strike. He played a pivotal role in organising the workers and negotiating with the authorities. Wałęsa would later become the leader of *Solidarność*.
3. Negotiations and the Gdańsk Agreement: After several days of protests and negotiations, the Polish government agreed to many of the workers' demands, including the right to form independent trade unions, the right to strike, and the release of political prisoners. On 31 August

1980, the Gdańsk Agreement was signed, which allowed the creation of *Solidarność* as the first independent trade union in the Eastern Bloc.

4. *Solidarność*'s Rapid Expansion: Following the success at Gdańsk, *Solidarność* spread rapidly across Poland, gaining millions of members from various sectors of society, not just in the shipyards, but also among intellectuals, students, and clergy. It became both a labour union and a broad social movement advocating for political reforms, human rights, and an end to the monopoly of communist rule.
5. The Polish Government's Response: Initially, the government of Poland, led by the Polish United Workers' Party, was unwilling to confront the growing union. However, the movement's popularity and power soon became a threat to the Communist regime. In December 1981, martial law was imposed by the government under General Wojciech Jaruzelski, and *Solidarność* was officially banned. Many of its leaders, including Wałęsa, were arrested, and the movement went underground. Despite this repression, *Solidarność* continued to function covertly and became a symbol of resistance to the communist regime, laying the groundwork for future political change.
6. The support by Pope John Paul II: Pope John Paul II, born Karol Józef Wojtyła on 18 May 1920, in Wadowice, Poland, was the first Polish pope and the first non-Italian pope in 455 years. His papacy, from 1978 to 2005, is one of the longest in history, lasting twenty-seven years. John Paul II played a pivotal role in the global Catholic Church, and his influence extended far beyond religious boundaries. John Paul II's impact was especially significant in his native Poland. In 1979, during his first papal visit to Poland, he delivered a series of stirring speeches that inspired the Polish people to stand up to the oppressive communist regime. His message of hope, dignity, and human rights helped energise the Polish people and created a sense of unity that would later buoy the *Solidarność* movement in the 1980s. The pope's moral authority and support for the workers' struggle provided immense encouragement to the leaders of *Solidarność*, including Lech Wałęsa, who credited John Paul II with inspiring the movement's peaceful resistance against Communism. John Paul II's unwavering support for freedom, human rights, and religious liberty played a crucial role in undermining the Communist regime and fostering a climate for political change in Poland. By the mid-1980s, the broader geopolitical environment began to change.
7. The rise of Mikhail Gorbachev: In 1985, Mikhail Gorbachev became the leader of the Soviet Union and introduced reforms such as *glasnost* (openness) and *perestroika* (restructuring), signalling a shift away from the strict control of Eastern Europe that had characterised the Cold War. Gorbachev made it clear that the Soviet Union would no longer intervene militarily in the internal affairs of its satellite states, effectively withdrawing the threat of military force. These shifts made it easier for reformist movements like *Solidarność* to push for change, and Western support for democratic movements in Eastern Europe became more pronounced.

By the mid-1980s, *Solidarność* had become a major force in Poland's struggle for freedom and democracy. Its activities contributed to the eventual fall of communism in Poland in 1989, and it played a significant role in the broader collapse of communist regimes across Eastern Europe. Lech Wałęsa went on to become the first democratically elected president of Poland in 1990. Today *Solidarność* remains a symbol of non-violent resistance and the power of collective action in the fight for human rights and democracy.

Russia and its authoritarian past

Vladimir Lenin's Bolshevik state was not that dissimilar to the Czar's rule when it came to repression. In fact, Lenin's government proved to be harsher than the Czars had ever been. Joseph Stalin's rule (1924–53) was even more severe. Current estimates by Russian scholars as to the number of people who perished as a result of Stalin's regime stand at around 20 million. The only one to beat that record is Adolf Hitler. The communist state that followed under Nikita Khrushchev (beginning in 1953) and Leonid Brezhnev (in 1964) was, in many ways, not as repressive as the Stalinist period, but the system had not altered substantially enough for the population of the Soviet Union to enjoy the benefits that come from living in a free society. In that communist 'utopia', individuals could not question or criticise the state. Doing so was to risk ostracism, alienation or even imprisonment. People also lived in virtual fear that someone would inform on them if they were overheard complaining about the state or said the 'wrong thing'.

Free travel was not permitted and individuals could not enjoy the benefits that come from economic independence, except for high party officials who received rewards of which the common Soviet citizen could only dream. In essence, the autocracy of the Czars and dictatorship of the Leninist and Stalinist period gave way to the oligarchy of the old guard in the Central Committee of the Communist Party. Throughout the communist period, citizens of the USSR would spend hours standing in bread lines or queues at the local department store, hoping to be able to purchase provisions or scarce consumer goods. This was because most of the nation's GDP was going to the production of military hardware.

Why did Russia end up as a kleptocracy?

When Brezhnev died in 1982, another old-timer from the Central Committee, Yuri Andropov, was elected General Secretary of the Communist Party. Andropov died in 1984 after serving less than two years, at which point another old-timer, Konstantine Chernenko, was elected. Chernenko lasted an even shorter time than Andropov, dying in 1985, not even a year after assuming office. Members of the Central Committee thereupon chose a candidate who was significantly younger than most of the old guard who had served up until then. The hope was that this new General Secretary would not have to be replaced in a couple of years. This turned out to be Mikhail Gorbachev. Gorbachev was born in 1931 of a Russian father and Ukrainian mother. Employing what he called *glasnost* and *perestroika,* Gorbachev set about trying to reorganise the Soviet economic and political system. The job seemed insurmountable, but Gorbachev began to make slow progress.

However, the changes that he was implementing seemed so progressive and democratic that in 1991 the hardliners in the communist party attempted a coup against Gorbachev. The coup ultimately failed. That failure led directly to the collapse of the USSR and the formation of the Russian Federation under Boris Yeltsin. The establishment of the Russian Federation in 1991 seemed to bring hope that perhaps the long Russian 'authoritarian winter' might break, and democracy could finally take hold. Unfortunately, two things occurred that quickly halted that swing towards democracy. First, instead of trying to support the newly created democratic institutions in Russia, the United States declared victory in the Cold War and went about establishing itself as the sole superpower in the world. Secondly, the appointment of Vladimir Putin as president of the Russian Federation in 1999 (after Yeltsin retired) eventually relegated Russia's newly born democracy to a slow death.

Putin, a KGB hardliner and a true believer in the Soviet communist system, worked slowly at first, crippling and undermining the newly created democratic institutions in Russia. In this he took the old Benito Mussolini adage 'If you pluck a chicken one feather at a time, no one will notice'. So, following this method, Putin usurped the democratic checks and balances in the country and slowly created the kleptocracy that exists in Russia today. Putin was not alone in this. He had help from people who felt as he did. The Weimar Republic was also undermined by officials who resented democracy and longed for a return to the rule of the Kaiser. Still others wished a new authoritarian leader to emerge. These men worked against the republic from within, subverting the government. The parallels here between the failed Weimar Republic and the failed attempt to bring true democracy to Russia are obvious.

Where was the United States?

Following the collapse of the USSR, the United States involved itself in several conflicts, some of which were not of its own making, like

Saddam Hussein's invasion of Kuwait in 1991 and the 2001 attack on America by Al Qaeda. But in 2003 the United States elected to invade Iraq. This was a war of choice that ultimately proved to be costly and debilitating to the US in terms of lives lost, the huge financial expense of the conflict, and the loss of political capital around the world. George Bush Jr opted for a pre-emptive policy that said the United States would act if it saw a threat in the making. This unnecessary conflict also helped to destabilise the delicate political balance in the Middle East. While it was true that Al Qaeda was responsible for attacking the United States on 11 September 2001, its presence was in Afghanistan, not Iraq. In order to justify the invasion of Iraq, the US government accused Saddam Hussein of having weapons of mass destruction. Hussein was also blamed for conspiring with Al Qaeda, even though those in the US government knew very well that he was a secular tyrant, who would not have allowed a fundamentalist theocratic movement like Al Qaeda into his country.

By 2003 Saddam was no longer a threat to the United States or even to his Arab or Persian neighbours. After his defeat in 1991, he had been content to remain within the borders of Iraq and butcher his own people. However, the neo-conservatives under the George Bush Jr administration saw an opportunity for regime change, under the guise of the pre-emptive policy and of fighting Al Qaeda. They felt this change could occur at the point of a gun, and that ousting Hussein would alter the political landscape of the Middle East in favour of the United States. The political situation of the Middle East did change after the invasion of Iraq, but this is not the change for which the neo-conservatives had hoped. The nation that in the end benefitted most from Saddam Hussein's fall was the Islamic Republic of Iran. Today Iraq has close relations and partners with Iran, while the United States has lukewarm relations with Iraq. At great cost in human life and financial expense, the United States has inadvertently aided a sworn enemy (Iran).

Hubris, it seemed, had taken the United States to a place where it was completely invested in what would become the longest conflict that America had ever fought. Initially in Afghanistan, only small American forces were employed, backed up by local warlords whose allegiance was not guaranteed. The United States had used few forces at the start of the Afghan war because it was saving the bulk of the troops for the invasion of Iraq. As a result, the one chance to capture Osama bin Laden early, at Tora Bora, was lost because one of America's Afghan 'allies' was bought off and turned a blind eye while bin Laden and his cohorts slipped away. Mistakes were also made in Iraq once the country was occupied.

The first mistake was placing a minority Shiite leader to head the new Iraqi government. After a lifetime of being abused by the Sunni majority, the Shiites were dying for payback. Nouri al-Maliki began to favour the Shiite, while the Sunni were marginalised. Another mistake was the US government's decision to disband the entire Iraqi Army, using the Coalition Provisional Authority. The Iraqi Army employed hundreds of thousands of Sunnis. The consequences of demobilising so many Sunni men would prove to be detrimental. These decisions, and others, led directly to further alienation and resentment by the Sunni population. Many former Iraqi soldiers, now out of work, and seeing their country led by a Shiite leader bent on weakening the power of the Sunni majority, were easily radicalised. These ex-Iraqi Army soldiers became ready recruits for a new terrorist organisation: ISIS. Slowly but steadily, attacks against US troops in Iraq began to increase.

The demise of the fledgling Russian democracy

While the United States was distracted with its Iraqi adventure, Russia was struggling to establish its democratic institutions. The period 1991–99, I would venture to say, was very similar to the period of the Weimar Republic in 1921–33. A nation that was only accustomed to one form of authoritarianism or another (Germany in 1921 and Russia in 1991) was asked to accept democratic institutions and to embrace them willingly. As stated earlier, like the Weimar Republic, there were people in the new Russian government who opposed democracy. The principal opponent in Russia's bid for liberalism was Vladimir Putin. When he was appointed President of the Russian Federation (after Boris Yeltsin retired), he was in a perfect position to attack that nascent Russian democracy from within. Just like Putin was given the position of President of the Russian Federation in 1999, Hitler was given the position of Chancellor of Germany in 1933, and just like Putin, he began to undermine the Weimar Republic until he obtained the dictatorship that he wanted. Again, the parallels between both men are obvious.

Putin was a child of the communist system and was wholly indoctrinated in the principles that had kept the USSR together. Using patience and the dirty tricks of his former KGB trade, he employed bribery, coercion, blackmail, and even worked with the Russian and Chechen mafia to eliminate or intimidate politicians, industrialists, and reporters, forcing them to bend to his will. Those who refused to be subverted were killed. Those critics whom Putin could not reach because they were living outside of the Russian Federation were eventually killed as well. It became quite common for Russian dissidents to be poisoned with Polonium-210 by the Federal Security Service of the Russian Federation (FSB) agents, many of whom were former KGB members. For example, Russian dissident Alexander Litvinenko was poisoned in 2006. In 2015, another dissident, Boris Nemtsov, was assassinated while taking a walk near the Kremlin. Those who are in the know claim that it was the Chechen mafia that killed Nemtsov. The person who benefited most from Nemtsov's murder was Putin. While living in the United Kingdom, Sergei Skripal and his daughter were poisoned using Novichok in 2018.

In 2020 Alexei Navalny, a brave critic of Putin, was poisoned. He survived, only to be charged with false corruption charges that sent him to jail for thirteen years. Navalny died on 16 February 2024. He was only 47 years old. Many warned Navalny not to return to Russia for fear of what would happen. Nevertheless, this brave critic of Putin refused to be cowed. Like so many before him, he paid the ultimate price for defending democracy in Russia. Since the start of the Second Chechen War (in 2000) and today, more than 200 Russian politicians and reporters from television and print media have been assassinated in Russia, a number that parallels the number of moderate and left-leaning German politicians and newspaper editors who were killed by right-wing assassins during the period of the Weimar Republic. Slowly, Putin has destroyed or usurped the new democratic institutions in Russia, including a free press. Adolf Hitler did the same thing.

The Russian parliament has become simply a rubber stamp for Putin's wishes and desires in much the same way that members of the Reichstag became a rubber stamp for Hitler. Newspaper and TV reporters in Russia must toe the line and only present to the Russian people the version of history and events that Putin wants to show them. This is yet another parallel with Hitler's Third Reich. Once he was certain that his position as President of the Russian Federation was secure for another twenty years, Putin lamented openly that the collapse of the Soviet Union was the greatest calamity to befall the world in the twentieth century. We hear today, as the Russian invasion of Ukraine continues to wreak destruction, pain, misery, and death, that the majority of Russians support Putin's war and his version of events. The ludicrous and spurious accusation by Putin that he is eliminating Nazis from the Ukrainian government is simply an excuse for aggression.

Unfortunately, he is believed by the majority of Russians. It's not merely the *babushkas* who believe him, but middle-aged people and even young adults. This is because Putin has turned what were independent and impartial Russian news outlets into the political mouthpiece of his regime. Those who are not fooled do not dare to speak openly. The situation has not been helped by the fact that the majority of the Russian people have not experienced true democracy and its advantages for any serious amount of time. Not knowing any better, perhaps some Russians actually prefer the harshness and repression of a police state, simply because it is familiar to them. Professor Jeffrey Herff, an expert on the history of the Weimar Republic, remarked in 1986 that the Weimar Republic 'was a republic without republicans'. This was echoed by Sebastian Ulrich in a work that was released in 2009.[2]

Both claimed that the German people at the time were only accustomed to authoritarian rule, and therefore were less inclined to support a democratic government when it was offered to them, especially when there were anti-democratic agents working from within to undermine that very democracy. This is the same scenario that Russia has experienced since 1999. It is also another reason why democracy was not firmly embedded in Russian society. Granted, there were some in Russia who tried to defend the newly created independent institutions, like a free press. Many who did so were targeted and paid the ultimate price. Putin and his cronies made sure of that, and that democracy would not flower in Russia. Taking all of this into account, we can say that the parallels between the history of the Weimar Republic and the Russian Federation are undeniable.

A forgotten lesson from the past

While the United States was spending much human capital and economic effort being the sole superpower of the world, fighting both a war of consequence and a war of choice, what it should have been doing was supporting Russia's young democracy by all means. Frankly, America dropped the ball. The United States forgot its own history. Back in 1918, when the First World War ended, President Woodrow Wilson wished to aid the newly established democracies of Europe that had been created from the ashes of four former empires. He wanted to do this by sending both money and experts to those new democratic nations in Europe. Two things put a stop to this. First, Wilson had a stroke towards the end of his second term that incapacitated him for about a year. Second, the US Congress refused to allocate any funds towards supporting the new democracies of Europe. Instead, the United States became isolationist and ignored Europe altogether.

Within twenty years (by 1938), the only true democracy left in central Europe was Czechoslovakia.[3] In that same year, Adolf

Hitler's threats yielded appeasement from the West yet again.[4] At the Munich Conference he was able to acquire the Sudetenland, a stretch of frontier border between Germany and Czechoslovakia that contained a sizeable *volksdeutsch* (ethnic German) population. The Sudetenland also happened to contain the principal mountain defences for Czechoslovakia. At Munich, Édouard Daladier of France and Neville Chamberlain of the United Kingdom didn't even bother inviting the Czechs to the negotiating table. Benito Mussolini, who really had nothing to do with the problem, showed up at the meeting uninvited, but was given a seat, while the Czechs, whose future was being decided, were left out.

When the Germans acquired the Sudetenland, they effectively stripped the country of its defensive fortifications along the Czech–German border. Months later, in March 1939, Hitler's armies quietly marched in and took over what was left of the Czechoslovakian nation. Hitler's troops entered Prague during a heavy snowstorm, which ironically intimated the dark period ahead for the Czech people. Had the United States supported the new democracies of Europe after the First World War, things might have had a different outcome. In 1991, instead of declaring victory in the Cold War, the United States should have assured that victory over the USSR by supporting democracy in Russia by any and all means possible.

Edmund Burke was right

We can speculate that things might have been different if in 1991 the United States had concentrated on making sure that democracy would take a firm hold in Russia. Today the nation of Ukraine, and indeed, all peaceful nations of the world, are suffering from Russian aggression, directly or indirectly, either at the point of a gun, or through rising food and fuel prices, all because for years many nations turned a blind eye to Russia's bullying. Ukrainians are dying by the thousands and people around the world are starving because the war is affecting grain shipments. The world had to suffer the Second World War because Hitler was appeased from 1934 until 1938, as he became stronger and more dangerous. Putin has been emboldened by the apathy and lethargy of the West. Europe in particular has had a large dependence on Russian oil and natural gas. This has led the nations of Europe to ignore Russia's growing belligerence in exchange for a steady energy supply. The Russian Army, long known for its brutality and heartlessness, devastated Grozny, the capital of Chechnya in 1994. This army also did horrible things in Georgia when Russian-backed separatists in the South Ossetian

Oblast declared their independence from Georgia in 2008 and sought Russian 'protection'.[5]

The heinous tactic of targeting civilians, as seen in Ukraine, was perfected by the Russian Army during the Syrian civil war in 2016. Entire cities in Syria were levelled by Russian artillery and air strikes. In particular, hospitals and schools were targeted as a way of demoralising their opponents. In the twisted logic of tyrants, killing the children of your enemy limits the rise of future soldiers who will oppose you. Even chemical weapons were used against the Syrian civilian population. Although President Obama warned Bashar al-Assad of Syria that employing chemical weapons was a line he should not cross, Assad, who benefitted from the protection of the Russian Army, employed those chemical weapons to horrific effect.

The United States and others condemned this barbaric act, but in the end, nothing was done by any Western leader, just as nothing had been done when the Russians committed war crimes in Chechnya and in Georgia. Employing terror and targeting the civilian population has become part of the *modus operandi* of the Russian Army. That sounds awfully familiar if we think back on the Nazi period with its politicised army, which committed untold war crimes. During the Second World War the Third Reich kidnapped tens of thousands of Nordic-looking children from all across Europe. They did so in order to raise them as Nazis. Today, Putin's regime has admitted to stealing as many as 700,000 Ukrainian children, under the guise of protecting them from the war. The woman in charge of coordinating this massive effort is Maria Lvova-Belova, one of Putin's stooges. Stories are now filtering out of Russia that indicate Putin has ordered the indoctrination of these Ukrainian children in order to raise them as Russians. Again, the parallels between what the Nazis did and what Putin is doing are there for anyone to see.

Empty promises

In 1991, when the Soviet Union collapsed, both the newly created Russian Federation and the United States made a promise to Ukraine that if it would give up its nuclear arsenal (there were nuclear missiles stationed in Ukraine), the United States and the Russian Federation would guarantee and protect the territorial integrity of Ukraine's borders. In February 2014 Vladimir Putin ordered the invasion and occupation of the Crimea and its annexation from Ukraine for the Russian Federation. This was followed up on 6 April 2014, when Russian-backed separatists began a war against the Ukrainian government in the Donbas region of eastern Ukraine. The attempt aimed to wrest control of this eastern Ukrainian province, rich in minerals and industrial capacity, from Ukraine and unite it with Russia. Russia supplied these separatist rebels with an abundance of military equipment and continue to do so today. It appears then, that Ukraine might have done better had it kept its nuclear arsenal as a deterrent to any would-be invader, rather than depending on the empty promises of both the United States and the Russian Federation to guarantee its borders.

As with all other acts of Russian aggression, the United States and Europe's leading powers employed words of condemnation in 2014, but not much else. This is exactly what happened between 1934 and 1938. Was it a surprise to the United States and the European nations that, after years of turning a blind eye to what Putin was doing, he felt emboldened enough to invade another sovereign nation? In order to find an excuse to swallow up the rest of Ukraine, Putin has made the baseless accusation that the country is being run by Nazis. This is truly a classic case of psychological projection, given that Ukraine's president, Volodymyr Zelensky, happens to be Jewish, and the only person behaving like a Nazi happens to be named Putin. Just as the Western leaders had appeased Hitler for years, culminating in the signing of the infamous Munich Agreement, so has the West appeased Putin by allowing him to run roughshod over his neighbours for years.

With the formal invasion of Ukraine on 24 February 2022, the birds of appeasement and economic pragmatism have come home to roost, and only too late has the West realised that Putin needs to be confronted. Only when Hitler's forces marched into what was left of Czechoslovakia in March 1939, ending that nation's liberty, did the British Prime Minister, Neville Chamberlain, and France's Prime Minister, Édouard Daladier, finally realise that Hitler, like all schoolyard bullies, needed to be opposed. The months between September 1938 and March 1939 have gone down in history as a testament to what happens when democracies fail to confront tyranny. We must now also add February 2014 to this shameful list. Confronting Hitler much earlier might have avoided war, or at least reduced the terrible cost in lives that the Second World War brought. By the same token, opposing Putin earlier might have also prevented further Russian aggression. If he were alive today to witness the tragic events unfolding in Ukraine, Edmund Burke, the Irish-born British statesman, would have repeated his famous warning: 'All tyranny needs to gain a foothold, is for people of good conscience to remain silent.' Again, the parallels between the Nazi period and now are uncanny.

The same old dream of empire building

Today we are faced with a Hitler wannabe in the guise of the Russian President. Putin's goal is no less than the re-establishment of a Russian empire like the one that existed during the time of the USSR. Realising that he can't live forever, and contemplating how Russians will remember him, Putin is attempting to re-establish the territorial boundaries of what used to be the USSR as his legacy. Like all other tyrants before him, his goal will ultimately fail, but not before tens of thousands, or even hundreds of thousands of innocent people lose their lives. At home in Russia, there are stirrings of dissent, but Putin's police state is now firmly entrenched. In 2017 he created the *Natsional'naya gvardiya* (National Guard), known as the Special Police Force. This organisation is a police formation of some 340,000 soldiers, whose members are only answerable and loyal to Putin himself. This paramilitary organisation sounds very similar in make-up and allegiance to Hitler's SA Storm Troopers, or even the SS. Now, the only way that Putin will fall from power is if military affairs take a further bad turn for Russia. Putin knows that his future as leader of the Russian Federation depends on victory in Ukraine, no matter what that victory might cost. If Putin is thwarted in taking Ukraine, he will lose power and most likely his life. Therefore, he will continue to act ruthlessly and show no mercy.

His past track record suggests he will be willing to sacrifice everything, including the lives of the Russian people, to obtain that victory. Recently, some politicians in the West have been pushing the Ukrainian government to make peace with Russia. This has been echoed loudly by the new American president, who appears to be a Putin admirer. What these career politicians and demagogues do not comprehend (or choose not to understand), is that allowing Putin to keep what land he has stolen from Ukraine will only encourage him to continue his aggression at a later date. The temporary peace will also give him time to re-equip and retrain the Russian Army. The Ukrainians understand that they cannot compromise or try to reason with a man like Putin. To Putin, compromise and reason are signs of weakness. The only thing he understands is raw, brute force. That is the measure of the man. In this, he is accompanied by a legion of Russian tyrants who came before him, going all the way back to Ivan the Terrible. Putin is merely the latest Russian tyrant.

Poland's government is doing all it can to support the Ukrainian nation in its defence against Russian aggression. In fact, many democratic countries are doing the same. They all realise that they have a stake in the Russian–Ukrainian conflict. As a result of this support, the war it seems, will last longer than Putin expected. Hopefully, Putin's attempt at empire building will fail. In the meantime, those politicians, generals, and rich oligarchs around Putin, who support his kleptocracy, are waiting to see if the Russian Führer suffers more military reversals, or if the West abandons Ukraine. If history is a harbinger, then this Russian war of aggression will decide not only Ukraine's future, but Putin's ultimate place in history. Just as the Nazis failed at building an empire in the East, Putin too, it is hoped, will fail in his attempt to create an empire along the lines of his beloved USSR. Dr John Gray's observation that history is cyclical has to be considered, given the many parallels between the Nazi period and now. If Putin suffers more military reversals on the battlefield, like Hitler discovered, he may find himself inside a house of cards that is about to collapse on him. Benito Mussolini's famous quote, 'a regime, of whatever kind, collapses only under the weight of defeat' will then have been proven true.

Dr Antonio J. Muñoz,
14 February 2025

INTRODUCTION – A DIFFERENT KIND OF WAR

Asymmetrical Warfare and Murder

Why was it that Nazi Germany was unable to create an eastern empire that many historians agree could have supplied land and resources that would have kept the Third Reich alive for a thousand years? The answer lies in the nature of the Nazi system itself. During the Second World War, Nazi policy regarding the combating of partisans, especially in Poland and the USSR, involved the tactic of *kollektive Gewaltmassnahmen*.[1] The manner in which the Germans treated the conquered peoples of the East was also far harsher than their treatment of west European or Scandinavian peoples under German rule. This policy of *kollektive Gewaltmassnahmen* punished all for the acts of a few. For example, an attack by guerrilla forces against German units or interests made the local population near that attack as responsible as the guerrillas themselves.

This and other German policies dealing with civilian and military matters would eventually work to undermine German rule in the East. The idea behind *kollektive Gewaltmassnahmen* was the German belief that, fearing reprisals, the local population in an occupied region behind German lines would inform on the partisans before the guerrillas had a chance to launch any attacks against German interests. In addition, several orders created shortly before the start of the Russian campaign, collectively referred to by historians as the *Verbrecherbefehle* (criminal orders), were meant to give an air of 'legality' to such policies as *kollektive Gewaltmassnahmen* that were criminal and illegal in wartime. These official announcements would quickly become standard policy in the East. They would also end up costing the lives of many civilians.

With the invasion of the Soviet Union on 22 June 1941, various Nazi ideologies were used that would come together in a deadly cocktail that would shape the German struggle in the East. Anti-Polish and anti-Jewish sentiments were already causing the deaths of thousands in German-occupied Poland. When the USSR was invaded, Poland's agony increased, as the Nazis bore down harder on the Polish people in order to safeguard the rear of the advancing German armies in the USSR. The idea that the Jewish, Romani, and Eastern European people were inferior to Germans, and natural enemies of Germany, made it easier for the Nazis to prosecute the occupation of Poland and the Russian campaign in a more barbaric manner. In effect, dehumanising these people made it easier for Germans to kill them. It's an established fact that anti-Semitism was the principal factor in the Nazis' eventual decision to attempt to murder the entire Jewish population of Europe. Christopher Browning states that the society in which Germans lived at the time was imbued with a steady dose of anti-Semitic propaganda, which denigrated and marginalised the Jews to the point where they began to be seen as less than human and, by extension, life not worth living (*lebensunwertes leben*):

> As *Leutnant* Drucker said with extraordinary understatement, 'Under the influence of the times, my attitude to the Jews was marked by a certain aversion.' The denigration of Jews and the proclamation of Germanic racial superiority was so constant, so pervasive, so relentless, that it must have shaped the general attitudes of masses of people in Germany, including the average reserve policemen.[2]

Just as importantly, however, Christian Streit has described very persuasively how anti-communism was 'a factor of crucial importance' in the process of creating an extermination policy during the period prior to and during the Russian campaign.[3] A perfect example of this is the infamous commissar order, which gave all German troops, irrespective of branch of service or rank, the ability to execute any and all Red Army commissars either right after capture or immediately after interrogation. Not many authors know that this order, instituted basically for the invasion of the USSR, was also employed in occupied Poland. All members of the Polish communist underground were considered, in effect, political commissars. While the Nazis had behaved harshly towards the Polish nation from 1939 to 1941, their cruelty only increased as their campaign in the Soviet Union unfolded.[4]

This increased in tempo as the war turned against the German invader. Poland would not be spared the full brunt of the Nazis' wrath. On the contrary, as soon as the German invasion of the Soviet Union began, Poland would feel the full weight of this *vernichtungskrieg* (war of annihilation). Repression begets cruelty, and the Germans would increase their campaign of terror against the Polish nation as the war in the East progressed. In effect, these criminal orders allowed the *Ostheer* (eastern army) to operate under a completely different set of rules than those that had been employed when the Wehrmacht (German Armed Forces) conquered Western Europe.[5] In this new form of warfare, simply being a Jew became synonymous with being a partisan. As such, all Jews were subject to execution on sight.

In addition, the Russian military and civilian population would have no legal protection from killings of any kind. Since the USSR had never signed the Geneva Convention on the treatment of captured enemy prisoners, the Nazis considered they had *carte blanche* in treating all captured enemy combatants and civilians in whichever way they wished. This included the use of immediate executions if it was deemed necessary by the local German commander, meaning that the lowest-ranked German soldier (even a lowly corporal) had the right to execute captured prisoners if he deemed it necessary. Nazi ideology, coupled with what was virtually a mandate to kill, fused together in the Russian campaign to create the *Weltanschauungskrieg* (ideological war) against what the Nazis referred to as the 'Judeo–Bolshevist' threat. Given such wide latitude, the struggle in the East would be unprecedented in terms of its intensity, ferocity, and brutality. With the Nazi belief that the Jewish race was a polluting factor in German life and *lebensunwertes leben*, this idea was now further expanded upon to suit the circumstances of the war in the East. This was accomplished (as stated earlier) by making the killing of Jews synonymous with fighting the partisans.

Hitler even said that the war in the East was an opportunity to kill all those they felt opposed them. The belief that *jeder Jude ist ein guerrillakampfer* ('every Jew is a guerrilla fighter') was hammered home by officers not only within the SS and *Ordnungspolizei* (Order Police), but the entire Wehrmacht. As if to reaffirm this view, Wilhelm Keitel issued the following order, dated 16 December 1942, regarding the combating of partisans. The command seemed to reiterate the criminal orders completely – almost a year and a half after the German invasion. A portion of the order reads:

> The troops therefore have the right and the duty to use, in this fight, any means, even against women and children, provided they are conducive to success. Scruples, of any sort whatsoever, are a crime against the German people and against the front-line soldier who bears the consequences of attacks by bands and who cannot understand why any should be shown to them or their associates. These principles

> must serve as a basis for operations against bands in the East. No German participating in action against bands or their associates is to be held responsible for acts of violence either from a disciplinary or a judicial point of view. Commanders of troops engaged in action against the bands are obliged to see to it that all officers of units under their command be immediately and thoroughly notified of this order, that their legal advisers be immediately acquainted therewith and that no judgments be passed which are in contradiction thereto.[6]

This policy made it easy for regular German army troops to (1) work side by side with SS units fighting the partisans and assist the *SS-Einsatzgruppen* in eliminating the Jewish population, and (2) commit crimes against the Jewish and non-Jewish population under the guise of combating the guerrillas. Romani were added to the category of *lebensunwertes leben*, so they too would be targeted wherever they were encountered. In many instances these murders were carried out independent of the SS mobile killing units. Even rear area army garrison commands have been shown to have cooperated with the SS and to have undertaken operations against Jews and Romani on their own initiative. The above order, issued by Keitel, stipulated that no soldier was to be punished for any acts that he committed while under the pretext of fighting the guerrillas and keeping order behind the lines. In addition, women and children were specifically mentioned as not being an exception to this rule.

What Keitel meant is clear enough: the killing of women and children in the East would be permitted. Notice also that all of this served, as he put it, as 'a basis for operations in the East', meaning that the war and the tactics that the *Ostheer* was employing in Poland and the Soviet Union were unique to this particular region of Europe. Was this the case because the Germans saw the Eastern Europeans as subhuman and less worthy of life? Was it hatred of Polish identity? Was it because Josef Stalin did not ascribe to the Geneva Convention? Was it anti-communist hatred? Was it the brutalisation that occurred on the Eastern Front, as Omer Bartov and others have argued, that contributed to the barbarisation of the German soldier? Was it anti-Semitism? Was it hatred of the *Zigeuner* (gypsies)?

The answer (sadly) is all of the above. All of these representative biases and bigotries were inflamed by Nazi propaganda and indoctrination. The Germans brought these biases to the East, and when coupled together with criminal military orders, permitting brutality and mass murder, they engendered in the German occupation army in Poland and elsewhere (including the *Ostheer*), a feeling that immoral conduct would be condoned. A major role in combating the partisans in Poland and the USSR was played not only by SS and police forces, but by the *Ostheer*. This included ancillary and volunteer auxiliary units of the German Army. In addition, Keitel's *befehl* (order) also reinforced the OKW (*Oberkommando der Wehrmacht* – the Armed Forces High Command) directive against communist insurrection in occupied territories. This order was issued on 16 September 1941. On 10 October 1941 the infamous 'Reichenau Order' was issued, detailing the conduct of troops in the eastern territories. An important part reads as follows:

> The most important objective of this campaign against the Jewish–Bolshevik system is the complete destruction of its sources of power and the extermination of the Asiatic influence in European Civilisation ... Therefore, the soldier must have full understanding for the necessity of a severe but just revenge on subhuman Jewry. The Army has to aim at another purpose, i.e., the annihilation of revolts in hinterland which, as experience proves, have always been caused by the Jews ... This is the only way to fulfil our historic task to liberate the German people once forever from the Asiatic–Jewish danger.[7]

In 2004, Ben Shepperd published a work detailing the war guilt of principally two such German units: two security divisions as they operated in central Russia from 1941 to 1943.[8] Although his work covered only two security divisions, the author argued that their behaviour proved how National Socialist indoctrination, combined with the brutality of the war in the East, created the conditions that allowed for widespread murders under the guise of combating the Soviet partisans. Shepperd's approach was to build his case from the bottom up, by illustrating a consistent pattern of action within the battalions and regiments of these security divisions. His study was important because it reinforced existing research on the criminal excesses of the Wehrmacht in the East. In Poland, the anti-partisan war was waged just as cruelly and just as heartlessly.

The book, however, would have been aided further if Shepperd had been able to cite other cases in similar German rear-area and front-line commands, to support the theory that this type of behaviour in the *Ostheer* was widespread and commonplace throughout the entire width and scope of the Eastern Front. By citing examples of atrocities committed by these units, Shepperd showed how, in the region of central Russia and Belarus, the degenerative brutality that National Socialism caused, when combined with the constant and vicious combat of the war in the East, worked to harden the German soldier and accustomed him to murder, even illegal killings.[9] This work will argue that similar criminal behaviours were perpetrated by German rear-area security forces throughout the East, including Poland, and what comprised the USSR at the time.

My research has affirmed what Dr Shepperd and other academics refer to as the brutalisation theory. But this is just one piece of the puzzle if we are to understand Nazi *Ost* policy. In this work, I have covered a wider area, citing numerous examples from the occupation of Poland, the Baltic States, and western Ukraine. The conclusions provide verifiable evidence of this widespread practice of criminal conduct, which was condoned and encouraged by the Nazi civilian administration in the East. Like Shepperd and other researchers, I have worked from the bottom up by going through reels of captured German records detailing the history of these rear-area forces that operated in the East from 1939 until 1944. Cases also abound of front-line troops behaving criminally during anti-guerrilla sweeps. All of what happened in the East was in keeping with a strategy prepared before the invasion. *Generalplan Ost* was a Nazi plan developed as a blueprint for the genocide and democide that would take place in the East as a precursor to German colonization. This plan required the Germans to be brutal and ruthless in the East. Employing the typical German penchant for fulfilling obligations, the *Ostheer* carried out this order to horrific effect.

The debate over German Army criminality in the East

Gerald Reitlinger is one of the earliest, if not the first, historian to have brought up the subject of possible participation of the German military in the heinous murders of the Jewish population of Poland and the USSR. Prior to this early work, the only substantive reference to this German Army and Holocaust connection were the High Command trials that occurred within the context of the Nuremberg War Crimes Trials of 1946–48. Reitlinger pointed to this in his ground-breaking 1956 study, *The SS: Alibi of a Nation*.[10] He began there, and others followed after him, with further proof that it wasn't just the Jewish people who were targeted, but the civilian population as a whole, and the *Ostheer* was knee-deep in it all. With this work, Reitlinger established a foundation upon which others would follow and contribute, in much the same way that the base of a house is built, and other workers later add the walls and roof. The crux of his argument was that by blaming all of the evils committed by the Nazi regime on the SS, the German nation (and therefore the army) as a whole could be exculpated from any guilt. Reitlinger followed that classic work four years later, in 1960, with *The House Built on Sand: The Conflicts of German Policy in Russia, 1939–1945*.[11] In it, he detailed how the Nazi leaders and their German Army counterparts had prepared for a different kind of war in the Soviet Union.

The criminal orders made the campaign different, in that these orders were a virtual licence to kill. In this he was repeating points already made by Alexander Dallin in *German Rule in Russia, 1941–1945: A Study of Occupation Policies*, in which Dallin described the 'Commissar Decree' among other documents linking the German Army to the Holocaust and the illegal killings of the general population.[12] Reitlinger pointed to documents written to senior German Army commanders by the Nazi leadership – collectively referred to by historians as the 'criminal orders', which provided the *Ostheer* with its 'mandate' to allow for the killing of the local population, especially the Jewish population.

These orders document how German military courts would not apply to Russian civilians, how the SS and police units were to work outside military commands, and also included the infamous Commissar Order and the Barbarossa Jurisdiction Order, to name a few. The Jurisdiction Order in effect gave virtual *carte blanche* to any German soldier fighting in the East to shoot or kill anyone that was categorised as being either an 'agitator', 'partisan', 'partisan helper', 'saboteur', 'political commissar', or 'Jew', without fear of prosecution by any German court or tribunal. As stated earlier, the terms 'partisan' and 'Jew' were made synonymous, since treatment of both groups would be the same: execution. While many former German Army officers point to the fact that no order originated from the Wehrmacht that specified that the Jewish population was to be targeted for premeditated murder, historian Yitzhak Arad was correct when he stated that because Jews were included in the list of those persons who could be shot on sight, the effect was the same as if the Wehrmacht itself had written the order for the murder of the Jewish population.[13]

The Criminal Orders, therefore, directly link the Holocaust in Poland and the USSR to the German Army. Reitlinger related how shortly after the start of the Russian campaign, a meeting was held on 16 July 1941, in Angerburg in East Prussia. In attendance were Göring, Keitel, Rosenberg, Lammers, Bormann, and Adolf Hitler. The Führer, Reitlinger explained, 'declared that Stalin had ordered partisan warfare behind the German front'. Hitler also commented that this partisan war gave them the ability to eliminate everyone who opposed them.[14] This, of course, not only included the Jews, but anyone considered by the Nazis as an enemy. As a result, on 22 July 1941, a new expanded order was put forth by Hitler and added to the Barbarossa Jurisdiction

Order, which stated implicitly that where SS and other security forces were not available, the German Army itself was to take all measures necessary, even draconian steps, to control the rear areas and those who populated them. They were also to eliminate the partisan threat or 'other dangers' that placed the German Armed Forces or the war effort at risk. This, Reitlinger wrote, 'became the German soldier's charter for anti-partisan warfare'.[15]

In spite of these early and impressive starts, the study of this German Army connection to the Holocaust and other illegal murders in the East did not really begin to be considered fully until the mid-1980s. It was then that Professor Omer Bartov published his now-classic work, *The Eastern Front, 1941–45, German Troops and the Barbarisation of Warfare*. In it, he proposed that the rigours of the Eastern Front, that is, the very nature of the warfare being fought between the Soviet Union and Nazi Germany, as well as pre-existing Nazi ideology, quickly accustomed the typical German soldier to brutalisation, which made it easier for him to kill Jewish and non-Jewish civilians, captured soldiers, and partisans with little thought to the legality or morality of his actions. Indeed, as stated decades before by Reitlinger and Dallin, the 'criminal orders' gave members of the German Army, from high-ranking officers down to even the lowly *landser*,[16] the feeling that any action taken under the pretext of these orders would protect them from punishment by any German Army military tribunal.[17]

Bartov's incisive work was followed up three years later, in 1989, by a study titled *The German Army and Nazi Policies in Occupied Russia* by Professor Theo J. Schulte. Dr Schulte proposed that not only had the German Army been complicit in the Holocaust, but that it was part of a Nazi aim that sought 'the total destruction of another society as a fundamental prerequisite for the refashioning of German society'.[18] Here, Schulte was echoing the thoughts of historian Michael Geyer, who argued that the war of ideologies, the *Weltanschauungskrieg*, was not just fought with mere words, but was practised in the East with physical vigour.[19] Two years later in 1991, Yitzhak Arad reappraised the various criminal orders and expounded and developed on their implications as part of the Yad Vashem Yearbook Series. This important article added 'cement' to the arguments that authors like Bartov and Schulte were developing. Even when discussing the non-military leadership that ruled the German Eastern empire, we see the same ideology and action. Why did it take several decades from the publication of Reitlinger and Dallin's works for them to be followed by further research on the criminality of the Wehrmacht in the East? This is an important question.

It is beyond the scope of this work to go into the personal, social, or political reasons why the topic remained relatively dormant for so many years, but in 2007 professors Ronald Smelser and Edward Davies published a study that proposed several reasons for this apparent twenty-year hiatus on the topic.[20] Although this study was fraught with numerous assumptions, the authors did conclude correctly that the Cold War may have played a role in sanitising the German Army from its complicity in the horrors perpetrated in the East. This was done in order to use the full capacity of a revitalised West German state to help block Soviet aggression and intentions during the Cold War.[21] Throughout this period, Smelser and Davies argue, an entire myth about the valour and chivalry of the Wehrmacht was created by numerous American and European writers. In addition, at the end of Second World War various powers were scrambling to grab as many Nazi scientists as they could get their hands on.

The Americans and Russians were the biggest hoarders of German scientific knowledge. Professor Werner von Braun, the Nazi scientist who worked at Peenemünde perfecting the V-1 and V-2 rockets, and who later helped the United States reach the moon, immediately comes to mind. The Cold War was also a time when former Nazis, some involved in the Holocaust, were sought by Western intelligence agencies because of their supposed knowledge of the Soviet Union and its people. An important study with regard to understanding how it came to pass that 80 million Germans fell sway to Hitler and the Nazis and aided in the destruction of European Jewry came when Christopher R. Browning published his definitive study, *Ordinary Men: Reserve Police Battalion 101 and the Final Solution in Poland*.

Dr Browning's study of the Holocaust in Poland through the eyes of the men of Reserve Police Battalion 101 has become a must read for those trying to understand *haShoah* (the Holocaust), the German mindset that allowed it to happen, and the overall German occupation policies in Poland. A few years later, in 1995, German author Paul Kohl published a little-circulated work called *Der Krieg der Deutschen Wehrmacht und der Polizei 1941–1944*. In it, he argued that indeed, the German Army had followed the *Führerprinzip* ('Leader Principle') of the *Weltanschauungskrieg* to its inevitable conclusion.[22] Following the work by Kohl, Walter Manoschek edited a book in 1996 titled *Die Wehrmacht im Rassenkrieg: Der Vernichtungskrieg Hinter der Front* (*The [German] Armed Forces in the Race War: The War of Annihilation Behind the Front*). The numerous contributors to this work, which included such notables as Raul Hilberg, Manfred Messerschmidt, Wolfram Wette, Christian Streit, Hans Safrian, Hannes Heer, Bertrand Perz, Ela Hornung, and Reinhold Gärtner, referenced incidences that occurred in the Soviet Union, but went a step further by describing the political and propaganda preparations and conditioning Germans were subjected to by the Nazi state before they even set foot on Soviet soil.

Manoschek also managed to document a comparable occurrence of a German army atrocity in Serbia, thus further cementing the truth of unlawful activities prevalent in the Nazi-era German Army.[23] Willi Dreßen had also recorded Wehrmacht atrocities in Serbia and Russia in an article published in the 1993 edition of the Yad Vashem Yearbook Series.[24] The numerous eyewitness reports in his book cemented those accounts with apparent indelible ink. That same year Hannes Heer and Klaus Naumann edited and published an extremely important study, *Vernichtungskrieg: Verbrechen der Wehrmacht 1941 bis 1944* ('War of Annihilation: Crimes of the [German] Armed Forces 1941 to 1944'), that propelled the topic of German Army complicity in atrocities to a whole new level by attacking the question from the top and bottom – that is, by presenting not only documentary evidence of guilt, but showing in a very lucid and straightforward manner how the very nature of the Nazi regime worked to create the conditions leading to complicity from all corners of the Wehrmacht and civilian apparatus.[25]

The book turned out to be so popular and important that in 2000 it was translated into the English language in annotated format.[26] *Vernichtungskrieg: Verbrechen der Wehrmacht 1941 bis 1944* proved very successful in the US, but interest was especially high in Germany, where there was a growing awareness of what had been a taboo subject until 1990: German army complicity in atrocities and sanctioned murder. An exhibit was eventually created that toured Germany for many years in the 1990s and was considered extremely controversial.[27] German military veteran groups protested that this exhibition was negatively painting too broad a stroke on the Wehrmacht. A huge, oversized volume was produced in 2002: *Verbrechen der Wehrmacht: Dimensionen des Vernichtungskrieges 1941–1944* ('Crimes of the Armed Forces: Dimensions of the War of Extermination').

Its 764 pages are chock full of documents, photographs, reports from diaries, interviews, eyewitness accounts, and other documentary evidence about the crimes of the German Army during the Nazi period. The sheer size and scope of this volume attests to the extent of the German Army's participation in these crimes, for surely if today the institute that produced it, the *Hamburger Institut für Sozialforschung* (Hamburg Institute for Social Research), could have amassed such a work, what other crimes were committed during Second World War that, for lack of evidence, we shall never know about? That same year

Wolfram Wette, who until then had been a contributing writer on this topic, published his first single and full study on the subject, translated into the English language as *The Wehrmacht: History, Myth, Reality*.[28] In it, Wette studied not only the top generals and middle-management officers but read reports and testimonials from the lowly privates as well. In his closing analysis, he stated:

> In recent years we have gained greater insight into the experience of the 'average Joe' in uniform, meaning the many millions of enlisted men and non-commissioned officers who participated in the exterminationist campaign on the eastern front. Many of them followed the generals' ideological guidelines reluctantly, while others supported the campaign on the basis of their own convictions. Recent research has revealed a considerable amount of agreement with and support for the regime's goals at the bottom of the military hierarchy. Very few summoned the courage to resist this war – to the extent that it was possible at all. While the Wehrmacht was officially dissolved after the capitulation of 8 May 1945, that did not put an end to its history. Some believe that only after that date did the Wehrmacht achieve its ultimate victory, namely, in its struggle to preserve its image as an army with 'clean hands' in the eyes of the public both at home and abroad. The myth of the Wehrmacht lived on. The policy of apology evident in the memoirs of former generals – in concert with like-minded people in West Germany – worked successfully for decades.[29]

Wette reached the conclusion that, perhaps by 2002 – the year when his work was published and several years after the *Hamburger Institut* exhibit, Germany was now ready to admit that the legend of the Wehrmacht's 'clean hands' could finally belong to the past.[30] However, old habits are hard to break. During the mid-1990s, an American political scientist would reopen the old wounds caused by German war guilt that perhaps the travelling exhibit on Wehrmacht crimes had merely opened slightly. So heated and controversial was this author's assertion to be that the national media both in the United States and in Europe picked up on it and carried the story for months. That author's name was Daniel J. Goldhagen, and the debate about the German Army's war guilt was about to expand to the German nation's war guilt as a whole.

By the early 1990s, the question over the extent of German Army complicity in *haShoah* almost certainly helped to partly inspire Goldhagen's work, *Hitler's Willing Executioners: Ordinary Germans and the Holocaust*.[31] Goldhagen's book sold more than 80,000 copies in its first print run – catching the attention not only of academics but the general public. American and European media covered the story about the controversy that the book produced. It also stirred up a hornets' nest of arguments among academicians for and against the theory that Goldhagen proposed. In the book he argued that the majority of Germans were willing participants in the Holocaust because of their predisposed negative conditioning towards Jewry. Accusations and counter-arguments appeared from every corner of academia. Julius H. Schoeps edited the first work that appeared in Germany to counter Goldhagen's argument: *Ein Volk von Mordern? Die Dokumentation zur Goldhagen-Kontroverse um die Rolle der Deutschen im Holocaust* ('A Nation of Murderers? Documentation Concerning the Goldhagen Controversy about the Role of Germans in the Holocaust').[32] Not all of the recriminations to Goldhagen's book came from Germany. Domestic scholars like Fritz Stern, a German–Jewish refugee who, at the time Goldhagen's work was released, was teaching at Columbia University, had some tough criticism to dish out as well. Stern's counter-argument seemed as persuasive, as did the strength of his words:

> Goldhagen singles out those murderers who were 'ordinary Germans' and who, he insists were motivated solely by their 'cognitive model' of the Jew. He then moves from specific and harrowing examples to a grotesque extrapolation: having examined the acts of some hundreds or perhaps even thousands of people, he insists that almost all Germans were moved by the same hatred, approved the killing, and would have acted in like fashion if chance had so decreed. As he writes, '... the institutions treated here ... should permit the motivations of the perpetrators in those particular institutions to be uncovered, and also allow for generalising both to the perpetrators as a group and to the second target group of this study, the German people.' The leap from individual cases to the German people at large is unpersuasive, but necessary for his indictment of his 'second target group'.[33]

That was but a taste of the argument that all Germans were willing participants in the Holocaust, based on several hundred or several thousand Germans who willingly took part. Dr Stern was pointing out the fact that you cannot assume that 80 million Germans were willing participants based on thousands who did have a leading role in the Holocaust. This argument was reinforced when further research about the complicity of German army units in the Holocaust began to be studied in greater detail (which began in the mid-1980s). It only affirms the continued importance of researching this topic even today. The implication of Goldhagen's work is clear: all Germans bear responsibility for the deaths of 6 million Jews. Thus, Goldhagen stirred many passions that have very real personal, social, and political implications. Geoffrey P. Megargee's work *War of Annihilation: Combat and Genocide on the Eastern Front, 1941* is perhaps one of the better studies to be released, and referred to what Goldhagen was claiming. In it, Megargee merges some of the theories expounded by Goldhagen, arguing that Germans in general were predisposed to the kind of annihilation war waged in Russia. Most academics, however, have only proven the guilt of the Wehrmacht during the war. In his conclusions, Megargee states, according to his premise, the crux of German Army guilt:

> In order to ensure their victory, the generals also helped lay the plans for Hitler's vision of an exterminationist war. Later they would claim that the SS was solely responsible for the crimes in the east, but in fact the military's role was crucial. At the most basic level, the crimes could never have taken place if the Wehrmacht had not conquered the ground, but the generals' culpability extends well beyond that fact. They encouraged their soldiers in an attitude that placed little or no value on the life of Soviet civilians, in fact, they ordered their men to use the harshest conceivable means to establish German dominance. They planned for the deliberate starvation of millions of people and for forced labour by millions more. They laid the groundwork for the fatal neglect of Soviet prisoners of war, whose care was their responsibility by international law. And they played a key role in planning for the elimination of the Communist leadership and intelligentsia, including those in uniform, as well as anyone who resisted German rule. That last goal provided the perfect cover for the *SS Einsatzgruppen* and other killing units to murder anyone whom they saw as a threat, including hundreds of thousands of Jewish men, women, and children. Since most of the military's leaders believed that Jews were fundamentally hostile and dangerous, they were able to persuade themselves, with little apparent difficulty, that killing all the Jews was necessary to secure the conquered territories.[34]

The only drawback to Megargee's book is that he only used published works, and as a result could only come to conclusions from observations and assessments of other authors. However, he laid out exactly what the Wehrmacht generals did that stained their escutcheon of honour forever. Another important work regarding German attitudes and decisions made in the East was published a year earlier, in 2005. It was titled *Abgehort: Deutsche Generale in britischer Kriegsgefangenschaft 1942–1945* ('Monitored: German Generals in British War Captivity 1942–1945'). This work, edited by Sönke Neitzel, is a massive compilation of secret conversations taped by British intelligence of German officers held in British PoW camps from 1942 to 1945. The book was thought important enough to be translated into the English language in 2008. The importance of this study is that in many of these secret conversations German officers talked openly of the annihilation war in the East. Not knowing that they were being recorded, they showed emotions ranging from arrogant joy to total indifference. One such example from the book describes a conversation secretly recorded in a PoW camp by the British on 6 May 1945, between *Generalleutnant* Karlimilian Siry, the former commander of the German *246. Infanterie-Division*, and *Generalstabsintendant* Pauer of the *OKH* (*Oberkommandos des Heeres*, the Army High Command).[35] Pauer just listened while Siry expounded on how he would have handled the massive PoW problem that the *Ostheer* had to deal with during the Russian campaign:

> Siry: One mustn't admit it openly, but we were far too soft. All these horrors have landed us in the soup now. But if we'd carried them through to the hilt, made the people disappear completely – no one would say a thing. These half measures are always wrong. In the East I suggested once to the *Korps* [command] thousands of PoW were coming back, without anyone guarding them, because there were no people there to do it. It went quite well in France, because the Frenchman is so degenerate that if you said to him: 'You will report to the PoW collecting point in the rear' the stupid idiot really did go along there. But in Russia there was a space of 50–80 km, that is to say a 2 to 3 days' march, between the armoured spearheads and the following close formations. No Russians went to the rear, they lagged behind and then took to the woods left and right, where they could live all right. So, I said: 'That's no good, we must simply cut off one of their legs, or break a leg, or the right forearm, so that they won't be able to fight in the next four weeks and so that we can round them up.' There was an outcry when I said one must simply smash their legs with a club. At the time, of course, I didn't really condone it either, but now I think it's quite right. We've seen that we cannot conduct a war because we're not hard enough, not barbaric enough. The Russians are that all right.[36]

This outlook did not just arise out of the blue. The Nazis had nine years (1933–1941) to imbue the German nation with a hatred of Jewry and the Slavic people in the East. This hatred was nurtured, fed, and finally legalised by a series of orders that, when combined with anti-Semitic and anti-communist ideology, worked to create conditions that caused criminality on a grand scale. However, we must admit that there existed in the German nation (and indeed, in most European countries) a base level of antipathy by the gentile community towards the Jewish people. Religious anti-Semitism had existed in Europe for hundreds of years. What made the Nazi period different was that racial anti-Semitism was now added, in much the same way that one adds more kindling to a fire. The Nazis were able to exponentially increase that basic anti-Semitic sentiment to the point of madness.

There is no doubt now that the German Army bears a good portion of the guilt for the horrors that occurred in the East. The outcome of the debate as to the degree of that war guilt on the part of the Wehrmacht is still incomplete. This work will hopefully add additional bricks and mortar to the studies mentioned in this introduction, but more precisely, it provides additional documentation to Dr Timothy Snyder's *magnum opus, Bloodlands: Europe Between Hitler and Stalin,*[37] and Mark Mazower's equally important study, *Hitler's Empire: How the Nazis Ruled Europe.*[38] The documentation herein affirms a cruel and extremely genocidal comportment on the part of the Germans, that was particular to these regions of Eastern Europe. This comportment was led by an ideology of exclusion and genocide. It was also the very reason why ultimately Germany was not able to establish an eastern empire as envisaged in *Mein Kampf.*

Chapter 1

GERMAN PREPARATIONS FOR THE INVASION AND OCCUPATION OF POLAND

Drang nach Osten [Spread to the East].

German zeitgeist from the nineteenth century

The growth of German security forces

When the Second World War began on 1 September 1939 Heinrich Himmler called up 91,500 police reservists from the 1901–09 age group. This group had not yet been subjected to the Wehrmacht draft, so Himmler was free to take these men to augment his SS and police forces, which he, rightly, believed would be needed to enforce control over the newly conquered territories.[1] However, the Army soon placed a demand on men going into the police forces. Himmler was forced to hand over two police regiments that had been recently created in Danzig and 8,000 regular policemen, who now helped to form the *Feldgendarmerie* (military field police force) for the *Heer* (German Army).

Up until then, the *Feldgendarmerie* had only consisted of three military police battalions: *Feldgendarmerie-Bataillone 682, 683,* and *685.*[2] The two police regiments created in Danzig were created from *SA* (*Sturmabteilung*) members. Eventually the storm troopers-turned policemen helped to form *60. Infanterie-Division (motorisiert).*[3] On 11 October 1939, Himmler composed an order requesting the expansion of the police battalions by 26,000 men. This would not be the last call-up of recruits into the German police forces. The following table lists the police battalions raised between 1939 and 1941:

Table 1. Police battalions established by the Third Reich, 1939–1941

Police Battalion	Created	Region	Higher Command	% Mobile
Pol. Btln. 2	1939	*Ostfront* (Eastern Front)	*281. Sicherungs-Division*	motorised
Pol. Btln. 32	4/1941	Klattau *Böhmen und Mähren*	*Polizeiregiment Böhmen*, in the 'Czech Protectorate'[4]	m/b[5]
Res. Pol. Btln. 45	6/1941	*Ostfront*	HSSuPF Süd[6]	m/b[7]
Res. Pol. Btln. 53	1941	*Ostfront*	HSSuPF Nord	motorised
Res. Pol. Btln. 64	1939	Belgrade, Serbia	HSSuPF Serbien, then: Militärbefehlshaber Serbien	motorised
Res. Pol. Btln. 65	4/1941	*Ostfront*	*285. Sicherungs-Division*	motorised
Pol. Btln. 67	10/1939	The Hague (Holland)	BdO Niederland	motorised
Pol. Btln. 68	6/1940	The Hague (Holland)	BdO Niederland	motorised
Pol. Btln. 82	4/1941	*Ostfront*	*454. Sicherungs-Division*	motorised
Pol. Btln. 84	4/1941	Hollenschau *Böhmen und Mähren*	Polizeiregiment Mähren, in the 'Czech Protectorate'[8]	motorised
Res. Pol. Btln. 105	9/1939	*Ostfront*	*207. Sicherungs-Division*	motorised
Pol. Btln. 131	9/1939	*Ostfront*	*403. Sicherungs-Division*	motorised
Pol. Btln. 203	5/1940	Holland	BdO Niederlande	motorised
Pol. Btln. 251	10/1940	Kongsvinger, Norway	*Polizeiregiment Südnorwegen*[9]	motorised
Pol. Btln. 252	1941	Bergen, Norway	*Polizeiregiment Südnorwegen*	motorised

Police Battalion	Created	Region	Higher Command	% Mobile
Pol. Btln. 253	1940	Oslo, Norway	*Polizeiregiment Südnorwegen*	motorised
Pol. Btln. 254	6/1940	*Ostfront*	BdO,[10] then HSSuPF z.b.V.	motorised
Pol. Btln. 255	6/1940	Halden, Norway	*Polizeiregiment Nordnorwegen*[11]	motorised
Pol. Btln. 256	12/1940	Harstadt, Norway	Polizeiregiment Nordnorwegen	motorised
Pol. Btln. 301	1940	Warsaw, Poland	Polizeiregiment Warschau[12]	motorised
Pol. Btln. 302	9/1940	Drontheim, Norway	Polizeiregiment Nordnorwegen	motorised[13]
Pol. Btln. 303	1941	*Ostfront*	HSSuPF Süd	bicycle
Pol. Btln. 304	1941	*Ostfront*	BdO, then HSSuPF z.b.V.	m/b[14]
Pol. Btln. 305	9/1940	Kielce, Poland	*Polizeiregiment Radom*[15]	bicycle
Pol. Btln. 306	10/1940	Lublin, Poalnd	*Polizeiregiment Lublin*[16]	bicycle
Pol. Btln. 307	1941	*Ostfront*	HSSuPF Mitte	motorised
Pol. Btln. 308	1941	Biala-Podlaska, Poland	*Polizeiregiment Lublin*	motorised
Pol. Btln. 309	1941	*Ostfront*	*221. Sicherungs-Division*	motorised
Pol. Btln. 310	10/1940	Czentoschau, Poland	*Polizeiregiment Radom*	motorised
Pol. Btln. 311	1941	*Ostfront*	*444. Sicherungs-Division*	motorised
Pol. Btln. 312	9/1940	Spillum, Norway	*Polizeiregiment Nordnorwegen*	motorised[17]
Pol. Btln. 313	1941	Zamosz, Poland	*Polizeiregiment Lublin*[18]	motorised

Police Battalion	Created	Region	Higher Command	% Mobile
Pol. Btln. 314	1941	*Ostfront*	HSSuPF Süd	motorised
Pol. Btln. 315	1941	*Ostfront*	BdO, then HSSuPF z.b.V.	bicycle
Pol. Btln. 316	1941	*Ostfront*	HSSuPF Mitte	m/b[19]
Pol. Btln. 317	1940	*Ostfront*	*286. Sicherungs-Division*	motorised
Pol. Btln. 318	1941	*Ostfront*	*213. Sicherungs-Division*	motorised
Pol. Btln. 319	1941	*Ostfront*	HSSuPF Nord	m/b[20]
Pol. Btln. 320	1941	*Ostfront*	BdO, then HSSuPF z.b.V.	bicycle
Pol. Btln. 321	11/1940	*Ostfront*	HSSuPF Nord	bicycle
Pol. Btln. 322	1941	*Ostfront*	HSSuPF Mitte	bicycle

In fact, by 1 August 1940, the total strength of the entire German police force would amount to 254,454 men.[21] Himmler justified the order to call for an additional 26,000 police recruits in October 1939 by citing the need for the SS and police to properly garrison Poland. This new influx of police recruits created thirty-eight additional police battalions. Of the 26,000 new recruits, 9,000 were born between 1918 and 1920, while 17,000 had been born between 1909 and 1912. The remaining 6,000 recruits were actually *Volksdeutsche* (ethnic Germans) who were recruited from the former Czech Republic as well as from Poland. Police battalions numbered '251' to '256' contained men from the 1918–20 age groups, while police battalions numbered '301' to '325' contained men from the 1909–12 age groups.

In 1940 the police battalions numbered '251' to '256' would be earmarked for the occupation of Norway. Police battalions numbered '301' to '325' were designated for duty in rump Poland. That is, the region of Poland that had not been absorbed into the Reich and which the Germans referred to as the GG *(Generalgouvernement)*.[22] Police battalions numbered '61' to '64' were created from men coming from the region of the Rhineland and Westphalia, while police battalions numbered '101' to '103' were formed in the city of Hamburg, under the *Wehrkreis* X (10th Military District).[23] By 1 September 1939, Himmler's police force amounted to 131,000 men.

SS and *Ordnungspolizei* forces earmarked for Poland

For the invasion of Poland, Himmler organised his SS and police forces into several *Kampfgruppen* (battlegroups). Following in the wake of the German invasion of Poland on 1 September 1939, Himmler sent in police, SS, SD, and security police forces, which were to occupy all conquered areas and impose the German regime by whatever means necessary. Even before the campaign in Poland had concluded, these security forces were fanning out across the country, arriving in captured localities sometimes only hours or minutes behind the leading German military units. In most instances, these security forces brought with them lists of individuals or organisations deemed a threat to the Nazi state. For the invasion, the *Befehlshaber der Ordnungspolizei* (Commander of the Order Police) had grouped their police battalions into six major police *Kampfgruppen* (battlegroups). These in turn were attached to the various German army groups.[24] Most of these police battalions contained a staff company plus three police rifle companies. However, some contained four rifle companies. Although these battalions were already numerically numbered, they were given Roman numerals to simplify their designation for the duration of the Polish campaign. They were all motorised and were organised as follows:

Polizeigruppe 1 – Oberst der Polizei Dr Friedrich Wolfstieg.[25]
I Polizei-Bataillon (i.e. Polizei-Bataillon 92)
II Polizei-Bataillon (i.e. Polizei-Bataillon 63)
III Polizei-Bataillon (i.e. Polizei-Bataillon 171)[26]
IV Polizei-Bataillon (i.e. Polizei-Bataillon 81)
V Polizei-Bataillon (i.e. Polizei-Bataillon 62)

Polizeigruppe 2 – Generalmajor der Polizei Herbert Becker.[27]
I Polizei-Bataillon (i.e. Polizei-Bataillon 101)
II Polizei-Bataillon (i.e. Polizei-Bataillon 102)
III Polizei-Bataillon (i.e. Polizei-Bataillon 103)
IV Polizei-Bataillon (i.e. Polizei-Bataillon 42)
V Polizei-Bataillon (i.e. Polizei-Bataillon 71)

Polizeigruppe 3[28] *– Oberstleutnant der Polizei* Hermann Franz.[29]

Polizeigruppe 4 –
I Polizei-Bataillon (i.e. Polizei-Bataillon 2)
II Polizei-Bataillon (i.e. Polizei-Bataillon 3)
III Polizei-Bataillon (i.e. Polizei-Bataillon 4)
IV Polizei-Bataillon (i.e. Polizei-Bataillon 91)
Polizei-Bataillon 41[30]
I. SS Totenkopf Reiterabteilung (First SS Death's Head Cavalry Battalion)

Polizeigruppe 4 z.b.V.[31] This police battlegroup was led by *Brigadeführer und Generalmajor der Polizei* Karl Pfeffer-Wildenbruch. It was under the German Military Commander for the captured city of Poznan.[32]
I Polizei-Bataillon (i.e. Polizei-Bataillon 61)

Polizeigruppe 5[33] – This police group was led by *SS-Brigadeführer und Generalmajor der Polizei* Arthur Mülverstedt[34] (the General Inspector of the *Schutzpolizei*).[35]
I Polizei-Bataillon (i.e. Polizei-Bataillon 1)
II Polizei-Bataillon (i.e. Polizei-Bataillon 6)[36]
Polizei Reiter Abteilung 5 (5th Police Cavalry Battalion)

Polizeigruppe Eberhardt – This brigade-size unit was led by *Generalmajor der Polizei* Friedrich Georg Eberhardt. The police brigade was organised in the following manner:

Polizeiregiment 1 (Police Regiment 1)
I. Bataillon
II. Bataillon
III. Bataillon
13. Kompanie

14. Kompanie
Reiter zug (cavalry platoon)
Nachrichten zug (communications platoon)
Polizeiregiment 2
I. Bataillon
II. Bataillon
III. Bataillon
13. Kompanie
14. Kompanie
Reiter zug [37]
Nachrichten zug

The SS, SD, and Gestapo forces were organised into Einsatzkommandos, which in turn were grouped into Einsatzgruppen, or Special Action Groups. The following list gives each *Einsatzkommando* and *Einsatzgruppe* according to which SS officer controlled each unit, and which German army it was attached to:

14. Armee
Einsatzgruppe I – led by *SS-Brigadeführer* Bruno Streckenbach.
Einsatzkommando 1/I – Led by *SS-Sturmbannführer* Dr Ludwig Hahn.
Einsatzkommando 2/I – Led by *SS-Sturmbannführer* Erwin Mueller.
Einsatzkommando 3/I – Led by *SS-Sturmbannführer* Dr Alfred Hasselburg.
Einsatzkommando 4/I – Led by *SS-Sturmbannführer* Dr Karl Brunner.
Gestapo Sonderkommando (30 men) – This platoon-sized unit was led by *Kriminalkommissar* (Criminal Inspector) Johann Schmer.

10. Armee
Einsatzgruppe II – Commanded by *SS-Obersturmbannführer* Dr Emanuel Schäfer.
Einsatzkommando 1/II – Led by *SS-Obersturmbannführer* Otto Sens.
Einsatzkommando 2/II – Led by *SS-Sturmbannführer* Karl Rux.

8. Armee
Einsatzgruppe III – Commanded by *SS-Sturmbannführer* Dr Herbert Fischer.
Einsatzkommando 1/III – Led by *SS-Sturmbannführer* Dr Wilhelm Scharpwinkel.
Einsatzkommando 2/III – Led by *SS-Sturmbannführer* Dr Fritz Liphardt.

4. Armee
Einsatzgruppe IV – Commanded by *SS-Brigadeführer* Lothar Beuthel.
Einsatzkommando 1/IV – Led by *SS-Sturmbannführer* Helmut Bischoff.
Einsatzkommando 2/IV – Led by *SS-Sturmbannführer* Dr Walter Hammer.

3. Armee

Einsatzgruppe V – Commanded by *SS-Standartenführer* Ernst Damzog.

Einsatzkommando 1/V – Led by *SS-Sturmbannführer* Julius Gräfe.

Einsatzkommando 2/V – Led by *SS-Sturmbannführer* Dr Robert Schefe.

Einsatzkommando 3/V[38] – Led by *SS-Sturmbannführer* Dr Walter Albath.

***Militärbefehlshaber in Westpreußen* (Military Commander West Prussia)**

Einsatzkommando 16 – Led by *SS-Oberführer* Dr Otto Rasch[39]

Einsatzkommando 16 was located in West Prussia and led by *SS-Obersturmbannführer* Rudolf Träger. *Einsatzkommando 16* had four principal sub-commands, *three 'Teilkommando'* and *one SD Kommando*:[40]

Teilkommando Gdingen (Gdansk) – led by *Kriminal Kommissar* (Criminal Commissioner) Friedrich Class.

Teilkommando Bromberg (Bydgoszcz) – led by *SS-Sturmbannführer* Jakob Lölgen.

Teilkommando Thorn (Torun) – led by *Kriminalkommissar* Hans-Joachim Leyer.

SD Kommando 16 – Led by an SD officer, *SS-Sturmbannführer* Franz Röder.

Deutscher Militärkommandant Posen (German Military Commander Posen)

Einsatzgruppe VI – led by *SS-Oberführer* Erich Naummann.

Einsatzkommando 1/VI – led by *SS-Sturmbannführer* Franz Sommer.

Einsatzkommando 2/VI – led by *SS-Sturmbannführer* Gerhard Flesch.

14. Armee

Einsatzgruppe z.b.V. von Woyrsch[41] *(Einsatzgruppe VII)* – commanded by *SS-Obergruppenführer* Udo von Woyrsch, with:

Einsatzkommando A – led by *SS-Brigadeführer* Otto Hellwig.[42]

Einsatzkommando B – led by *SS-Oberführer* Dr Hans Trummler.[43]

SS Heimwehr Danzig Bataillon – This was a special SS battalion, mostly composed of ethnic Germans living in Gdansk (Danzig). It was originally designated as *III. Sturmbann/SS-Totenkopfstandarte 4.*[44] After the Polish campaign it was absorbed into the newly forming *3. SS Infanterie-Division 'Totenkopf' (motorisiert).*[45] This SS battalion was led by *SS-Obersturmbannführer* Hans Friedemann Götze. The Regimental Adjutant was *SS-Obersturmführer* Harro Westermann (Nazi Party No. 3,553,657 & SS No. 71,356). Westermann was killed in Danzig on 12 September 1939.

SS-Totenkopfstandarte 2 'Brandenburg' – This was the *SS-Totenkopfstandarte 4* under *SS-Gruppenführer* Günther Pancke and his adjutant, *SS-Standartenführer* Paul Nostitz. This unit was under the German *8. Armee* command. It contained four battalions with four companies per battalion. In addition, it had a communications company. It was employed in Poland under *Einsatzgruppe 3*, in the area of *8. Armee*. A part of the unit was absorbed into the *3. SS Infanterie-Division 'Totenkopf' (motorisiert)* in mid-October 1939. That same month, the regiment was renamed *SS Totenkopf Standarte 5*. The initial three commanders were (in order): *SS-Obersturmbannführer* Michael Lippert, *SS-Standartenführer* Otto Reich, and *SS-Standartenführer* Paul Nostitz

Biographical notes on the Einsatzgruppen officers

The following are brief biographies of the officers in command of these SS, SD, and Police formations:

Dr Walter Albath was born on 7 December 1904. His Nazi Party number was 1 719 177. His SS membership number was 260 971. He was promoted to *SS-Standartenführer* on 9 November 1943. After the Polish campaign he served as Inspector of the Security Police and SD in Düsseldorf.

Lothar Beuthel served on the staff of the Security Police and SD in Posen (Poznan).[46] He was accused of committing atrocities in Poland, first on 10 September 1939 while serving in his Einsatzkommando and in conjunction with *Polizei-Bataillon 6*. This included the shooting of 500 Polish communists and members of the intelligentsia in Bromberg (Bydgosczcz) on 9 September 1939, and the shooting of 1,700 people in the Campinos Forest near Posen from 7–8 December 1939.

Helmut Bischoff was born on 1 March 1908. His Nazi Party number was 203 122. His SS membership number was 272 403. He was a holder of the Death's Head honour ring and Iron Cross, 2nd Class. In 1940 he served as Director of the Gestapo while stationed in Posen. He was promoted to the rank of *SS-Obersturmbannführer* in the SD on 21 June 1943. In December 1943, he was appointed as head of security for Germany's *Rachewaffen* (Vengeance Weapons) programme tasked with protecting the building installation where the V1 and V2 rockets were built. In addition, he led SD men in the Mittelbau-Dora Concentration Camp, which was actually a sub-camp of Buchenwald Concentration Camp, before becoming a separate camp in 1944. The actual factory was located in a series of connecting underground tunnels underneath Kohnstein Hill, near Nordhausen, in the Harz mountrains of Thuringia. It was there that the V2 rockets were built. On 9 February 1945 he was made *Kommandant der Sicherheitspolizei z. b. V.* (Commander of the Security Police for Special Employment) for the V2 programme. One unsubstantiated source states that in 1944 he was transferred into the ranks of the *Waffen-SS* and demoted to the rank of *SS-Untersturmführer* (Second Lieutenant) for some infraction. The story goes that he was attached to the *1. Kompanie (Volkswagen Schwadron)* of *SS Aufklärungs Abteilung 8* of the *8. SS Kavallerie Division 'Florian Geyer'*. Serving in that unit, he won the second highest German military decoration, the *Deutsches Kreuz in Gold* (German Cross in Gold) on 30 December 1944. This occurred supposedly while the *8. SS Kavallerie Division 'Florian Geyer'* was surrounded in Budapest, Hungary. If that is true, Bischoff would have to have been inducted into the *Waffen-SS* no later than the summer of 1944.

Dr Karl Brunner was born on 26 July 1900. His Nazi Party number was 1 903 386, while his SS membership number was 107 161. He was promoted to *SS-Brigadeführer und Generalmajor der Polizei* on 9 November 1942. On 15 September 1943 he was appointed to lead *SS und Polizeiführer Alpenland.* This SS command was based in Bozen (Bolzano), Italy. Given his post, he worked closely with *SS-Oberführer und Oberst der Polizei* Hans Griep.[47] Brunner would also hold the title of *Inspekteur der Sicherheitspolizei und des SD* (Inspector of the Security Police and SD) in Salzburg, from February 1940 to April 1944.

Ernst Paul Heinrich Damzog was born on 30 October 1892. His Nazi Party number was 5081001. He had a relatively early SS member ship number: 36 157. He became *Inspekteur der Sicherheitspolizei und des SD in Posen* (Poznan) on 23 October 1939. He was then assigned as Inspector of the Security Police and SD in the staff of the *Höhere SS und Polizeiführer Wartheland* (Higher SS and Police Leader *Wartheland*) in Posen, from 20 November 1939 until 10 February 1945. He was promoted to *SS-Brigadeführer und Generalmajor der Polizei* on 21 June 1944.

Dr Herbert Fischer was born on 30 December 1904. He did not belong to the Nazi Party, but he was a member of the SS. His membership number was 267 238. He was holder of the Death's Head honour ring. He died on 31 December 1945. From 1937 to 1938, Fischer served in the Legion Condor in Spain. His position was head of the GFP – *Geheim Feldpolizei Gruppe* (Secret Field Police Group) for the Condor Legion. At the time, he held the rank of *Feldpolizeidirektor* (Field Police Director). The group of detectives led by him and subordinate to the *Abwehr* was listed under the designation S/88/Ic. It consisted of between ten to fifteen police officers. His deputy here was Wilhelm-Heinrich Schmitz (born 1908), who served with him for several months. The principal mission of his secret field police unit was to interrogate captured Republican soldiers, but in particular German members of the communist Thälmann Battalion. On 11 September 1938, Fischer was promoted to *SS-Hauptsturmführer,* and on 20 April 1941, to *SS-Sturmbannführer.*

Gerhard Flesch was born on 8 October 1909. His Nazi Party number was 3 018 617, while his SS membership number was 267 300. He was promoted to *SS-Obersturmbannführer* on 30 January 1944. He was holder of the War Service Cross, 1st Class, and Iron Cross, 2nd Class. He served in the RSHA (*Reichssicherheitshauptamt* – the Reich Main Security Office). From September 1939, Flesch was leader of *Einsatzkommando 2/VI,* which was stationed in Posen. Like many in the *Einsatzkommando* units, he took part in *Unternehmen Tannenberg,* the elimination of Polish intelligentsia and leaders in the areas of Poland that Nazi Germany annexed.

Julius Gräfe was born on 10 September 1910. His Nazi Party number was 4 277 440. His SS membership number was 120 509. He served in *Stammabteilung 68* (Cadre Battalion 68) when he joined the SS. He became an *SS-Sturmbannführer und Major der Polizei* on 15 September 1941.

Dr Ludwig Hahn was born on 23 January 1908. He had a relatively early Party membership number (194 463), and SS number (65 823). He was appointed as *Inspekteur der Sicherheitspolizei und des SD Warschau* (Chief of the Security Police and SD in Warsaw). Hahn had a network of agents within the Polish resistance. For his work, he was promoted to *SS-Standartenführer* (Colonel) on 20 April 1944.

Dr Walter Hammer was born on 30 June 1907. His Nazi Party number was 3 196 199, while his SS membership number was 280 155. He was bearer of the *Reichsführer-SS* Honour Ring. As part of the *Einsatzgruppen* of the Sipo (*Sicherheitspolizei,* Security Police) during the invasion of Poland, Hammer was appointed leader of *Einsatzkommando 2* of *Einsatzgruppe IV* (leader *SS-Brigadeführer* Lothar Beutel). This consisted of two *Einsatzkommandos: Einsatzkommando 1/IV,* led by *SS-Sturmbannführer und Regierungsrat* Helmut Bischoff, and *Einsatzkommando 2/IV,* led by *SS-Sturmbannführer und Regierungsrat* Dr Walter Hammer.

Dr Alfred Hasselberg was born on 30 August 1908 and died in the city of Frankfurt am Main on 3 April 1950. He was promoted to *SS-Sturmbannführer* on 26 September 1938. His Nazi Party number was 2 837 238, and his SS membership number was 272 286. He was a lawyer by trade. He apparently had some type of disciplinary issues while working for the *Geheimstaatspolizei* (the State Secret Police). After 1938, he was not promoted to a higher rank within the SS. According to another SS officer, *SS-Obersturmbannführer* Johannes Müller, Hasselberg was expelled from the Gestapo in 1939 and transferred into the Luftwaffe.

Otto Hellwig was born on 24 February 1898. His Nazi Party number was 2 155 331. His SS number was 272 289. He was promoted to *SS-Brigadeführer und Generalmajor der Polizei* on 30 January 1943. In December 1944 he was promoted to *SS-Gruppenführer und Generalleutnant der Polizei.* From the end of October 1942 to May 1943 he held the post of *SS und Polizeiführer Zhitomir.* In that capacity, he was responsible for burning down 108 villages between October 1942 and January 1943. From June 1943 until July 1944, he held the post of *SS und Polizeiführer Bialystok.* In December 1944 he became deputy commander of *SS-Oberabschnitt 'Nordost'* (whose headquarters were located in Königsberg). He held that post until the end of the war.

Dr Fritz Liphardt was born on 3 May 1905. His Nazi Party number was 2 653 601. His SS membership number was 280 121. He was holder of the War Service Cross, 2nd Class, and the Iron Cross, 2nd Class. From November 1939 to October 1943, Liphardt was placed in charge of the post of *Kommandeur der Sicherheitspolizei und des SD (KdS) Radom.* He was promoted to *SS-Obersturmbannführer* on 9 November 1942. Beginning in November 1943 until the spring of 1945, he was head of the *Gestapo* in Stettin (Szczecin).

Erwin Müller was born 19 June 1903. His Nazi Party number was 306 903. His SS membership number was quite low (14 677). In 26 November 1941 he was the commander of *Einsatzkommandos 'R'*, which at the time was stationed in Zhitomir. From 10 February 1943 to March 1944 he was leader of *Einsatzkommando der VoMi in Gebiet Transnistrien* (VoMi Task Force in the Transnistria Region). The abbreviation 'VoMi' stood for *Volksdeutsche Mittelstelle* (Ethnic German Liaison Office). He was promoted to *SS-Standartenführer* on 1 August 1944. A report from Department I A5 of the RHSA (*Reichssicherheitshauptamt,* Reich Security Maun Office) dated December 1944 stated that Müller had been missing since autumn 1944. Most likely this occurred as a result of the Red Army advance into Romania, beginning in the late summer of 1944 and continuing into the autumn.

Erich Naumann was born on 29 April 1905. His Nazi Party number was 170 257, while his SS membership number was 107 496. He was a holder of the Death's Head honour ring, War Service Cross, 1st Class, and Iron Cross, 1st Class. He was made Inspector of the Security Police and SD in Nuremberg. He was promoted to the rank of *SS-Brigadeführer und Generalmajor der Polizei* on 9 November 1942. He commanded *Einsatzgruppe 'B'* during the Russian campaign from November 1941 until 1943, when he was named as the new *Kommandeur der Sicherheitspolizei und des SD im Nederland.* He was condemned to death during the Nuremberg War Crimes Trials on 8 April 1948. He was hanged in Landsberg prison on 8 June 1951.

Dr Otto Rasch was born in Friedrichsruh on 7 December 1891. He joined the Nazi Party in 1931 (Party Number 620 976), and joined the SS in 1933 (Membership Number 107 100). He was *Inspektor der Sicherheitspolizei und des SD im Königsberg*, in East Prussia, before the war. The attack on the German Pitschen Forestry station, planned by the SD to look like a Polish army attack on German soil, was headed by Dr Rasch. On 14 December 1940 he was promoted to the rank of *SS-Brigadeführer und Generalmajor der Polizei*. He became the leader of *Einsatzgruppe 'C'*, which was operating in Ukraine during the Russian campaign. He was charged for being responsible for ordering the shooting of thousands of Jews in Kiev in September 1941. He quarrelled with *Generalkommissar für Ukraine*, Erich Koch, and shortly thereafter was removed from his post. He was given leave and succeeded in prolonging his leave in Germany indefinitely. Late in the war he was offered the post of *Höherer SS- und Polizeiführer für Frankreich–Norditalien*, but refused the position in favour of becoming the Mayor of Wittenburg and Director of the Continental Oil AG Company. Following the war, he contracted Parkinson's disease. He was tried in the Nuremberg War Crimes trials of 1946–48, but was judged too ill to continue in September 1947. He died of Parkinson's disease on 1 November 1948.

Karl Heinz Rux was born on 3 September 1907. His Nazi Party number was 1 444 292, While his SS membership number was 231 696. At the time of the Polish campaign, he was an *SS-Sturmbannführer*. Rux was unique among the *Einsatzgruppen* and *Einsatzkommando* officers during the Polish campaign in that he had been born in German lands that were later ceded to Poland by the Treaty of Versailles. He was born in the city of Bromberg (Bydgoszcz), and had only settled in Schneidemühl, Germany, after his family chose to flee Polish rule.[48] He was promoted to *SS-Obersturmbannführer* on 9 November 1942. He was a bearer of the Death's Head honour ring.

Dr Wilhelm Scharpwinkel was born on 4 December 1904. He was a holder of the War Service Cross, 2nd Class, and the Death's Head honour ring. His Nazi Party number was 1 053 578. His SS membership number was 290 803. On 1 October 1936 Scharpwinkel was inducted into the *Geheimstaatspolizei (Gestapo)*. From November 1940 to August 1942, he was in charge of the *Staatspolizeistelle* (State Police Office) that was located in the city of Wilhelmshaven. Then, beginning in September 1942 until the end of the war, he was in charge of the *Staatspolizeileitstelle* (State Police Headquarters) in Breslau, Silesia. He was promoted to *SS-Obersturmbannführer* on 20 April 1943. He was also *Inspektor der Sicherheitspolizei und des SD im Breslau (SS-Militärbezirk Nr. VI)*.

Dr Robert Schefe was born on 23 August 1909. His Nazi Party number was 1 027 861, while his SS membership number was 267 268. He held the Death's Head honour ring and Iron Cross, 2nd Class. He joined the Nazi Party in 1932 and by 1934 was already a member of the *Sicherheitsdienst* (SS Security Service). From September 1938 to February 1940, he was in charge of the *Staatspolizeistelle Allenstein* (State Police Office in Olsztyn). Serving in Poland from August to November 1939, he led *Einsatzkommando 2* of *Einsatzgruppe V*. It was this murder *Kommando* that killed the Polish intelligentsia in Poland. Beginning in March 1940 and continuing until January 1942, Schefe was head of the *Gestapo* in the city of Łódź. He was promoted to *SS-Obersturmbannführer* on 21 June 1943. Schefe then served as leader of *Gruppe V A (Reichskriminalamt)* in the *Reichssicherheitshauptamt* in Berlin until March 1943. He ended the war as the head of the *Kriminalpolizei* (criminal police) in Berlin.

Dr Emanuel Schäfer was born on 15 July 1895. His Nazi Party number was 4 659 879, while his SS membership number was extremely low: No. 280. He was promoted to *SS-Oberführer und Oberst der Polizei* on 21 June 1943. He became the head of the SS Security Police and SD command in Belgrade, Serbia, and was then stationed in Trieste, in north-east Italy. He withdrew his SS and police forces from Trieste as Tito's Partisans began their assault on the city in April 1945. He reached Austria and went into hiding until he was discovered in April 1951, when a de-Nazification court sentenced him to twenty-one months of hard labour for having been a member of the Gestapo. He was charged with gassing 6,000 Jews from the Semlin camp near Belgrade, and sentenced to six and a half years' imprisonment in Cologne Schwurgericht in October 1953. He was released in 1955.

Otto Sens was born on 14 April 1898. His Nazi Party number was 278 102. He had a relatively low SS membership number: 23 662. He became Inspector of the Security Police and SD in Stettin, located along the Oder River, which formed part of *SS-Bezirk XIII* (SS District 13). In February 1934 he was head of the *Anhaltischen Politischen Polizei* (Anhalt Political Police), which was later renamed the *Staatspolizeistelle Dessau* (Dessau State Police). From September to November 1939, Sens was the leader of *Einsatzkommando 1* of *Einsatzgruppe II*, which was responsible for murdering Polish intellectuals and Jews. Later he was transferred to serve as a member of the *Sicherheitspolizei und des SD (BdS) in Krakau* (Security Police and the SD in Kraków). From October 1940 until June 1941, Sens was head of the *Staatspolizei Kattowitz* (Katowice State Police). In July 1941 he became the head of the *Staatspolizei Koblenz* – a choice job and a relatively quiet post in the city of Koblenz, which lies at the confluence of the Rhine and Moselle rivers. He remained there until the end of the war. He was promoted to *SS-Standartenführer* (SS Colonel) on 20 April 1944.

Franz Sommer was born on 30 November 1897. His Nazi Party number was 2 266 842. His SS membership number was 272 578. He was holder of the Death's Head honour ring, Iron Cross, 2nd Class, Wound Badge in Bronze, Honour Cross for Front Fighters, and Clasp of the Iron Cross, 2nd Class. From 1931 he was in charge of the *Politische Polizei* (Political Police) in Oberhausen. He held the same command in the city of Düsseldorf beginning in 1933. He joined the SS in 1936. At the start of the invasion of Poland, Sommer was head of *Einsatzkommando 1*, which was a part of the larger *Einsatzgruppe VI*. His *Einsatzkommando* also took part in the murder of Polish Jews and intellectuals. He was promoted to *SS-Obersturmbannführer und Hauptmann der Reserve* on 9 November 1940. That same month Sommer became the head of the *Kriminalpolizeileitstelle* in the city of Köln. He remained there for several years, then in 1944 he applied for and received a leave of absence to visit Davos, Switzerland, ostensibly for a lung ailment. Wisely, he did not return to Germany until after the war had ended. He later lived in Düsseldorf and passed away quietly in 1980.

Bruno Streckenbach was born in Hamburg in 1902. He joined the Nazi Party in 1930 and the SS organisation in 1931. He was promoted to *SS-Gruppenführer* (SS Major-General) in 1941. In 1939, he became commander of the *Reichssicherheitsdienst im Generalgouvernement*. In 1941 he was appointed chief of *Abteilung I* (Department I – Personnel) in the *Zentralamt für Reichssicherheit* (Central Office for Reich Security). In January 1944 he took command of the *8. SS Kavallerie Division 'Florian Geyer'*. From June 1944 he assumed the post of commander of the *19. Waffen Grenadier Division der SS (Lettische Nr. 2)*. At the end of the war, he became a prisoner of the Soviet Union and was repatriated to the West in 1955.

Rudolf Träger (or Tröger,[49] depending on sources) was born on 23 April 1905. His Nazi Party number was 2 434 089. His SS number was 261 192. A lawyer by trade, he spoke four languages (German, English, French and Spanish). He led *Einsatzkommando 16* into Poland, while *SS-Oberführer Dr* Otto Rasch remained the titular head of *Einsatzkommando 16*. At the time of the Polish campaign, he was an *SS-Sturmbannführer*. He was sent to the SD post in Chemnitz and was later promoted to *SS-Obersturmbannführer*. He was killed on 18 June 1940, apparently serving under *60. Infanterie-Division (motorisiert)* during the final phase of the French campaign. Träger's adjutant during the Polish campaign was *SS-Sturmbannführer* Franz Röder.[50]

Udo von Woyrsch was born on 24 July 1895. He served during the First World War as a first lieutenant, then as an officer of the Frontier Protection Service. He organised the SS in Silesia. He was holder of the Death's Head honour ring, Iron Cross, 1st Class, War Service Cross, 1st

Class, Honour Cross for Front Fighters, and Golden Honour Cross of the Nazi Party. His Nazi Party number was 162 349. He had a very low SS membership number: 3 689. He was promoted to *SS-Obergruppenführer und General der Polizei* on 1 January 1935. He was on the personal staff of the *Reichsführer-SS* (National Leader of the SS). He served as commander of *SS-Oberabschnitt Südost* in Silesia. In September 1939 he led *Einsatzgruppe VII* into Poland. During his service as an *Einsatzgruppe* commander in Poland, his unit was sent to the Katowice area in mid-September 1939 to 'pacify' the region and ended up murdering some 500 people. Acting on Himmler's orders, he began deportations of Upper Silesian Jews on 21 September 1939. These operations brought von Woyrsch into conflict with Field Marshal Gerd von Rundstedt, the chief German army military commander in that region, who managed to stop Himmler's plans for a time. Because of this conflict, on 20 April 1940, von Woyrsch was recalled to Germany and appointed leader of the *Höherer-SS und Polizeiführer 'Elbe'* command, and commander for *SS-Oberabschnitt 'Elbe'*. Due to continued conflict with the Wehrmacht, Himmler removed him from his two posts on 13 February 1944 and assigned him to the *Reichsführer-SS* immediate staff. According to all accounts, he was part of the entourage that escorted Himmler all over north-west Germany from April to May 1945.

Dr Hans Trummler was born on 24 October 1900. He had a very early Nazi Party number: 73 599. His SS number was 254 581. At the time of the Polish campaign, his rank was that of *SS-Standartenführer*. He was head of the *SS-Sicherheitspolizei und SD-Kommando* in Wiesbaden before being posted to an *Einsatzkommando* for employment in the Polish campaign. He was promoted to the rank of *SS-Oberführer und Oberst der Polizei* on 9 November 1941 – long after the Polish campaign was over. Trummler commanded the Frontier Police and the 'Hochlinden defenders' in the staged Polish attack on the German radio station at Gleiwitz. He was bearer of the Golden Honour Ring of the Nazi Party, Honour Cross for Front-fighters, War Service Cross. 2nd Class, and Iron Cross, 2nd Class. At the end of the war, *SS-Oberführer und Oberst der Polizei* Hans Trummler led an SS battlegroup under the control of the *XIII. SS Armeekorps* operating against the Western allies.[51]

The mission of the security forces in Poland

When the German SS, police, and SD units fanned out behind the advancing German Army during the Polish campaign they had several missions to accomplish. Their principal role was to eliminate or incarcerate actual or potential enemies of the Reich. The code name for the operation that would target for elimination around 61,000 Poles (considered the elite of the Polish intelligentsia) was *Unternehmen Tannenberg*. Another role was to prepare the vast expulsion of Polish citizens from the newly created *Reichsgau Wartheland* – the region of western Poland that had been part of Germany before it had been handed over to Poland by the Treaty of Versailles. The *Wartheland* encompassed the city of Posen (Poznan) and the surrounding region.

Their third mission was the collection and eventual liquidation of the Polish Jewish population. The first step was to round up the Jewish people and place them in various ghettos in anticipation of their extermination. Their fourth mission was to combat the rise of a guerrilla movement. All four missions were intertwined and connected, and from the beginning German security forces did not bother to differentiate between any of these four separate categories.

In the case of eliminating actual or potential enemies of the Reich, the SD (*Sicherheitsdienst*) and Gestapo had compiled a fairly extensive list of names of suspected enemies.[52] This list varied for every *Einsatzgruppe, Einsatzkommando, Teilkommando,* and German police unit, depending on the town, city, and region in which they operated. The list contained names of Polish politicians, people considered part of the Polish intelligentsia, as well as prominent civic and important military leaders. A perfect example of this mission was *Teilkommando Bromberg* (Bydgoszcz), which was led by *SS-Sturmbannführer* Jakob Lölgen and was responsible for eliminating 'enemies of the Reich' as directed by the SS list compiled for the city of Bydgoszcz. Between 30 October and 10 November 1939, *Teilkommando Bromberg* executed or expelled the following people using their 'Bydgoszcz' list:[53]

Table 2. Polish citizens killed or expelled from Bydgoszcz, 30 October–10 November 1939

Prominent civilians	Killed	Evacuated	Dismissed
Civic leaders	73	68	66
Public notaries	3	2	1
Pharmacists	2	-	5
Lawyers	-	1	1
Bankers	13	3	10
City officials	1	-	4
Other, various officials	2	1	4

Teilkommando Bromberg was assisted by 370 members of the German Army, 150 men of the NSKK – the *Nationalsozialistisches Kraftfahrkorps* (National Socialist Motor Transport Corps), eighty policemen, and 150 ethnic Germans from the Bydgoszcz *Selbstschutz*.[54] What happened in Bydgoszcz was repeated hundreds of times, all over Poland. Of the approximately 9 million Polish citizens living in the Polish regions annexed by Germany, approximately 560,000 were already earmarked for evacuation to the so-called *Generalgouvernement* (General Government, hereafter referred to as the GG). The GG had been created using Polish territory not earmarked for absorption into the Reich. The GG was considered rump Poland. This forced deportation began almost from the start of the war.

Figure 1. The German military districts as they appeared in 1939. When Poland was conquered, two additional military districts were created from annexed Polish territory.

Between 1 and 16 December 1939, 80,000 Polish citizens (both Jews and non-Jews) were sent to the GG. By 1 May 1940, the following people had been killed or sent to the GG from the *Wartheland* region and surrounding areas:[55]

From East Prussia: 30,000 Jews
From Silesia: 24,000 Jews
From Danzig-West Prussia (Jews and non-Jews): 40,000
From the newly created *Reichsgau Wartheland* (Jews and non-Jews): 90,000
People killed in the annexed territories: 45,000

People killed in the GG: 7,000
Grand Total: 236,000.[56]

Of the above figure, 52,000 were killed and 186,000 were forcibly evacuated from territories annexed by Germany.[57] By the end of 1940, at least 325,000 people from the annexed Polish lands had been expelled and forced to resettle in the GG.

An excuse for murder

Even before the German campaign in Poland ended, Nazi allegations of Poles abusing ethnic Germans surfaced. *SS-Brigadeführer* Lothar Beuthel, the commander of *Einsatzgruppe IV*, reported to *Reichsführer-SS* Heinrich Himmler that 'Bydgoszcz's ethnic German inhabitants could no longer be found'.[58] In addition, he reported several instances of Poles killing ethnic Germans within the city, and said that those few *Volksdeutsche* who could be found were '*Vollständig eingeschüchtert*' ('completely intimidated'). These reports of attacks against the ethnic German community soon reached the ears of Adolf Hitler, who flew into a rage and told Himmler to order that reprisal shootings should take place in Bydgoszcz in order to avenge the Germans killed there. Apparently, there was some truth to the allegations about the ethnic German community in Poland being targeted by frustrated Poles, who saw them as 'Fifth Columnists'. However, the incidence of Poles attacking ethnic German Poles was small, and the Polish government had no official programme geared to subjugate and cow the ethnic German community. Of the one million-plus ethnic Germans living in Poland,[59] only about 5,437 had been positively identified as having died from Polish acts of persecution, while another 45,000 were unaccounted for or otherwise missing.[60]

By the end of the war, about 500,000 ethnic Germans who had been considered Polish citizens before 1 September 1939 ended up serving in the Wehrmacht in one capacity or another. *Einsatzkommando 1/IV*, led by *SS-Sturmbannführer* Helmut Bischoff, a sub-unit of *Einsatzgruppe IV*, was the first to arrive in Bydgoszcz after the German Army had moved on. The SS formation entered the city on 5 September 1939. Earlier, in the neighbouring town of Naklo, Bischoff had encountered ethnic Germans who had been killed. Enraged, he took out his frustration on a hapless Polish looter, whom he personally shot.[61] Two days later, after hearing that a German soldier and a policeman had been killed by unknown assailants, he ordered the execution of thirty-four Polish citizens. It stands to reason that most ethnic Germans living in Poland were eventually accounted for, since the Germans made good use of them during the war.

Most of these Polish citizens of German descent were grouped into three separate types of ethnic Germans.[62] The Germans recruited perhaps 300,000 Category I ethnic German Poles. Around 110,000 Category II ethnic German Poles were also conscripted into the German Armed Forces.[63] Finally, about 90,000 Category III ethnic German Poles were drafted into the German Army. By contrast, 380,000 Poles served in the Polish Home Army (*Armija Krajowa*, abbreviated as AK) during the war.[64] What all this means is that while the case could be made that Poles killed ethnic German citizens in Poland after the German invasion, these incidences were nevertheless an aberration. The number of Nazi retaliation murders of Polish citizens was wholly out of proportion and far outnumbered the killings of ethnic German Poles.

In their expulsion of Jews and other Polish citizens from the annexed territories, the Germans employed not only the SS, Sipo, and SD, but *Ordnungspolizei* units as well. When war broke out between Germany and the Soviet Union, and the eastern half of Poland came under German control, these forced evacuations of regions earmarked for German colonisation continued. A perfect example can be seen in the actions of *Polizei-Bataillon 322*. Charged with clearing sections of the Bialystok region, a brief look at its actions in a one-week span, from 25 July–2 August 1941, shows how these deportations took place, and the vast number of people whose lives were affected. Below is a small section of the war diary for the battalion:

> 25 July 1941 – Cleansing operation in the Bialowieza Forest region. 183 families (921 people) evacuated from the villages and towns of Budy, Terenyski, and Pogorzelce, about 4, 6, and 9km north-west of the Bialowieza Forest.
> 26 July 1941 – Cleansing operation. 200 families (1,240 people) evacuated from the villages and towns of Masievo-Nove, Lanczyno, Czolo, and Zamocze, about 13km north of the Bialowieza Forest.
> 27 July 1941 – Cleansing operation continues in same area.
> 28 July 1941 – Cleansing operation. 160 families (945 people) evacuated from the villages and towns of Brovsk, Ploso, Cychovola, Tuszenianka, Niemierzianka, and Jazwiny, about 20km north of the Bialowieza Forest.
> 29 July 1941 – Cleansing operation. 100 families and 577 people evacuated.
> 30 July 1941 – Cleansing operation. 320 families and 1,133 people evacuate.
> 31 July 1941 – Cleansing operation. 1,619 people plus 200 Russian PoWs moved. Forty-five Polish and Russians were shot for supposedly being communist functionaries.
> 2 August 1941 – Seventy-two people apprehended, of whom thirty-six were executed.[65]

Establishing the SD station posts in Poland

After the fall of Poland, the special *Einsatzkommandos* formed were dissolved and their personnel were dispersed all over occupied Poland into SD station posts. These were located in areas annexed by Germany, and those that became a part of the GG. The troops under the various *Einsatzkommando* units were posted throughout the country. For example, *Einsatzkommando 16* helped to create *Stapoleitstelle Danzig* (Police Control Centre Gdansk), *Stapoleitstelle Bromberg* (Bydgoszcz), and *Stapoleitstelle Graudenz* (Grudziad).[66] *Teilkommando Gdingen*, also known as Gotenhafen, or Gdynia in Polish, went to that Polish city after which it was named. Likewise, *Teilkommando Bromberg* was posted to Bydgoszcz, while *Teilkommando Thorn* was posted to Torun.

Figure 2. The partitioning of Poland and annexation of Polish territory.

The staff of *Einsatzgruppe VI* became the nucleus for the *Inspektor der Sicherheitspolizei und SD im Posen. Einsatzkommando 1/VI* became *Stapostelle*

Łódź (State Police Office Łódź), *Einsatzkommando 2/VI* became *Stapostelle Posen* (Poznan). The staff of *Einsatzgruppe V* went on to become the nucleus for the *Inspektor der Sicherungspolizei und SD im Posen. Einsatzkommando 1/V* went on to become *Stapostelle Hohensalza* (Inowroclaw) and Drogusovo. *Einsatzkommando 2/V* did the same, becoming a *Stapostelle* in Pultusk and Makow. *Einsatzkommando 3/V* was used to staff *Stapostelle Soldau, Plonsk,* and *Siedlce. Einsatzgruppe IV* became the nucleus of the *Kommandeur der Sicherheitspolizei und SD im Warschau* (Warsaw) and also helped to form the same in Bialystok (after the German invasion of the USSR).[67] Similarly, *SS-Obersturmbannführer* Mühle became *Kommandeur der Sicherheitspolizei und SD im Lublin,* and *SS-Obersturmbannführer* Heim the *Kommandeur der Sicherheitspolizei und SD im Krakau.*

Figure 3. When Nazi Germany conquered Poland, it created two military districts from Polish territories it annexed: *Danzig-Westpreussen* (District 20), and *Wartheland* (District 21). A third area, labelled Zichenau, was annexed to East Prussia.

Many former *Einsatzgruppen* and *Einsatzkommando* officers went on to take positions within the police administration in the GG. The commander of *Einsatzkommando 2/III*, Dr Fritz Liphardt, was still the *Inspektor der Sicherungspolizei und SD im Radom* in 1944. Other ex-*Kommando* officers who were inspectors of the SiPo (abbreviation of *Sicherheitspolizei*, the SS Security Police), and *Sicherheitsdienst*, included Karl Rux in Bydgoszcz, Ernst Damzog in Poznan, Dr Ludwig Hahn in Warsaw, and Erwin Müller in Lublin. Erwin Müller would be replaced by *SS-Sturmbannführer* Dr Pirtz in 1943. All of the other commanders were eventually posted to other duties. The men that had been employed in the special action groups were thus dispersed among the conquered Polish cities and towns. The German Order Police similarly set up commands and posts throughout the countryside. The Nazi Party was tasked with controlling the civilian administration of what the Germans referred to as the GG.

Figure 4. The German military districts as they appeared in 1940.

In the special region of Zichenau that was annexed by the Reich, civilian Nazi Party leaders were eventually installed. You can see the transition from military to civilian control by the men who ruled this region of annexed Polish territory:

Zichenau Administrative District – Head of the civil administration (South-east Prussia Special Staff Area):

6 September 1939: *SS-Brigadeführer* Heinz Jost (from Berlin).
10 September 1939: *Landeshauptmann* Helmut von Wedelstädt (from Königsberg).

District President, Zichenau Administrative District:

26 October 1939: *Leiter der Zivilverwaltung, Gouverneur* Helmut von Wedelstädt.
24 November 1939: *Vizepräsident des Exekutivrat, SA-Standartenführer* Dr Hermann Bethke.
April 1940: *Regionaler Organisations- und Ausbildungsleiter der NSDAP* Paul Dargel (from Königsberg).
November 1940: *Regionaler Organisations- und Ausbildungsleiter der NSDAP* Paul Dargel (from Zichenau).
1 September 1941: *Vizepräsident der Regierung* Clemens Roßbach (from Zichenau).

The Generalgouvernement (GG)

The GG comprised the Polish territories that were not annexed and incorporated into the Reich. The civilian administration of the GG was headed by *Generalgouverneur* Dr Hans Frank. Frank, who had been appointed in October 1939, was a prominent Nazi lawyer who was now put in charge of four basic districts that made up the GG.[68] The seats of these four administrative districts were located in the Polish cities of Warsaw, Kraków, Lublin and Radom. When the USSR was invaded, a fifth district, Galicia, was created, with the administration located in Lemberg (Lviv in English, but spelled Lwów in Polish).[69] Not counting the district of Galicia, Frank was in charge of about 90,000 sq km of land and around 34 million Poles. Through Frank, the German administration oversaw the establishment of work camps and the creation of Jewish ghettos throughout the GG. Extermination camps were also established where the Nazis planned to eliminate the Jewish people after collecting them in the ghettos. Four out of the six death camps were located in the territory of the GG.

Food rations were also set by Frank's administration. In most cases where Polish citizens were concerned, the rations were meagre, but in the case of the Jewish population it was set so people would slowly starve to death. When the Polish underground began sabotage, assassinations, and raids against the German occupation government and military, it was Frank's office that established the *kollektive bestrafung* (collective punishment) that justified the *kollektive gewaltmaßnahmen* (collective forced measures). This policy caused the deaths of thousands of Polish civilians who were shot in reprisal for Polish resistance activities. The German attempt to garrison their eastern domains with SS and police forces soon ran into a manpower problem. Faced with mounting partisan resistance in Poland, the Baltic States, Belarus, Ukraine and Russia, the Germans resorted to the recruitment of men from various European populations, including Poland.

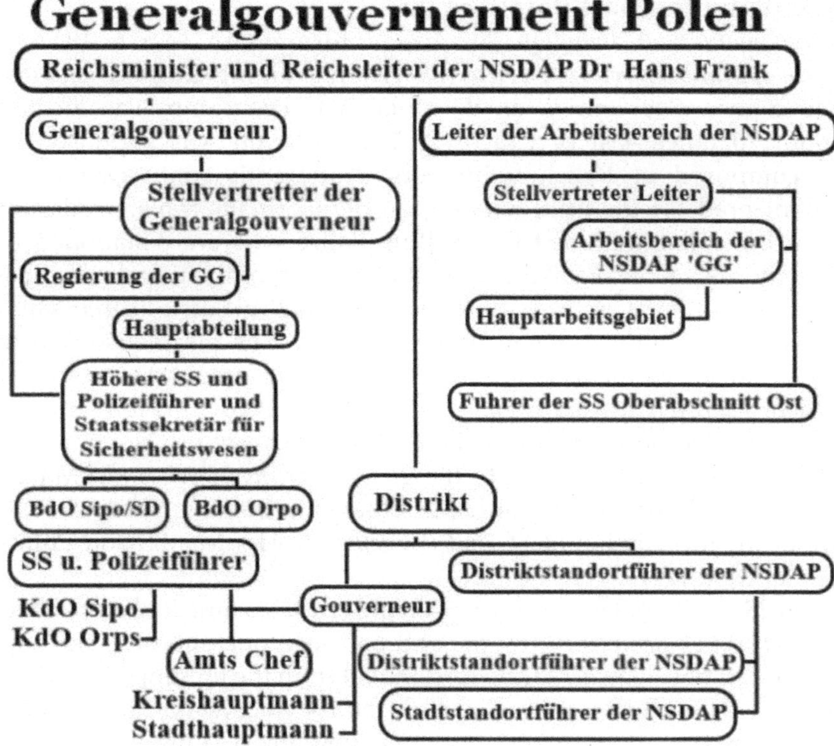

Figure 5. Structure of the Nazi civilian administration of the General Government in Poland.

Frank's government was also made responsible for guarding, housing and feeding the growing number of Jews that were placed in ghettos in every major Polish city in the GG. When the Germans began to deport

Jews not only from the Reich but other parts of Europe to the GG, the feeding, accommodating and guarding of these people became an even bigger nightmare. For example, at the Wannsee Conference, held in a suburb of northern Berlin on 20 January 1942, the issue of overcrowding was brought up by Dr Josef Bühler, who attended the meeting and represented Hans Frank. Bühler was told in no uncertain terms that how to handle the overcrowding was his (and Frank's) problem to deal with. Assisting Frank in administering the GG were Arthur Seyss-Inquart, who became Frank's deputy, and Dr Josef Bühler, who was appointed Secretary of State in the GG.

Schutzmannschaft Bataillon 202

Schutzmannschaft Bataillon 202 began forming in March 1942 at *SS-Truppenübungsplatz 'Debica'* (SS Troop Training Ground 'Debica', which was also known as 'Heidelager'). The camp was located about 70 miles east of Cracow.[70] The battalion was supposed to be composed of Polish volunteers. Apparently, only two Poles volunteered for the unit, whereupon the Germans transferred men from the collaborationist Polish Blue Police who were stationed in the city of Cracow. By April 1942 the strength of the battalion was a paltry 360 men. The formation was stationed in Lutsk in that same year. The battalion became depleted when half the men deserted to the Polish partisans belonging to the 27th Home Army Division, which operated in that area. Based on this incident, the Germans made the decision to transfer the unit to Belarus at the beginning of 1943. There it was attached to the *286. Sicherungs-Division* in March 1943. In April that same year it was billeted in Borisov. There it came under the jurisdiction of *SS und Polizeiführer Mogilew* (SS and Police Leader Mogilev).

On 28 April 1943 it was once again moved. This time it was attached to *Sicherungs-Regiment 44* for anti-partisan operations. The unit performed poorly, warranting its removal from the fighting. It appears that it was withdrawn from combat and sent to serve guard duty in eastern Poland from May to November 1943. Military necessity, however, forced the Germans to employ it in combat once more in December 1943. In that month, the battalion was transferred for combat operations against partisans in western Ukraine. It was used initially against partisan units made up primarily of Jews and former Soviet soldiers who were operating in the forests of the Kolbuszowa region. This time the battalion performed well enough not to be withdrawn from battle. This was on account of the fact that Ukrainian volunteers had been added. In January and February 1944, *Schutzmannschaft*

Bataillon 202 was employed under *Kampfgruppe Prützmann*. In March it took so many losses that the battalion had to be withdrawn once again. In early June 1944 the unit was officially disbanded. One unsubstantiated report indicates that in January 1945 about 150 former Polish Blue Police members of the battalion withdrew into the Reich alongside the German Army, no doubt to escape possible retribution by the Poles or Russians.

Chapter 2

GARRISONING POLAND AND POLISH RESISTANCE TO NAZI RULE, 1939–1944

German garrison forces

The newly established *Wehrkreis XX* and *XXI* (20th and 21st Military Districts), created from annexed Polish territory, were quickly filled with all manner of German Army, Air Force, SS, and police forces, as well as every paramilitary organisation in the Nazi regime. These territories were to be Germanised. One Nazi organisation that was quickly established in these annexed lands was the *Allgemeine-SS* (General-SS) organisation, which contained standing battalions and regiments of SS members. Several of these SS regiments were transferred or were ordered created for service in *Wehrkreis XX* and *XXI*.[1] All of these regiments belonged to the SS organisation. Himmler's SS empire was actually established very quickly. At the end of 1929 the SS contained barely 1,000 men. One year later that number had risen to 2,700. On 1 March 1931, the SS still numbered only 2,727 men. The year in which the SS really began to grow was 1932. In August that year, it comprised 25,853 men and by the end of 1932, the SS had grown to around 52,000 men. In 1934 the *Allgemeine-SS* was created as a separate force from the other branches of the SS. These included the SS concentration camp guards, which belonged to the *SS Totenkopf Standarte*, and the front-line SS combat troops of the *SS Verfugungstruppe*.[2]

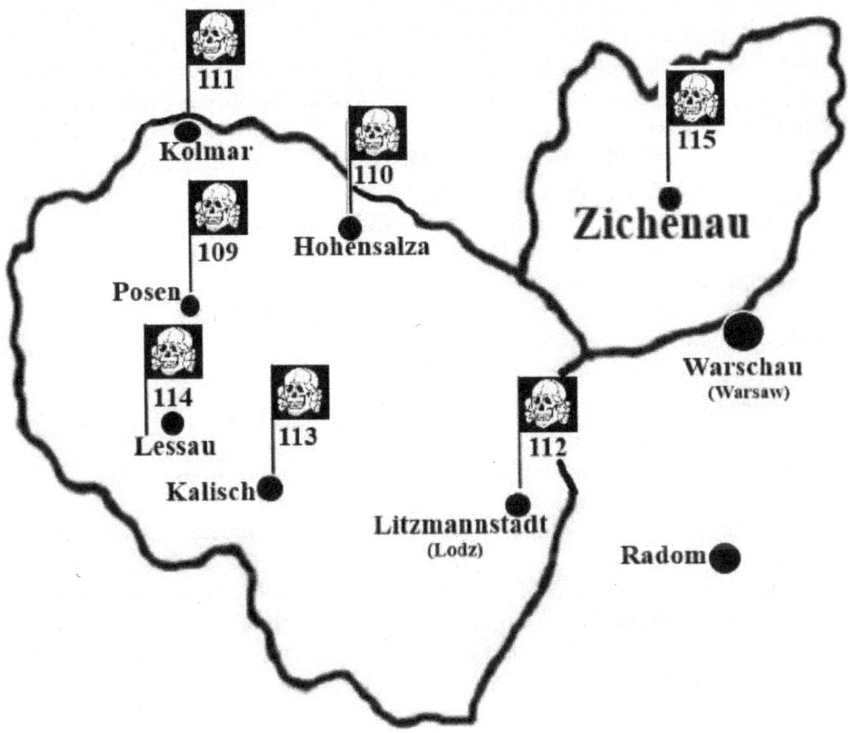

Figure 6. General SS regiments stationed in *Wehrkreis XXI* and in the Zichenau region.

By 1935 the total number of SS men had risen to 164,863. In the beginning of 1945, the *Allgemeine-SS* could still count on 48,500 men in its regiments. By the end of the war (8 May 1945) that number had dropped to some 40,000. The *Allgemeine-SS* regiments used in the annexed Polish territories were organised along the same lines as the *Allgemeine-SS* in the rest of the Reich. They were stationed in the following cities and towns and led by the following officers:[3]

SS-Standarte 109, led by *SS-Obersturmbannführer* Wilhelm Götze (1943–45): Posen (Poznan)
SS-Standarte 110, led by *SS-Sturmbannführer* Karl Schulz (January 1942–May 1945): Hohensalza (Inowroclaw)
SS-Standarte 111, led by *SS-Sturmbannführer* Otto-Wilhelm Lange (May 1944–May 1945): Kolmar (Chodzież)
SS-Standarte 112, led by *SS-Sturmbannführer* Willi Markus[4] (March 1941–May 1945): Litzmannstadt (Łódź)

SS-Standarte 113, led by *SS-Standartenführer* Heinz Mozek[5] (1942–1944): Kalisch (Kalisz)
SS-Standarte 114, led by *SS-Obersturmbannführer* Fritz Leonhardt (1941–October 1944), then *SS-Sturmbannführer* Martin Beckmann (December 1944–1945): Leslau (Włocławek)
SS-Standarte 115, led by *SS-Obersturmbannführer* Paul Exner[6] (1941–August 1944): Zichenau (Ciechanów)
SS-Standarte 116, commander unknown: two *Sturmbann* in Bromberg (Bydgoszcz) and one located in Nakel. The officers in charge of these three battalions were as follows:

I. Sturmbann: SS-Sturmbannführer Wilhelm Fasthoff – Stationed in Bromberg (Bydgoszcz)
II. Sturmbann: SS-Sturmbannführer Christian Schnug – Stationed in Bromberg (Bydgoszcz)
III. Sturmbann: unknown – Stationed in Nakel (Nakel powiedział)

SS-Standarte 117, led by *SS-Obersturmbannführer* Johann Schlechl (1938–45): Konitz (Chojnice)
SS-Standarte 118, led by *SS-Hauptsturmführer* Hans Modrow (June 1940–August 1942): Preussisch-Stargard (Starogard Gdański)
SS-Standarte 119, led by *SS-Obersturmbannführer* Otto Böttcher (1941–45): Graudenz (Grudziądz)
SS-Standarte 120, led by *SS-Hauptsturmführer* Karl Kohlmeyer (1 January 1940–31 December 1940), then *SS-Sturmbannführer* Karl Schulz (1 January 1942–8 May 1945: Kulm (Chełmno)
SS-Standarte 121, led by *SS-Sturmbannführer* Hans-Günther Holzel (1941–44)

The *Allgemeine-SS* (General-SS) regiment, *SS-Standarte 113*, is a good case study for the actual number of troops available to these SS regiments at any one time. One must remember that many of the men who comprised these SS regiments were constantly being called up for military service by all branches of the Wehrmacht. Although these regiments were not prominent and have been basically ignored by most historians, they did play a role in aiding the German occupation of Poland and in fighting the growing partisan threat. They also took part in the persecution of the Jewish population in Poland.

Figure 7. *Allgemeine-SS* regiments in *Wehrkreis XX*.

For example, on 16 June 1940 in the town of Kutno, the Nazis rounded up the Jewish population and forced them into the town's ghetto. During the process the Germans used the local *Gemeindekriminalpolizei* (Municipal Criminal Investigative Police). The *Ordnungspolizei* was also represented by way of the *Schutzpolizei* and *Gendarmerie* forces deployed. Finally, the *III. Sturmbann* (3rd Battalion) of *SS-Standarte 114* was also employed in rounding up the Jewish people of the town and escorting them into the ghetto.

116

Figure 8. A typical cuff band from the SS Death's Head Regiment. This one is from the 116th Regiment. The cuff band was worn on the lower left sleeve of the field jacket.

As the following table explains, each *Allgemeine-SS* regiment had a 'authorised strength' – men who were officially listed as part of the regiment, and an actual strength – men who were actually available. The actual strength was the number of available SS men the regiment could employ if necessary. As can be seen by the average over the years, *SS-Standarte 113* could muster fewer than 500 men at any one time. Five hundred men was equivalent to a battalion in strength. This regiment, therefore, which on paper was supposed to contain three battalions, could barely muster one at any given time:[7]

Table 3. Strength of *SS-Standarte 113*, 1941–1945

Date	Authorised Strength	Actual Strength
30 June 1941	920	657
31 December 1941	1,005	581
30 June 1942	1,097	543
31 December 1942	1,118	497
31 December 1943	1,140	295
30 June 1944	1,146	281
Average	1,071	476

Whenever these *Allgemeine-SS* regiments were employed in an operation, their average actual strength was about a battalion-sized battlegroup. These regiments were vital to the German occupation as they often augmented the strength of German forces in the major cities. The most common way that these units were used was as *Hilfspolizei* (auxiliary policemen). Beginning in 1943, they were employed more and more in the field, taking part in anti-partisan sweeps. In this capacity they supplemented whatever police forces that were employed against the guerrillas. Strengths for two other regiments exist: *SS-Standarte 116* and *SS-Standarte 117*. If we compare the average number of actual troops available from all three SS regiments (*113*, *116*, and *117*), we get an average strength of 488 men. Again, we see that the normal strength of these regiments was just under 500 men. We must also remember that these were part-time members who would meet once a week. Their employment in the field would have been strictly on an emergency basis:[8]

Table 4. Strength of *SS-Standarte 116*, 1941–1945[9]

Date	Authorised Strength	Actual Strength
30 June 1941	1,380	1,012
31 December 1941	1,373	888
30 June 1942	1,389	681
31 December 1942	1,388	604
31 December 1943	1,381	511
30 June 1944	1,373	422
Average	1,380	398

Table 5. Strength of *SS-Standarte 117*, 1941–1945

Date	Authorised Strength	Actual Strength
30 June 1941	740	501
31 December 1941	751	408
30 June 1942	745	304
31 December 1942	731	259
31 December 1943	716	191
30 June 1944	708	150
Average	732	302

In addition to the *Allgemeine-SS* regiments, there were other SS forces stationed in Poland. In May 1940, these other SS units included several *SS Wach-Bataillonen* (SS Guard Battalions) and *SS-Totenkopfstandarten* (SS Death's Head regiments). *SS Wach-Bataillon 5* was located at *SS-Truppenübungsplatz 'Westpreußen'* (SS Troop Training Ground 'West Prussia'), located north-east of Könitz (Chojnice).[10] *SS Wach-Bataillon Oranienburg* was stationed at *SS-Truppenübungsplatz 'Debica'*. This SS training camp was later officially renamed as *SS-Truppenübungsplatz 'Heidelager'* on 15 March 1943. It was located east of Debica, in Galicia (south-eastern Poland). *Reichsführer-SS* Heinrich Himmler also stationed several additional SS Death's Head regiments in Poland:

SS-Totenkopfstandarte 8, led by *SS-Brigadeführer* Franz Breithaupt[11]
SS-Totenkopfstandarte 11, led by *SS-Standartenführer* Prof. Dr Karl Diebitsch[12]
SS-Totenkopfstandarte 12, led by *SS-Obersturmbannführer* Hans W. Sacks[13]
SS-Totenkopf-Reiterstandarte 1, led by *SS-Standartenführer* Hermann Fegelein[14] with:
- *I. Kavallerie-Abteilung*, led by *SS-Hauptsturmführer* Gustav Lombard: Warsaw
- *II. Kavallerie-Abteilung*, led by *SS-Hauptsturmführer* Albert Faβbender: Warsaw

SS-Totenkopf-Reiterstandarte 2, led by *SS-Sturmbannführer* Franz Magill with:
- *I. Kavallerie-Abteilung*, led by *SS-Hauptsturmführer* Herbert Schönfeldt: Cracow
- *II. Kavallerie-Abteilung*, led by *SS-Hauptsturmführer* Reinhold von Mohrenschildt: Lublin

By the start of the Russian campaign, these *SS-Totenkopfstandarte* had been placed under the *Kommandostab Reichsführer-SS* (Command Staff of the National Leader of the SS), and in the summer of 1941 were committed to battle in the USSR. The *Allgemeine-SS* regiments remained in the towns and cities where they were stationed, but their strengths varied from year to year as their members were called up to serve in the armed forces. They were used basically as a supplemental reserve to the regular army and police forces stationed around the country, but were always considered an auxiliary force.

Table 6. SS Death's Head Regiments under the Headquarters of the *Reichsführer-SS*, autumn 1940 to summer 1941.

Death's Head Regiment	Location	Officers	NCO	Men	Total
SS-Totenkopfstandarte 8	Cracow	48	337	1,751	2,136
SS-Totenkopfstandarte 11	Radom	55	349	2,008	2,412
SS-Totenkopfstandarte 12	Poznan-Treskau	46	251	2,296	2,593
SS-Totenkopf-Reiterstandarte 1	Warsaw	79	318	3,115	3,512
SS-Totenkopf-Reiterstandarte 2	Cracow-Lublin				

In addition to these SS forces under the control of the *Kommandostab Reichsführer-SS*, the *Waffen-SS* had several guard battalions stationed in training bases in and around the countryside. Garrison troops in Poland also included army training and reserve forces that were eventually posted there.

Additional police reinforcements

In order to augment the Order Police in Poland, Himmler recruited 6,000 *Volksdeutsche* to serve in the *Ordnungspolizei*. The five police battalions that were created utilising a sizable number of these ethnic German men were the following:[15]

Polizei-Bataillon 210
Polizei-Bataillon 309
Polizei-Bataillon 311
Polizei-Bataillon 318
Polizei-Bataillon 319

Polizei-Bataillon 309 and *Polizei-Bataillon 311* had been created from ethnic Germans from Poland, while the other three were formed from *Volksdeutsche* personnel from the *Sudetenland* and the rest of occupied Czech territory. Later, four additional police battalions were established principally using ethnic Germans. These included:

Polizei-Bataillon 316
Polizei-Bataillon 317
Polizei-Bataillon 320
Polizei-Bataillon 321

Again, most of the recruits came primarily from former Czech territories like the Sudetenland and the German 'Protektorat von Böhmen und Mähren'.[16] By 4 November 1939, four police regiments had been created from the police battalions performing occupation duty in Poland. These regiments and battalions were organised as follows:[17]

Polizeiregiment Warschau:
- *Polizei-Bataillon Warschau I* (formerly *Polizei-Bataillon 301*)
- *Polizei-Bataillon Warschau II* (formerly *Polizei-Bataillon 304*)
- *Polizei-Bataillon Warschau III* (formerly *Polizei-Bataillon 307*)

Polizeiregiment Radom:
- *Polizei-Bataillon Radom* (formerly *Polizei-Bataillon 309*)
- *Polizei-Bataillon Czestochowa* (formerly *Polizei-Bataillon 310*)
- *Polizei-Bataillon Kielce* (formerly *Polizei-Bataillon 305*)

Polizeiregiment Krakau:
Polizei-Bataillon Krakau I (formerly *Polizei-Bataillon 311*)
Polizei-Bataillon Krakau II (formerly *Polizei-Bataillon 321*)
Polizei-Bataillon Tarnow (formerly *Polizei-Bataillon 303*)
Polizei-Bataillon Reichshof[18] (formerly *Polizei-Bataillon 314*)
Polizeiregiment Lublin:
Polizei-Bataillon Lublin (formerly *Polizei-Bataillon 306*)
Polizei-Bataillon Zamosz (formerly *Polizei-Bataillon 313*)
Polizei-Bataillon Biala-Podlaska (formerly *Polizei-Bataillon 308*)

Overall command of police forces in the GG was through the *Befehlshaber der Ordnungspolizei-Generalgouvernement,* or BdO-GG.[19] This command headquarters was located in the city of Krakau (Cracow), also in the GG.[20] Each district in the GG had a 'KdO' *(Kommandeur der Ordnungspolizei),* or Commander of the Order Police. The German police officers who led the BdO during the war varied. Some of these officers served in the capacity of BdO in the GG more than once:[21]

BdO Generalgouvernement (Krakau):
Oberst der Gendarmerie Emil Höring (1–24 October 1939)
Generalmajor der Ordnungspolizei Herbert Becker (25 October 1939–September 1940)
Generalleutnant der Ordnungspolizei Paul Riege (October 1940–21 August 1941)
Oberst der Gendarmerie Rudolf Müller (22 August–November 1941)[22]
Generalmajor der Ordnungspolizei Gerhard Winkler (December 1941–April 1942)
Generalleutnant der Ordnungspolizei Herbert Becker (May 1942–July 1943)
Generalmajor der Ordnungspolizei Hans-Dieter Grünewald (October 1943–March 1944)
Generalmajor der Ordnungspolizei Fritz Sendel (8–22 March 1944)
Generalleutnant der Ordnungspolizei Emil Höring (23 March 1944–January 1945)

The German police officers in charge of the various KdOs *(Kommandeur der Ordnungspolizei)* within the GG had the dual role of being the commander of the local police regiment. Thus, if we list the regimental commanders for each police regiment stationed in the GG, they should also be the KdO commanders for the period of time in which they served as the CO of the particular regiment in question. During the occupation, the following police officers served as commanders of the police regiment stationed in each of the following regions:

KdO – Krakau: *Polizeiregiment Krakau* (later renamed *Polizeiregiment* 23)
Oberst der Schutzpolizei Max Montua, (September 1939–February 1940)
Oberstleutnant der Schutzpolizei Werner Spitta, (February 1940)
Oberst der Schutzpolizei Hermann Keuper (March 1940–6 November 1941)
Oberstleutnant der Schutzpolizei Andreas May (7 November–12 December 1941)
Oberstleutnant der Schutzpolizei Richard Gaβler (13 December 1941–30 July 1942 – died)
Oberstleutnant der Gendarmerie Werner Bardua (1 August 1942–17 April 1944)
Oberst der Gendarmerie Felix Bauer (April 1944–14 November 1944)
Oberstleutnant der Schutzpolizei Franz Heitsinger (15 November–1945)

KdO – Radom: *Polizeiregiment Radom* (later renamed *Polizeiregiment* 24)
Oberst der Schutzpolizei Ferdinand Heske (Nov 1939–Nov 1940)
Generalmajor der Polizei Paul Worm (Oct 1940–June 1942)
Oberstleutnant der Schutzpolizei Walter von Soosten (November 1942–20 April 1943)
Oberstleutnant der Schutzpolizei Russel (21 April 1943–9 April 1944)
Major der Gendarmerie Erich Schwieger (10 April–14 July 1944)
Oberst der Schutzpolizei Felix Bauer (15 July 1944–22 October 1944)
Oberstleutnant der Schutzpolizei Borgsen (23 Octoberr–2 December 1944)
Oberstleutnant der Schutzpolizei Richard Paust (3 December 1944–January 1945)

KdO – Lublin: *Polizeiregiment Lublin* (later renamed *Polizeiregiment* 25)
Oberst der Schutzpolizei Walter Griphan (February–November 1941)
Oberstleutnant der Schutzpolizei Walther von Soosten (November 1941–May 1942)
Oberstleutnant der Schutzpolizei Hermann Kintrup (June 1942–1943)
Oberstleutnant der Schutzpolizei Josef Vogts (16 February–14 July 1944)
Oberstleutnant der Schutzpolizei Hermann Kintrup (June 1942–28 October 1943)
Oberstleutnant der Schutzpolizei Konrad Rheindorf (29 October 1943–October 1944)
Oberst der Schutzpolizei Rudolf Haring (October 1944–21 February 1945)

KdO – Warsaw: *Polizeiregiment Warschau* (later renamed *Polizeiregiment* 22)
Standartenführer und Oberst der Polizei Karl J. H. Brenner (1939–1940)[23]
Oberstleutnant der Schutzpolizei Karl Montua (1940–July 1941)
Oberstleutnant der Schutzpolizei Joachim Petch (August 1941–May 1942)
Oberstleutnant der Schutzpolizei von Zamory (June 1942–February 1943)
Oberstleutnant der Schutzpolizei Rudolf Haring (April 1943–4 July 1944)

KdO – Lemberg (Lviv / Lwów): *Polizeiregiment Galizien* (existed 1941–1942)
Oberstleutnant der Schutzpolizei Joachim Stach (11 August –11 November 1941)[24]
Major der Schutzpolizei Franz Heitzinger (12–15 November 1941)[25]
Oberstleutnant der Schutzpolizei Joachim Stach (16 November–12 December 1941)

Major der Schutzpolizei Franz Heitzinger (13 December 1941–8 January 1942)[26]
Oberstleutnant der Schutzpolizei Joachim Stach (9 January–May 1942)[27]
Oberstleutnant der Schutzpolizei Walther von Soosten (June 1942–July 1943)
Oberstleutnant der Schutzpolizei Franz Heitzinger (August 1943–1944)[28]

In July 1942 the German SS and police forces in the GG were substantially augmented by the arrival of several police regiments, some of which had been formed from existing police battalions in the GG, with additional personnel brought in from the Reich. No additional *Ordnungspolizei* personnel were assigned to the district of Galicia and no separate police regiment was established until 1943. *SS-Gruppenführer and Generalleutnant der Polizei und Waffen-SS* Fritz Katzmann, leader of the *SS und Polizeiführer Galizien* command, initially could only count on two *Schutzpolizei* companies in the city of Lemberg. These two companies were on loan from the town of Gliwice. He later acquired (on loan) two police battalions from *Polizeiregiment Radom*. The commander of *Polizeiregiment Galizien, Oberstleutnant der Schutzpolizei* Joachim Stach, became the first to assume the post of *Kommandeur der Ordnungspolizei* (KdO) for Galicia. In July 1942 *Polizeiregiment Galizien* was disbanded. The commander of the *Schutzpolizeileitstelle* in Lemberg for most of the German occupation was as follows:

Kommandeur der Schutzpolizei im Lemberg – Major der Schutzpolizei Fritz Weise (October 1941 to 2 July 1944)[29]

By August 1940 a total of seven other *Ordnungspolizei* battalions were assigned to the western Polish territories that Germany annexed, while an additional thirteen police battalions were stationed in German-occupied Poland (GG). The seven police battalions in the newly annexed territories of *Wartheland* and *Danzig-Westpreussen* amounted to sixty-three officers and 3,500 NCOs and enlisted men. The thirteen police battalions stationed in the GG included 219 officers and 8,245 NCOs and enlisted men.[30] In the German military structure, the *Wartheland* region, which was part of the annexed Polish territories, became the *Wehrkreis XX* (20th Military District). Polish lands annexed and labelled *Danzig-Westpreussen* became the *Wehrkreis XXI* (21st Military District).

The GG itself was divided into four main districts: Warsaw, Radom, Cracow, and Lublin. A fifth district, Galicia, was added in 1941. This last district was created from a part of western Ukraine and had been formed after the German invasion of the Soviet Union on 22 June 1941. All of these police battalions took part in the forced expulsion and relocation of hundreds of thousands of Polish citizens who, as we shall see, were evacuated from these annexed regions in order to make way for the eventual Germanisation of these lands. In these annexed regions, the German Order Police also had their BdO commands with lower-ranking KdO posts, which in turn controlled the locally posted German *Ordnungspolizei* battalions and regiments. As a rule, only one order police regiment was posted to each KdO. Each regiment had between three and four police battalions. In the *Warthegau* region *(Wehrkreis XXI)*, the BdO was stationed in Posen (Poznan). The *Danzig-West Preussen* region *(Wehrkreis XX)* had a BdO command located in the city of Danzig (Gdansk). The following Order Police commanders were known to have been posted to these two BdO posts:

BdO Posen *(Wehrkreis XXI):*
Generalmajor der Ordnungspolizei Oskar Paul Knofe (November 1939–29 June 1942)[31]
Generalmajor der Ordnungspolizei Walther Hille (30 June 1942–13 December 1943)
Generalmajor der Ordnungspolizei Hans Podzun (14 December 1943–February 1944)
Generalmajor der Ordnungspolizei Dr Walter Gudewill (March 1944–January 1945)[32]
BdO Danzig *(Wehrkreis XX):*
Generalmajor der Ordnungspolizei Leo von Falkowski (September 1939–16 November 1943)
Generalmajor der Ordnungspolizei Franz Diermann (16 November 1943–3 January 1944)[33]
Oberst der Schutzpolizei Walter Strehlow (3 March 1944–29 May 1944)
Generalmajor der Ordnungspolizei Dr Johannes Hachtel (13 June 1944–March 1945)

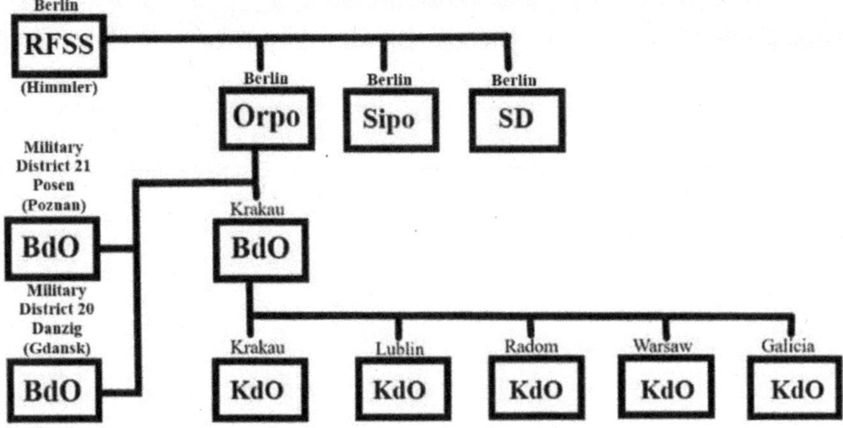

Figure 9. The structure of the German Police Command in Poland.

Danzig was also the city where a *Höhere SS und Polizeiführer* headquarters was located. That command was led by the following officers:

Höhere SS und Polizeiführer Danzig-Westpreussen (Wehrkreis XX)[34]
SS-Obergruppenführer und General der Polizei Richard Hildebrandt (21 September 1939–20 April 1943)
SS-Gruppenführer and Generalleutnant der Polizei und Waffen-SS Fritz Katzmann (20 April 1943–April 1945)
Chief of Staff: *SS-Standartenführer* Karl Thier (9 October 1939–1942)[35]
Kommandeur der Selbstschutz Danzig: SS-Oberführer Ludolf von Alvensleben (9 October 1939–April 1944)[36]

The various *SS und Polizeiführer* headquarters had a special relationship with the German *Ordnungspolizei* due to their ability, because of Himmler's explicit orders, to employ not only SS units, but police forces as they were needed.

This right of control was not limited to the use of police units against partisans and regular enemy forces. The SS also employed the numerous German and auxiliary police units in rounding up and transporting Jews to concentration camps and in helping with the actual liquidation of Jews and others, like the Romani, whom the Germans considered 'undesirables'. *SS-Oberstgruppenführer und Generaloberst der Polizei* Kurt Daluege was the head of the Orpo *(Ordnungspolizei)* up until 1943, when he was forced to retire due to an out-of-control drinking problem. After the war, Daluege testified that from 1941 until 1943 the *Ordnungspolizei* was fully involved in the mass deportations of people to concentration camps and in the mass murder of the Jewish population.[37] In fact, professor Eric Haberer indicated this inter-relationship of SS and police commands when he wrote about the practice the Germans had of assigning SS and police officers with dual command roles.[38]

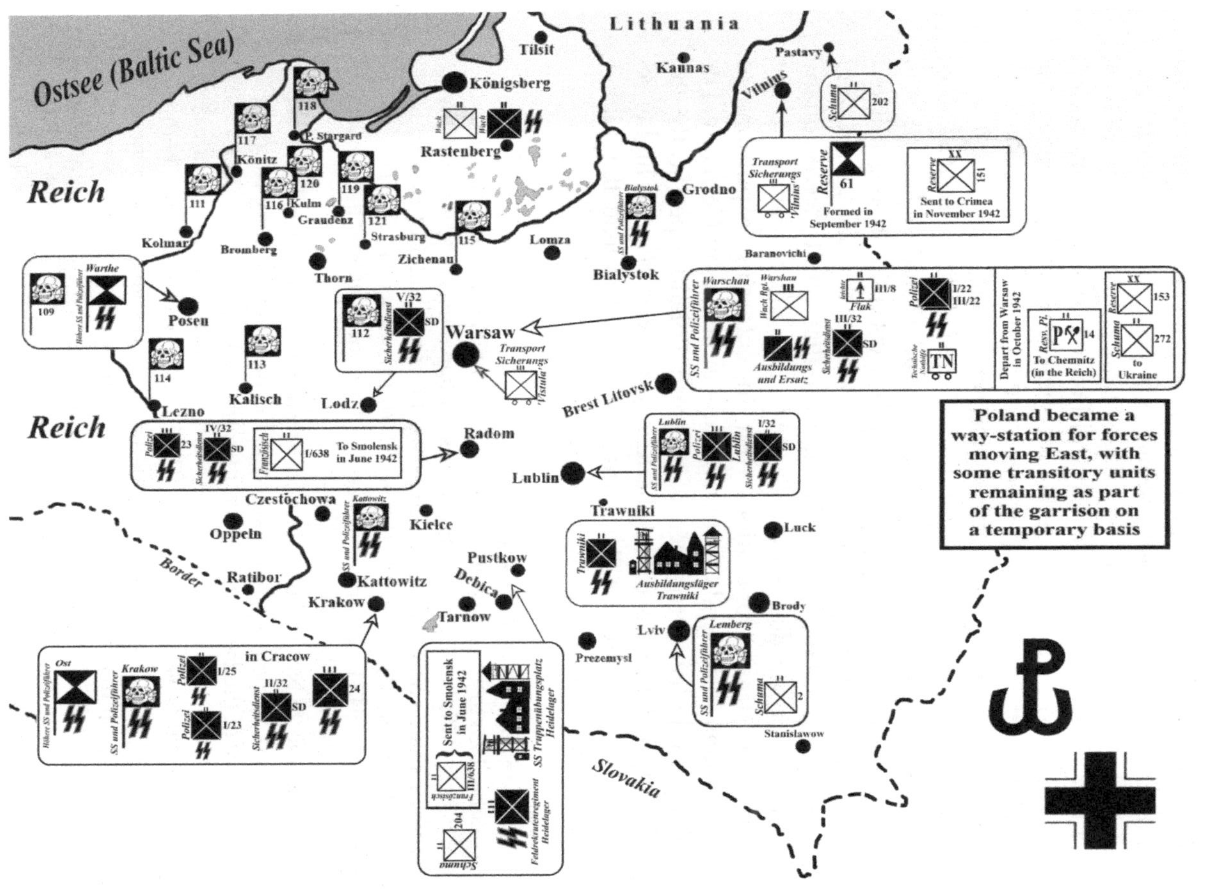

Figure 10. Location of SS and Police forces in Poland in 1941.

For example, in the occupied territories, the *Gendarmerie Gebietsführer* (Rural Police District Commander) would also be assigned the post of *SS und Polizeigebietsführer* (SS and Police District Leader). This practice was followed up and down the chain of command. Below the *Gendarmerie Gebietsführer* were the various posts of the *Gendarmerie Hauptmannschaft* (local town or village rural police post) as well as the *SS und Polizei Standortführer* (SS and Police Garrison Commander), which would normally be located in the same town as the *Gendarmerie Hauptmannschaft*.[39] Professor Haberer showed that many *Gendarmerie* officers in charge of the local *Gendarmerie Hauptmannschaft* also held the title of commander of the *SS und Polizei Standortführer*. The *SS und Polizeiführer* (SS and Police Leader) and *Höhere SS und Polizeiführer* (Higher SS and Police Leader) commands also utilized the *Gemeindepolizei* (Municipal Police), as well as the *Gendarmerie* and the *Landespolizei* (State Police). Foreign auxiliary units were equally employed when needed by the *SS und Polizeiführer* command, not only in anti-partisan operations, but in enforcing expulsions of Polish civilians from lands that were now annexed by Germany. For the occupied Polish territories of western Poland, specifically the region that the Germans called the *Reichsgau Wartheland*, a higher SS command was established. The officers assigned to lead this higher SS headquarters during the war were as follows:

Höherer SS und Polizeiführer Warthe

9 October 1939 to 8 November 1943 – *SS-Gruppenführer und Generalleutnant der Polizei Wilhelm Koppe.* Koppe was simultaneously inspector of the *Sicherheitspolizei* and SD while also being the commander of *Höherer SS und Polizeiführer Warthe. Inspekteur der Sicherheitspolizei und des SD.*

9 November 1943 to 28 January 1944 – *SS-Obergruppenführer und General der Polizei* Theodor Berkelmann.

29 January to 26 November 1944 – *SS-Brigadeführer und Generalmajor der Polizei* Heinz Reinefarth (Not located in Poznan, but working from the Berlin office of the *Hauptamt der Ordnungspolizei*).

27 November 1944 to January 1945 – *SS-Gruppenführer und Generalleutnant der Polizei Willy Schmelcher*. Schmelcher's most recent posting before coming to Poznan was as leader of the *SS und Polizeiführer Shitomir* (Zhitomir) command. He held that command from September to November 1943. In October 1943 Schmelcher was also made responsible for the *Technische Nothilfe* department in the main *Ordnungspolizei* HQ, located in Berlin. He held that post until the end of the war. In that capacity he found a way to leave Poznan and travel to Berlin before the Red Army encircled the city on 10 February. He thus avoided being caught when the city fell to the Russians on 23 February 1945.

It appears that it was common for many of the German Order Police personnel to hold dual Police/SS ranks throughout the war. In April 1943 *Reichsführer-SS* Heinrich Himmler even went so far as to order that the Order Police regiments were to be prefixed with the SS runes. This paper decree may seem of little importance, but it clearly shows the close relationship that had developed since 1933 between the SS organisation and the German police. For all intents and purposes, the German police were indeed a part of the SS. Their actions during the war attest to this and are fully documented in this work. Based on this close cooperation between the Orpo and the SS,[40] a record of the SS commands in the GG should be noted since they had the power to employ police forces:

BdS *(Befehlshaber der Sicherheitspolizei) für den Generalgouvernement:*
SS-Brigadeführer Bruno Streckenbach (1 November 1939–14 January 1941)
SS-Oberführer und Oberst der Polizei Eberhard Schöngarth (14 January 1941–June 1943)
SS-Oberführer und Oberst der Polizei Dr Walter Bierkamp (June 1943–February 1945)
Höherer SS und Polizeiführer Ost – HQ: Kraków
SS-Obergruppenführer und General der Waffen-SS Friedrich Wilhelm Krüger (4 October 1939–8 November 1943)
SS-Obergruppenführer und General der Polizei Wilhelm Koppe. (9 November 1943–April 1945)[41]
SS und Polizeiführer Warschau – with:
Kommandeur der Ordnungspolizei:
Major der Schutzpolizei Karl Mantua (25 October 1939–10 June 1941)[42]
Oberstleutnant der Schutzpolizei Joachim Petsch[43] (27 November–December 1940)[44]
Kommandeur der Schutzpolizei: ?
SS-Obersturmbannführer und Oberstleutnant der Schutzpolizei Karl Daume (26 October 1939–March 1940)
Oberstleutnant der Schutzpolizei Alfred Jarke 1941–43)
Kommandeur der Gendarmerie: ?
Note: Often, whoever led the KdS command would also lead the KdG *(Kommandeur der Gendarmerie)* post.
Commanders of the *SS und Polizeiführer Warschau* post:
Hauptquartier Warschau (HQ Warsaw) –
SS-Gruppenführer Paul Moder (14 November 1939–August 1941)
SS-Oberführer Arpad Wigand (4 August 1941–21 July 1942)
SS-Oberführer Dr Ferdinand von Sammern Frankenegg (22 July 1942–16 April 1943)
SS-Oberführer Jürgen Stroop (17 April 1943–24 September 1943)

SS-Brigadeführer Franz Kutschera (25 September 1943–30 January 1944)[45]
SS-Oberführer Walter Stein (2 February 1944–30 March 1944)
SS-Oberführer und Oberst der Gendarmerie Paul Otto Geibel (31 March 1944–January 1945)[46]
***Kommandeur der Sicherheitspolizei in Warschau* (KdS)**
SS-Brigadeführer Lothar Beuthel (30 September–23 October 1939)[47]
SS-Standartenführer und Oberst der Polizei Josef Meisinger 23 October 1939–1 March 1941.
SS-Obersturmbannführer Ludwig Hermann Karl Hahn[48] (2 March 1941–October 1944)
SS und Polizeiführer Lemberg (Lviv/Lwów) – with:
Headquarters: Lemberg (Lviv/Lwów)
Commanders:
SS-Oberführer und Oberstleutnant der Polizei Fritz Katzmann (November 1939–April 1943)
SS-Standartenführer Willi Ost (20 April 1943–28 July 1943)
SS-Oberführer und Generalmajor der Polizei Theobald Thier (29 July 1943–24 February 1944)
SS-Brigadeführer und Generalmajor der Polizei Christoph Diehm (25 February 1944–16 September 1944)[49]

Kommandeur der Gendarmerie:
Oberstleutnant der Gendarmerie Dr Alois Schertler (1941–43)
Oberstleutnant der Gendarmerie Franz Gansinger (1943–25 October 1944)[50]
Kommandeur der Schutzpolizei:
Major der Ordnungspolizei Fritz Weise (October 1941–2 July 1944)
Kommandeur der Ordnungspolizei: Oberst der Schutzpolizei Joachim Stach (1941–1942)

SS und Polizeiführer Krakau (Cracow) – with:

Kommandeur der Ordnungspolizei:
Oberst der Gendarmerie Felix Bauer (5 July 1944–22 October 1944)
Kommandeur der Gendarmerie:
Oberst der Gendarmerie Felix Bauer (5 July 1944–22 October 1944)

Headquarters: Cracow
Commanders:
SS-Gruppenführer Karl Zech (24 November 1939–30 September 1940)
SS-Oberführer Hans Schwedler (October 1940–August 1941)[51]
SS-Oberführer Julian Scherner (4 August 1941–28 February 1944)[52]
SS-Oberführer und Generalmajor der Polizei Theobald Thier (1 March 1944–January 1945)[53]
SS und Polizeiführer 'Radom'
SS und Polizeiführer 'Lemberg'
Kommandeur der Sicherheitspolizei in Kraków[54]
SS-Sturmbannführer Bruno Müller (September–November 1939)
SS-Standartenführer Walther Huppenkothen (November 1939–January 1940)

SS-Sturmbannführer Ludwig Hermann Karl Hahn (January–July 1940)
SS-Obersturmbannführer Ludwig Rudolf Karl Großkopf (August 1940–April 1943)
SS-Obersturmbannführer Heim (May 1943–1944)
SS-Obersturmbannführer Rudolf Batz (1944–January 1945)
SS und Polizeiführer Lublin – with:
Kommandeur der Schutzpolizei:
Major der Schutzpolizei Melcher (July 1940–?)
Kommandeur der Ordnungspolizei:
Major der Ordnungspolizei Ziehe (October 1939–?)
Kommandeur der Gendarmerie:
Major der Gendarmerie Genz (1939–11 January 1940)
Major der Gendarmerie. Hahnzog (12 January 1940–?)
Kommandeur der Sicherheitspolizei:
Regierungsrat SS-Sturmbannführer Dr Alfred Hasselberg (December 1939–1940)
SS-Standartenführer Walther Huppenkothen (February 1940–?)
Headquarters: Lublin
Commanders:
SS-Gruppenführer Odilo Globocnik (9 November 1939–15 August 1943)
SS-Gruppenführer und Generalleutnant der Polizei Jakob Sporrenberg (16 August 1943–November 1944)
SS und Polizeiführer Radom – with:
Kommandeur der Ordnungspolizei:
SS-Brigadeführer Paul Worm (October 1940–June 1942)[55]
Kommandeur der Gendarmerie:
Major der Gendarmerie Fievet
Headquarters: Radom
Commanders:
SS-Brigadeführer und Generalmajor der Polizei Fritz Katzmann (30 November 1939–August 1941)
SS-Oberführer Carl-Albrecht Oberg (8 August 1941–11 May 1942)
SS-Oberführer und Oberst der Polizei Dr Herbert Böttcher (12 May 1942–January 1945)
Kommandeur der Sicherheitspolizei und der Sicherheitsdienst fur den Distrikt Galizien
SS-Sturmbannführer Helmut Tanzmann (July 1941–March 1943)
SS-Obersturmbannführer Dr Josef Witiska (8 March 1943–30 July 1944) or:
SS-Obersturmbannführer Dr Josef Witiska (8 March 1943–9 September 1944)
Kommandeur der Ordnungspolizei Distrikt Galizien – Lemberg (Lviv/Lwów)
Oberst der Schutzpolizei Paul Worm (1941)
Oberst der Schutzpolizei Joachim Stach (1941–42)
Oberstleutnant der Schutzpolizei Walter von Soosten (1942–43)
Oberst der Schutzpolizei Gustav Schubert (1943–44)

Kommandeur der Gendarmerie Distrikt Galizien[56]
Oberstleutnant der Gendarmerie Alois Schertler (1941–43)
Oberstleutnant der Gendarmerie Franz Gansinger[57] (1943–44)
Kommandeur der Schutzpolizei Distrikt Galizien[58]
Oberst der Schutzpolizei Fritz Weise (1941– 44)
SS und Polizeiführer Bialystok – with:[59]
Headquarters: Bialystok
Commanders:
SS-Standartenführer Werner Fromm (18 January 1942–30 January 1943)
SS-Brigadeführer und Generalmajor der Polizei Otto Hellwig (20 May 1943–18 July 1944)
SS-Oberführer und Oberst der Polizei Heinz Roch (18 June 1944–22 October 1944)
***Kommandeur der Sicherheitspolizei Litzmannstadt* (Łódź)**
SS-Obersturmbannführer Otto Bradfisch (26 April 1942–December 1944)

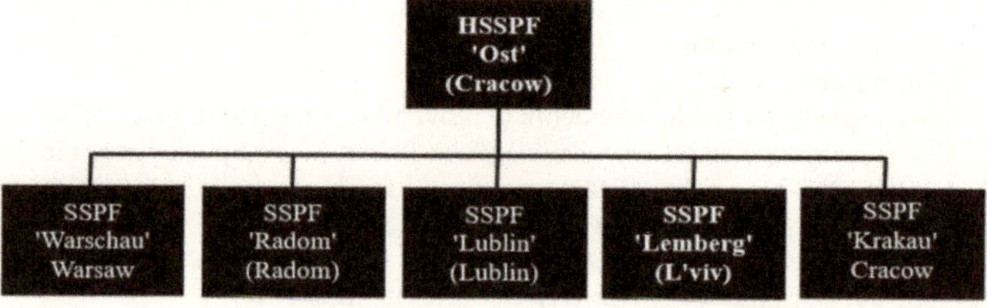

Figure 11. The SS command structure in Poland.

German Ordnungspolizei battalions in Poland

Further German order police battalions made their appearance in Poland and remained on occupation duty for various periods of time and in different locations throughout the occupied countryside. In some instances, these police battalions were withdrawn and sent to the Reich for refreshment and replenishment before they were either returned for a second tour of duty in Poland or ordered to another region of occupied Europe. The following table lists those police battalions that performed occupation duty in Poland between 1939 and 1945. Those battalions that were in Poland for only a month or were 'in transit' through the Polish countryside were not listed.

The battalion in question may have served less than a year even though they were listed for the entire year. For example, *Polizei-Bataillon 307* arrived in Poland in autumn 1939 but was listed simply as having served in Poland in 1939. Similarly, it went on to serve in the invasion of the Soviet Union in the summer of 1941, but was listed as is having been a part of the German police garrison in Poland for that year. *Polizei-Bataillon 307* was withdrawn from Russia in the beginning of 1942 and returned to Poland, so it was also listed as having served in Poland in 1942. Thus, even though this police battalion operated in the USSR from mid-1941 until the beginning of 1942, it is shown in this table as if it served continuously in Poland. This table, therefore, should be seen as a rough estimate of German police forces in Poland from year to year and not as an exact figure.

Table 7. Police battalions serving in Poland, 1939–1945.

Battalion No.	1939	1940	1941	1942	1943	1944	1945
1	■						
2	■						
3	■						
4	■						
5	■						
6	■	■					
8	■	■					
10	■	■					
11	■	■					
12	■						
13		■					
21	■						
22	■						
32			■				
41	■	■	■	■	■	■	
42	■						
43	■	■					
51	■						
53				■	■	■	
61[60]	■	■	■	■			
62	■	■			■	■	
63	■						
64	■						

Battalion No.	1939	1940	1941	1942	1943	1944	1945
65							
67							
71							
72							
73							
74							
81							
83[61]							
84							
91							
92							
93							
101[62]							
102							
103							
104							
106							
111							
132							
133[63]							
171							
181							
301[64]							
303							
304							
305							
306							
307[65]							
308[66]							
309							
310							

Battalion No.	1939	1940	1941	1942	1943	1944	1945
311							
313							
314							
316							
321							
323							
GB 1[67]							
GB 2[68]							
PRB 3[69]							
	1939	1940	1941	1942	1943	1944	1945
Total:	43	32	17	20	17	15	5[70]

In January 1940, the number of *Ordnungspolizei* battalions in occupied Poland were numerous. The four police battalions stationed in *Wehrkreis XX* (*Danzig-West-Preussen*) were: *Polizei-Bataillon 13*, *Polizei-Bataillon 64*, *Polizei-Bataillon 71*, and *Polizei-Bataillon 91*.

Three police battalions were stationed in *Wehrkreis XXI* (*Warthegau*): *Polizei-Bataillon 41*, *Polizei-Bataillon 101*, and *Polizei-Bataillon 132*.

Fourteen police battalions were stationed in the GG: *Polizei-Bataillon 6*, *Polizei-Bataillon 8*, *Polizei-Bataillon 10*, *Polizei-Bataillon 11*, *Polizei-Bataillon 43*, *Polizei-Bataillon 61*, *Polizei-Bataillon 62*, *Polizei-Bataillon 72*, *Polizei-Bataillon 73*, *Polizei-Bataillon 92*, *Polizei-Bataillon 102*, *Polizei-Bataillon 103*, *Polizei-Bataillon 104*, and *Polizei-Bataillon 106*.

By November 1940, the police battalions stationed in the GG had been exchanged for the following formations:[71]

Polizeiregiment Warschau
- *Polizei-Bataillon 301*
- *Polizei-Bataillon 304*
- *Polizei-Bataillon 307*

Polizeiregiment Krakau
- *Polizei-Bataillon 311*
- *Polizei-Bataillon 321*
- *Polizei-Bataillon 303*
- *Polizei-Bataillon 314*

Polizeiregiment Lublin
- *Polizei-Bataillon 306*
- *Polizei-Bataillon 313*

Polizeiregiment Radom
Polizei-Bataillon 309
Polizei-Bataillon 310
Polizei-Bataillon 305
Polizeiregiment Galizien[72] CO: *Oberstleutnant der Schutzpolizei* Joachim Stach[73]
Polizei-Bataillon 133[74]
Polizei-Bataillon 254[75]
Polizei-Bataillon 315[76]

In July 1942 and April 1943, the German *Ordnungspolizei* reorganised the existing police battalions into regiments and even managed to create newly formed police battalions. In some cases, some of those battalions and regiments were transferred out of Poland within a short time. For example, *Gendarmerie-Bataillon 1 (motorisiert)*,[77] recently organised, was sent to Belarus in July 1942 under *Reichsführer-SS* Heinrich Himmler's personal orders.[78] At the time, this Gendarmerie battalion was led by *Major der Gendarmerie* Erich Schwieger.[79] The history of this unit is interesting as it operated almost exclusively on Polish territory. This battalion was created in Warsaw on 24 June 1942. The formation initially consisted of 400 men. Later, when a fourth company was added, the number of men rose above 500. It consisted of the headquarters company, a motorcycle platoon, a communications platoon and three companies of around 130 men each. Each company had three platoons.

In November 1942, the unit was spread out in and around Biała Podlaska, Lubartów and Zamość. However, the headquarters of this formation changed location numerous times. The battalion was fully motorised and equipped. As such, it was one of the more formidable and effective anti-partisan formations in the German arsenal. Like many police units from the Second World War, the battalion also committed war crimes. From 3 to 4 December 1942 the unit took part in an anti-partisan operation between Lubartov and Partsev. *Polizeiregiment 22* and *Polizei-Kavallerie-Bataillon 3* also took part, as well as the Lubartov Gendarmerie. The operation netted seventy-seven partisans killed and seventy-four Jews murdered in the forest region between the two towns.[80]

Beginning on 6 July 1943 a *4. (schwer) Kompanie* was created for the battalion, and became the heavy weapons company. It was divided into an light machine gun platoon, a heavy (100mm Nebelwerfer 35) infantry mortar platoon, and an armoured reconnaissance platoon made up of four pre-war Austrian Steyr armoured cars. The armoured car platoon was formed later in the year.[81] Between 14 July and 16 August 1944, the battalion lost nine men killed, seventy-five wounded, and fourteen missing in the region of Grodno, Bialystock and the East Prussian border. This was according to a report by *Hauptmann der Schutzpolizei* Kurt Winneberger, *Organisation Abteilung /Ia (3).*

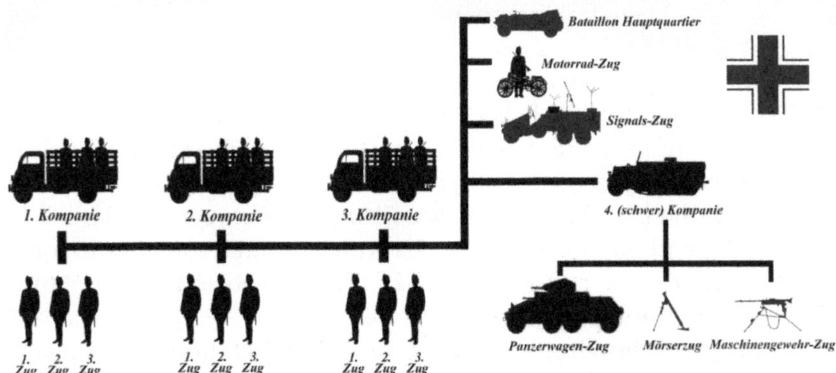

Figure 12. Gendarmerie-Bataillon 1 (motorisiert), June 1942. (*Author's line drawing*)

On 15 August 1944, the battalion was located adjacent to *Brigade Anhalt*. The Anhalt police brigade was composed of *SS-Polizeiregiment 2, I. Bataillon* of *SS-Polizeiregiment 17* and *I. Bataillon* of *Polizei-Schützenregiment 34*. At this time, *Gendarmerie-Bataillon 1 (motorisiert)* was temporarily made subordinate to *Brigade Anhalt*. Other minor formations employed in this police battlegroup were *Gendarmerie-Zug 6 (mot.), Gendarmerie-Zug 7 (mot.), Gendarmerie-Zug 11 (mot.), Gendarmerie-Zug 12 (mot.), Gendarmerie-Zug 13 (mot.), Gendarmerie-Zug 19 (mot.), Gendarmerie-Zug 49 (mot.),* and *Gendarmerie-Zug 50 (mot.)*. The eight motorised Gendarmerie platoons amounted to around 180 men, or the strength of one reinforced company. On 17 November 1944 the battalion contained twenty officers and 991 NCOs and enlisted men. At this time, it was located around the town of Sulejów, in the Radom District, and attached to *Korück 532 (9. Armee)*. Other police forces under *Korück 532* at this time were *I. Bataillon* of *SS-Polizeiregiment 11*, and *III. Bataillon* of *SS-Polizeiregiment 23*. On 14 October 1944 the Germans established *Division z.b.V. 603* and it was made a part of *Heeresgruppe A*. *Gendarmerie-Bataillon 1 (motorisiert)* was attached to this divisional staff beginning in January 1945 and stationed near the southern Polish town of Radomsko, in the *Generalgouvernement*.[82]

In July 1942 *Polizeiregiment Lublin* traded *Polizei-Bataillone 306* and *313* for *Polizei-Bataillone 65, 67,* and *101,* which became the *I., II., and III. Bataillone* in the regiment. That same month *Polizeiregiment Galizien* was disbanded, and its battalions were transferred to other duties. As stated earlier, various police battalions spent time garrisoning Poland. *Polizeiregiment Warschau,* the precursor of *Polizeiregiment 22,* had originally been formed using *Polizei-Bataillon 6, Polizei-Bataillon 8,* and *Polizei-Bataillon 72.* This changed in November 1940 when these three battalions were replaced by *Polizei-Bataillon 301, Polizei-Bataillon 304,* and *Polizei-Bataillon 307.*[83] In July 1942, *Polizeiregiment Warschau* was redesignated as *Polizeiregiment 22.* Once again, its police battalions were exchanged. *Polizei-Bataillon 41* and *Polizei-Bataillon 53* now became the *I.* and *III. Polizei-Bataillone* of *Polizeiregiment 22,* while several independent police companies were gathered together to form *II. Polizei-Bataillon* of *Polizeiregiment 22.* There were numerous other police battalions and police regiments that were created and organised in Poland. The following units were raised and stationed in Poland between 1942 and 1944:

Table 8. Police companies, battalions and regiments created in Poland, 1942–1944

Police Formation	Region	Battalions
Polizeiregiment 22[84]	Poland, then Belarus	*41, 53, III Btln.*[85]
Polizeiregiment 23[86]	Poland	*307, II, III Btln.*[87]
Polizeiregiment 24[88]	Poland, then White Russia	*83, 93, 153 Btln.*
Polizeiregiment 25[89]	Poland	*65, 67, 101 Btln.*
Galizien SS[90] *Freiwilligen Regiment 4 (Polizei)*[91]	Galicia, Poland, partly in Holland, then Ukraine	*I, II, II Btln.*
Galizien SS Freiwilligen Regiment 5 (Polizei)[92]	Galicia, Poland, then Ukraine	*I, II, II Btln.*
Galizien SS Freiwilligen Regiment 6 (Polizei)[93]	Galicia, Poland	*I, II, II Btln.*
Polizei-Schützenregiment 32[94]	Galicia, Poland	*III/17, 206 Schuma*
Polizei-Schützenregiment 34[95]	Bialystok, Poland	*I, II, III Bataillone*
Gendarmerie Battalions	Region	Companies
Gendarmerie-Bataillon 1 (mot.)[96]	Poland	*1, 2, 3 Kompanien*

Gendarmerie-Bataillon 2 (mot.)[97]	Poland	*1, 2, 3 Kompanien*
Police Cavalry Formations	Region	Cavalry Squadrons
Polizei-Reiter Bataillon 3[98]	Poland	*1, 2, 3 Schwadrone*
Polizei Reiter Schwadron Galizien[99]	Galicia	Galizien
Polizei Reiter Schwadron Lublin[100]	Lublin	Lublin
Kosaken Reiter Zug der Polizei Krakau[101]	Cracow	Krakau[102]
Polizei Geschütz Batterie Lublin[103]	Lublin	One battery
Polizei Geschütz Batterie Galizien 1[104]	Galicia	One battery
Polizei *Geschütz Batterie Galizien* 21[105]	Galicia	One battery
Polizei Granatwerfer Kompanie Krakau[106]	Cracow	Krakau[107]
Polizei Wachbataillon I[108]	Posen (Poznan)	1, 2, 3 Co.
Polizei Wachbataillon II[109]	Litzmannstadt (Łódź)	1, 2, 3 Co.
Polizei Wachbataillon XX[110]	Posen (Poznan)	1, 2, 3 Co.
Polizei Wachbataillon Warschau[111]	Warsaw	1, 2, 3, 4 Co.
Polizei Wachbataillon Krakau[112]	Cracow	1, 2, 3 Co.
Polizei Landesschützen Bataillon I[113]	Bialystok	1, 2, 3 Co.
Polizei Landesschützen Bataillon XXI[114]	Posen (Poznan)	1, 2, 3 Co.
Grolmann Miliz Bataillone (Polizei) Nr. 1–18[115] + [116] + [117]	Posen (Poznan)	*drei (1,2,3) Kompanien pro Bataillon*

In addition to these police infantry, cavalry, and artillery forces, *Reichsführer-SS* Heinrich Himmler ordered that the major police regiments stationed in Poland be equipped with some armoured units. These armoured forces began their operations as small platoon-sized units. In some instances, direct orders from Himmler were given that eventually sent an armoured car platoon from the Reich to the *Ordnungspolizei* forces in Poland. In another instance, some police battalions in Poland had an established 'heavy' company that initially contained armoured cars and motorcycles and later still would be equipped with light tanks captured during the Polish campaign. The Austrian-made Steyer armoured car model was first used by the German Army in 1938. Some of these Steyer armoured cars were not handed over to the *Ordnungspolizei* until late 1939. Several TP-7 light tanks had been captured by the German Army during the Polish campaign, and were likewise handed over to the police in the spring and summer of 1940:

Figure 13. In spring 1940, the German Order Police received their first armoured units: a platoon of four Austrian Steyer AGDZ armoured cars and a platoon of three ex-Polish Siedmiotonowy TP-7 tanks. (*Author's line drawing*)

As 1939 turned into 1940, the police regiments garrisoning the GG were given an armoured component. These armoured police units were to be attached to one of the three police battalions in each regiment, usually the *I. Bataillon*. For example, in November 1940 three police battalions, *Polizei-Bataillonen 301, 304,* and *307*, contained three motorised rifle companies apiece. In addition, *Polizei-Bataillonen 301* (i.e., the *I. Bataillon* in the regiment), had a *4. Kompanie (Schwer)*, which contained (a) a company troop, (b) two heavy machine gun platoons, and (c) an armoured car platoon made up of four Austrian-made Steyer armoured cars. *Polizeiregiment Krakau*, which had four police battalions (*Polizei-Bataillon 311*, *Polizei-Bataillon 321*, *Polizei-Bataillon 303*, and Polizei-Bataillon *314*), was also allotted an armoured section. This came in the form of four Steyer armoured cars.

Again, the *I. Bataillon* of this regiment (ex- *Polizei-Bataillon 311*), received the armoured cars. In June 1940, *Polizeiregiment Radom* contained *Polizei-Bataillone 51, 111, 305,* and *309*, which were operating as the *I., II., III.,* and *IV. Bataillone* of the regiment (respectively). That same month, another four-vehicle armoured car platoon was assigned to this police regiment and attached to the *I. Bataillon* (aka, *Polizei-Bataillon 51*). This armoured complement was stationed in the town of Pionki, near Radom.[118]

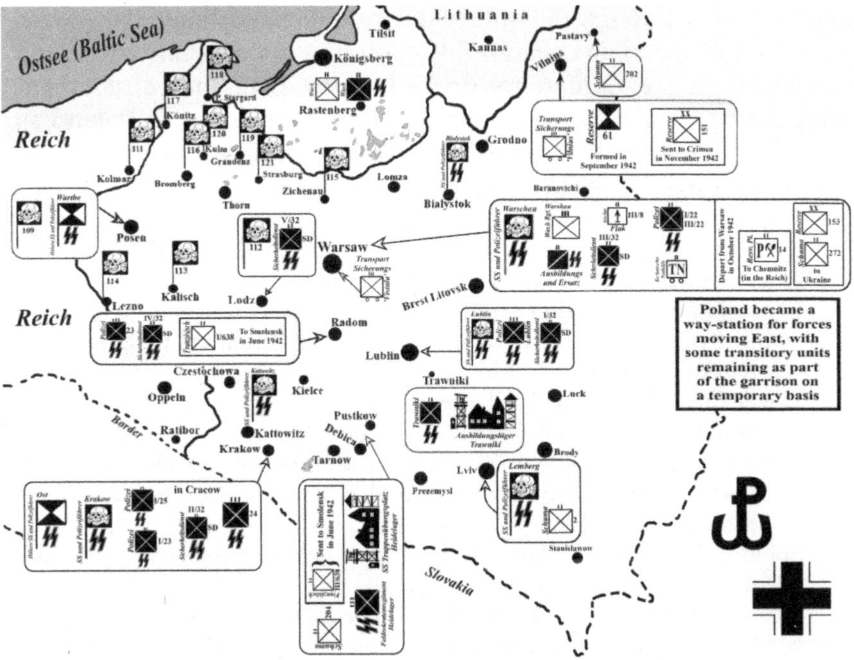

Figure 14. SS and Order Police forces in Poland in 1942.

In addition to this armoured car unit, the *II. Bataillon* (the ex-*Polizei-Bataillon 111*) of *Polizeiregiment Radom* had an armoured platoon of three captured Polish TP-7 tanks. These three vehicles would eventually end up being used by *Polizeiregiment Mitte* during the Russian campaign, beginning in June 1941.[119] In fact, the armoured platoon that in 1940 was serving with *Polizei-Bataillon 111* in and around Kielce was withdrawn from that battalion and assigned to *Polizei-Bataillon 305* in January 1941. At the same time, the armoured car platoon operating with *Polizei-Bataillon 51* was similarly withdrawn and assigned to *Polizei-Bataillon 309*. *Polizeiregiment Lublin* was also assigned an armoured component in the spring of 1940. The platoon assigned was also a four-vehicle unit that contained Steyr armoured cars. The platoon was initially attached to *Polizei-Bataillon 104* and later operated with *Polizei-Bataillon 73.*

The Holocaust in action in Poland

The killing of Polish Jews began almost from the very start of the Polish campaign in September 1939. Individual cases of Germans murdering Jews and entire units doing the same occurred, but the mass murder of the Jewish population on an industrial level did not begin until sixteen months later. Although the official decision to exterminate the Jewish people of Europe in an organised fashion was not officially presented until the Wannsee Conference on 20 January 1942, the employment of the Final Solution to the Jewish questions was begun in Poland as early as December 1941. A total of six major extermination camps were established there. These included:

1. Chełmno (in operation from December 1941 to January 1945)
   a) Estimated deaths: 152,000 to 200,000 people
   b) Chełmno was the first extermination camp, where victims were mostly Jews from the Łódź ghetto, along with Romani people and others. They were killed in gas vans.
2. Bełżec (in operation March–December 1942)
   a) Estimated deaths: 430,000 to 500,000 people
   b) Bełżec was one of the first camps to use stationary gas chambers. Most victims were Jews from Poland, Ukraine, and other parts of Eastern Europe.
3. Sobibór (in operation May–July 1942, then again from October 1942 to October 1943)
   a) Estimated deaths: 170,000 to 250,000 people
   b) Sobibór also used gas chambers, primarily killing Jews, including those from the Lublin District, as well as Romani people.
4. Treblinka (in operation from July 1942 to August 1943)
   a) Estimated deaths: 700,000 to 900,000 people
   b) Treblinka was one of the deadliest camps. Most of the victims were Jews from the Warsaw ghetto, as well as Jews from other parts of Poland and beyond.
5. Maydanek (in operation September 1942 to July 1944)
   a) Estimated deaths: 78,000 to 235,000 people
   b) Majdanek (Maidanek) served both as an extermination camp and a concentration camp. Victims included Jews, Poles, Soviet prisoners of war, and others. The camp had gas chambers, and many died from forced labour, starvation, or disease.
6. Auschwitz-Birkenau (in operation from March 1942 to January 1945)
   a) Estimated deaths: 1.1 million to 1.5 million people
   b) Auschwitz-Birkenau, the largest and most infamous of the Nazi camps, was responsible for the deaths of a vast number of people, including Jews (the vast majority), Romani people, Soviet prisoners of war, and others. The majority were killed in gas chambers, but many also perished from forced labour, starvation, and disease.

Key murder operations

Aktion Reinhard, 1942–43 (Operation Reinhard)

The purpose of *Aktion Reinhard* was aimed at no less than exterminating the entire Jewish population of the GG. It was the most systematic and large-scale operation to exterminate Polish Jews. The key components were as follows:

1. Bełżec, Sobibór, and Treblinka: These extermination camps were actually built for the operation. Jews from all over Poland were deported to these camps, where most were murdered in gas chambers.
2. Deportations: Jews were rounded up from towns and ghettos in the General Government and sent to these camps, where over 1.7 million Jews were killed.

Unternehmen Höss, 1941–44 (Operation Höss)
The purpose of *Unternehmen Höss* was aimed at targeting the mass murder of Jews in Auschwitz-Birkenau, where the notorious SS officer Rudolf Höss was commandant. The key components were as follows:

1. In Auschwitz Rudolf Höss set out to kill as many Jews as the camp could possibly process. Given that Auschwitz-Birkenau was the largest extermination camp, Jews from all over Europe, including Poland, were brought there and systematically killed. It was part of the broader strategy of mass murder using gas chambers and forced labour. Around 1.1 to 1.5 million Jews were killed here.

Die Liquidierung des Warschauer Ghettos, 1942 (Liquidation of the Warsaw Ghetto)
The purpose of the operation was the liquidation of the Warsaw Ghetto, where the largest Jewish population in Poland resided. It began in July 1942. The key components were as follows:

1. The Nazis began deporting Jews from the ghetto to the Treblinka extermination camp, and many were murdered in mass shootings or in the ghetto itself. This operation led to the deaths of around 300,000 Jews from the Warsaw ghetto.
2. Further resistance occurred in April 1943, when the remaining Jews in the ghetto offered resistance (the Warsaw Ghetto Uprising), and fought back when the Nazis attempted to finalise the ghetto's destruction. After the uprising was crushed, the remaining population was deported or killed.

Aktion Lublin, 1942–43
Aktion Lublin was part of the Nazi efforts to clear the Jews from the Lublin region, which included mass killings and deportations to death camps. The key components were as follows:

3. Thousands of Jews were rounded up and either shot or sent to camps like Majdanek (which was both a concentration and extermination camp) for execution or forced labour.

4. A large proportion of the Jews from this region were murdered as part of the operation.

Die Liquidierung des Krakauer Ghettos, 1943 (Liquidation of the Kraków Ghetto)

The purpose of this operation was the elimination of the Kraków ghetto, which was home to a significant Jewish population. was liquidated as part of the larger SS effort to exterminate Jews in Nazi-occupied Poland. They key components of the operation were as follows:

1. Jews were rounded up and either sent to extermination camps or killed in mass shootings in the ghetto itself.
2. The liquidation of the Kraków ghetto culminated in the deportation of thousands of Jews to Auschwitz.

Aktion Werwolf, 23 June to August 1943[120]

Aktion Werwolf was a 'pacification and displacement' operation carried out by the Germans in the Zamość region from June to August 1943, during which from 30,000 to 60,000 Poles from 171 villages were expelled. From 22 to 24 June 1943, approximately 5,000 Jews from Bendzin and from Sosnowitz were deported to Auschwitz. Beginning in August 1943, the last ghettos of eastern Upper Silesia were liquidated. Afterwards, the Nazis labelled this area '*Judenfrei*' (free of Jews). The key components were as follows:

1. The resettlements took place in the Zamość region and were the most brutal actions of the German administration there, aimed at completely 'clearing the area' of Poles to make way for German colonisation.
2. The operation employed more than 10,000 troops, which included *154. Reserve-Division, 174. Reserve-Division,* elements from seven police regiments, a police cavalry battalion, *Gendarmerie-Bataillon 1 (mot.)* and *Gendarmerie-Bataillon 2 (mot.),* military police, the SS, a few *Ostlegionen* battalions, and Ukrainian auxiliary police.

Unternehmen Erntefest, 3–4 November 1943 (Operation Harvest Festival)

This two-day operation was one of the largest mass executions of Jews that took place in Nazi-occupied Poland. The following were the key components of the operation:

1. During *Unternehmen Erntefest,* the SS and police executed up to 43,000 Jews, mainly from the Lublin District, in what was one of the largest single-day massacres of the Holocaust.

2. This was basically a follow-up operation to *Aktion Lublin* (1942–43).
3. The victims were killed by shooting at several killing sites, including at Majdanek and other locations.

Many German SS and police forces took an active role in the murders. One of those units was *Gendarmerie-Bataillon 1 (mot.)*. A gendarme by the name of Heinz Houben, from Dortmund, was assigned to *Gendarmerie-Bataillon 1 (mot.)* in Poland in late summer 1943. He served as a marksman and driver. He recalled the shooting in Poniatowa on 4 November 1943 (part of Operation Harvest Festival). At Poniatowa, around 15,000 Jews were murdered that day:

> One day we had to drive from Lublin to a forest area and surround it. (…) We motorists were also called in to this barrier. I was assigned to a machine gun as gunner. After our cordon had been completed, shooting began inside the forest, which lasted longer. (…) After a few hours, the barrier was lifted and we drove back to the accommodation in Lublin. (…). Under the direction of Police Major Kurt Sack, a firing squad consisting of men from the Lublin Security Police killed the inmates of Poniatowa. Eight other Dortmunders had belonged to the (1st) Gendarmerie Battalion.[121]

Unternehmen Zamosc, 1942–43 (Operation Zamość)

This was an ethnic cleansing operation of the Polish population of Zamojszczyzna. The operation was also referred to as *Unternehmen Himmlerstadt*. The operation was aimed at forcibly resettling the Polish population and exterminating the Jews in the Zamość region. The following were the key components:

1. The plan called for the annexation of large parts of Eastern Europe, including Poland.
2. The expulsions had been outlined in *Generalplan Ost*. It was the Nazi regime's secret blueprint for the colonisation and transformation of Eastern Europe.
3. Finally, the operation included the mass deportations of Poles from the region. Some Poles would go to forced labour. This included the non-Jewish Polish population. Jews were to be sent to extermination camps.
4. Finally, the plan called for large numbers of ethnic Germans to be settled in the newly acquired territories to replace the native population.

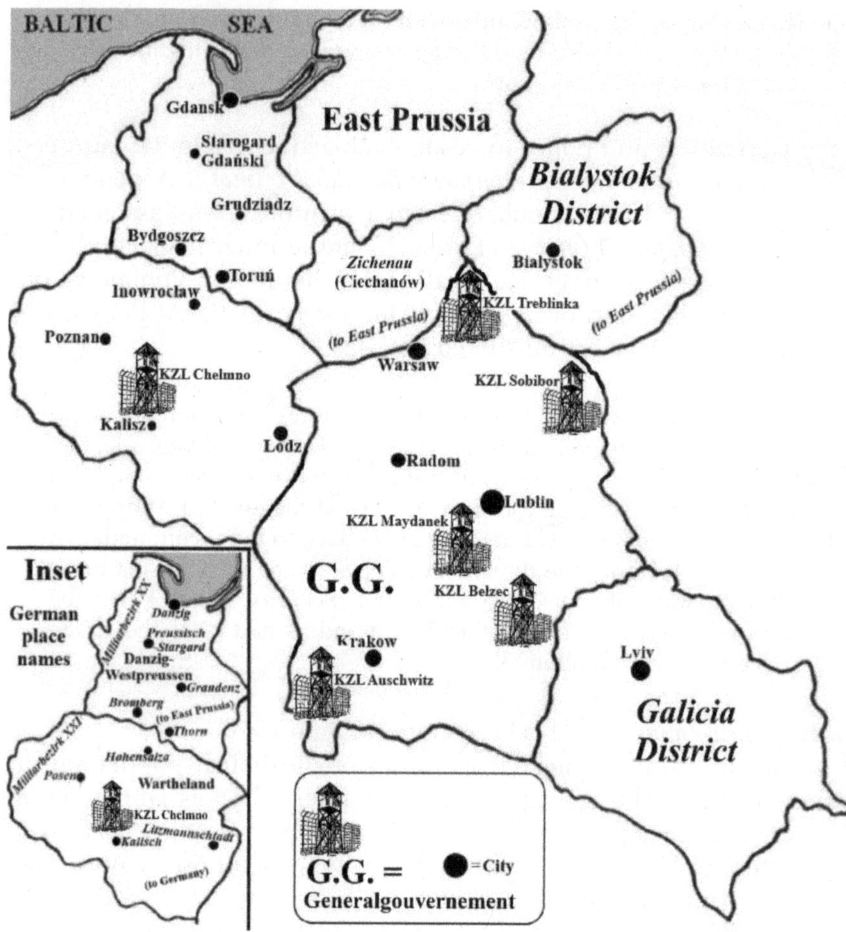

Figure 15. Location of Nazi extermination camps in Poland, including the annexed Polish territories. The implementation of the Holocaust in Poland was begun as early as December 1941.

These various Nazi operations were integral parts of the Third Reich's genocidal policies in Poland, contributing to the systemic extermination of a large segment of the Jewish and non-Jewish population. The mass murder of Jews, particularly in extermination camps like Auschwitz, Bełżec, Sobibór, and Treblinka, remains one of the darkest chapters in human history. Approximately 5,600,000 to 6 million Poles were killed during the war. Of that number, 3 million were Polish Jews. These figures prove that the Nazis not only targeted the Jewish Polish population for extermination; but they also desired to kill as many non-Jewish Polish citizens – all in an attempt to remove them from confiscated Polish lands earmarked for German colonisation.

1941–42

The plan to exterminate Poland's Jews was a systemic plan that was developed in steps. One of those 'steps' was *Aktion Reinhard*. The SS officer who was tasked with this mission was 37-year-old *SS-Gruppenführer* Odilo Lothar Ludwig Globocnik. As stated earlier, the Germans constructed three extermination camps specifically to accomplish this operation: Bełżec, Sobibór, and Treblinka. In addition, several shooting *Aktionen* (actions) took place between December 1941 and all of 1942 to supplement the murder by gassings that was going on in the three killing centres. The operation was always the same. German SS and police forces would encircle an entire Jewish community and march them off to the nearest forested area, where they were forced to dig either a large pit or individual graves, after which they would be shot, usually en masse. Between 1940 and mid-1942, starvation and disease took an additional 83,000 Jewish lives in the Warsaw ghetto. The deportations to extermination camps began in 1942. By that year, three additional extermination camps had been made operational.

Between March 1942 and November 1943, the Germans killed 1,526,500 Jews in three camps: Sobibor, Treblinka, and Belzec, as part of *Aktion Reinhard*. In total, somewhere between 1.7 and 2 million people were exterminated during *Aktion Reinhard* and related killing operations.[122] In 1943, one of the extermination camps, Auschwitz, had expanded to include an additional four crematoriums. The camp became two camps: Auschwitz I and Auschwitz II. At peak capacity, each extermination camp in Poland could gas and incinerate up to 12,000 people per day. Academic estimates of the number of people killed at the Auschwitz Extermination Camp is about 1,100,000. Of that number, around 100,000 were gentiles. Overall, approximately 2,700,000 Jews were murdered at these six extermination centres. About 2 million Jews were killed in mass shooting operations in Poland, the Baltic States, Belarus, Ukraine and Russia. Perhaps about 800,000–1 million Jews were killed in labour camps, other concentration camps, and in various ghettos all across Eastern Europe.

Another 250,000 Jews were murdered outside of the camps and ghettos in systemic violence against Jewish communities. The total therefore is around 6 million human beings who were systematically murdered. Overall, the estimated number of people that the Nazi regime murdered between 1933 and the end of the war in April 1945 is a staggering 17 million.[123] That figure does not include the 15 million who died in battle. Another 21 million people died as a result of collateral damage from the war, that is, being killed as a non-combatant in the midst of the war.

Auxiliary occupation forces in Poland

The Polish Blue Police

Not much data has been forthcoming regarding the command structure of the auxiliary police units which aided the occupation of Lviv. We do know that *Hauptmann der Gendarmerie* Dallmann was *Kommandeur der Gendarmerie in Lemberg* (Commander of the Rural Police in Lviv), and was to supervise the Ukrainian Police forces in the area. It is known that the *5. Ukrainisches Polizeikommissariat* (5th Ukrainian Police Commissariat), which was part of the Lviv region, was headed by Ukrainian *Hauptmann* (later *Major*) Yuri Torbych. The auxiliary police forces that the Germans raised in every occupied country also played a role in the Jewish Holocaust. They only varied to the degree in which they participated. Eastern Europe (like Western Europe) had a long history of religious anti-Semitism. In the second half of the nineteenth century, the rise of racial anti-Semitism only served to increase the hatred of Jews. During the Second World War, those anti-Semitic feelings were exponentially expanded, especially given the Nazi policy towards the Jews.

Therefore, the auxiliary police in Galicia (as elsewhere) were active in assisting the Germans in the destruction of Polish Jewry. In one particular incident, Major Torbych's Ukrainian police assisted the Lviv Gestapo and Gendarmerie in liquidating the Jewish ghetto in Strahovetz in 1942.[124] But the Ukrainian auxiliary police were not the only ones who supported the Nazis. In Poland, there were several auxiliary police forces that aided the German occupation. In addition to the aforementioned SS and police units, the Germans allowed the puppet Polish government to maintain a Polish auxiliary police force. That formation's title was *Policja Granatowa,* which literally translates to 'Navy Blue Police', but meant 'Blue Police', so named after the colour of their uniform.[125] At least 16,000 Poles served in this force during the occupation. One reliable source says that the number was even higher. According to Jan Grabowski, by 1943 the Blue Police numbered 20,000 men:

> The police corps was purged of 'politically and racially unreliable' elements, all higher officers were fired or demoted and were replaced by German policemen. During the first months of occupation the ranks of the PP grew quickly, reaching 10,000 officers and men in the beginning of

> 1940, and, at its peak in late 1943, more than 20,000. The Polish resistance, or the so-called Polish underground state, gave the Polish policemen its reluctant blessing to enter the new formation, urging them at the same time to do their best to protect the interests of the Polish nation. The 'Blue Police', as the PP came to be known for their dark blue uniforms, thus were the only militarised and armed Polish formation the Germans allowed to continue operating in occupied Poland.[126]

The strength of the Blue Police rose from 8,700 in February 1940 to 11,000 in April 1941 and 12,000 in November 1942. It reached its peak strength of some 20,000 men in 1943. According to a report written by *SS-Oberführer* Walter Bierkamp, approximately 2,000 out of the 20,000 *Policja Granatowa* were ethnic German Poles.[127] In October 1941 a school for Polish policemen was established in the town of Nowy Sacz, with the aim of training recruits. All Blue Police, regardless of whether they were former members of the pre-war Polish State Police or new recruits, were issued revolvers and rifles and wore their Polish Police pre-war uniforms with the Polish insignia removed.

The German authorities gave the Polish police the duty of dealing primarily with criminal activities, but they were also used widely in combating smuggling and black marketeering and in measures taken against the Jewish population. The Polish police patrolled the ghettos inside the GG, and searched for Jews who had escaped from the ghettos and camps and had sought refuge among the Polish population in the towns and cities or in the forests. The Polish police played a particularly important role in Warsaw, the centre of the opposition movements in occupied Poland. In June 1942 there were sixty officers and 3,150 NCOs and men of the Blue Police stationed in Warsaw. The Polish police commanders in Warsaw were Marian Kozielewski (October 1939 to May 1941), Aleksander Reszczynski (May 1941 to March 1943), and Franciszek Przymusinski (March 1943 until the Warsaw Polish uprising in 1 August 1944). All these police officers had the rank of lieutenant colonel in the police.

The Polish police were used to guard the gates of the Warsaw ghetto and other Polish city ghettos. In Warsaw alone, a force of 400 Blue Police was assigned to patrol the ghetto. In the suppression of the Warsaw Ghetto Uprising in 1943, 367 Polish Blue Police were employed under the German command of *SS-Gruppenführer* Jürgen Stroop. The Polish Blue police also sought out Jews who had escaped from the ghetto to the 'Aryan' side of the city, while assisting the Germans in seizing Poles on the streets of Warsaw for forced labour in Germany. From 1942 onwards, the Blue Police were employed in the struggle against the partisans. Their losses in that year were eighty-four dead and ninety wounded. In June 1942 a special Polish police battalion, *Schutzmannschaft Bataillon 202*, was deemed ready to fight against the guerrillas near Lviv. It had been created in March 1942.

On 27 July 1944, after the liberation of the Lublin district by communist forces, the *Polski Komitet Wyzwolenia Narodowego* (Polish Committee for National Liberation) issued an edict disbanding the Blue Police and terminating its service, stating it to have been an entity that had served the Nazi occupation. In its place a new Polish police force was created, the *Milicja Obywatelska* (Civil Militia).

The Polish Blue Police, although considered unreliable by the Germans, actually took part in helping the Nazis round up Jews for transport to extermination camps, as well as rounding up Polish civilians for forced labour in the Reich. Although not all Blue Police members cooperated so fully, many did, and some with great zeal. Other Blue Police members actually refused to carry out orders, but refusing to carry out an order always carried with it great risk. In some instances, Blue Police members assisted the Polish underground and also helped Polish Jewry.

All the various groups of the Polish underground aggressively condemned the overall behaviour of the Polish Blue Police because of the scope of its collaboration with the Germans, its general practice of extortion, the moral degradation it demonstrated, and its large-scale participation in the persecution and massacre of the Jews. Several particularly active policemen were executed by the underground for collaborating with the Nazis, including the Warsaw police commander Lieutenant Colonel Reszczynski and the police officer, Captain Roman Swiecicki. In the final analysis, it can be said that the Blue Police actually made the job of occupying Poland easier for the Nazis. Within this assessment, it was correct to judge the Polish Blue Police as a collaborationist organisation, even though not every single member of this force was an anti-Semite or supported the Nazi cause. In fact, some men used their position within the Blue Police to aid Polish patriots and help Jews evade capture. Unfortunately, the same allegation of collaborating can be levelled at many of those who served in the Jewish Order Police.[128]

The Jewish Order Police

The Germans employed Jewish policemen to help them round up fellow Jews to be sent to their deaths in concentration camps. They operated in all the ghettos set up by the Nazis. Service in the Order Police, as the Jewish police force was called, allowed the Jewish member to survive (at least for a time) and avoid the deportation to a death camp. In Warsaw alone, there were an estimated 2,000 members of the Jewish Order Police by July 1942. It is not until recently that this sad and delicate subject has begun to be broached by scholars. The role of Jews in *ha Shoah* is therefore only now coming to light. This is because to understand it requires that a special set of questions be asked about why these Jewish men betrayed their own people by aiding the Nazis.

These questions are painful and difficult to answer. Was it simply to save one's skin? Did the person try to profit in some way from his position? Was he known for being someone who would try and help those about to be deported or otherwise arrested, or did he become a willing and enthusiastic participant in the round-ups? These are but a few basic questions that are, frankly, hard to gauge the answer to. In any event, the participation of the Order Police in rounding up the Jewish population for transport to extermination camps is a sad chapter in the history of the Jewish people.[129] These men were under the command of Jewish Order Police Colonel Józef Sherinsky, a Jewish convert to Christianity whose real name was Shenker.[130] Sherinsky was detested by the Jewish population of the Warsaw Ghetto. He wasn't hated for the fact that he was serving the Germans to save his skin, for many others were doing the very same thing, but because he was profiteering from the plight of the Jewish population.

His conversion to Christianity certainly didn't win him any supporters within the Jewish community. Sherinsky was eventually assassinated by a fellow Order Police member on the orders of the Jewish Fighting Organisation. Major Jakub Laikin, a Jewish lawyer and another convert to Christianity, was the vice-commander of the Warsaw Jewish Order Police. Police Captain Reuven Shmerling was on Sherinsky's staff. At peak strength, the Warsaw Order Police contained 2,500 members. Another 600 Jewish Order Police were stationed in Łódź, while 500 were aiding the Nazis in Lublin.[131] According to famed historian, Dr Raoul Hilberg (2 June 1926–4 August 2007), there was never a lack of volunteers who wished to join the Order Police since service in this collaborationist force meant that the Jewish volunteer was guaranteed high pay, steady meals, and most important of all, the chance to survive the deportations and murders for a little while longer. In essence, service in the Order Police meant survival for many Jewish men, if only temporarily.

The *Selbstschutz* and *Sonderdienst*

Most ethnic German Poles had been drawn initially into the *Selbstschutz* (Self-Defence) set up shortly after the collapse of Polish resistance along the lines of the Nazi *SA* – the *Sturmabteilungen,* or Storm Trooper battalions. Governor Hans Frank had ordered the creation of the *Selbstschutz* so that the *Volksdeutsche* community in Poland could serve:

> Himmler had authorised the German Order Police headquarters to establish locally based Selbstschutz units in the annexed western territories of Poland. For the Government General, he appointed an SS and Selbstschutz commander, subordinate to the Higher SS and Police Leader (Höherer SS und Polizeiführer, HSSPF) for the Government General, SS-Obergruppenführer Friedrich-Wilhelm Krüger. Between November 1939 and April 1940, some 12,600 ethnic German men were recruited into Selbstschutz units under command of the SSPF for each of the four districts of the Government General.[132]

The *Selbstschutz* eventually numbered about 45,000 ethnic German Poles between the ages of 18 and 40. The effective date of activation for the *Selbstschutz* was 30 November 1939. We know some of the commanders of the *Selbstschutz,* but the list is not complete. The *Selbstschutz* commander for the Lublin District was *SS-Standartenführer* Walter Gunst. By December 1939 a *Selbstschutz* battalion made up of five companies was established there. Counting all officers, NCOs, and enlisted men, the strength of the battalion was somewhere between 800 and 1,000.[133] The *Selbstschutz* was also directly implicated in the persecution of the Jews. On 22 April 1940 *SS-Gruppenführer* Odilo Globocnik, the head of the SS und Polizeiführer Lublin command, ordered that the *Selbstschutz* be used in an additional capacity. They were to guard the labour camps that held the Jewish forced labourers. The *Selbstschutz* would eventually guard a total of six camps containing approximately 2,700 Jewish labourers.

Figure 16. The cuff band of the *Sonderdienst* was worn on the lower left sleeve of the field blouse.

These Jewish forced labourers had been put to work on regulating the Bug River by the *Wasserwirtschaftsinspektion* (Water Economy Inspectorate) for the Biala-Podlaska District.[134]

In April 1940 Hans Frank ordered the *Selbstschutz* officially disbanded and the following month he decreed the establishment of the *Sonderdienst* (Special Service), which was to become Frank's special police in Poland. The basic unit in the *Sonderdienst* was the *Sturm*, which contained thirty men and was equal to an American platoon of the Second World War. A *Sturmkompanie* contained four *Sturm* and was thus roughly the size of a small company. A *Sturmbataillon* (Assault Battalion) contained three or four *Sturmkompanie*.

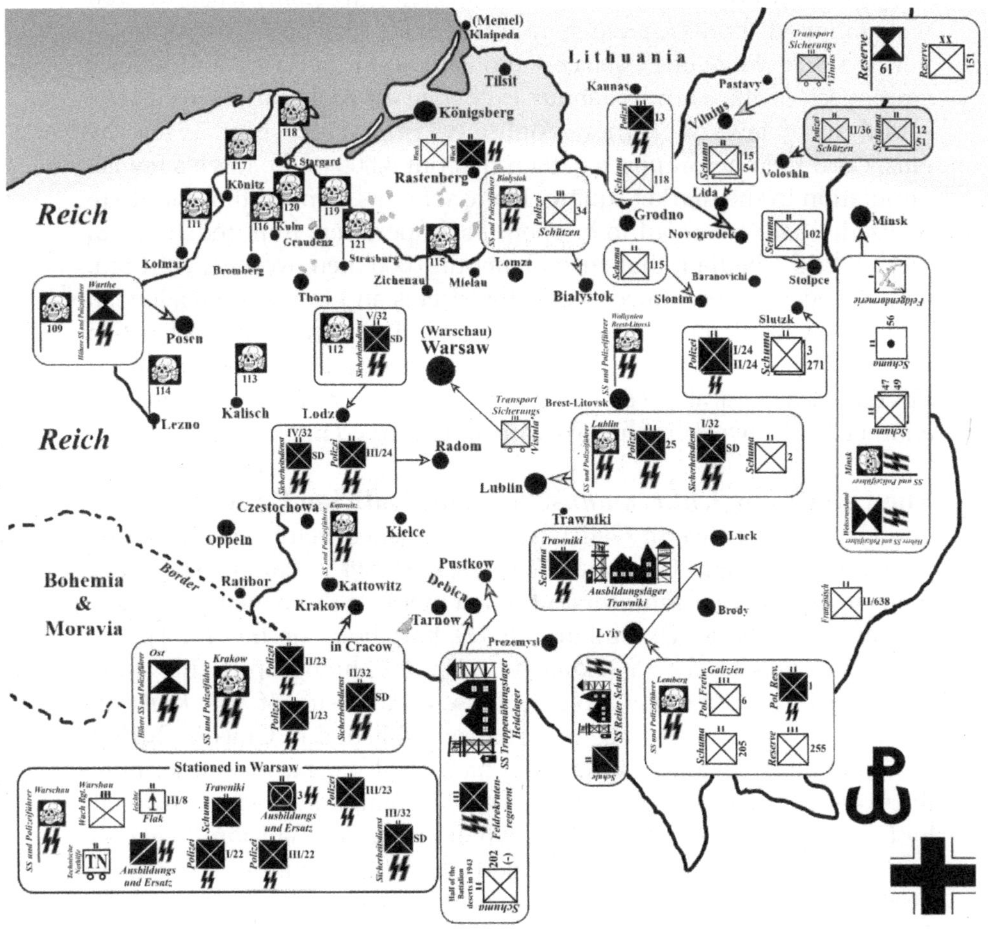

Figure 17. SS and Order Police forces in Poland, 1943.

Frank employed these locally raised ethnic German troops as guards for civil and military buildings and installations, among their many duties. Frank's control of the *Sonderdienst* ended in August 1942 when *Reichsführer-SS* Heinrich Himmler ordered that the organisation be assigned to the control of *SS-Obergruppenführer* Friedrich-Wilhelm Krüger.[135] One large-scale employment of the *Sonderdienst* while under Frank's control occurred on 11 June 1942, when a special round-up of Jews took place in Tarnow. The city of Tarnow had a pre-war Jewish population of around 25,000, about 45 per cent of the city's total population. The operation was so large that the security services sought assistance from the local police as well as the district police. A company of *Waffen-SS* troops, commanded by *SS-Hauptsturmführer* Klienow, that was stationed at *SS-Truppenübungsplatz Debica,* also participated.

The *Sonderdienst,* the *Baudienst* (Polish Labour Service), and several employees of the Tarnow labour exchange all took part as well. The round-up of Jews in Tarnow continued from 11–19 June 1942. The Nazis and their accomplices gathered about 3,000 of the town's Jewish population in the market square. Panic set in as some of those in there realised what was about to happen. In desperation, hundreds tried to escape. In the bedlam that ensued, about 3,000 men, women, children, and old people were murdered in the streets and in the town's Jewish cemetery, where many had taken refuge. Those who did not try to run away were taken out of the town to a forest near the village of Zbylitowska Góra, about 6 miles south-west of Tarnow. It was there that another 7,000 Jews were shot to death and dumped into a shallow grave.

The Ukrainian *Schutzmannschaft* and Galician Police

The Ukrainian police in Galicia was established before the Germans ever raised a single Ukrainian *Schutzmannschaft* battalion. They had their own particular uniform and when many of these men were later transferred over to Ukrainian *Schuma* battalions or the *14. Waffen Grenadier Division der SS (ukrainische Nr. 1),* photographs still show them wearing Ukrainian police blouses. An issue of the *Krakauer Zeitung,* a German language newspaper published in Cracow during the occupation, dated 27 June 1941, had a full-page article describing the visit of Governor Hans Frank to a Ukrainian Police School headed by Ukrainian Police Colonel Dr Kubiyovytsch. The Galician Police, as the Ukrainian police forces were called, reached a strength of 1,800 men by the end of 1941. Several Galician police regiments were eventually formed in 1943.

Most were ultimately absorbed into the *14. Waffen Grenadier Division der SS (Galizien Nr. 1),* while some were employed in police battlegroups and soon thereafter destroyed in combat. Two *Schuma* battalions, numbered *'203'* and *'204'*, were raised from Ukrainian personnel in autumn 1942 and the early part of 1943 and served in Poland. According to one source, *Schutzmannschaft Bataillon 204* provided guards for a concentration camp located near the town of Pustków, approximately 132km (88 miles) east of Cracow.[136] In July 1943 *Schutzmannschaft Bataillon* 204, whose commander was *SS-Sturmbannführer und Major der Schutzpolizei* Karl Hennessen, was reinforced with 800 men. in June 1944, the battalion was transferred over to the Ukrainian *14. Waffen Grenadier Division der SS (Galizien Nr. 1)* as replacements.

Schutzmannschaft Bataillon 203 had been trained in a camp near the village of Pulawy, in the GG. This camp, like the one near the village of Trawniki, became a training centre for eastern volunteers who wanted to serve in the Nazi *Hilfspolizei*. In March 1942 the camp held 1,250 auxiliary policemen – recruited mainly from Russian PoW camps. By September 1942, the Germans had trained some 2,500 volunteers divided into two recruit training battalions. These two battalions were under the command of *SS-Untersturmführer* Will Franz and *SS-Untersturmführer* Johann Schwarzenbacher. Although it was unusual for second lieutenants to lead entire battalions, in this case it was normal, given that both battalions were made up of foreign volunteers. Before the war was over the Trawniki camp would train about 5,000 men.

In September 1942 the 300 men of *Schutzmannschaft Bataillon 203* completed their training in Pulawy. The commander of this unit was *Hauptmann der Schutzpolizei* Walter Koch,[137] and he led it until 17 January 1944. This *Schutzmannschaft* battalion was made subordinate to *SS-Polizeiregiment 25*. The battalion was stationed from 1942 to 1944 in the Wolka Prefecture, a suburb located in north-eastern Lublin. On 23 March 1944 seventeen members of the battalion deserted with their weapons and several *Panjewagen* (horse-drawn carts). In June 1944 the battalion was still under the control of the *Ordnungspolizei* in Lublin.

Other Ukrainian *Schuma* battalions were also created for specific employment in Poland. *Schutzmannschaft Bataillon 205* was a *Wach* (guard) unit raised from Ukrainian volunteers in Lemberg (Lwów).[138]

The battalion was assigned to *Oberfeldkommandantur 365* and was still in that city by June 1944. A police rifle regiment, *Polizei-Schützenregiment 34*, was formed in April 1943 for service in the Bialystok District of north-eastern Poland. The *Polizei Schutzenregiment* was the brainchild of the German Order Police. They were created because there simply weren't enough German police regiments to manage the growing partisan threat. They consisted of one battalion of German police and two battalions of foreign volunteer police. The *I. Bataillon* in these police rifle regiments contained Germans, while the *II.* and *III. Bataillone* were to be composed of foreign volunteers (usually Ukrainians). In this way, the Germans were able to raise more police regiments.

In May 1944 several other Ukrainian *Schuma* battalions were also raised for service in Poland. These included the *Schutzmannschaft Bataillon 207,* as well as three *Plastun* (Cossack infantry) battalions numbered '*209*', '*210*', and '*211*'. *Kosaken Schutzmannschaft Bataillon 209* served in Warsaw, while *Kosaken Schutzmannschaft Bataillon 210* and *Kosaken Schutzmannschaft Bataillon 211* operated in the area in and around Radom. The last battalion created in Poland was *Schutzmannschaft Bataillon 212,* a Ukrainian unit that became operational in June 1944 and was eventually destroyed in April 1945.

German Army occupation forces

The German Army also provided forces for the occupation of Poland. These included three specific rear area commands. The lowest was the *Ortskommandantur I, II,* and *III* (local commandant of the military government; where *Ortskommandantur I* was battalion level, *Ortskommandantur II* and *III* were company level. The next highest administrative command was the *Feldkommandantur,* or field command military government, which was a headquarters of regiment or brigade level. The next highest after that was the *Oberfeldkommandantur,* which was a military government headquarters at division level.[139] In addition, numerous reserve and replacement units were eventually posted to garrison duty in Poland. This also included numerous training bases that provided recruits as well as new combat units for the *Heer.*

Table 9. German Army units garrisoning the *Generalgouvernement,* 1939–1945.

Formations listed by town or city	1939	1940	1941	1942	1943	1944	1945
Nowa Dęba[140]							
Sturmgeschütz Ersatz Abteilung 400				X[141]	X[142]		
Stolpce (Stowbtsy)[143]							
Division Nr. 141				X[144]	X	X[145]	
Landshut (Łańcut) in the GG[146]							
154. Reserve-Division				X	X	X	

Formations listed by town or city	1939	1940	1941	1942	1943	1944	1945
Janow[147]							
Turkistanische Arbeits Ersatz Abteilung				X			
Freiwilligen (Turkistanische) Ausbildungs und Ersatz Brigade					X	X[148]	
Jedlnia[149]							
Turkistanische Legion[150]				X	X	X[151]	
Legionovo							
Turestanische Legion[152]				X	X	X	
Pulawy							
Armenische Legion				X[153]	X	X	
Rozan							
Infanterie Ersatz Bataillon 493		X[154]					
Wach-Bataillon 654			X[155]				
Sanok							
III. Btln. der Festungs Pionier Stab 18				X[156]			
Modlin							
II. Bataillon/Infanterie Regiment 721			X[157]	X			
Gren. Ersatz u. Ausb. Bataillon 493[158]					X	X	
Kielce							
Sicherungs-Bataillon 692					X[159]	X	X[160]
Sicherungs-Bataillon 688						X[161]	
Landesschützen-Bataillon 619			X[162]	X	X[163]		
Sicherungs-Regiment 609					X[164]	X	
Ersatz Brigade 203			X[165]				
Sicherungs-Bataillon 689						X[166]	
Sicherungs-Bataillon 954					X[167]		

Formations listed by town or city	1939	1940	1941	1942	1943	1944	1945
Litzmannstadt (Łódź)							
Reserve Grenadier Bataillon 323			X[168]	X			
Transport Begleit Regiment Posen			X[169]				
Sarny							
Landesschützen-Bataillon 637			X[170]			X	
Landesschützen-Bataillon 988		X[171]					
Wieruschow							
Infanterie Ersatz Bataillon 484	X[172]						
Wesola (Warsaw)							
Nordkaukasiche Legion				X[173]	X	X	
Warsaw							
Landesschützen-Bataillon 564			X[174]				
Festungs Infanterie Regiment 8						X[175]	X
Landesschützen-Bataillon 476			X[176]	X	X		
Landesschützen-Bataillon 918				X[177]	X	X[178]	
Landesschützen-Regiment 33				X[179]	X[180]		
Festungs Maschinengewehr Bataillon 24							X[181]
Infanterie Regiment 88		X	X	X	X		
Festungs Infanterie Regiment 88						X[182]	X
Festungs Maschinengewehr Bataillon 25						X	X[183]
Wach Regiment Warschau		X[184]	X	X	X	X	X
Sicherungs-Bataillon 944					X[185]	X	
Sicherungs-Bataillon 945					X[186]	X	
Landesschützen-Bataillon 996			X[187]	X	X	X	
Landesschützen-Bataillon 997			X[188]	X	X	X	X[189]
Landesschützen-Bataillon 998			X[190]				

Formations listed by town or city	1939	1940	1941	1942	1943	1944	1945
Skierniewice							
Turkestanisches Inf. Bataillon 450				X[191]			
Infanterie Ersatz Bataillon 478		X[192]					
Infanterie Ersatz Bataillon 500[193]					X[194]		
Grenadier Ersatz Regiment 500						X	
Malkinia							
Landesschützen-Bataillon 616				X[195]			
Smolewice							
Reserve Infanterie Bataillon 162					X[196]	X	
Łowicz							
Landesschützen-Bataillon 909				X[197]			
Tarnow							
Sicherungs-Bataillon 965					X[198]	X	
Zamosc							
Reserve Infanterie Bataillon 414				X[199]	X	X	
Ersatz Bataillon 414				X[200]	X	X	X
Reserve Infanterie Bataillon 385			X[201]	X	X	X	
Lemberg (Lviv) (Lwów)							
Sicherungs-Bataillon 693					X[202]	X	
Reserve Grenadier Regiment 255				X[203]	X	X[204]	
Reserve Infanterie Bataillon 455							
Infanterie Regiment 612			X[205]				
Regiment 'Lemberg'						X[206]	
Transport Sicherungs-Bataillon 595				X[207]			
Sicherungs-Bataillon 693					X[208]	X	X

Formations listed by town or city	1939	1940	1941	1942	1943	1944	1945
Sicherungs-Bataillon 1004						X[209]	
Landesschützen-Regiment 'Lemberg'				X[210]	X	X	
Landesschützen-Bataillon 310	X[211]		X[212]	X[213]	X	X[214]	
Landesschützen-Bataillon 405			X[215]	X	X	X	
Landesschützen-Bataillon 887			X[216]	X	X	X	
Landesschützen-Bataillon 888			X[217]	X	X	X	
Landesschützen-Bataillon 990			X[218]	X	X	X[219]	
Zloczow							
Gren. Ers. u. Ausb. Bataillon 385[220]				X[221]			
Lublin							
Ersatz Brigade 203			X[222]				
174. Reserve-Division				X[223]	X	X	
Wach-Bataillon 653		X[224]					
Landesschützen-Bataillon 636			X[225]	X	X	X	
Infanterie-Regiment 653		X[226]					
Landesschützen-Bataillon 617			X[227]				
Landesschützen-Bataillon 619			X[228]	X	X[229]	X	
Infanterie Regiment 655		X[230]					
Wach-Bataillon 655		X	X[231]				
Landesschützen-Bataillon 636			X[232]				
Landesschützen-Bataillon 991			X[233]	X	X	X[234]	
Landesschützen-Bataillon 992			X[235]	X	X	X	
Radom							
359. Infanterie-Division					X[236]		
SS-Totenkopfstandarte 11	X[237]	X					
Landesschützen-Bataillon 561				X[238]			
Landesschützen-Bataillon 913				X[239]	X	X	
Landesschützen-Bataillon 914				X[240]	X	X	
Landesschützen-Bataillon 915				X[241]			

Formations listed by town or city	1939	1940	1941	1942	1943	1944	1945
Landesschützen-Regiment 65			X[242]	X	X	X	X
Krakau (Cracow)							
Division z.b.V. 601						X[243]	X
Infanterie Regiment 644		X[244]	X[245]				
Landesschützen-Bataillon XVII/V	X[246]	X	X				
Landesschützen-Bataillon XIV/VIII	X[247]	X[248]					
Landesschützen-Bataillon II/X	X[249]	X[250]					
Landesschützen-Bataillon XV/XIII	X[251]	X[252]					
Wach-Bataillon I[253]			X[254]	X	X	X	X[255]
Wach-Bataillon II[256]			X[257]	X	X	X	X[258]
Divisionsstab z.b.V. 425	X[259]	X					
SS-Totenkopfstandarte 8	X[260]	X	X				
SS-Totenkopfstandarte 10		X[261]	X				
Lancut							
154. Reserve-Division				X[262]	X	X	
Kruszyna							
Kommandeur der Ostlegionen[263]				X[264]	X	X	
Rovno							
Landesschützen-Bataillon 528						X[265]	X[266]
Auschwitz							
Landesschützen-Bataillon 515	X	X[267]					
Chelm							
Landesschützen-Bataillon 405			X[268]				

The Polish Home Army

There were several distinct guerrilla organisations fighting the German occupation in Poland. First and foremost was the *Armia Krajowa* (AK, Polish Home Army). The AK represented the Polish government in exile. Then there was the Soviet-backed *Gwardia Ludowa* (GL, People's

Guard). This was a separate guerrilla force under the control of the Polish communist party, with their own military units who took their orders from Moscow. In addition, there were two more significantly important Polish guerrilla movements. One of them was the leftist *Armia Ludowa* (AL, People's Army). By 1943, both the GL and AL had been merged. The other was the very nationalist, anti-Semitic, right-wing *Narodowa Sily Zbrojne* (NSZ, National Armed Forces). The strengths of these various guerrilla organisations varied from time to time. At its height in late 1943, the NSZ had anywhere between 15,000–18,000 men under arms all across the country.

This nationalist movement often fought the communists and even engaged in fighting Jewish partisans until March 1944 when about 10,000–15,000 were accepted into the ranks of the AK with the agreement that no more attacks would be launched against other Polish units – no matter what their political or religious affiliation may be. The AK grew slowly but steadily from 1939 onwards. In January 1943 the AK had a small, modest military organisation numbering only around 3,000 active combatants split up into forty-two formations. By the spring of 1943 it would boast of having 2,000 more.

In August 1944 it could boast of having some 38,000-plus men fully trained and equipped. Given that at the time the AK consisted of about 400,000 members, most, it would seem, were willing volunteers but wholly unarmed. An AK company usually contained 100 men, while a platoon was supposed to be composed of thirty men. The units were dispersed as follows: four companies in the district of Radom, four companies and four platoons in the district of Cracow, two companies and two platoons in Polesie, six companies and five platoons in the Lublin district, five companies and three platoons in the Nowogrodek area, two companies in Vilnius (Vilna), one platoon in Wolyn, and one company and one platoon in Bialystok.

Finally, there was a company of AK men in Łódź and a platoon in Rzeszow. The total amounted to twenty-five companies and seventeen platoons. The Polish communist People's Army had been organised in June 1941 but no major combat units existed until autumn 1941. The communist-backed *Gwardia Ludowa* was not officially formed until March 1942. Its strength never exceeded 3,000 Polish volunteers but they were supported and supplied by Joseph Stalin's NKVD intelligence service in 1942, and the Red Army and Red Air Force in 1943 to 1945. The Jewish leader Hanka Szapiro-Sawicka was the chief organiser and head of the Youth Struggle Organisation within the AL. About 5,000 Soviet nationals were in the ranks of the AL from 1942 until 1945.

The strength of the AL also grew steadily, although the strength of the GL/AL never exceeded 7,000–9,000 men at peak strength in 1944. Actual Polish participation in the GL in 1942 was somewhere in the neighbourhood of 2,000–3,000 men. The years 1942–43 saw the employment of nine GL units in the Kielce region. Of this number, three were purely Jewish units and one was predominantly Jewish, while Jews constituted a large proportion of membership of two additional GL units. During the entire war, perhaps as many as 5,000 Jewish fighters fought in the ranks of the GL. An interesting note is the fact that Jewish partisans were also to be found in purely Soviet guerrilla formations. Exactly ninety-two Soviet partisan units had Jewish commanders.

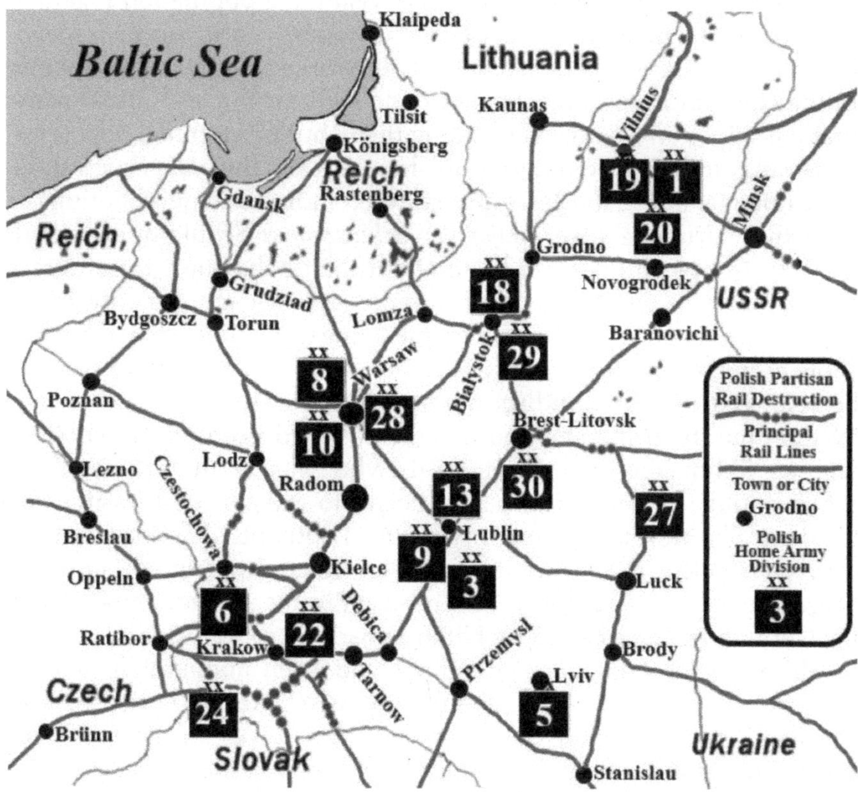

Figure 18. This map shows the various Polish Home Army divisions and their area of operations in 1944. It also includes concentrations of railway destruction activities in 1942–44. A significant amount of materiel and rolling stock was either destroyed or damaged by the Polish Home Army.

Major guerrilla actions in Poland

From the very beginning of the German invasion the Polish people resisted the Nazis by ignoring orders and decrees, sabotaging the German war effort through delays, routing trains on to wrong tracks, setting warehouses on fire, cutting telephone lines, setting off bombs, and even carrying out individual acts of assassination against selected German officers and civilian officials or targets of opportunity. One of the earliest attacks attributed to Polish guerrilla activity behind the German lines occurred in Konskie on 12 September 1939. A few days earlier, some Germans from a reconnaissance unit had been killed by Polish guerrilla snipers as they reconnoitred the city. This act incensed the German army unit that entered Konskie on 12 September. They gathered a large group of the city's Jewish male population together and forced them to dig graves in the town's park for their dead comrades. The Jews were beaten as they worked and the atmosphere in the German Army unit did not bode well for the Jews. It is likely that the snipers were not even among them, but this typified how Jews were randomly singled out for punishment when the real perpetrators were not available. Non-Jews also suffered indiscriminate shootings.

In this particular case, *Major der Schutzpolizei* Schulz approached the *Heer* troops and berated them about their behaviour. He ordered that the Jews be released, whereupon the Jews began to run away. At this moment an army lieutenant by the name of Kleinmischel fired two shots at the fleeing Jews and felled one. The German army formation he belonged to started indiscriminately firing at the fleeing men and by the time the firing stopped, twenty-two had been murdered. The famous filmmaker Leni Riefenstahl, who was in the city making a film about the Polish campaign, began to cry after witnessing the incident. She never completed her film. Leutnant Kleinmischel was court-martialled, primarily due to Major Schulz's testimony and his insistence, but was pardoned and released in the general amnesty for the German military issued by Hitler in early October 1939.[269]

Although the behaviour of Schulz had been honourable, it was nevertheless atypical of the manner in which the majority of the German police forces would conduct themselves in Poland and elsewhere. At the very least, the local Polish population, especially the Jewish population, was subject to daily acts of humiliation. At worst, the German police took part in indiscriminate or planned mass arrests and murders. Hundreds of period photographs and reports attest to this and are indisputable evidence of German atrocities.

The actual creation of the Polish *Armia Krajowa* occurred almost at the start of the German occupation, but it grew slowly. The official date, however, appears to have been in February 1942. There had been a brief period in early 1940 when a Polish partisan force named *Hubal* had operated in the GG, specifically in the region bounded by the cities of Łódź, Kielce, Radom, and Warsaw. This force was relatively small, perhaps 200–300 men. It was attacked towards the end of March 1940 by a combined Gestapo, Gendarmerie, and Wehrmacht force and was wiped out.[270] After this, the AK scaled down its operations until autumn 1942, when they considered their units strong enough to once again try and carry the war against the German occupation army, if only in the countryside.

The AK numbered only 5,000 trained members at the start of the occupation, and had only grown to about 20,000 trained members by the spring of 1943, with 60,000 unarmed volunteers.[271] In 1943, the leader of the AK was Stefan Rowecki. However, he was arrested in June 1943, so another officer, Leopold Okulicki, was selected to lead the AK. As stated earlier, AK membership was probably around 80,000 people in 1943. For 1944, the best estimate as to the size of the AK is around 400,000. One must remember, however, that the majority of these volunteers lacked weapons and training. The AK received very few weapons from the Western powers, a clear opportunity missed by the British and Americans to create mayhem for the Germans.

Though the killings of Polish guerillas and civilians did not deter the Polish Home Army from attacking the German forces in built-up areas, they did realise that there was no chance that they could liberate a city or cities without losing considerable numbers of men and weapons. Besides, even if they could manage such a feat in 1942, the Allied and Russian front lines were hundreds of miles away and German forces could draw on considerable troops inside Poland and in the *Reich* for reinforcements, which could retake any captured city rather quickly. Accordingly, open warfare in the cities was not a possibility in 1942. The AK leadership did launch several significant operations during the course of the war. These special undertakings had code names and specific goals that the AK needed to achieve. The principal AK operations were as follows:

a) Operation Belt. Attacks against German border outposts between the General Government region and the annexed Polish territories. The operation lasted from August 1943 to March 1944. The results seemed insignificant, with fewer than twenty German outposts destroyed and the German guards either killed or driven away. But the AK was able to achieve this with few casualties.
b) Operation Tempest. This was a plan by the AK to attack and capture major Polish cities in the summer of 1944, as the German military was preoccupied with the Red Army, whose front lines appeared to be advancing quickly.

c) Operation Sharp Gate. This was actually part of Operation Tempest and ran from 7–14 July 1944. The objective was for the AK 1st and 19th Divisions to capture Vilnius before the Red Army could do the same. The two Polish AK divisions were grouped into five principal combat groups and arrayed just south-east of Vilnius. The situation at the time only allowed for about 5,000 out of 12,500 AK soldiers to be within striking distance of the town. The battle was eventually won by the Red Army, which employed mechanised formations that quickly captured the town.
d) The Lviv Uprising. Like Operation Sharp Gate, this uprising, which began in the city of Lviv on 23 July 1944, was part of Operation Tempest. As happened in Vilnius, the leading Red Army tank units reached the outskirts of Lviv on 22 July 1944. The AK units inside the city aided the Russians in taking the city. The operation ended on 27 July when the Red Army disarmed the AK troops.
e) The Warsaw Uprising. The battle to reclaim the Polish capital began on 1 August 1944, and lasted sixty-three days until 2 October, when AK units fighting in the city were ordered to surrender. This uprising requires special attention and will be discussed in a separate chapter.

With regard to Operation Tempest, the AK command ordered that larger combat formations be established. In this way, companies formed into battalions, battalions created regiments, and regiments were grouped into partisan divisions. These units were to concentrate on eastern Poland, which was closer to the front lines of the Russian Front. Specifically, the AK divisions were to take special attention to block major German Army avenues of withdrawal. The operation began in March 1944. It appears however, that only one Polish division, the 27th, commanded by Major Wojciech Kiwerski, had success in attacking German forces in the district of Volhynia in any major way.

The rapid advance of the Red Army and the unwillingness of Stalin to tolerate an independent pro-Western Polish military force doomed Operation Tempest to failure. Kovel was taken by a combination of the 27th Division and Red Army forces, but after initial contact, the Russians seemed to distance their military units away from the AK fighters, who then became vulnerable to German counter-attacks. Although a city uprising by the AK did not take place until August 1944 when the Home Army tried to expel the Germans from Warsaw, they nevertheless were very active. The sheer number of losses suffered by the AK in fighting the Nazi occupation testifies greatly to the degree in which the Polish underground was involved. Between 1 September 1939 and 31 July 1944, the AK lost 62,133 officers, NCOs, and enlisted men in battles with the Nazi occupation army.[272]

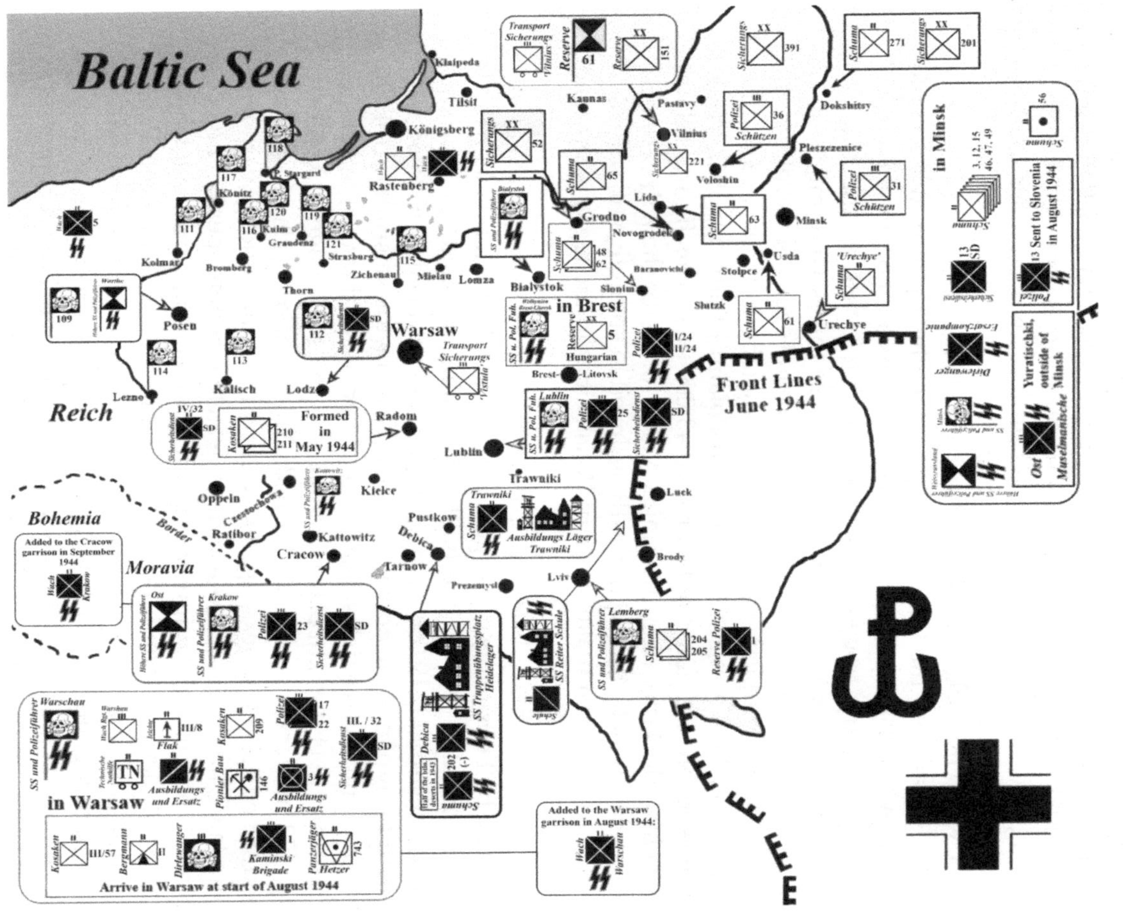

Figure 19. SS, Order Police, and German Army occupation forces in Poland, June 1944.

In addition to this figure, the Polish uprising in Warsaw (between 1 August and 2 October 1944) cost the Home Army an additional 14,221 officers, NCOs and men killed, wounded, and captured. Before the occupation would be over, an estimated 150,000 Germans would be killed, but not before 5,384,000 Polish citizens would lose their lives on account of Nazi aggression. This number also includes Polish Jews murdered. German police and other security forces stationed in Poland throughout the war never decreased. In fact, by December 1942 the total number of *Ordnungspolizei* troops in the GG amounted to 11,400 men, while the *Sicherheitspolizei* stood at 2,200.

Thus, between the Orpo and Sipo, Himmler's police forces could count on 13,600 men. The Germans could also count on another 16,337 foreign auxiliary troops who were serving either in the Galician police or *Schutzmannschaft* battalions. These forces were made up of Ukrainian, Lithuanian, Latvian, Belarusian, and even Polish volunteers. Those forces, coupled with the 13,000 members of the Polish Blue Police and the German police force in Poland in autumn 1942, could be reasonably estimated to be around 43,000 men. This figure did not even include Army rear-area units, *NSKK* forces, or the *Allgemeine-SS* regiments, which, although greatly reduced in strength, still served to help garrison most major western Polish cities in the regions annexed by Germany.

Between 1 January 1941 and 30 June 1944 the following damage was inflicted by Polish guerrillas against Nazi occupiers: 6 trains damaged, 803 trains delayed in overhaul, 732 trains derailed, 979 railway trucks destroyed, 19,058 damaged, and 443 set on fire, 638 separate disruptions of electric power in Warsaw (i.e. factory disruption), 4,326 German military vehicles destroyed or damaged, thirty-eight bridges blown up, twenty-eight planes damaged, 1,167 gas storage tanks blown up, 122 military warehouses burned, 25,145 various acts of sabotage performed, 5,733 attacks against German military and government personnel, hundreds of thousands of defective or non-operating pieces of war materiel and equipment produced in factories and slave labour camps all across Poland. What these figures show is that the Polish guerrillas were active in the struggle to liberate their country from foreign occupation. The Polish people paid a very heavy price during the almost six years that their country was occupied. From 1 September 1939 to 8 May 1945, Poland lost nearly 6 million citizens and soldiers, of which, according to noted author Gerald Reitlinger, nearly 2,600,000 were Polish Jews.

Chapter 3

COMPLICITY IN ATROCITIES BY THE GERMAN ARMY, SS AND POLICE FORCES IN POLAND, 1939–1944

Man is the cruelest animal.

Friedrich Nietzsche

Nazi punitive operations

The Germans began anti-guerrilla operations and 'punitive' or 'punishment' operations almost from the start of the occupation. In addition, major sections of Polish society were forced to evacuate certain provinces that Germany had annexed. This included the forced expulsion of both Polish Jews and gentiles. The first of these forced evacuations occurred in late September 1939 when about 20,000 Polish Jews were forced to cross the San River and they were sent from the recently established GG into the USSR. The next was the evacuation of Gdynia (Gdansk, or Danzig) of Polish Jews and gentiles. They were expelled and sent south to be accommodated in towns and cities of what became known as *Wehrkreis XXI 'Danzig-West Preussen'*. This was a part of western Poland that the Germans had annexed. Between November 1939 and 20 January 1941, the Germans evacuated from *Danzig-West Preussen* and the *Wartheland* – another region of western Poland annexed by Germany and referred to as *Wehrkreis XX* – an estimated 342,729 Polish citizens.[1] They were all expelled and forced into the established GG.

This figure included both Jews and non-Jews. In May 1940 *Reserve Polizei-Bataillon 101* was transferred from Hamburg, Germany, and sent to the *Wartheland* region to take part in these massive deportations. There the battalion took part in forcibly expelling the population for five months.[2] Other German *Ordnungspolizei* battalions also took part in these expulsions and 'relocations'. In addition, between 9 November and 17 December 1940 an additional 20,646 Polish citizens were sent to the GG from the Zichenau region of Poland, which had likewise been annexed by the Third Reich. This area lay between Warsaw and the Prussian border.

In eastern Upper Silesia, an area of the Reich bordering southern Poland, an additional 17,415 'undesirables' were evacuated to the GG from 23 November to 14 December 1940. This expulsion was part of *Generalplan Ost* by the Germans. The deportations that occurred between 1939 and 1940 from *Wartheland, Danzig-Westpreußen,* and *Ost-Oberschlesien,* were organised by *SS-Obersturmbannführer* Hermann Alois Krumey.[3] Krumey was the head of the *Umwandererzentralstelle* (the central office for immigrants – UWZ). In this capacity, he was responsible for organising the expulsions. *SS-Gruppenführer* Odilo Globocnik brought him to the Lublin District in late 1942 in order to help him organise the massive deportations there as well.

The next wave of forced expulsions began on 30 January 1941, in which an additional 19,226 people were expelled from the *Wartheland* and sent to the GG. This expulsion ended on 15 March 1941, only to be followed by an even larger displacement between 16 March 1941 and 21 January 1942. Between that time period, 111,600 people were relocated within the borders of the *Wartheland* for military and political reasons. Another 23,815 people were expelled from the city of Schieratz (Sieradz) between 1 April and 1 November 1941. They were allowed to remain in the *Wartheland.* Between 22 April 1941 and 31 December 1942 another internal relocation occurred, this time in the Danzig–West Preussen region, where 19,312 Polish citizens were forcibly moved. Another, more massive, relocation within the *Wartheland* occurred from 22 January to 31 December 1942, when 99,074 Poles were internally relocated. Beginning in 1941, these forced evacuations and relocations became deadlier when shooting actions began.

The first was launched in the GG in 1941 and ran into 1942. By the time it was over, 171,000 Polish citizens (the vast majority of them Jews) were dead. Another operation, launched in the *Wartheland* and titled *Unternehmen Feldarbeiter* (Operation Field Workers), took place from 2 March to 23 June 1942. The death toll of this drive was another 171,947 people. *Aktion Zamosc* occurred between 28 November and

31 December 1942 in the Lublin District. It took an estimated 33,832 additional lives. *SS-Gruppenführer* Odilo Globocnik had established several special concentration camps to house the people from the Zamosc region. These camps were operational from 27 November 1942 to 19 January 1944 and included:

1. **Zwierzyniec** – A major transit and internment camp used for the temporary detention of displaced Polish civilians before further deportation.
2. **Zamość** – A transit and selection camp where Polish families were categorised for forced labour, Germanisation, or deportation.
3. **Sitno** – A camp used for detaining Polish civilians, including children, before their fate was decided.
4. **Budzyń** – Initially a subcamp of Majdanek, later turned into a forced labour camp used for Polish prisoners, including those from Zamość.
5. **Majdanek** – Although primarily an extermination and labour camp, Majdanek was also used for processing and deporting Polish civilians from the Zamość region.

These camps were part of the broader Nazi effort to Germanise the Zamość region by expelling the Polish population and replacing them with German settlers. Many Polish civilians, including children, were sent to labour camps, concentration camps, or designated for *Lebensborn* programmes if deemed racially suitable for Germanisation. The *Zweigstelle Zamosc* camp was typical:

> Its inmates were held in 16 barracks that were separated by barbed wire. All came from Zamosc County. Between 28 November and 3 December 1942, it had housed nearly 10,000 inmates from 60 villages as part of the first phase of the Zamosc Lands action, which lasted from November 1942 until March 1943, and affected 116 villages and some 41,080 people.[4]

It appears that *Aktion Zamosc* had been ordered due to the intensive activity of the so-called peasant battalions, the *Bataliony Chpskie* (BcH for short).[5] The BcH began to be steadily augmented with more Home Army (*Armia Krajowa*) volunteers, but it was the communist-led *Armia Ludowa* (People's Army) or AL that won the race to absorb the BcH force that was operating in the Lublin District. The AL partisan forces continued guerrilla activities in this region in 1943 and 1944. In 1942 it was the independent BcH that had been giving the Germans so much trouble, especially in the Zamosc area. Between 1942 and 1943 another 63,000 people were relocated from the eastern part of Upper Silesia, while 28,465 people from the Bialystok District were similarly handled within the same time period. In total, between 1939 and 1940, some 200,000 Polish citizens would be expelled from Eastern Upper Silesia.

This included both ethnic Poles and Jews, many of whom were forcibly removed from their homes as part of the Nazis' policy to Germanize the region and eliminate Polish presence. From 15 January to 23 March 1943, exactly 14,739 people from the Lublin District were sent to concentration camps under Odilo Globocnik's control. *Aktion Werwolf* also took place in the Lublin District. It occurred between 26 June and 13 July 1943 and was a massive deportation campaign of the Christian Polish population that had apparently been ordered on the direct orders of *Reichsführer-SS* Heinrich Himmler. Historians apparently differ as to how many people were expelled and/or killed outright. Based on all the varying figures, a good guess would be that around 5,000 people were killed and 60,000 were expelled. In addition to the large-scale forced evacuations already mentioned, the Germans also launched the following known 'punitive' actions in Poland from March 1940 until December 1944.

Table 10. German 'punitive/pacification' Operations in Poland, 1940–44

Date	Location: town, city, region	District	People Killed	Type of Troops
1940				
30 Mar.–18 Apr.	Mechlin, Tomaszow	Radom	40	Gestapo, Gendarmerie, and Wehrmacht
30 Mar.–11 Apr.	Hucisko Chlewickie, Konskie	Radom	25	SS
4 April	Galki Krzeczonowskie, Starachowice	Radom	62	Gestapo, Gendarmerie, and Wehrmacht
4 April	Stefankov, Starachowice	Radom	72	SS
6 April	Stadnicka Wola, Konskie	Radom	26	Gestapo, Gendarmerie, SS
7 April	Miedzierna, Kielce	Radom	30	Gestapo, Gendarmerie, SS
7–8 April	Adamov, Konskie	Radom	20	Gestapo, Gendarmerie, SS
7–8 April	Krolewiec, Konskie	Radom	81	Gestapo, Gendarmerie, SS
8 April	Szalas, Kielce	Radom	92, includ-ing children as young as 12	Gestapo, Gendarmerie, SS
11 April	Skloby, Konskie	Radom	228	Gestapo, Gendarmerie, SS
14 April	Jozefow, Serokomla, Radzyn Podlaska	Lublin	191	Gestapo, Gendarmerie, SS
30 May	Rudno, Radzyn Podlaska	Lublin	49	SS

Date	Location: town, city, region	District	People Killed	Type of Troops
16 June	Radawiec Duzy, Lublin	Lublin	27	Gestapo, Selbstschutz
1941				
22 June	Siolko, Dabrova	Bialystok	15	Wehrmacht
22 June	Janovka, Augustov	Bialystok	54	Wehrmacht
25 June	Slochy Annopolskie, Siemiatycze	Bialystok	57	Wehrmacht
26 June	Stoczek, Zablotczyzna, Bielski Podlaska	Bialystok	?	Wehrmacht
30 July	Miklaszevo, Bielski Podlaska	Bialystok	?	Wehrmacht
30 July	Minkovka, Olechovka, Bielski Podlaska	Bialystok	5	Wehrmacht
31 July	Narew, Haynovka	Bialystok	42	SS
21 Aug.	Gruszki, Guszczewina, Bielski Podlaska	Bialystok	?	Wehrmacht
14 Sept.	Tarnopol, Bielski Podlaska	Bialystok	?	Wehrmacht
1942				
20–28 Feb.	Kryniczki, Orlov, Krasnyastav	Lublin	35	Gendarmerie
15 March	Sobien, Konskie	Radom	28	SS
18 March	Karolin, Radom	Radom	62	Gestapo, Gendarmerie, and Wehrmacht
24 April	Wiski, Derecwiczna, Radzyn Podlaska	Lublin	41	Gestapo. Gendarmerie

24 April	Rudno, Radzyn Podlaska	Lublin	40	Gestapo, Gendarmerie, SS
10, 20, and 25 May	Wiszenki, Zamosc	Lublin	All 3 days: 26	Gendarmerie
18 May	Lezno, Leszcanka, Chełmno	Lublin	65	Gestapo, SS
21–22 May	Tuchanie, Cholm	Lublin	62	?
16 June	Raysk, Bielski Podlaska	Bialystok	149	Gestapo, Gendarmerie, SS
20 June	Potoczek, Zamosc	Lublin	41	SS
3 August	Kulno, Bilgoraj	Lublin	100	Gendarmerie
22 Sept.	Budziska, Radzyn Podlaska	Lublin	24	Gestapo
26 Sept.	Komarov, Zamosc	Lublin	51	Gendarmerie, SS, Ukrainian Ordnungsdienst
29 Sept.	Osowek, Krasnik	Lublin	43	Gestapo, Gendarmerie, SS
30 Sept.	Goliszowiec, Krasnik	Lublin	41	SS
30 Sept.	Kochany, Krasnik	Lublin	41	Gestapo, Gendarmerie, SS and Wehrmacht
3 Oct.	Pikule, Krasnik	Lublin	51[6]	Gendarmerie, SS
3 Oct.	Kalenne, Krasnik	Lublin	58	Gendarmerie, Waffen-SS
20 Oct.	Sterdyn, Sokolov	Warsaw	72	Gendarmerie, Wehrmacht
28 Oct.	Obrocz, Zamosc	Lublin	28	Gendarmerie
18 Nov.	Bochotnica, Pulawy	Lublin	45	Gendarmerie, SS
22 Nov.	Zbedowice, Pulawy	Lublin	88	Gendarmerie, SS
27–28 Nov.	Grezovka, Radzyn Podlaska	Lublin	29	Gendarmerie

Date	Location: town, city, region	District	People Killed	Type of Troops
6 Dec.	Ciepielov Stary, Starachowice	Radom	33[7]	SS
7 Dec.	Bialka, Radzyn Podlaska	Lublin	96	SS
11 Dec.	Kitov, Zamosc	Lublin	180	Gendarmerie, and Ordnungsdienst[8]
20–29 Dec.	Rachodoszcze, Zamosc	Lublin	46	Gendarmerie, Ukrainian Ordnungsdienst, and a Sonderdienst unit
Dec. 24	Bialowieza, Bielski Podlaska	Bialystok	300	?
Dec. 25	Laszczow, Zamosc	Lublin	75	Gestapo, Gendarmerie, SS
29 Dec.	Bialowola, Zamosc	Lublin	52	Gestapo, Gendarmerie, SS
1943				
4 Jan.	Nielisz, Zamosc	Lublin	62	Gendarmerie, SS, and Schutzpolizei
4 Jan.	Krzak, Zamosc	Lublin	28	Gendarmerie
27-29 Jan.	Dzieraznia, Zamosc	Lublin	76	Gendarmerie
28 Jan.	Huta, Dzieraznia	Lublin	88	Gendarmerie
29 Jan.	Sumin, Zamosc	Lublin	50	Gendarmerie
2 Feb.	Roza, Zamosc	Lublin	36	Gendarmerie
4 Feb.	Pardysovka, Bilgoraj	Lublin	38	Gendarmerie, SS, and Waffen-SS
5 Feb.	Lendo Wielkie, Pulawy	Lublin	36	Waffen-SS, Luftwaffe
7 Feb.	Pienki, Siedlce	Warsaw	30	SS
10 Feb.	Alexandrov, Bilgoraj	Lublin	28	Gendarmerie, Wehrmacht

18 Feb.	Wielka, Wies Laki, Konskie	Radom	27	Gendarmerie, SS
6 Mar.	Raczyna, Yaroslav	Krakau	27	?
7 Mar.	Kaszyce, Yaroslav	Krakau	136: 57 men, 52 women, 27 children	Gestapo, Gendarmerie, Ukrainian. Ordnungsdienst
8 Mar.	Rokietnica, Yaroslav	Krakau	45	Gestapo, Gendarmerie
15–16 Mar.	Skronina, Sobien, Kornica	Radom	86 burned alive	Gendarmerie
18 Mar.	Rozaniec, Bilgoraj	Lublin	68	Gendarmerie, SS, and Wehrmacht
23 Mar.	Wieworka, Debica	Krakau	23	Gestapo, Gendarmerie, Bahnpolizei
28–30 Mar.	Wywloczka, Zamosc	Lublin	11	Gendarmerie, Wehrmacht
21–22 Apr.	Luta, Konskie	Radom	27	Gendarmerie
7 May	Dabrowa Gorna, Poduchowa, Starachowice	Radom	29	Gendarmerie
8 May	Dabrowa Dolna, Skarbona, Starachowice	Radom	59	Gendarmerie
8 May	Boncza, Wolka Boniecka, Krasnystaw	Lublin	34	Gendarmerie
9 May	Przewrotne, Reichhof	Krakau	52	Gendarmerie, Blue Police
11 May	Skalka Polska, Yedrzeyow	Radom	93, includ-ing 42 children	Gendarmerie, Schutzpolizei, Sonderdienst
18 May	Szarayovka, Bilgoraj	Lublin	58 burned alive	Gendarmerie, Ukrainian Schutzmannschaft

Date	Location: town, city, region	District	People Killed	Type of Troops
24 May	Zuchowiec, Gebice, Starachowice	Radom	72	Gendarmerie
26 May	Rachanic, Zamosc	Lublin	39	Gendarmerie
26 May	Mniov, Raszovka, Serbinov, Poglodov, Kielce	Radom	50	SS, Gestapo, Gendarmerie
29–30 May	Kulno, Bilgoraj	Lublin	82	SS
1 June	Bopdzentyn, Kielce	Radom	39	Gestapo, Gendarmerie, SS
1 June	Sochy, Bilgoraj	Lublin	200	Schutzpolizei, Luftwaffe
1 June	Starovina, Reichhof	Lublin	44	Sicherheitspolizei, and Gendarmerie
2 June	Ispina, Bochina	Krakau	25	Gendarmerie, Wehrmacht
3 June	Struzki, Opatov	Radom	96	Gendarmerie, Sonderdienst
3 June	Polyawice, Miechow	Krakau	60	Gestapo, Gendarmerie
4 June	Zarogov, Miechov	Krakau	23	Gestapo, Blue Police
4 June	Nasiechovice, Miechov	Krakau	70	Gendarmerie, Sonderdienst, Schutzpolizei
12 June	Policzna, Radom	Radom	33	Gestapo, Gendarmerie, and Sonderdienst
13 June	Hucisko, Reichhof	Krakau	24	Gestapo, Wehrmacht
20 June	Wola Zarczycka, Yaroslav	Krakau	76	Gendarmerie
23 June	Czemierniki, Radzyn Podlaska	Lublin	25	Gendarmerie

23 June	Krayno Parcele, Kielce	Radom	28	Gendarmerie
24 June	Maydan Novy, Bilgoraj	Lublin	28	SS, Galizien Polizei
30 June	Debno, Yedrzeyov	Radom	29	Gendarmerie, Wehrmacht
30 June–2 July	Popovka, Bialystok	Bialystok	37, including 17 children	Gendarmerie
1 July	Kaszov, Krakau	Krakau	26	Gendarmerie, SS, SD and Galizien Polizei
2 July	Osuchy, Bilgoraj	Lublin	34	Gendarmerie
3 July	Maydan Stary, Bilgoraj	Lublin	65, including 44 women and children	SS, Galizien Polizei
3–4 July	Bor Konovski, Starachowice	Radom	42	SS Kavallerie Regiment 17
4 July	Liszki, Krakau	Krakau	30	Gestapo, Gendarmerie, SS, Sonderdienst, Wehrmacht
9 July	Bobrova, Debica	Krakau	36	Sonderdienst
9 July	Golce, Kurzyna, Reichhof	Krakau	31	SS, Wehrmacht
9 July	Yarocin, Krasnik	Lublin	36	SS, Wehrmacht
9 July	Maydan Golczanski, Krasnik	Lublin	87	SS, Wehrmacht
9 July	Mostki, Krasnik	Lublin	29	SS, Gendarmerie
12 July	Baltov, Pulawy	Lublin	36	Gendarmerie, Luftwaffe
12–13 July	Michniov, Kielce	Radom	203	SS, Gendarmerie

Date	Location: town, city, region	District	People Killed	Type of Troops
13 July	Sikory-Tomkovieta, Lomza	Bialystok	49, including 14 children	Gestapo, Gendarmerie, and Wehrmacht
13 July	Zavady, Lomza	Bialystok	28	Gendarmerie Abteilung 1
13 July	Laskoviec, Lomza	Bialystok	29	Gestapo
17 July	Krasovo-Czestki, Lomza	Bialystok	257, including 83 children	Gendarmerie Abteilung 1
18 July	Vola Zoblienska, Reichhof	Krakau	38	Gendarmerie, SS
20–21 July	Radvanovice, Krakau	Krakau	30	Wehrmacht
24 July	Sulkovice, Harbutovice, Krakau	Krakau	26	Gestapo, Gendarmerie, SS
5 Aug.	Virkovice, Zamosc	Lublin	30	Gestapo, Gendarmerie
15 Aug.	Zagaye, Miechov	Krakau	68	Gestapo, Gendarmerie, SS, Galizien Polizei
26 Aug.	Yasionovo, Grodno	Bialystok	58	Gestapo, Gendarmerie and Wehrmacht
Aug. 26	Maly Plock, Lomza	Bialystok	23	Gestapo
10 Sept.	Talczyn, Radzyn Podlaska	Lublin	74	Gestapo, Gendarmerie, and Wehrmacht
11 Sept.	Tczov, Radom	Radom	31	Gestapo, Gendarmerie
11 Oct.	Voronicze, Sokolka	Bialystok	65	Gestapo, Gendarmerie

17 Oct.	Zavaly, Moldava, Debove Pole	Radom	63, including 25 children	Wehrmacht
17 Oct.	Volka Modrzeyova, Starachovice	Radom	50, including 21 children	Gendarmerie
22 Oct.	Lysakovo, Krasnik, Maydanek	Lublin	40, of whom 37 were killed in Maydanek	Wehrmacht
11 Nov.	Gebice, Zuchoviec, Starachovice	Radom	30	Gendarmerie
23 Nov.	Bichinov, Yedrzeyov	Radom	44	Gendarmerie, Wehrmacht
10 Dec.	Biskupice, Krakau	Krakau	25	Gendarmerie, Sonderdienst, Blue Police
21 Dec.	Vnory-Vandy, Lomza	Bialystok	28	SS, Wehrmacht
31 Dec.	Karpiovka, Krasnik	Lublin	45 burned alive	Gestapo, Gendarmerie
1944				
12 Jan.	Klodne, Neu-Sandez (Novy Sacz)	Krakau	28	Gestapo, Gendarmerie
28 Jan.	Lyszkovice, Krakau	Krakau	26	SS, Gendarmerie
1–2 Feb.	Borov, Vola Goscieradov, Karasiovka, Szczecyn, Volka Szczecyn, Lazek Chalovski, Lazek Zaklikovski	Lublin	1,060	Gendarmerie, SS, Galizien Polizei

Date	Location: town, city, region	District	People Killed	Type of Troops
6 Feb.	Czech, Radonsko	Radom	32 burned alive	Gestapo, Gendarmerie, Ukrainian Ordnungsdienst
24 Feb.	Piotrovin, Zamosc	Lublin	23 burned alive	Ukrainian Ordnungsdienst
28 Feb.	Vannaty, Garvolin	Warsaw	108[9]	Gestapo, Gendarmerie, Ostlegionen from Pulawy
1 March	Leokadiov, Pulawy	Lublin	40	Ostlegionen from Pulawy
7–8 Mar.	Yamy, Boyki, Lublin	Lublin	200	Wehrmacht
8 March	Yablon-Dobki, Lomza	Bialystok	95	Gendarmerie
17–18 Mar.	Tarnoszyn, Hrubieszov	Lublin	37	Galizien Polizei
27 March	Smoligov, Hrubieszov	Lublin	66	Gendarmerie, SS
27 March	Gozdov, Hrubieszov	Lublin	30	Galizien Polizei
1 April	Obroviec, Hrubieszov	Lublin	34[10]	Galizien Polizei, SS, SD
3–4 Apr.	Zagorze, Krakau	Krakau	32	Gestapo, Gendarmerie
24 April	Pavlov, Cholm	Lublin	15	Luftwaffe
5 May	Marynin, Cholm	Lublin	19	Wehrmacht
9 May	Zerechov, Petrikau (Petrikov)	Radom	6	Gendarmerie, SS, Blue Police
9 May	Momoty Gorne, Krasnik	Lublin	35	Wehrmacht, Luftwaffe
9 May	Smarkov, Kielce	Radom	25	Gendarmerie
22–24 May	Tokary, Krasnyastav	Lublin	3	Luftwaffe
27 May	Filipovka, Kuyavy	Warsaw	32	Gendarmerie

5 June	Olszanka, Krasnyatav	Lublin	97	Wehrmacht[11]
12 June	Harasiuki, Bilgoraj	Lublin	40	*Kalmückisches Kavalleriekorps*
13 June	Usice, Krasnik	Lublin	28	Wehrmacht, Luftwaffe
14 June	Lakoc, Barlogi, Pulawy	Lublin	12	Gendarmerie
20 June	Yanoviec, Pulawy	Lublin	30	Gendarmerie
22 June	Yanovka, Sudauen	Gumbinnen	53	Wehrmacht
22 June	Yaminy, Sudauen	Gumbinnen	24	Gestapo, Galizien Polizei
24 June	Boroviec, Lukova, Bilgoraj	Lublin	43	Ostlegionen
24–25 June	Osuchy, Bilgoraj	Lublin	40 [12]	Wehrmacht
5 July	Gesianka Borova, Minsk Mazur	Warsaw	70	SS, Gestapo
7 July	Vola Groyeka, Opatov	Radom	30	Ordnungspolizei
9 July	Komarovka, Biala-Podlaska	Lublin	6	Gendarmerie
22 July	Plebania Vola, Makoszka, Biala-Podlaska	Lublin	23	SS, Ostlegionen, Wehrmacht
23 July	Chlaniov, Vladislavin, Krasnyatav	Lublin	60	SS, Galizien Polizei
24–26 July	Tryczovka, Bialystok	Bialystok	27[13]	Wehrmacht
28 July	Opatoviec, Miechov	Krakau	31	Gestapo, Wehrmacht, Galizien Polizei
28–29 July	Uyscie Yezuicjie, Tarnov	Krakau	36	Galizien Polizei
29 July	Korczyna, Krosno	Krakau	40	SS, Wehrmacht

Date	Location: town, city, region	District	People Killed	Type of Troops
1–2 Aug.	Ksiaz Vielki, Miechov	Krakau	12	Gestapo, Gendarmerie
20–23 Aug.	Porabka, Neu-Sandez	Krakau	12	Gendarmerie
4 Aug.	Bokiny, Bialystok	Bialystok	25	129. Infanterie-Division
5 Aug.	Nur, Ostrov	Warsaw	120	Gestapo, Wehrmacht
5 Aug.	Skalbmierz, Miechov	Krakau	96[14]	Gendarmerie
6 Aug.	Poreba Dzierznia, Miechov	Krakau	39	Gestapo, SS
9 Aug.	Sklody Borove, Lomza	Bialystok	49	Galizien Polizei
12 Aug.	Daleszyce, Kielce	Radom	23	Wehrmacht, Vlasov toops
15 Aug.	Minoga, Barbaka, Miechov	Krakau	51	Gendarmerie, Galizien Polizei
16 Aug.	Grzedy, Grayevo	Bialystok	29	Wehrmacht
17 Aug.	Svaryszov, Yedrzeyov	Radom	49	Gendarmerie, Galizien Polizei
20 Aug.	Skrzydlna, Neu-Sandez	Krakau	23	SS
31 Aug.	Krusze, Warsaw	Warsaw	148	SS
2 Sept.	Radoszyce, Konskie	Radom	34	Gestapo, Gendarmerie
16 Sept.	Lipnik, Krakau	Krakau	10	Gestapo, Gendarmerie, and Wehrmacht
17–18 Sept.	Visniova, Czeslav, Krakau	Krakau	83, includ-ing 33 children	Gestapo, Gendarmerie, and Wehrmacht
18 Sept.	Pogorzany, Neu-Sandez	Krakau	51	SS, Ordnungspolizei

24 Sept.	Barycz, Kielce	Radom	33	Gendarmerie
24 Sept.	Yamna, Tarnov	Krakau	57	Gendarmerie, SS, Galizien Polizei, and Wehrmacht
30 Sept.	Grebosze, Kielce	Radom	28	SS
30 Sept.	Kaliga, Kielce	Radom	26	Gendarmerie, SS, Ukrainian Schutzmannschaft
27 Oct.	Nienaszov, Krosno	Krakau	20	Wehrmacht
28–30 Oct.	Szalas, Kielce	Radom	70	Gendarmerie, SS, Wehrmacht
1 Nov.	Gruszoviec, NeuSandez	Krakau	34	SS
7 Nov.	Bydgov, Konskie	Radom	22	Wehrmacht
28 Nov.	Zygmuntov, Konskie	Radom	35	Unknown Wehrmacht units
29 Nov.	Zavadka, Krakau	Krakau	12	Ukrainian Schutzmannschaft
13 Dec.	Sadki, Miechov	Krakau	13	Wehrmacht
13 Dec.	Trzonov, Miechov	Krakau	49	Gendarmerie, Ordnungspolizei, Wehrmacht
23 Dec.	Ochotnika Dolna, Neumarkt	Krakau	51	SS
31 Dec.	Nielawice, Lomza	Bialystok	56	562. Volksgrenadier Division

The above table clearly demonstrates just how important and involved the German Gendarmerie force was in the murder of Polish civilians. The local Gendarmerie posts and their motorised platoons, as well as the two principal motorised Gendarmerie battalions employed in Poland, were very active, not only in launching 'punitive' operations but in taking part in major anti-partisan drives. On the subject of the complicity of the *Ordnungspolizei* in war crimes as a whole, this is now established. Below is a sampling of *Ordnungspolizei* battalions and regiments whose members were prosecuted after the war for war crimes. The following table is therefore not a complete listing, but is comprehensive enough to show that the German police in the Second World War were an active participant in individual as well as in large-scale murder operations, and fully invested in *haShoah* (the Holocaust).[15]

Table 11. Police units implicated in atrocities in Poland and the USSR, 1939–44

Police Unit	Victims	Region	Dates
Gendarmerie-Zug (mot.) No. 7	Soviet and Polish PoWs, Jews, Romani, and other civilians	Novogrudok, Bielowiec, Bodzentyn, Debno, Grabkov, Huta-Sklana, Yeziorko, Klonov, Krasnik-Vysokie, Nova-Slupia, Opoczno, Parczew, Psary-Podlesy, Svietla-Katharczyna, Tarczek, Voiciechov, WolaSzczygielkova, Vyvoz, Zvolen	Dec. 1941, August 1942–December 1944
Gendarmerie-Zug (mot.) No. 16	Soviet partisans, Jews, and other civilians	Borysovka (Borisov), Kobryn (Assisted in the killing of 4,250 Jewish men, women, and children in the Kobryn Ghetto),[16] and the region of Petrikovka	23 September 1942, 15 October 1942, 4 March 1943
Gendarmerie-Zug (mot.) No. 62	Soviet and Polish PoWs, Jews, Romani, and other civilians	Novogrudok, Bielowiec, Bodzentyn, Debno, Grabkov, Huta-Sklana, Yeziorko, Klonov, Krasnik-Vysokie, Nova-Slupia, Opoczno, Parczew, Psary-Podlesy, Svietla-Katharczyna, Tarczek, Voiciechov, WolaSzczygielkova, Vyvoz, Zvolen	December 1941, August 1942–December 1944
Gendarmerie Bataillon 1 (motorisiert)	Polish and Soviet partisans, Jews, and other civilians	Novogrudok, Bielowiec, Bodzentyn, Debno, Grabkov, Huta-Sklana, Yeziorko, Klonov, KrasnikVysokie, Nova-Slupia, Opoczno, Parczew, Psary-Podlesy, SvietlaKatharczyna, Rokietnica, Kaszyce, Zvady, Krasovo-Czestki, Tarczek, Voiciechov, Wola-Szczygielkova, Vyvoz, Zvolen	July 1942–December 1944
Reserve-Polizei-Kompanie Köln	Polish Jews and other civilians	Warsaw	May 1943–1944
Polizei-Wach-Bataillon Łódź	Polish Jews	Łódź	April 1941–April 1943

Police Unit	Victims	Region	Dates
Polizei-Bataillon 6	Polish civilians	Hostages were shot in Bromberg (Bydgoszcz)	10 September 1939
Polizei-Bataillon 9	Soviet civilians	Shitomir (250 men)	1941
Reserve Polizei-Bataillon 11	Soviet Jews	Smolevichi (30 Jews), Slutsk (300 Jews) on orders of the commander of the *707. Infanterie-Division* for alleged support of the local partisans	October 1941
Polizei Bataillon 13[17]	Latvian Jews and other civilians	Libau, Priekule, Aizpute, Skeden (by Libau), Windau (Ventspils) – 3,000 Jews and other Latvian civilians suspected of being members of the Communist Party	July 1941–March 1942
Polizei-Bataillon 21	Latvian Jews	Riga (25,000 Jews in the Rumbuli Forest)	December 1941
Polizei-Bataillon 22	Polish Jews and other civilians	Torun (Thorn) – specifically, Fort No.7 in the city	1940
Polizei-Bataillon 44	Polish Jews and other civilians	Łódź (77 people in two separate dates)	23–24 November 1939
Reserve-Polizei-Bataillon 41	Polish Jews and other civilians	Łódź (107 Poles killed here between October-November 1939), Kutno,Poznan, Zamosc region, Krasnik, Warsaw, Chlewiska, Trawniki	11 October 1939–November 1943[18]
Reserve-Polizei-Bataillon 45	Soviet Jews	Berdichev, Chorol, Kiev, Sslawuta, Schepetovka, Sudylkov, Vinnitsa (a total of 2,400 Jews during its drive through Ukraine)	July–November 1941

Polizei-Bataillon 61	Polish Jews	Warsaw (110 Jews shot in reprisal for shootings of policemen and Wehrmacht soldiers)	7 June 1942
Reserve-Polizei-Bataillon 69	Soviet Jews and other civilians	Dowsk, Peklana, Luminiec (1,000 Jews shot assisting the SD in Luminiec)	1941–October 1942
Reserve-Polizei-Bataillon 82	Polish and Soviet partisans, Jews, and other civilians	Karwin, Chrzanow, Knyashitschi,Kolzovka, Krasniy-Ugol, Krasniy-Bor, Orlovka, Rshaniza, Syelo, Staraya Lavschina, Subovka, Suchodol, Tschervonoye, Verchnyaya-Rshaniza, Bryansk region, Gremyatsch, Kattowitz, Shitomir	March 1940–July 1942
Polizei-Bataillon 91[19]	Polish and Soviet Jews	Ostrov (in November 1939 360 men, women, and children were shot in reprisal for a major fire allegedly started by Jews), Krynki, Jerschitschi	November 1939–1942
Polizei-Bataillon 93[20]	Polish civilians	In Warsaw (35 men and five women shot)	26 August 1943
Reserve-Polizei-Bataillon 101[21]	Polish and German Jews	Jozefow, Konskovola, Serokomla, Miedzyrzec, Lomazy, Komarovka, Parczew, Kock, Lukov, Maydanek, Poniatowa, Radzyn, Vohyn, Biala-Podlaska (about 38,000 Jews shot in total)	July 1942–November 1943
Polizei-Bataillon 304	Polish / SovietJews, civilians, PoWs	Warsaw, Krakau, assisting in the shooting of 17,200 Jews in the Cracow District,[22] Starakonstantinov, Vinnitsa, Laidyschin, Gaisin, Kirovograd region, Kirovograd, Uman, Snamenka, Kiev	October 1940–April 1941, 4 January 1941, 10 August 1941
Polizei-Bataillon 306	Polish and Soviet PoWs, Jews, and other civilians	Lublin (shooting six polish villagers after an unsuccessful mopping up operation, individual shootings of seven Jews for violating a residential restriction decree, and the shooting of two escaped Soviet PoWs), Biala-Podlaska (5,000 Soviet PoWs by the Huisinka Forest)	February 1941, September 1941–November 1942

Police Unit	Victims	Region	Dates
Polizei-Bataillon 307	Soviet civilians	Mogilev (shooting of several children suspected of being partisan scouts and helpers)	October 1941
Polizei-Bataillon 309	Polish and Soviet PoWs, Jews, and other civilians	Bialystok, Dobryanka (shooting of a civilian, Soviet PoWs, and hundreds of Jews on the day the German Army entered Bialystok. Burning alive as well as shooting of at least 700 Jews in the main synagogue of Bialystok. The shooting of at least 25 Jews near Dobryanka)	27 June 1941, 17 September–3 October 1941
Polizei Bataillon 310 (III. Bataillon der Polizeiregiment 15)	Polish and Soviet Jews and other civilians	Brest, Chmieliszcze, Oltusz-Lesnia, Zablocie	19 November 1940, 23 September 1942, 15–16 October 1942, 23 October 1942
Polizei Bataillon 314	Soviet Jews and other civilians	Macieyov, Holoby, Dniepopetrovsk (mass murder of Jews in these three localities), Kharkov [23]	July–October 1941, March 1942
Polizei Bataillon 316	Polish & Soviet partisans, Jews, and other civilians	Bialystok, Bobruisk, Mogilev, region south of Baranovichi (9 July 1941), Cholm (24 Feb. 1944 during *Aktion 1005*)	9 July 1941, 24 February 1944
Polizei-Bataillon 322	Polish and Soviet partisans, Jews, and civilians	Baranovichi, Barssuki, Bialovice, Bialystok, Minsk, Mogilev	July - October 1941

SS-Polizeiregiment 2	Soviet partisans and civilians	Region west of Lepel, area of Kodianov–Nalibok Forest, Begomiel-Dockschitsi, Minsk	20 October 1942–26 April 1944
Polizeiregiment 8	Czech civilians	Czech region	1944–1945
Polizeiregiment Süd [24]	Soviet Jews	Area around Kiev (100 Jews), Brody (60 Jews)	July–September 1941
SS-Polizeiregiment 13	Partisan PoWs	Persmanhof (Upper Carnolia)	August–September 1944
Polizeiregiment 15	Polish/Soviet Jews, PoWs, and other civilians	Borysovka,[25] Zablocie, Chmieliszcze, Oltusz-Lesnia, Jaswin, Hwosniza–USSR	23 September–28 October 1942
Polizeiregiment 17	Polish Jews	Lublin District (1,000 Jews killed assisting the local SD)	1944
Polizeiregiment 26	Soviet Jews	Glebockie Ghetto	20 August 1943
Polizeiregiment 36 [26]	USSR civilians	Kiev, Minsk, Molodechno, USSR	1943

During the Nuremberg war crimes tribunals numerous eyewitness testimony was presented. This included victims, perpetrators and even bystanders who witnessed these atrocities. The following is a report taken from the transcripts of the tribunal dated Monday, 18 February 1946. It details just one of the above listed operations and its human cost:

> **Report from the battalion commander:**
> 1. Mission: the 9th Company must destroy the village of Borysovka, which is overrun by partisans.
> 2. Forces: Two platoons of the 9th Company of the 15th Police Regiment, one platoon of gendarmes of the 16th Motorised Regiment, and one tank platoon from Beresina-Kartushka. I emphasize, your Honours, that the expedition included a tank platoon from Beresy-Kartuska. Against whom were these tanks and the two platoons supposed to operate? We find an answer to this question in the following item of this report:
> 3. Execution of Mission: the company assembled on the evening of 22 September, 1942, in Dyvyn. During the night from 22 to 23 September 1942, they marched from Dyvyn in the direction of Borysovka. The village was encircled from the north to the south by two platoons at 4 a.m. … At daybreak the entire population of the village was assembled by the village elder. After an investigation of the population with the assistance of the Security Police and the SD from Dyvyn, five families were resettled in Dyvyn. The remainder were shot by an especially detailed squad, and buried five hundred metres to the north-east of Borysovka. Altogether, 169 persons were shot, consisting of 49 men, 97 women and 23 children.
>
> **Prosecutor:** I consider that these quotations are so eloquent that I can conclude the reading of this document and, omitting two pages, pass on to the next part of my statement. I beg the Tribunal to look at Page 119 of the document book, which contains the report of the 'Extraordinary State Commission on the Destruction caused by the German fascist invaders in the Stalinsk Region'.[27]

By the time in which these murders took place, *Polizeiregiment* 15 was missing its *I. Bataillon*. It was therefore operating with only the *II.* and *III. Bataillon*. The above testimony was from the battalion commander of *III. Bataillon*. During the regiment's operations against partisans in this area, Polish and Soviet civilians were repeatedly shot. At the end of October 1942, parts of the regiment were involved in clearing the ghetto in Pinsk.

The Partisan War intensifies: 1941–43

At the end of December 1942, *SS-Obersturmbannführer* Mühle, the head of the Sipo and SD forces in the Lublin District, listed the number of guerrilla attacks that had been made in his region alone. The number of partisan attacks was quite telling. It indicates an increase in Polish guerrilla activity and, as the following table also describes, these attacks increased in number in the early months of 1943:[28]

Table 12. Partisan attacks in the Lublin District, January 1942–April 1943

January 1942	96
February 1942	61
March 1942	120
April 1942	300
May 1942	780
June 1942	1,140
July 1942	600
August 1942	800
September 1942	1,600
October 1942	300
November 1942	500
December 1942	900
January 1943	1,296
February 1943	1,600
March 1943	2,306
April 1943	2,320

Although it appears that the autumn months saw a slight reduction in the number of partisan attacks in the district, they nevertheless increased dramatically from January 1943. Lublin can be considered an average district. It is almost a certainty that throughout the area of the GG, guerrilla attacks increased on a similar scale. On 10 December 1942, *SA-Sturmbannführer* Dr Herbert Hummel,[29] the District Representative and Deputy Governor for the GG in Warsaw, wrote the following sombre report regarding the growing partisan menace and the political and military situation in the Warsaw District:

> The current political situation in the Warsaw District displays two main aspects: 1) Increased activity on the part of the Polish resistance. 2) The organisation of the partisans and guerrilla bands. In October 1942 there have been noteworthy acts of sabotage on the part of the Resistance

> Movement. On the 7th and 8th of October in many of the railway junctions around Warsaw, acts of sabotage have taken place which have resulted in the derailment of service trains. Hand grenades were thrown at the I Club and the station restaurant. A number of leaflets have been distributed of Hitler bearing the title: 'The Greatest Liar in the World'. Regarding the Resistance Movement, it can be stated that in recent months it has been reinforced from outside the [Warsaw] District and that the internal divisions of this movement are receiving weapons. Our reprisals have consisted of imprisoning fifty communists, the imposition of a fine of 1,000 Zlotys on the city of Warsaw and the inauguration of a curfew from 7:30 pm In October there were 256 cases of banditry, and 286 cases were reported in November. In general, they were not crimes of a political nature but perpetrated by criminal gangs which have grown stronger as a result of the evacuation of the Jews. Jews on the run have joined these gangs, in particular young Jewish girls. We are waging a pitiless war against these gangs but so far, we have been unable to liquidate them.
> Dr Hummel. [30]

On 16 February 1943, the deputy governor for Warsaw also noted the strength of the SS and *Ordnungspolizei* in the GG and questioned if these forces were sufficient based on the increase in guerrilla activity. At the time the strength of the SS and police was 11,400 policemen and 2,250 SS and *Sicherungspolizei*, for a total of 13,650 men. This figure was only fifty men more than the strength of the Orpo and Sipo forces in the GG in December 1942.[31] By September 1943 the numbers of *Ordnungspolizei* in the GG had been reduced to only 10,000 men. Based on continued reports of increased partisan activity, additional reinforcements were eventually brought into the GG at the direct orders of *Reichsführer-SS* Heinrich Himmler:

> Please make available at once the regiment of Police Griese from Marseilles, b) three further battalions of police will be sent to the General Government to restore the situation, c) From the three battalions which will be transferred to me from the Security Police divisions, two battalions will be assigned to the General Government which will be replaced later by others. Not for a few weeks will I be able to dispose of further battalions of police composed in part of cadres, d) I shall then reinforce the Security Police of the General Government by 250 men.
>
> The strength of the police force will thus amount as follows:
> 1) Regiment Griese: 2,000 men.
> 2) 3 Heimat (home) battalions: 1,800 men.
> 3) 3 battalions from the security divisions: 1,800 men.
> 4) Security Police: 250 men.

> In this way the German police force will comprise about 19,500 men. I must stress that in the General Government I have at my disposal 1,700 men from the SS formations belonging to the reserve units. They will be used in future, as well as the other formations, for minor actions, as for example for street fighting in the Warsaw Ghetto. The operation of evacuating about 300,000 Jews remaining in the General Government is not to be interrupted but is to be carried out to the end at the greatest possible speed. Although the evacuation of the Jews is the cause of these momentary disorders this will eventually become a basic factor in the pacification of this region.
> Heinrich Himmler[32]

The *Polizeiregiment Griese*, which Himmler referred to, was raised under the BdO *(Befehlshaber der Ordnungspolizei)*, or Supreme Commander of the Order Police in Marseilles, France, in April 1943 and renamed and numbered *Polizeiregiment 28 'Todt'*.[33] This regiment began forming in November 1942 and had been assigned a regimental commander who had previously led *Polizei-Bataillon 323*. This turned out to be *SS-Sturmbannführer der Reserve und Oberst der Polizei* Bernhard Griese, hence the reference to the regiment as *Polizeiregiment Griese* during its initial organisation. *Polizeiregiment 28 'Todt'* initially contained *Polizei-Bataillon 62* and *Polizei-Bataillon 69*, which became the *I. Bataillon* and *II. Bataillon* in the regiment respectively. The *III. Bataillon* was created from scratch for this regiment. It is interesting to note that even though Himmler promised to send *Polizeiregiment 28 'Todt'* to Poland, he eventually sent *Polizeiregiment 4* instead. This unit had been raised six months earlier in June 1942 and stationed in Paris.

The *Polizeiregiment 4* had been formed using *Polizei-Bataillon 316*, *Polizei-Bataillon 323*, and *Polizei-Bataillon 62* acting as the *I.*, *II.*, and *III. Bataillone* respectively. In 1942 *Polizei-Bataillon 316* had been operating in Upper Carnolia, Slovenia, when it was moved to France. *Polizei-Bataillon 323* was operating in Poland before it too was ordered to France. One source states that the headquarters for the regiment was not created until April 1943.[34] *Polizei-Bataillon 62*, which had been acting as the *I. Bataillon* of *Polizeiregiment 28 'Todt'*, was detached and assigned as the *III. Bataillon* of *Polizeiregiment 4*. At that time, a new *I. Bataillon* was created from scratch for *Polizeiregiment 28 'Todt'*. This battalion was created based on an influx of new police recruits and a transfer of experienced NCOs from the Reich.

At the start, *Polizeiregiment 4* was led by *Oberstleutnant der Schutzpolizei* Bolko von Schweinichen, but his command of the unit ended on 15 April 1943. Afterwards, it was *Oberstleutnant der Schutzpolizei* Erich Skoworonnek who assumed control of the regiment. He in turn led the unit until July 1944, when *Oberstleutnant der Schutzpolizei* Walter Danz assumed control. By June 1943, *Polizeiregiment 4* was in the GG. In December 1944 it was attached to *SS Polizei Kampfgruppe Hannibal,* an emergency police formation which had been fighting on the front lines since the summer of 1944, along the Polish–Russian–East Prussian border. *SS Polizei Kampfgruppe Hannibal* also had an artillery component in its organisation: *Polizei Geschütz Abteilung I* (three artillery batteries).

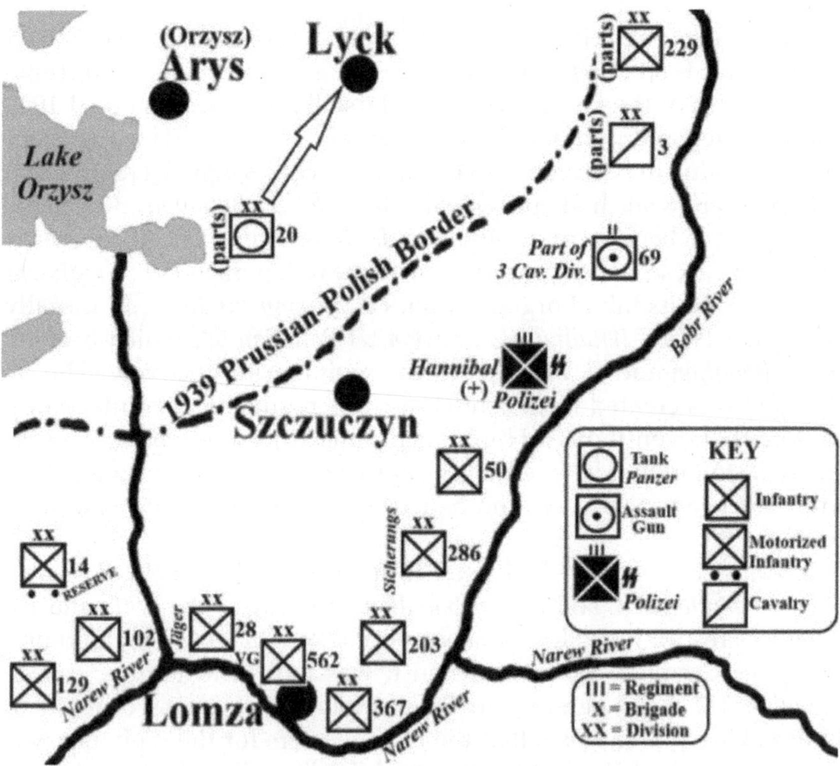

Figure 20. *SS Polizei Kampfgruppe Hannibal* in December 1944.

These reinforcements included *Polizeiregiment 22,* with three police battalions. This regiment had its headquarters in Warsaw, while *Polizeiregiment 24* was stationed in Lemberg (Lviv/Lwów). Its three police battalions were located in Kattowitz, Lemberg, and Łódź. *Polizeiregiment 23* and *Polizeiregiment 25* had also been organised in the summer of 1942 and stationed in Lublin and Cracow respectively. *Polizeiregiment 25* was spread over the outlying towns and cities of Reichshof (Rzeszów), Lwów, Radom, Czestochowa, and Kielce. All of these regiments had been raised from the existing named police regiments created in Poland in November 1939. In April 1943 two more police regiments were organised for use in the GG. These included *Polizei-Schützenregiment 34* and *Polizei-Schützenregiment 35.* As stated previously, these regiments had been organised on a two to one ratio of Ukrainian battalions to one German battalion. The *I. Bataillon* of these police rifle regiments contained the German personnel, while the *II.* and *III. Bataillones* were composed of Ukrainian volunteers, with a sprinkling of German and Ukrainian officers and NCOs. The regimental headquarters was predominantly German. *Polizei-Schützenregiment 34* was initially led by *Oberstleutnant der Polizei* Martin Dietz. The regiment was to operate in the area in and around Bialystok, that is, that part of eastern Poland that had been titled the 'Distrikt Bialystok'. This region was to have eventually become a part of East Prussia had the Nazis won the war.

Polizei-Schützenregiment 35 was commanded by *Oberstleutnant der Polizei* Martin Valtin. It was assigned to the area in and around Łódź. However, in early 1944 this regiment was transferred to eastern Galicia, where it was disbanded on 25 March 1944, after experiencing fierce front-line action. Remnants of the unit were absorbed into *SS-Polizeiregiment 10.* Another police regiment was also sent to Poland. This was *SS-Polizeiregiment 11,* which made its appearance in the GG in April 1944. It was stationed in Lemberg (Lviv / Lwów). It was employed between July and September 1944 as an emergency front-line combat unit under the control of the *LVI. Panzerkorps*. Its *II.* and *III. Bataillones* were finally destroyed and disbanded in November 1944, while the *I. Bataillon, SS-Polizeiregiment 11* survived only to be destroyed in the fighting for Chełmno a month later.

There were other formations that arrived in Poland in 1943 and were placed at the disposal of the local SS and police command. These had been brought up in order to try and counteract the growing partisan threat. One such unit was the *1. Kosaken Kavallerie Division,* which received its marching orders on 12 May 1943. Between 10,000 and 15,000 Cossacks left the city of Kherson (in Ukraine) and headed for Mielau (Mlawa), north-east of Warsaw, in the Zichenau region that Germany had annexed in 1939. An additional Cossack training camp was also soon set up in Mochowo, some 20km away from Mlawa. This Cossack division remained in this region of Poland until 17 September

1943, when it began its journey by train for its next assignment: fighting Tito's partisans in Yugoslavia.

An exotic German military unit in Poland

During the German invasion of the Soviet Union and subsequent occupation of captured territories, the German Army, purely out of military necessity, established numerous auxiliary police and self-defence formations raised from the local population. The minority non-Russian groups, especially the Kalmyks, Cossacks, and Tartars, were given special consideration and attention by the Germans, and were permitted to establish self-defence units. One of the most interesting would eventually become known as the *Kalmückisches Kavalleriekorps* (abbreviated to KKK). This formation would become one of the most exotic foreign volunteer units in the Wehrmacht. The Kalmyks were a Mongolian race of people scattered throughout Central Asia and extending westward into southern Russia.[35] They were nomads, possessing herds of horses, cattle, and sheep.[36]

The Kalmyks migrated to the Volga Steppes a short time before 1700, and then again in response to a Chinese 'invitation' seventy-one years later (1771). The resistance of the Kazaks to Russian expansion on the northern steppe was greatly weakened by this Kalmyk migration. The story of the Kalmyks has been forever immortalised in Thomas De Quincey's classic essay, 'Revolt of the Tartars'.[37] The word 'Kalmyk' literally means 'to remain' in the Turkish language. The Kalmyk people were a remnant of the Oirat Mongol Confederacy, which had stubbornly fought over control of Peking between 1450 and 1650. Later they were used as pawns in the inevitable power struggles between China and Russia. Surprisingly, the Kalmyks were never absorbed into Turkdom, nor did they embrace the Islamic faith.

They were in fact, the only German Army military unit made up completely of Buddhists of the 'Greater Way'.[38] In summer 1942, the *16. Infanterie-Division (motorisiert)* captured Elista, the capital of the Kalmyk Autonomous Soviet Socialist Republic, which Joseph Stalin had established in 1935. The division had been assigned the task of keeping a link between German forces fighting in the Caucasus and those German units in and around the city of Stalingrad. The division quickly set up shop in this Kalmyk capital, and began sending long-range reconnaissance patrols from Uta, a staging town east of Elista.[39]

It wasn't long before the Russians began partisan operations inside the Kalmyk ASSR, which included the entire expanse of the Kalmyk

Steppe. The 'Ic' of *16. Infanterie-Division*, Major Poltermann, requested permission from the divisional commander to raise a local volunteer militia from the nomadic Kalmyk tribes that would help them to guard the flanks. *Oberstleutnant* Bernd von Freytag-Loringhoven, who at the time was in Poltava, quickly made some phone calls and located an interpreter for him who had knowledge of the Kalmyk people and best of all, could speak their language fluently.[40] This officer turned out to be *Sonderführer* (Special Officer) Dr Otto Doll, whose real name was Otmar Rudolf Werva.[41] Another source states that his real name was Rudolf Vrba.[42]

Doctor Doll quickly organised what would initially be referred to as the *Kalmyken Verbände Dr Doll*, but which was eventually named as the *Kalmückisches Kavalleriekorps*, abbreviated to KKK within the German Army. The formation followed the German withdrawal from Russia throughout the period 1942–44, and in January 1944 the *Kalmückisches Kavalleriekorps* came under the control of *Oberfeldkommandantur 372* in Lublin, Poland.[43] In February 1944 the KKK was attached to the *213. Sicherungs-Division* for operational purposes.[44] The Kalmyk volunteers were now relegated to performing anti-guerrilla operations against the Polish underground army. In this new environment the Kalmyks encountered a different climate and fauna. The dry, wide-open steppes were long gone – replaced by woods, marshes, and hills that were unfamiliar to them. Their employment in these new surroundings would lower the effectiveness of the Kalmyk units, although alongside their beloved commander Dr Doll, they continued to do their best. In June 1944 the unit was still in the Lublin District, where a large anti-partisan operation was launched against guerrillas entrenched in the Bilgoraj Forest. The Germans had amassed a sizeable force for the drive, which included the following formations:

Ground units:

Sonderdienst-Bataillon
CO: *SS-Sturmbannführer* Helmut Pfaffenroth.
Sonderdienst Bataillon
CO: *Rechtsrat* Dr Jänsch.
154. Reserve-Division
CO: *Generalleutnant* Friedrich Altrichter
174. Reserve-Division
CO: *Generalleutnant* Friedrich Georg Eberhardt
213. Sicherungs-Division

CO: *Generalleutnant* Hubert Lendle[45]
Kalmückisches Kavalleriekorps (attached to *213. Sicherungs-Division*)
CO: Oberst Dr Doll
Landesschützen-Bataillon 115 (115th Regional Defence Battalion)
Gendarmerie-Bataillon 1 (mot.)
5th Hungarian Reserve Division[46]

Air Support: *1. Staffel der Luftwaffe Fliegergruppe 7*[47]

The Germans listed Polish Home Army losses as 898 killed, while '193 bandits and 531 bandit helpers' were apprehended. Axis losses were placed at 102 killed and 202 wounded. Captured equipment included two radio sets, eight light machine guns, three anti-tank weapons (bazookas), twenty-four machine pistols, two mortars, forty rifles, 230 hand grenades, 22,000 rounds of rifle ammunition, 2,500 rounds of machine pistol ammunition, 400kg of explosives, and 370 fuses.[48] There the KKK performed all too well, eliminating any guerrillas they found, but they had a reputation for stealing horses and supplies from the local population, and even from other units. This behaviour did not change and they continued to be misunderstood. The Germans continually failed to understand how the Kalmyks felt. These people, who had been uprooted from their ancestral home, had basically given everything up for the Germans, and felt that the Third Reich was indebted to them. Therefore, it was felt that the responsibility of the Germans was to supply the Kalmyks with their every need. If those needs were not met, then they felt justified in removing the property and livestock of the local peasants.

Pretty soon the local German authorities were complaining about the formation once again. In a way, you could not blame the Kalmyks for taking this attitude, but it made them seem more and more like the free-booters of the Thirty Years' War. It was in July that the KKK was committed to fighting on the front lines against regular Russian units. Tragedy befell the unit when its beloved and much-admired commander, *Oberst* Dr Doll, and some other Kalmyk leaders were killed during a partisan ambush. The loss of their German commander was so great that the unit became demoralised for a time and had to be withdrawn for several weeks. The interim commander was now to be *Oberstleutnant* Bergen. (in January 1945, *Oberst* Raimund Hörst would assume command).[49] Slowly, the unit's morale was once again raised, but not to the level at which it had been before Doll's death. On 6 July 1944, the KKK could count on the following forces and arms:

Table 13. Military equipment of the *Kalmückisches Kavalleriekorps* on 6 July 1944.

Officers	NCOs	Enlisted Men	Total
147	374	2,917	3,438
Horses / camels	rifles	pistols	machine pistols
3,802 / 798	2,166 [50]	246	163[51]
light MGs	60mm mortars	*Panjewagen*	PKW and LKW light trucks
21	9	500	8

In the autumn, the unit was stationed in the Radom district. The KKK was still there when in January 1945 the Soviet winter offensive began. The German front line cracked all across the front. It was during this chaotic period of the war that the Red Army forces finally trapped and conclusively defeated the *Kalmückisches Kavalleriekorps* near Kielce.[52] It was eventually decided that *Oberst* Eduard Bataev would assume command. What remained of the KKK after the Soviet January 1945 offensive withdrew into Austria in February 1945. It is interesting to note that shortly before the Soviet offensive in January 1945, the strength of the KKK had increased to around 5,000 men. This had been achieved by a large-scale conscription of all available men of Kalmyk descent from German PoW camps. This recruitment now brought in Crimean Tartars as well. Kalmyk men older than 45 years of age and younger than 18 had not been drafted into the unit before 1944.[53] By a combination of ruthless recruitment in the PoW camps and the employment of those too old or too young to serve, the formation attained brigade strength.

Interestingly, it appears that plans had been in the works to include the KKK in the *Kaukasicher-Waffen-Verbände der SS*, which at the time was in the process of forming in northern Italy. One unconfirmed report states that the *SS-Hauptamt* (SS Main Office) had, on 8 January 1945, authorised the transfer of the *Kalmückisches Kavalleriekorps* into the newly organised *Kaukasicher-Waffen-Verbände der SS*.[54] It would appear that the idea was dropped, either because of the Soviet winter offensive, which began a few days later, or on account of the fact that the KKK had already been earmarked for the Vlasov Army.[55] Perhaps it was on account of both these reasons. In any case, we shall never really know. The remnants of the *Kalmückisches Kavalleriekorps* withdrew through Silesia and eventually reached Austria in March 1945, when it was finally dissolved and its survivors were absorbed into General

Andrey Andreyevich Vlasov's 'Russian Army of Liberation'.[56] This occurred at *Truppenübungsplatz Neuhammer*, which was located near the Silesian town of Neuhammer am Queis.[57]

Jewish Bolshevism?

From all of the data and sources presently available, the indication is that an overwhelming number of Jews who participated in the partisan struggle, both in Poland and in the USSR, did so mostly under communist units, or in independent, all-Jewish formations. The Nazis had always loudly and openly stated their theory of a Judeo–Bolshevist plot, mainly for the political consumption of Europeans. Most people who had even the slightest bit of common sense found this supposed Jewish–communist conspiracy ludicrous, since Hebrew beliefs, like Christianity and Islam, run contrary to the harshness of communism. Why then did this Nazi theory of close cooperation or direct employment of Jewish volunteers in communist guerrilla movements prove to be true (at least technically) in Poland and the Soviet Union? The reason lies in what is basically a self-fulfilling prophecy created by the Nazis themselves. First of all, German actions against the Jews contributed directly to the creation of Jewish guerrillas. Faced with deportations, starvation, and extermination, all of the Jews who could escape the ghettos and flee into the countryside did so.

Once in the woods, it was just a matter of taking that extra short step to join the ranks of the partisans. Survival in the woods also depended greatly on joining a partisan group, as there was safety in numbers. Even stealing food to survive was made easier if you could claim you were confiscating the foodstuffs for the partisan band, i.e., for the war effort. Some authors have hinted that in Poland for example, the Polish Home Army tended to be anti-Semitic, and that is the reason why Jews rushed to join the communist AL/GL guerrillas. While this may have been true to some degree, it was by no means a major factor. Jewish men in particular were very vulnerable living in a town or major city; even those who could pass as gentiles could be revealed as Jewish if strip searched. Thus, in order to survive, hide, or fight, Jews had to flee major populated areas and seek refuge in the countryside.

There were Jews in the Home Army, most notably Henryk Wolinski, who headed the Jewish Bureau of the AK, but the vast majority of those wishing to avoid capture had to leave the towns and cities and flee to the forests in the countryside. As stated earlier, once in the countryside, it was deemed safer to join a partisan band than to wander alone. For the most part, they joined the communist guerrillas because for the time period 1939–1941, the AK remained mostly a city-bound force.

Thus, when the majority of the Jews escaping the cities reached the countryside, it was the (communist) GL who welcomed them. Only beginning in autumn 1942 did the AK start to establish a large presence outside of the cities. In addition, many, if not most of the Jewish guerrilla fighters joined the war effort not only to survive the war, but to exact revenge on their German tormentors. At a time when their people were being exterminated by a ruthless and relentless enemy, many Jews chose to fight in guerrilla units formed from what seemed to be the most keenly opposed political movement to Nazism.

Finally, there were Jews who were not religious or had turned away from their Hebrew beliefs and had accepted communism as their creed, just as some Jews chose to accept Christianity over Judaism. The range of motives as to why a human being decides to do something always has to be judged on a one-to-one basis. That being said, it appears that the overwhelming majority of Jews joined the communist partisans or formed their own guerrilla units for two basic reasons: (1) self-preservation, and (2) revenge. The Nazis have been ridiculed for attempting to make communism and Judaism synonymous as 'Judeo–Bolshevism'. However, they were in part and for purely circumstantial reasons as described above, correct in their assumption of Jewish participation in the communist guerrilla movement in Poland (and elsewhere for that matter).

The Nazis themselves created this self-fulfilling prophecy by giving the Jews of Europe only two choices: stay in the towns and cities and die, or run to the countryside to join a partisan unit and hopefully survive. The explanation for Jewish participation in communist units in the USSR is even simpler: the movement was, with the exception of the Ukrainian nationalist guerrillas, always under the control of the Communist Party. But anti-Semitism could sometimes also be found in Soviet partisan units. There are a number of cases of this happening.

Again, these occurrences should be judged on an individual basis, given that all human beings are a world unto themselves. Some people believed in communism, others did not. Some people were anti-Semitic, some were not. This also explains why, in many instances, Jewish guerrillas chose to form their own fighting groups, in order to avoid anti-Semitism. It is the very reason why Zionists sought to establish a Jewish state. In 1943 several entirely Jewish combat units were formed in Poland and the USSR. For the most part, they were well led and organised. These included the 'Kaganovitch' unit in Polesie, 'Ordjonikidze' Otriad in the Novogrudok Forest, the 'Zhukov' battalion in the Kapoli region, the 'Vengeance' formation in the Narotch woods, and the 'Struggle', 'Death to Fascism',

'Avengers',' and 'Victory' partisan units in the Vilna (Vilnius) region. These units were just a few of many that were organised. The 'Vengeance' unit, for example, was disbanded by the local communist commander (named Markov) on 23 September 1943, with the excuse that some people in this unit had 'no training'. The Jewish fighters were split up into non-Jewish partisan formations. The likely reason why most of these all-Jewish units were eventually disbanded whenever possible was that, in typical Stalinist fashion, they were not trusted completely.

The Ukrainian nationalist guerrillas

The relationship between the Ukrainian nationalist guerrilla movements (there were several) and the Germans had been an 'on again, off again' affair filled with disappointments for the Ukrainian Bandera and Melnyk movements, and missed opportunities for the short-sighted German policies regarding Ukraine (and the East in general). Cooperation between Germans and Ukrainians had been forthcoming from several sectors of the Ukrainian population and, indeed, from members in both the OUN-B (Bandera faction) and OUN-M (the faction under the more conservative Colonel Andrew Melnyk). A third Ukrainian guerrilla force was located in the Polesie region of Galicia, and headed by 'Taras Bulba', a pseudonym for Colonel Taras Borovets.[58] Colonel Borovets controlled a 10,000-man Ukrainian militia army in that region. In the summer of 1941, the commander of *213. Sicherungs-Division*, *Generalleutnant* René de l'Homme de Courbière, officially recognised his guerrilla force as a 'legitimate militia', which the Germans referred to as the '*Polissia Sich*'. In fact, it was this Ukrainian militia force that assisted the Germans in their anti-partisan operations in the district of Wolyn (Volhynia) in autumn 1941.

In eastern Ukraine, Galicia, and Vinnitsa, the Melnyk group assisted the Germans in recruiting a large number of Ukrainian men for the German auxiliary police force. Still others in the Melnyk group went on to Kiev and Zhitomir, where they formed part of the cadres for pro-Melnyk police organisations. The Ukrainian guerrilla group headed by Stephan Bandera was not as supportive, although there were exceptions like Anatoli Kabaida, the former leader of the OUN-B in Volhynia who joined the Ukrainian auxiliary police in Kiev. In certain instances, almost entire Ukrainian *Schutzmannschaft* battalions had been formed from ex-members of the OUN-B faction. Two such examples were the '*Nachtigall*' and '*Roland*' battalions, created by the German *Abwehr* (the German Armed Forces military intelligence service, headed by Admiral Wilhelm Canaris), which were later merged into the (ukrainische) *Schutzmannschaft Bataillon 201*. The *1. Kompanie* and *2. Kompanie*, which had been raised from volunteers from the Tarnopol region, had a particularly large percentage of ex-OUN-B men. Mention was made in one source that when raised, there were no proper uniforms available for this unit, and for a while they operated with civilian attire and armbands bearing the title *Schutzpolizei*.

Putting this partial or open collaboration aside, the OUN (especially the Bandera group) began to openly fight not only the communist and Polish guerrillas, but beginning in late 1942 and intensifying its efforts in 1943, went about attacking German units and positions as well. The goal of all Ukrainian nationalists, no matter what movement they were in, was to see a free and independent Ukrainian nation. They were separated by their views on how to go about achieving that goal. Some believed that independence could be gained through cooperation with the Nazis, while others thought otherwise. One example of a Ukrainian attack against the Germans is the assault on a slave labour camp near the village of Sviatoslav, close to the town of Skole. There the German Order Police had incarcerated all those local Ukrainians who refused to serve in the German auxiliary construction battalions. The camp was attacked by the OUN-B faction and the Ukrainians were freed. In the course of the battle many Germans were killed.

More spectacular were the ambushes and assassinations of German General Viktor Lutze, Polish General Karol Wacław Świerczewski, and Red Army Colonel-General Nikolai Fyodorovich Vatutin by members of the OUN-B. By German estimates, the OUN-B faction had an estimated 40,000 men by mid-1943. Evidence that the Germans feared the growing Ukrainian OUN menace is found in their launch of an anti-partisan drive in the Polish district of Volhynia in May 1943. That area that had been annexed to the German Civil Administration in Belarus (White Russia), but to Ukrainian nationalists was considered to be the southern half of 'Ukrainian Galicia'. Indeed, on 27 November 1943 two German divisions detected the movement of a Ukrainian UPA regiment of some 600 men. In response, elements of these two Nazi divisions swept through the villages of Maidan, Posich, and Zavityin near the town of Bolekhiv.

In December 1943 the Germans launched another major anti-partisan drive in the Kropyvnyk–Mizun area near the Carpathian foothills against an *OUN* battalion of some 300 men. According to one source, the Germans employed two entire regiments. Still, cooperation between the Germans and the UPA (Ukrainian Insurgent

Army) has been documented as late as 1944. For example, a document from *SS-Kampfgruppe Prützmann* dated 4 August 1944 and written by Prützmann's 'Ic', *SS-Sturmbannführer* Schmitz, discussed how the Germans supplied seventy to eighty rifles and 10,000 rounds of rifle ammunition to the local UPA group.[59] Ukrainian nationalist sources state that by May 1944 the UPA had around 80,000 fighters within its ranks, plus an additional 20,000 men hailing from other nationalities, making a grand total of 100,000 soldiers. The great weakness of the UPA lay in its lack of sufficiently trained officers, sufficient artillery, and other heavy weapons. After the end of the Second World War, the NKVD and in particular, the GPU (a section of the NKVD) fought the Ukrainian Insurgent Army well into the 1950s.

The war against the Polish partisans

The earliest employment of a large number of German SS and police forces arrayed against a Polish partisan group occurred in March 1940 in the region of Pilica, some 57km north-east of Katowice. At the beginning of November 1939, reports were received for the first time that a group of Polish soldiers had appeared in the forest area east of the Pilica. These were men who had refused to surrender, and were willing to continue the struggle by other means. In this they were ahead of the curve, for it would not be until 1942 that the Germans took serious notice of the growing Polish partisan threat. In the first months of 1940, this partisan group grew from an initial band of twenty soldiers to a company-sized force of about 150 men.

On 30 March 1940, the *SS und Polizeiführer Radom* command employed *Polizei-Bataillon 7* and *Polizei-Bataillon 51* against this guerilla force. From 26 April to 7 May 1942, *Polizei-Bataillon 51* was relocated to Reichshof (Rzeszow). From there it marched east and was deployed in central Russia.[60] *Polizei-Bataillon 51* was to be stationed in Mogilev. These two police battalions were led by *SS-Brigadeführer und Generalmajor der Polizei* Fritz Katzmann. The Germans sent these two battalions into the forest area east of Pilica, with the intention of finding the Polish partisan camp and destroying it.

One police battalion did not find the partisans, some of whom were said to be travelling on horseback. The other battalion encountered the main guerrilla group, but was forced to withdraw after taking sizeable losses. On 1 April 1940 a second attempt was made to destroy the partisan force. It was deemed that the first attempt had been made with few troops. In addition, the failure was also attributed to the fact that the German command had split into two groups. Finally, the fact that policemen were facing trained Polish soldiers also contributed

September 1939: German and Russian soldiers leisurely stroll around central Sambor (Lviv region). Most people know that Nazi Germany invaded Poland on 1 September 1939. Less well known is that the USSR also invaded Poland on 15 September 1939. The German and Russian dictators carved up Poland between them in much the same way that 167 years earlier, in 1772, the first partition of Poland took place between Prussia, Russia and Austria. (*Bundesarchiv*)

Execution of Polish hostages in Bromberg (Bydgoszcz) in late 1939. From the very beginning of the Nazi occupation, the German treatment of Poles was abysmal. (*District Museum Leona Wyczółkowskiego*)

Execution of Polish hostages in October 1939. From the very start of the occupation, the Nazis exacted a heavy toll in human lives for Polish acts of defiance and resistance to the German occupation. (*Bundesarchiv*)

Expulsion of the Polish population from western Poland. The region in question was the so-called *Wartheland*, which roughly bordered Inowroclaw, Lodz, Kaliz, and Poznan. Six hundred thousand Poles were displaced by the Nazis from German-occupied western Poland between 1939 and 1940. Seventy thousand Poles were banished by the Germans to the General Government from the *Reichsgau Wartheland* city of Poznań alone. (*Bundesarchiv*)

Occupation duty somewhere in a rural area of Poland, winter of 1939–40. Initially the German occupation forces faced little or no organised resistance. Beginning in the winter of 1941 and spring of 1942, guerrilla activity began to increase in the Polish countryside. (*Author's collection*)

As the Polish patriots began to target the infrastructure that allowed the Nazi war machine to function, the Germans found it necessary to bring additional security forces into the country and to garrison and patrol important military, supply and transportation hubs. Here we see two Order Police members assigned to guard a train station. (*Author's collection*)

Members of a German Order Police battalion shortly before being employed during Aktion Reinhard (Operation Reinhard), the planned elimination of all Jews from the General Government. The operation ran from March 1942 until November 1943. (Author's collection)

Deportation of Jews to Treblinka death camp from the Siedlce ghetto in 1942. This was part of Operation Reinhard. (*Bundesarchiv*)

SS Brigadeführer Odilo Lothar Ludwig Globocnik, who was tasked with carrying out Operation Reinhard in the *Generalgouvernement* (General Government). The Nazi plan for the extermination of Jews in occupied Poland resulted in the murder of approximately 1,700,000–2 million people. This operation, which included the establishment of extermination camps such as Sobibor, Belzec, and Treblinka, was a key component of the Holocaust. The exact number of victims is difficult to pinpoint due to the nature of the records and the scale of the atrocities, but the estimates generally fall within this range. (*Bundesarchiv*)

A machine gun team from Reserve Police Battalion 101. This battalion was stationed in Poland beginning in March 1941, and it was involved in various activities related to the enforcement of Nazi policies, including the implementation of the Final Solution. The battalion is particularly known for its role in the mass shootings of Jews and other civilians during the Holocaust. As such, they took part in numerous operations, including Operation Reinhard. (*Bundesarchiv*)

German motorised Gendarmerie in Poland. Two German motorised Gendarmerie battalions operated in Poland. Both took part in numerous atrocities during the occupation. (*Author's collection*)

Young Polish patriots. Boys and girls as young as 14 served in the Polish Home Army during the Warsaw uprising. (*Muzeum Powstania Warszawskiego* (*Museum of the Warsaw Rising*))

Not Germans, but actually Polish Home Army patriots during the Warsaw uprising. (*Muzeum Powstania Warszawskiego* (*Museum of the Warsaw Rising*))

Soldiers from Kolegium A of Kedyw on Stawki Street, in the Wola district during the Polish uprising (1944). They are dressed and armed in a mixture of Polish and German clothing and equipment. (*Muzeum Powstania Warszawskiego* (*Museum of the Warsaw Rising*))

The Russian collaborator *SS Brigadeführer* Bronislav Kaminski (arms behind his back), seen here conferring with German Order Police officers in 1944. Kaminski's brigade was partly committed to help crush the Polish uprising in Warsaw. There his men committed numerous atrocities against the Polish civilian population. The behaviour of his men was so reprehensible that even the Germans eventually ordered the unit's withdrawal from the city. This was not done out of kindness, but the presence of Kaminski's men in Warsaw was actually helping to stiffen Polish resistance. (*Bundesarchiv*)

The German campaign to fight the partisans on Polish territory (and elsewhere) continued into 1944. In that year, several Soviet partisan bands made successful efforts to establish themselves in eastern Poland. (*Bundesarchiv*)

Communications unit in a forest bunker, belonging to the 22nd AK Division, Zamosc region. (*National Archives, Kew Gardens, London*)

Home Army light submachine gun team, Zamosc region, 1943. (*National Archives, Kew Gardens, London*)

Home Army heavy machine gun from the First World War, acting in an anti-aircraft role, Zamosc region, 1943. (*National Archives, Kew Gardens, London*)

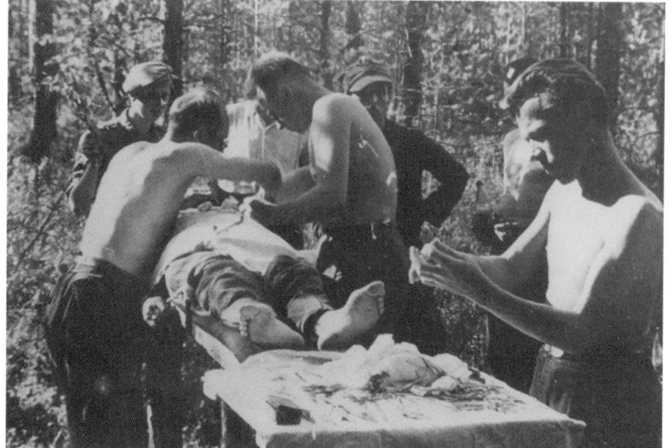
Home Army first aid station in the woods. An often-untold story of the partisan war is that of the brave doctors, nurses and orderlies who helped to save countless lives. (*National Archives, Kew Gardens, London*)

Dr Gryczolek, one of a score of brave Polish physicians who risked their lives to save fellow patriots. Here he is seen in a forest hospital camp in the Zamosc region, circa 1943. (*National Archives, Kew Gardens, London*)

Another unsung hero of the Polish Home Army – an orderly. His mission was to go into battle and bring back wounded Polish soldiers for the surgeons to operate on. (*National Archives, Kew Gardens, London*)

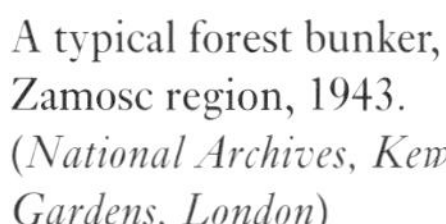

A typical forest bunker, Zamosc region, 1943. (*National Archives, Kew Gardens, London*)

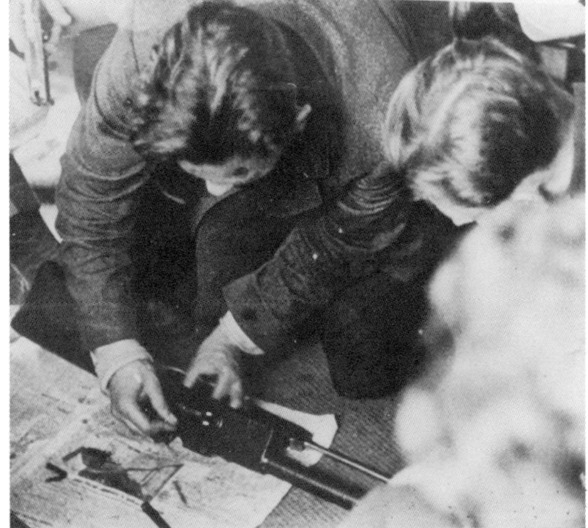

Learning to assemble and disassemble a weapon – part of AK training for new recruits. (*National Archives, Kew Gardens, London*)

New recruits fall in for inspection in the Zamosc region during 1943. (*National Archives, Kew Gardens, London*)

Soldiers of the AK 9th Division, Zamosc region, 1943. (*National Archives, Kew Gardens, London*)

A different view of that same light submachine gun squad from the AK 9th Division, Zamosc region, 1943. (*National Archives, Kew Gardens, London*)

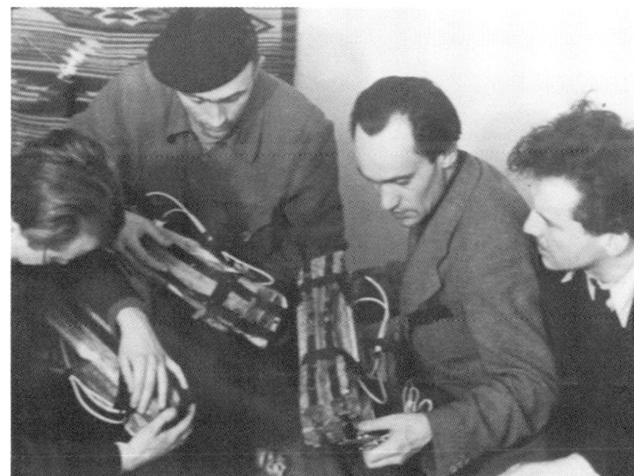

Demolition experts of the AK prepare explosives that will derail a German train, Zamosc region, 1943. (*National Archives, Kew Gardens, London*)

The handiwork of an AK demolition team: a derailed German military train. In the background you see two German soldiers. It took courage to take this photograph. (*National Archives, Kew Gardens, London*)

A different view of the same derailed train. A close examination of the photo reveals an SS guard, staring at whoever is taking the photo, and a dog is visible between the photographer and the SS guard. Railway employees are also seen in the photograph. (*National Archives, Kew Gardens, London*)

A Home Army soldier carrying a German MP-30 submachine gun. The gun was first produced in 1929 and was often referred to as the MP-34. (*National Archives, Kew Gardens, London*)

Polish Home Army soldiers in a village in the Novogrudok region, January 1944. (*National Archives, Kew Gardens, London*)

Operations against German forces, Novogrudok region, winter of 1943–44. (*National Archives, Kew Gardens, London*)

Novogrudok region, February 1944. A female (most likely an orderly or nurse) is seen in the centre. The Home Army was organised like a regular fighting force. It had infantry, cavalry, a few armoured vehicles, engineer, artillery, supply and medical services. (*National Archives, Kew Gardens, London*)

An officer in a Home Army Uhlan cavalry regiment, seen in the Novogrudok region in February 1944. (*National Archives, Kew Gardens, London*)

AK infantry forces during an operation in the Novogrudok area in February 1944. (*National Archives, Kew Gardens, London*)

AK infantrymen in the Novogrudok area, in February 1944, wearing winter camouflage clothing. (*National Archives, Kew Gardens, London*)

Members of an AK cavalry regiment in the Novogrudok region in February 1944. (*National Archives, Kew Gardens, London*)

A Soviet officer in May or June 1944. He appears to be none other than Oleksiy Fedorovych Fedorov, who led one of the most famous Soviet partisan brigades against the Germans in Belorussia and Ukraine. His brigade eventually penetrated into Polish territory in 1944. (*National Archives, Kew Gardens, London*)

Polish partisans from the Volhynia region in May or June 1944. (*National Archives, Kew Gardens, London*)

to the German defeat. For this reason, the following substantial units were gathered together into a battlegroup.

These units included: *SS-Totenkopfstandarte 8* (stationed in Cracow), *SS-Totenkopfstandarte 12* (stationed in Poznan-Treskau), *SS-Totenkopf Reiterstandarte, Polizei-Bataillon 7, Polizei-Bataillon 51,* and *Gendarmerie-Zug Radom (motorisiert)*.[61] An encirclement of the area was established through the towns and villages of Odrowaz, Wolow, Krasnao, Mniow, Samsonow, Jairow, Zagnansk, Suchedinow, Baranowicze. Katzmann, who had assumed the post of *SS und Polizeiführer Radom* in November 1939, was once again in command of this anti-partisan operation. On the night of 2 April 1940, a mounted group of the partisan force managed to break through the SS and *Ordnungspolizei* encirclement and headed west.

Those partisans who were on foot, however, were able to be either killed or captured. During the operation, the SS and police forces burned down the villages of Galki and Hucisko, and murdered its occupants. This incident, plus the failure of the police and SS units to completely destroy the entire partisan force, led to tensions between the SS command and the *Heer*. The year 1941 went by with few major operations launched against a sizeable partisan force. The Polish Home Army was only just organising itself, and what anti-German actions were being taken, were operations in the major cities and not the countryside. The Germans, for their part, were concentrating their SS and police forces on making sure that *Aktion Reinhard* was being fully implemented. In the cities, the SS and police focused on rounding up Jews and on imprisoning them in the Jewish ghetto in every Polish city.

The Germans also tried to disrupt the rise of any organised resistance to Nazi rule. The severity of the German reprisals against individual or group acts of sabotage, or the killing of Germans, increased in harshness as the year passed and the Russian campaign began. If you lived in a city or major town, it was always wise to minimise your time on the streets, given that the Germans had roving gangs of SS or police who would pick up Polish citizens and later execute them for every act of resistance. For killing a German, the Nazis executed 100 people. It didn't matter to the Nazis if you were simply an innocent civilian. What mattered was the body count that would be had for every anti-German act.

While major anti-partisan drives were undertaken during 1943 and 1944, other punitive operations were carried out, mainly in the districts of Radom, Lublin, Cracow, and Bialystok, with some in Warsaw as well. These retaliatory actions on the part of the Germans involved mainly civilians and ranged in the number of deaths that they caused, which varied from as little as two dozen to as many as several hundred Poles killed. This body count increased into the thousands when the Warsaw Uprising erupted in August 1944. All told about 33,970 victims of reprisal executions died in these regions.

These arbitrary round-ups and executions of hostages were meant to act as a deterrent to the guerrillas, but they never really worked. Quite the contrary, given they caused a sense of outrage on the part of the population and provoked more able-bodied Poles to join the ranks of the partisan bands in the forests and take part in resistance activities in the cities. For example, Jews who managed to escape the Vilnius and Kovno ghettoes helped to form the '*Nekama*' (Vengeance) Partisan Battalion out of perhaps 300–400 initial volunteers. Local Jewish guerrilla leaders in this region included Abba Kovner and Yosef Glazman. Local Soviet formations also included a 'Lithuanian' brigade of some 1,200 men that was composed mostly of Russians who had settled in Lithuania.

Table 14. Polish civilian deaths due to punitive actions, 1939–1945

Province	1939	1940	1941	1942	1943	1944	1945	City Total:
Bialystok	126	40	472	304	612	564	-	2,118
Bydgoszcz	2,996	187	32	31	3	226	106	3,581
Cracow	391	91	14	214	1,066	1,477	122	3,375
Gdansk	275	13	-	-	-	24	4	316
Kielce	182	-	45	309	1,968	1,437	61	4,002
Łódź	873	501	147	273	507	948	44	3,293
Lublin	214	350	319	1,708	2,445	1,519	-	6,555
Poznan	1,260	6	84	19	48	213	270	1,900
Rezeszow	53	21	83	144	1,422	569	-	2,292
Slask	1,136	71	3	66	80	160	76	1,592
Warsaw	663	128	8	593	1,141	1,710	726	4,969
Total:	8,169	1,408	1,207	3,661	9,292	8,847	1,409	33,970

All the while, the Germans were launching anti-partisan operations, launching punitive expeditions, and shooting hostages all across Poland. Even a special Luftwaffe group, known as *Fliegergruppe z.b.V.*

7 assisted in some of the anti-partisan operations that were conducted by the Germans in Poland from 1943 to1944.

Fliegergruppe z.b.V. 7

Figure 21. The various types of aircraft in Fliegergruppe z.b.V. 7. (*Author's line drawing*)

This air group was basically a reconnaissance air unit that initially contained three and later four types of aircraft.[62] These were the Arado Ar 95, the Fiesler Storch Fi 56, Heinkel He 60, and Junkers Ju 52 transport plane. This flight group was formed in 1942 and was under the direct command and control of *Reichsführer-SS* Heinrich Himmler.[63] Its sole purpose was to support anti-partisan operations. The formation would do this through air reconnaissance. In addition, valuable and important supplies and men could be airlifted from one place to another relatively quickly, if the need were to arise. Some of the pilots were SS members. As a result, the SS could now technically claim that they had their own air arm. To fully document the entire German campaign against the Polish guerrillas would require an entire book. What follows are brief descriptions of some of the major operations. For a complete list of all of the major German punitive and anti-partisan operations, please refer to the tables describing them.

Unternehmen Atilla

On 9 February 1943, the commander of the Security Police and SD in Radom launched *Unternehmen Attila,* which was aimed at destroying a battalion of the GL in the area of Wywoz, Zielonka, and Gozdzikow, plus other AK and BCh forces. Polish guerrilla forces amounted to around 800–1,000 men. This operation involved elements of the German Army, the *Gendarmerie-Bataillon 1 (mot.)* under the command of *Major der Gendarmerie* Erich Schwieger, and elements of the *Schutzpolizei* and a *Kommando* of the Sipo (*Sicherheitspolizei*) from Radom. The *Kommandeur der Sicherheitspolizei und SD Radom* was headed by *SS-Obersturmbannführer* Dr Fritz Liphardt. This Sipo platoon was led by *SD-Untersturmführer* Flath. The results of the operation were negligible, with only sixteen guerrillas killed and twenty-three apprehended. Only seven rifles and about 200 rounds of ammunition were captured. The People's Guard Battalion, which was the subject of this operation, was commanded by a Polish Jew named Rogulsky.

Unternehmen Ostersegen

Between 2 and 11 February 1943 *Gendarmerie-Bataillon 1 (motorisiert),* supported by elements of *SS-Polizeiregiment 25, Landesschützen-Bataillon 582,* and other minor SS and SD units totalling some 1,900 men, attacked the communist GL Battalion 'A. Mickiewicz' in the Zamosc-Bilgoraj area. This guerrilla unit had around 700–800 fighters. The sweep netted a body count of 159 killed but no weapons recovered. In the process, 156 farms were burned to the ground. It was obvious that the GL battalion had evaded destruction and that the Nazi units had only killed local civilians. On 4 February 1943, the same German force made contact with a company of the AK in the area of Lascowice, but this Polish guerrilla unit likewise withdrew and evaded capture.

Unternehmen Werwolf I und II

The Zamosc–Bilgoraj area was the subject of another, more intense anti-partisan sweep between 27 June and 11 July 1943. The code names for this two-part operation were *Werwolf I* and *Werwolf II*. The units involved in these two drives included the following forces: parts of *Polizeiregimenter 4, 13, 25, 26,* and *32, Schutzmannschaft Bataillone 203* and *252, Polizei Reiter Abteilung 3, Turkistanische Infanterie Bataillon 790,* and *Staffeln Flieger Gruppe 7.*[64] The renewed German attempts to engage and destroy the Polish partisans showed that the guerrillas were becoming better trained and better disciplined than they had been during the period 1941–42. The guerrillas showed that they could avoid a determined German anti-guerrilla drive, even when the Germans employed larger forces. On 24 October 1943, a combined force of some 3,000 men attacked a GL battalion in Diabla Gora. SS and police forces included *Schutzmannschaft Bataillon 206, Landesschützen-Bataillonen 994* and *995*, and *SS-Polizeiregiment 25.*

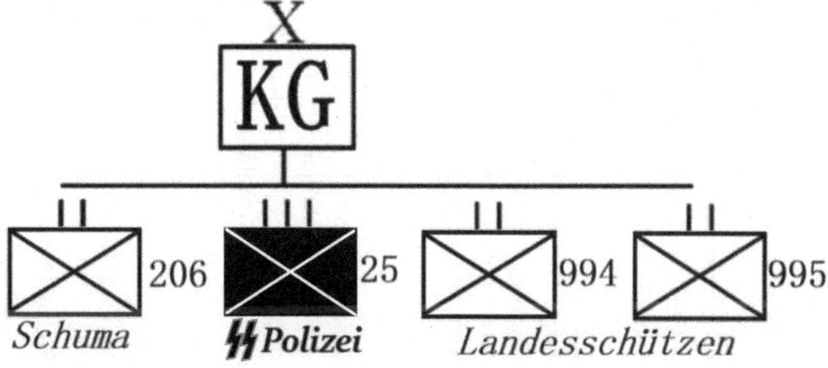

Figure 22. German Battlegroup by Diabla Gora, October 1943.

Unternehmen Memel

Three days later, on 27 October 1943, *Unternehmen Memel* was launched. *Memel* pitted the same SS and police forces, plus the addition of *SS-Polizeiregiment 17,* against an estimated 4,000-man Polish Home Army force code-named 'Gruppe Ponoury'.[65] Coincidentally, the German SS and police forces numbered about the same strength as the partisans. The fighting took place in the area around Starachowice. A report from the commander of *SS und Polizeiführer Krakau* (*SS-Oberführer* Julian Scherner), dated 16 September 1943, and addressed to the *Reichsminister fur die besetzten Ostgebiete* (National Minister for the Administration of the Eastern Territories), listed all of the guerrilla acts perpetrated in the Vholynia district from 9 to 14 June. It also mentioned that about 6,000 partisans were estimated to be operating in that area.[66] The following table provides a list of the major German anti-partisan operations against Polish guerrilla forces, including Russian insurgent units operating on Polish territory.

Table 15. Major anti-partisan operations in Poland, 1943–1944.

Code Name	Date	Region	German Forces	Partisan Units
1943				
Attila[67]	2–11 February	Zamosc–Bilgoraj	Polizeiregiment 25, Landesschützen-Bataillon 582[68] Gendarmerie-Bataillon 1 (mot.),38 Radom under:[69]	One AK battalion, 3rd BcH Company 'Grzmot', and one GL company
Ostersegen (Easter Blessing)	22–24 April	Parczew–Ostrov Lubelski	1. Staffeln-Flieger-Gruppe 740 plus parts of SS Polizei Regiment 25, Polizei-Schützen-Regiment 32, Landesschützen Bataillon 268, and Schutzmannschaft Bataillon 203	GL Battalion 'A. Mickiewicz'
Nachpfingsten (*Post-Pentecost*)	23 June–4 July	Parczew	Parts of Polizeiregiment 25, Polizeiregiment 32, and Schutzmannschaft Bataillon 203	GL Battalion 'A. Mickiewicz'
Werwolf I/ II (Werewolf I & Werewolf II)	27 June–11 July	Zamosc–Bilgoraj	Parts of Polizeiregimenter 4, 13, 25, 26, and 32, Schutzmannschaft Bataillon 203 and 252, Polizei-Reiter Abteilung 3,[70] Turkistanische Infanterie Bataillon 790, 1. Staffeln der Flieger Gruppe 7	Unknown number of AK, BCh, and GL units
Hermann (Herman)	15 July–5 August	Ivienic–Nalibok Forest Area[71]	1. SS Infanterie Brigade, SS Polizeiregiment 2, SS Sonder Regiment Dirlewanger, Polizei-Schützenregiment 31, Schutzmannschaft Bataillonen 15, 46, 47, 57, 271, Schuma Artillerie Abteilung 56, Polizei Panzer Kompanie 1 and 12, Gend. Zug 21[72]	Bielski Partisan unit

Vistula III (Named for the Vistula River)	1–10 August	Wolyn and Polesie	SS-Polizeiregiment 12, 13, and 26, Volgatartar Infanterie Bataillon 825, Kosaken Kavallerie Bataillon 102 (Oberst Kononov),[73] Luftwaffe Bombardierengruppe 6 der Luftflotte 6,[74] Polizei Panzer Kompanie 4[75]	Kovpak Partisan Brigade (3,500 men)
Karpaten (Named for the Carpathian Mountains)	30 July–25 August	Karpaty	Two regiments from the 154. and 174. Reserve-Division, Gendarmerie-Bataillon 1 (mot.),[76] SS-Polizeiregiment 4 and SS-Polizeiregiment 13	Kovpak Partisan Brigade
Brüll (Roar)	19–28 October	Zaklikovsko, Krasnik, Diabla Gora	Schuma Bataillon 206,[77] Landesschützen-Bataillon 994 and 995, SS-Polizeiregiment 25	Kovpak Partisan Brigade
Memel (Klaipeda)	27–29 October	Starachovichi	Gendarmerie-Bataillon 1 (mot.), SS-Polizeiregiment 17, SS Polizei Wach-Bataillon 5 (Debica)[78]	Ponary AK Gruppe (4,000 strong)
Ulanen (Ulan)	6–7 November	Dabrovka, Yaroslav	SS-Polizeiregiment 23, part of Polizei-Schützenregiment 32, Landesschützen-Bataillon 405	Ponary AK Gruppe (4,000 strong)
Sonnenschein (Sunshine)	19–21 December	Dabrovka, Bilgoraj	Polizei-Schützenregiment 32, Landesschützen-Bataillon 405	Ponary AK Gruppe (4,000 strong)
1944				
Ostsee (Baltic Sea)	2–14 January	Diabla Gora	SS-Polizeiregiment 14,[79] Gendarmerie-Bataillon 1 (mot.), Landesschützen-Bataillon 619, and Feldgendarmerie-Zug 62.	AK 'Burzy' and 'Wicht' Battalions and AL 'General Bern' Battalion

Code Name	Date	Region	German Forces	Partisan Units
Wintersport (Winter Sport)	4–10 January	Opole Lubelski	SS-Polizeiregiment 25, Landesschützen-Bataillon 992.	Unknown AL units
Waldkämmen	9–13 March[80]	Szczebrzeszyn–Zwierzyniec–Bilgoraj–Frampol south of Lublin[81]	SS Gendarmerie Bataillon 1 (mot.)[82] II. Bataillon of SS-Polizeiregiment 25, then later reinforced with: III. Bataillon of SS-Polizeiregiment 17[83]	2,000 men of the (Russian) Saburov Partisan Brigade.
Immergrün (Evergreen)	9–27 April	Chelm(no), Krasnystav	Part of Polizei-Schützenregiment 32, SS-Polizeiregiment 25, Landesschützen-Bataillon 991.	AL, BCh, and Soviet Kovpak Brigade
Maigewitter (May Thunderstorm)	5–16 May	Parczew, Krasnik	Part of 5. SS Panzer-Division 'Wiking', SS-Polizeiregiment 4, SS-Polizeiregiment 25, and 1. Staffeln Flieger Gruppe 7.	'Chepiga' Soviet Partisan Band (1,400 men) and a local AL band
Sturmwind I and *II* (Storm Wind I and II)[84]	8–25 June	Yanov Lubelski, Bilgoraj	Reserve-Division 154 and 174, part of Sicherungs-Division 213, Landesschützen-Regiment Stab 115, Landesschützen Bataillon 994 and 995, SS-Polizeiregiment 4, plus, Gendarmerie forces Bataillon 1 (mot.), *Kalmückisches Kavalleriekorps*,[85] part of the Hungarian 5th Light Division, 1. Staffeln Flieger Gruppe 7 + 1 Schlachtfliegerstaffel. This large force was launched against approximately 5,000 Polish and Soviet communist partisans in the area.	'Ziemia Lubelska' 1st and 'W. Wasilewska' AL Brigades, AL 'Pajdo' Battalion, and the 5th Soviet Partisan Battalion

Vagabund (Vagabond)	8–23 June	Radzyn Podlaski, Wlodawa, Cholm Parczew	Part of Polizei-Schützenregiment 32,[86] part of SS Polizeiregiment 4, SS-Polizeiregiment 25, Landesschützen-Bataillon 991 and 992.	Unknown number of Polish and Soviet partisan forces
Wirbelsturm (Whirlwind)	15–21 July	Parczew	Landesschützen-Bataillon 310, Lublin, 619, 887-88, 990, 991, 992, SS-Polizeiregiment 23, plus a battalion of Luftwaffe troops acting as infantry.	AL Brigade 'Swit' AL Brigade 'General Bern', and part of the Polish Home Army 27th Division
1. Herbstoffensive (1st Fall Offensive):	11 September–6 October	Kielce, Konskie	Forces under Korück 532:[87] Kosaken Schuma Bataillon 209, I. Bataillon der Polizei-Schützen-Regiment 34, Dirlewanger SS Brigade, Ostmuselmanische SS Regiment 1, Ost Reiter Abteilung 580, Kosaken Bataillon 572, Aserbeidschan Bataillon I/111, Korück 585: Sicherungs Regiment Ostland, and *Kalmückisches Kavalleriekorps* (in total, these forces amounted to about 10,000 men).	AL 3rd, 10th, and 11th Partisan Brigades, plus one battalion from the AL 1st Brigade, AK 2nd Division, AK 25th and 72nd Regiments (altogether about 1,200 AK men)
Waldkater (Forest Tomcat)	25–26 September	Kielce	Korück 581, with: Three (3) Landesschützen-Bataillonen, and SS Gendarmerie Bataillon 1. (mot.).	AK 25th and 2nd Regiments (altogether about 1,200 AK men).

Code Name	Date	Region	German Forces	Partisan Units
Sternschnuppe (Shooting Star)	26–30 September	Campinos Forest	Forces under Korück 532: Kosaken Schuma Bataillon 209, I. Bataillon der Polizei-Schützen-Regiment 34, Dirlewanger SS Brigade, Ostmuselmanische SS Regiment 1, Ost Reiter Abteilung 580, Kosaken Bataillon 572, Aserbeidschan Bataillon I/111	AK Group in the Kampinos Forest
Oktoberfest (October Festival)	6–9 October	Piotrkow Tribunalski	Polizei Wachbataillon 1, Landesschützen-Bataillon 317 and 843, Kampf Bataillon der 9 Armee (about 2,500 German troops).	AL 3rd Partisan Brigade
2. *Herbstoffensive* (2nd Fall Offensive):	17 September–18 October	Starachowice Wloszczowa	SS Panzer-Division Totenkopf, four Army battalions under the Feldkommandantur 620, two motorised Gendarmerie platoons.	AL 2nd, 10th, and 11th Brigades, two battalions of the 1st Brigade, three battalions of the BCh, plus the AK 25th Regiment
Kriemhild	18–20 October	Starachowice	Landesschützen-Bataillon 619, 898, 991, and 992, SS Gendarmerie-Bataillon 1 (mot.).	AL 10th Brigade

The Holocaust in Poland, 1943

The Warsaw Ghetto Uprising, April–May 1943

The final clearing of the Jewish ghetto in Warsaw began in April 1943. About 60,000–68,000 Jews remained in the ghetto by April 1943. As previously stated, the Nazis had systematically emptied out most of the ghetto between 1942 and 1943, sending the people there to various extermination camps. On 17 December 1942, the first public announcement of the Nazi attempt to murder Europe's Jewish population was made by the British government. If people didn't know before what was being done to the Jews of Europe, they knew now. Many Jews who were still alive now understood what 'resettlement' meant. Many resolved not to go to their deaths without a fight. This was the case with the remaining Jews in the Warsaw ghetto. During the battle, the Germans only captured seven Polish rifles, fifty-nine pistols, one Soviet rifle, one German rifle, plus several hundred actual and home-made hand grenades, including Molotov cocktails. With these meagre weapons, Jewish fighters in the Warsaw ghetto were able to hold out from 19 April to 16 May 1943. It took the Germans an entire month to break the Jewish resistance.

The German report filed after the battle also described the large quantities of explosives and machine gun ammunition that were found, although the Germans did not find any machine guns that could use it. *SS-Oberführer* von Sammern-Frankenegg was initially in charge of the deportations. The fighting began when Sammern-Frankenegg's SS and police units were ambushed as they attempted to enter the ghetto to deport the remaining Jews. The Jewish defenders were lightly armed but were very determined not to go to their deaths without a fight. The SS and police, including foreign auxiliaries, had simply marched into the ghetto not expecting any resistance. The disgraced Sammern-Frankenegg was immediately replaced by *SS-Brigadeführer* Jürgen Stroop, who had recently arrived from Galicia in south-eastern Poland. The forces employed against the Jewish fighters in the Warsaw ghetto (on a daily average) were as follows:

Table 16. Number of men employed by Stroop during the destruction of the Jewish ghetto in Warsaw, 1943.

Formation	Officers	Men
SS Panzergrenadier Ausbildungs und Ersatz Bataillon 3 'Totenkopf	4	440
SS Kavallerie Ausbildungs und Ersatz Bataillon 8	5	381
I. Bataillon/Polizeiregiment 22	3	94
III. Bataillon/Polizeiregiment 22	3	134
Technische Nothilfe Trupp	1	6
Polnische Polizei im Generalgouvernement (die 'Blau Polizei')	4	363
Polnische Feuerwehrleute	1	165
SS Sicherheitsdienst Zug	3	32
(leichte) Alarm Flak Batterie/III. Bataillon/Flak Regiment 8	2	22
Pioniereinheit der Panzerzüge/Reserve Bataillon 'Rembertow'	2	42
Reserve Pionier Bataillon 14 der 174. Reserve-Division	1	34
Ukrainische Hilfswilliger der Ausbildungs Bataillon Trawniki	2	335
Ein (1) Französisches panzer der Waffen-SS	1	
Zwei (2) Panzerspähwagen der Waffen-SS	2	
Total number of officers and men	31	2,048
Total average daily number of officers and enlisted men	31	1,262

Stroop compiled a daily series of reports and photographs, which he put together and presented to *Reichsführer-SS* Heinrich Himmler to show the SS leader what he had 'accomplished'. On 20 April 1943, Hitler's birthday, the following telegraph was sent by Stroop to the *Höhere SS und Polizeiführer Ost:*

> Warsaw, April 20, 1943
> From: The SS and Police Leader (SS und Polizeiführer) in the Warsaw District
> Ref. No.: I ab/St/Gr-16 07-Journal No. 516/43 Secret
> Re: Ghetto Operation
> To: The High SS and Police Leader East, Cracow
> Progress of the Ghetto Aktion on
> April 19, 1943:
> Closing of ghetto commenced at 03.00 hrs. At 06.00 hours the Waffen-SS was ordered to comb out the remainder of the ghetto at a strength of 16/850.[88] As soon as the units had entered, strong concerted fire was

> directed at them by the Jews and bandits. The tank employed in this operation and the two heavy armoured cars were attacked with Molotov cocktails. The tank was twice set on fire. This attack with fire by the enemy caused the units employed to withdraw in the first stage. Losses in the first attack were 12 men (6 SS men, 6 Trawniki men).[89] About 08:00 hours, the units were sent in again under the command of the undersigned.
>
> Although there was again a counter-attack, in lesser strength, this operation made it possible to comb out the blocks of buildings according to plan. We succeeded in causing the enemy to withdraw from the roofs and prepared elevated positions into the cellars, bunkers and sewers. Only about 200 Jews were caught during the combing-out operation. Immediately afterwards shock-troop units were directed to known bunkers with orders to pull out the occupants and destroy the bunkers. About 380 Jews were caught in this operation. It was discovered that the Jews were in the sewers. The sewers were completely flooded, to make it impossible to remain there. About 17:30 hours very strong resistance was met with from one block of buildings, including machine-gun fire. A special battle unit overcame the enemy, and penetrated into the buildings, but without capturing the enemy himself. The Jews and criminals resisted from base to base, and escaped at the last moment through garrets or subterranean passages. About 20:30 hours the external closure of the ghetto was reinforced.
>
> J. Stroop
> Commanding[90]

During the months' long battle, the Germans would lose a total of eighty-three SS men, eighty-eight policemen, ninety-seven Wehrmacht troops, and ninety-six *Schutzmannschaft* volunteers.[91] Jewish losses were estimated to be at least 7,000 killed in battle or executed after capture. However, total Jewish losses have been calculated to be 13,000, of which around 6,000 were non-combatants who were shot, burned alive, or suffocated by smoke when the Nazis set fire to the ghetto. After the battle, Stroop was transferred to Athens, Greece, to become the head of the *Höhere SS und Polizeiführer Griechenland* command. However, his actions in Warsaw became so infamous that even the Greek collaborationist government of Ioannis Rallis refused to work with him. In about a month he had to be replaced by *SS-Brigadeführer und General der Polizei* Walter Schimana. Schimana was appointed to the *Höhere SS und Polizeiführer Griechenland* post on 18 October 1943. Of the 1938 pre-war Polish census, which listed about 3,300,000 Jews living in the country, only around 380,000 remained by 1946.

The Bialystok Ghetto Uprising

In response to a partial '*Aktion*' against the Jewish population in the Bialystok ghetto in January 1943, the Jewish council there resolved to arm themselves. Arms were supplied by Jewish workers in German factories. Rifles and pistols were brought in; in one case even an automatic rifle was smuggled inside the ghetto. In addition, Jewish guerrillas in the ghetto were able to conduct two raids on German military arms warehouses, escaping with about seventy rifles. Clandestine factory workshops were also established, which produced weapons made from various materials and crude but lethal home-made grenades. A small Jewish partisan band even began operating in the forests around Bialystok from February 1943 onwards. By August of that year that partisan Otriad had grown to about 120–150 men.

By August 1943, 30,000–45,000 Jews remained in the Bialystok ghetto. Armed resistance to the German attempt to 'evacuate' the Jews from the ghetto began on 15 August 1943. Jewish guerrilla strength in the ghetto was perhaps some 300–400 men, of whom about 200 were only armed with pistols and crude hand grenades. The Germans had learned a costly lesson during the crushing of the Jewish ghetto in Warsaw. This time they had taken the precaution of surrounding the Bialystok ghetto with ample forces who were well armed. These forces included *Polizei-Schützenregiment 34*, along with the SS security police and SD command stationed in the town which amounted to perhaps 90–100 men, including foreign auxiliaries. Even so, the Germans eventually needed to employ German Army units.

According to one source, for a while, the Jews in the Bialystok ghetto held off part of the German *Division Nr. 461*, which at the time was led by *Generalleutnant* Richard Wenck.[92] The Jews in the ghetto were armed with twenty-five German rifles, 100 Soviet rifles and pistols, a few submachine guns, some hand grenades, one heavy machine gun, some dynamite, plus dozens of Molotov cocktails.[93] In addition, other Jews in the ghetto fought simply with knives, axes, and bayonets. The Bialystok ghetto uprising lasted from 16 to 20 August 1943. While the bravery and exploits of the Jewish resistance in the Warsaw ghetto uprising has been documented in detail and hailed as a noble effort, the resistance put up by the Jews of the Bialystok ghetto is less well known but no less important. To have held off an entire German division for about a week, and to do so with only enough weapons to arm a single company of men, was a remarkable accomplishment. The revolt at Bialystok was led by Mordecai Tenenbaum and Daniel Moszkowicz.[94]

Revolt at the Sobibor death camp

The Sobibor extermination camp had been established by the Nazis as part of *Aktion Reinhard,* the planned extermination of Polish Jews in the GG. The camp usually held about twenty-five SS officers and NCOs, and about 110–120 Ukrainian guards. The Sobibor camp used the forced labour of about 600 prisoners. Most Jews that arrived at the camp were quickly gassed and then buried in pre-dug pits as there were no crematoriums at Sobibor. If a prisoner was chosen to live, they had to take part in the killing process, whether it was collecting clothing from the victims or bringing them to the gas chamber while telling them they were about to take a shower. These Jewish men who worked at the camp were killed and replaced after four to eight weeks. On 14 October 1943 a revolt was begun that had been organised by Alexander Petchorski, a Russian Jew who had served in the Red Army.

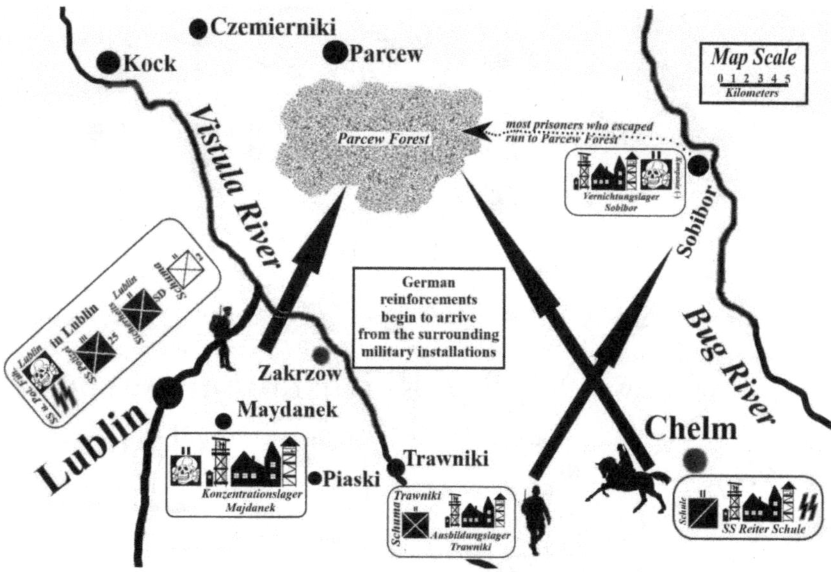

Figure 23. The Germans rushed reinforcements to Sobibor and the surrounding areas to hunt down the escaped prisoners.

The insurrection began in the early afternoon on 14 October, with prisoners quietly disposing of SS and Ukrainian officers and NCOs at various isolated locations. In addition, two Ukrainian guards were hacked to death. When several hundred prisoners reached the camp gates, they were confronted by an ethnic German guard from the Volga region of southern Russia, who shouted: 'You sons of bitches, didn't you hear the whistle? Why do you push around like a herd of sheep?'[95] As if reacting to these words, the entire group of Jewish prisoners set upon the guard with axes, which had up until then been hidden under their clothing. The guard was struck in the head and face numerous times, and fell instantly. At this time the general alarm was finally sounded and Alexander Petchorski, the leader of the uprising, knew that the moment to attempt the escape from the camp had arrived. He yelled: 'Forward, comrades. Forward for our Fatherland. For Stalin. Forward.'[96] The time was around 4.00 pm Upon hearing Petchorski's battle cry, about 600 Jewish prisoners now rushed forward, shouting 'Hurrah' at the surprised German and Ukrainian guards. The Germans and Ukrainians began to fire nervously and indiscriminately into the surging mob.

Figure 24. The regions of Jewish partisan activity, 1942–1944.

About 300 prisoners managed to escape, while around 200 were killed in the attempt. The remaining 100 or so men were apprehended inside the camp and executed when German military and police reinforcements arrived from Chełmno. These reinforcements turned out to be elements of *Polizeiregiment 25* and the *Sicherheitspolizei* command from Lublin. Many of the escaped prisoners made it to Parczew Forest, where they joined a local Polish guerrilla band. One of them, Semyon Rozenfeld, even managed to later join the Red Army. He had the honour of entering Berlin with Soviet forces when that city fell in early May 1945.

Figure 24 shows a map with the regions of Jewish partisan activity from 1942 to 1944. Although these areas were never completely controlled by the guerrillas, they did conduct sabotage activity and ambushes that took a toll on the Nazi occupation forces. The forests that were important in protecting these guerrillas are also presented in this map. About thirty Jewish partisan detachments (roughly company-sized units) operated on Polish soil throughout the war. The most famous Jewish partisan units in Belarus were the Bielski Brigade (1,200 members) and the Zoring Otriad (800 members). Altogether it is estimated that some 20,000–30,000 Jews fought as partisans either in Jewish guerrilla units or serving in non-Jewish partisan formations throughout Poland, the Baltic States, Ukraine, Belarus, and Russia.

Operation Tempest

From 1939 to 1943 the AK fought basically a limited offensive war, largely because German forces were substantial enough to prevent an all-out nationwide uprising. By late 1943, however, the situation in Poland had changed. Several Red Army partisan forces began to operate deep inside Polish territory with greater impunity. The Home Army was larger, better organised and armed than previously. Realising that the Red Army was but months away from entering Polish territory, the leadership of the Polish government in exile decided to prepare a contingency plan for the eventual return of the Red Army on Polish soil. In 1943, the Polish Home Army, in coordination with the Polish government in exile in London, prepared a general plan for retaking Polish territories once the Red Army (which was the closest Allied army to Poland) crossed into the pre-war Polish border region.

The plan was to attack German army positions all across the country employing the numerous Home Army divisions in coordination (if possible) with the Red Army. On 2 January 1944 the Soviet 2nd Belorussian Front crossed the pre-war Polish border and the operation was set in motion. Initially the plan seemed to work. On 6 April 1944 the city of Kovel was captured from the Germans with the coordination of the Polish Home Army and Red Army. Informed of what the Home Army was up to, Joseph Stalin ordered that the Red Army was to arrest AK units that showed themselves. The NKVD was tasked with eliminating the higher-ranking AK officers in a continued plan to remove any possible resistance to Soviet rule in Poland after the war. In spite of this, sporadic cooperation between the AK and Red Army took place during the rest of the spring and summer of 1944. For example, Vilnius was liberated due in part to Polish forces working in conjunction with the Red Army. On 23 July 1944 the AK rose in Lviv, just as the Red Army was approaching the city.

On 27 July the Red Army entered the city and immediately the NKVD began arresting AK representatives of the military and civilian government. Operation Tempest eventually proved a military success, because it aided in the liberation of Polish territory from the Germans, who suffered heavy losses in men killed, wounded, or missing as well as losses in rolling stock, munitions and equipment of all kinds. The operation, however, proved a political failure because Stalin ordered the arrest of AK officers and the disbandment of any AK units that showed themselves, thus stifling any attempt by the pro-Western Polish government in exile at creating an independent, democratic nation. What followed was forty-four years of domination by the USSR.

Chapter 4

THE GUERRILLA WAR IN POLAND IN 1944

We shall heal our wounds, collect our dead and continue fighting.

Mao Zedong

Russian partisans enter Poland

The new year brought the Eastern Front closer to the borders of occupied Poland. The first troops to arrive were the Soviet partisans, who up until then had been few in number. On 9 February 1944, the commander of the *Höhere SS und Polizeiführer Ost, SS-Obergruppenführer und General der Polizei* Wilhelm Koppe, contacted *SS-Brigadeführer* Hans Erich Voss, who was the commander of *SS-Truppenübungsplatz Heidelager*. This SS troop training ground was located just outside the town of Pustkow. In a telephone call, Koppe directed Voss to create an emergency battlegroup from forces available to him in his training base, in order to employ them in an anti-partisan operation. Voss, in turn, passed on the order to the forming *14. Waffen Grenadier Division der SS (Galizien Nr. 1)* that it was to immediately form a *Kampfgruppe* for an anti-guerrilla operation. The partisan force the Germans were aiming to destroy was the 1st Sydir Kovpak Ukrainian Partisan Division, under the command of Pyotr Vershigora. Colonel Vershigora had taken over command of this partisan force when its previous commander, Semyon Rudnev, had been killed in July 1943. The Kovpak partisan unit had entered the territory of the GG, where it had been operating with impunity.

The forming *14. Waffen-Grenadier-Division der SS (Galizien Nr. 1)* provided one infantry regiment and a battalion of artillery for the operation. The battlegroup also controlled a company of engineers and anti-tank guns. The anti-tank guns had been brought along because it was known that this particular Soviet partisan unit contained several captured tanks. The name of the emergency group formed to fight this guerrilla force was *Kampfgruppe Beyersdorff*, named after its temporary commander, *SS-Obersturmbannführer* Friedrich Beyersdorff, who was the deputy commander of the *14. Waffen Grenadier Division der SS*. This battlegroup remained operational from 16 February to 17 March 1944. Although many of the soldiers in this ad hoc formation were only raw recruits and not yet fully trained, the unit apparently performed well enough. The *Kampfgruppe* operated in and around the following towns and villages: Lubaczów, Bilgoraj, Zamosc, Bingley, Tarnogród, and Cieszanów. On 9 March 1944 the 2,000-strong *Kampfgruppe*, in conjunction with other SS and police forces from the region, encountered the main force of the Kovpak partisan unit near the town of Chmielnik.[1] By the afternoon several hundred members of this partisan force had been routed and dispersed.

Major anti-partisan drives in Poland in 1944

Polish guerrilla attacks against the German occupying forces increased in tempo and speed from 1943, when it was reported that 361 German Gendarmes had been assassinated by the Polish underground. This number increased dramatically a year later. In the first six months of 1944, Polish partisans killed 584 Gendarmes. On average during the year, in Warsaw alone, five Germans lost their lives each day. The year 1944 began with the assassination of *SS-Brigadeführer and Generalmajor der Polizei* Franz Kutschera, who was head of the *SS und Polizeiführer Warschau* command in the Polish capital. The assassination was bold as it was risky, given that Kutschera was killed as he was walking out of his own headquarters building on 1 February 1944. The planning and execution of the operation was done by the *Kedyw*, the acronym for *Kierownictwo Dywersji* (Directorate of Diversion).[2]

In reprisal, the Germans executed 300 innocent Polish civilians. The guerrilla war wasn't easy for the Poles, who admit to having lost 62,133 officers, NCOs, and men from the period 1 September 1939 up to the Warsaw Uprising. Between 1 September 1943 and 29 February 1944, the Polish Home Army lost 14,221 men. At the end of the German occupation of Poland, a total of around 150,000 Germans had been killed, but this figure pales in comparison to the 5,384,000 Polish soldiers and civilians who lost their lives between 1939 and 1945. The Germans were not about to sit idly by as the Polish guerrilla movement grew bolder and stronger. They did all they could to cow the population and intimidate the Polish people into submission. Throughout 1944 several anti-partisan operations were prepared and launched with varying forces and varying results. As always during these offensives, the local Polish civilian population suffered terribly.

The first of these operations began on 2 January and lasted until 14 January. It was code-named *Ostsee* (Baltic Sea) and launched in the region of Diabla Gora. It employed a Regional Defence formation of battalion strength, *Feldgendarmerie-Zug 62* (Military Field Police Platoon No. 62), *Gendarmerie-Bataillon 1 (motorisiert)*, and *SS-Polizeiregiment 14*. The intended targets were the AK 'Wichr' and 'Burzy' Battalions and the AL 'General Bern' Battalion. Simultaneously the Germans launched *Unternehmen Wintersport* (Operation Winter Sport), which ran from 4 to 10 January in the Opole Lubelskie region and was targeting some AL units there. The main forces used for this drive were another regional defence battalion and part of *SS-Polizeiregiment 25*. *Unternehmen Immergrun* (Operation Periwinkle) was launched on 9 April and would last until 27 April. The area for the operation was the Chelm (Chełmno) region, with the Polish partisan forces being made up of communist units – elements of the AL, BcH, and even Soviet guerrillas who had reached this region.

Unternehmen Maigewitter (Operation May Thunderstorm) followed *Immergrun* (Periwinkle) a month later, and lasted from 5 to 6 May. The area where it was launched was Parczew-Krasnik, and the Germans employed an air force fighter group as support, with the following forces: *SS-Polizeiregiment 4*, *SS-Polizeiregiment 25*, supported by part of *5. SS Panzer-Division 'Wiking'*. This large SS and police force was used against the estimated 1,400 Soviet and Polish (AL) guerrilla fighters under the partisan leader, whose *nom de guerre* was 'Chepiga'. In June 1944 the Germans launched a major anti-partisan drive that had two parts, code-named *Sturmwind I und II* (Storm Wind I and II). This operation centred on the estimated 5,000–6,000 Soviet and Polish partisans in the Janow, Lubelski, and Bilgoraj Forest regions. The total number of German–Axis forces would reach 30,000 plus and would employ some very exotic Axis units, including the all-Buddhist Kalmücken Kavallerie Korps. The operation is worth describing in some detail.

Background to the forces used in *Unternehmen Sturmwind I & II*

As noted previously, when the Germans established the GG, they used thousands of ethnic Germans as a vital manpower source to run the newly conquered Polish territories. Governor Hans Frank turned to these men for help as they had special knowledge of the country, people and language, having been Polish citizens of German ancestry. In May 1940 Frank set up a military organisation complete with its own uniform, called the *Sonderdienst*. At first, service in the *Sonderdienst* was voluntary, but that would be changed to compulsory in 1943. Ethnic Germans between the ages of 18 and 40 were eligible to join. The importance of this organisation in helping to run occupied Poland was so great that in August 1942 *Reichsführer-SS* Heinrich Himmler ordered that henceforth the *Sonderdienst* would come under the control of the *Höhere-SS und Polizeiführer Ost* command in the GG.

In 1943 the number of Polish citizens of ethnic German descent who were then serving in the *Sonderdienst* was 2,960 men. These were split into roughly company and battalion-sized units, which were controlled by the local SS command. *Rechtsrat* Dr Hermann Hammerle was in charge of the ethnic German community from Hungary and Romania (but he resided in Poland). Eventually he was made responsible for the *Volksdeutsche* in Poland as well. Below him, as the head of the *Sonderdienst* was *SA-Oberführer* Kurt Peltz, but it was *Oberst der Schutzpolizei* (Colonel of the Police) Fischer who would be in direct, day-to-day operational control of the companies and battalions. Peltz was also placed in command of the *Wehrdienst*. He kept the existing job that he previously had: *Führung der Geschäfte des Stabsführers des Führungsstabes der SA im Generalgouvernement* (Management Leader of the SA Command Staff in the GG). He had held this post from 1 February 1942, but was given permanent command on 1 February 1943. He was eventually promoted to *SA-Brigadeführer* on 20 April 1944.

On 8 May 1944, a meeting was held in Kraków to discuss the upcoming anti-partisan drives code-named *Storm Wind I* and *II*. Those present included Hans Frank, Governor General for Occupied Polish Territories, Dr Teitge, who was on Frank's staff, and *Oberst* Fischer, also on Frank's staff and in direct control of the *Sonderdienst*. *SS-Gruppenführer und Generalleutnant der Polizei* Emil Höring, who was Supreme Commander of the Order Police in the General Government, and *SS-Oberführer* Walther Bierkamp, Supreme Commander of the Security Police in the GG were also present. Bierkamp was also in charge of the *Polizei Hilfsdienst*, the so-called Polish Blue Police that was initially made up of pure Poles, but which was also composed of about 15 per cent ethnic Germans. In addition, a few Ukrainians from the Polish 'Galicia' District were injected into that organisation. *SA-Brigadeführer* Kurt Peltz, who was in overall charge of the *Sonderdienst* and *Wehrdienst*, was also present at this meeting. So was *Rechtsrat* Dr Hammerle, as well as *SS-Hauptsturmführer* Jordan, a representative from Heinrich Himmler. Professor Dr Brinckmann, another of Himmler's representatives, accompanied Jordan.

Finally, *SS-Sturmbannführer* Appell, who was in charge of the Polish *Baudienst* (Construction Service), was also present at this meeting. The *Baudienst* was composed entirely of Poles and was supposed to be used for construction purposes. However, it was also employed for various other purposes. Sometimes its members served as guards when Jews were being rounded up or were concentrated in one locality in anticipation of being transported to an extermination camp. The famous film director Roman Polanski was a young Jewish boy in Poland during the war. He remembered an experience that he had with a member of the *Baudienst* during the war. He had this to say about it:

> I remember that we were all gathered into the *Umschlagplatz* and were being guarded by men of the *Baudienst*. I wanted to escape. I approached a member of the *Baudienst* accompanied by a younger friend of mine and told the guard that we were hungry and that we promised to return to the *Umschlagplatz* if he would only allow us to return home so we could eat. The guard stared at us, and then motioned for us to go so we began to run, at which point the guard turned to us and yelled 'walk, don't run.' I'll never forget those words.[3]

It is obvious from this heartfelt account that this Polish member of the *Baudienst* was, at his core, a decent man. He knew very well that those two Jewish children were not coming back, and that they wanted to avoid deportation and the inevitable end that likely awaited them. Risking imprisonment or even his own life, he motioned for them to go. He even warned them how to behave by telling them to walk, not to run. Unbeknownst to him, he had performed a Jewish *mitzvah*, an absolute good deed.

But I digress. The meeting began with *SS-Sturmbannführer* Appell discussing the number of Polish workers available for the German war effort. While the number of Poles serving in the *Baudienst* was about 45,000 in January 1944, that figure dropped dramatically to only 24,000–25,000 men by February 1944. In May 1944 the number rose slightly to around 33,000, but this figure would reach a record low in August 1944 when the *Baudienst* would register only 3,000 Poles available for service, while the rest failed to appear for work. This was most likely related to the coming Warsaw Ghetto Uprising.

SS-Oberführer Bierkamp stated that approximately 2,000 of the 13,000 members of the Polish Blue Police were ethnic Germans and that in his opinion these men were completely reliable and ready for employment. *SS-Gruppenführer und Generalleutnant der Polizei* Emil Höring added that within the GG itself there were perhaps 15,000–16,000 foreign volunteers of numerous, diverse nationalities, and religions, all ready for action. *SS-Brigadeführer* Walther Bierkamp was familiar with the military situation as well as the available forces that could be sent against the Polish partisans. In a meeting held on 27 September 1943, he had proudly stated that between January 1940 and 31 August 1943, a total of 41,000 Poles had been apprehended and labelled *'partisan tater und helfer'* ('partisan culprits and helpers').[4] Bierkamp went on to discuss the guerrillas of the Bilgoraj Forest. He said that in the months of January and February 1944, the SS and police leader in Radom had identified various guerrilla formations that were apparently using the forest as their base of operations.

Bierkamp said that they had identified three separate groups: one of thirty to sixty men. While these figures seem deceptively small, the number of acts of sabotage in the Radom district was large, suggesting that a much larger partisan force was at work. Acts of sabotage in the Radom district were much greater than in the 'Galicia' district. In March 1944, for example, there had been 120 attacks against the railway line in Radom – an average of four attacks per day. Guerrilla activity all over the GG had grown since the beginning of 1944. Between 1 January and 31 March 1944, German anti-partisan sweeps had netted 10,700 prisoners and killed a further 3,219 people. This figure did not include hostage shootings, which was a separate figure altogether and has been presented in Table 14. By far the largest guerrilla formation in the Radom District was an all-Russian communist band of some 2,000–3,000 men. There was also a 300-man Soviet partisan force in the Rawa Ruska region of the District of Galicia.

The Galicia district was also the home of a Ukrainian nationalist UPA unit loyal to Stephan Bandera. In Galicia, partisan forces numbered about 2,000 men. The *Sonderdienst* contribution to the anti-partisan operation in the Bilgoraj Forest area included the use of two battalions under the command of *SS-Sturmbannführer* Helmut Pfaffenroth and Rechtsrat Dr Jaensch. Other formations that took part in this operation included the exotic *Kalmückisches Kavalleriekorps* (KKK), which had recently made their appearance in the Lublin District, beginning in July 1944, which we have already discussed.[5]

Other units included: the *154. Feldausbildungs-Division*, the *174. Reserve-Infanterie-Division*, part of the *213. Sicherungs-Division*, *Landesschützen-Regiment 115* (under *Oberfeldkommandantur Krakau*),[6] *SS-Polizeiregiment 4*, *Gendarmerie-Bataillon 1. (motorisiert)*, and parts of the 5th Hungarian Reserve Division. For air support, *1 Schlachtfliegerstaffel of Staffeln-Flieger-Gruppe 7* was available. There was also an unconfirmed report that a Ukrainian (Galician) SS police regiment took part in the operation. The Bilgoraj partisans suffered losses in the neighbourhood of some 2,000 men between May and June

1944, but managed to remain largely intact despite this. In late June the remaining 4,000 or so guerrillas moved to an area south of Drohobycz-Boryslaw. The following were the results of the anti-partisan drive:

> The Germans listed Polish Home Army losses as 898 killed, while '193 bandits and 531 bandit helpers' were apprehended. Axis losses were placed at 102 killed and 202 wounded. Captured equipment included two radio sets, eight light machine guns, three anti-tank weapons (bazookas), twenty-four machine pistols, two mortars, forty rifles, 230 hand grenades, 22,000 rounds of rifle ammunition, 2,500 rounds of machine pistol ammunition, 400 kg of explosives and 370 fuses.[7]

In the month of June, a large partisan unit of 800–1,000 men attacked a Polish *Baudienst* battalion and killed most of its German cadre. The unit was completely routed and its Polish workers, fearing reprisal, fled. A large German police regiment gave chase but to no avail. At the same time that *Sturmwind I* and *II* were being launched, another anti-partisan drive was also under way. Code-named *Vagabund* (vagabond), it began on 8 June and lasted until 23 June. The principal regions in question were the Radzyn, Podlaski, Wlodawa, and Chelm (Chełmno) areas. By June 1944 the eastern Polish provinces were either in Soviet hands or were being threatened by them. Volhynia had already been overrun. This region had seen the destruction of numerous German and locally raised police units, beginning in 1944 and continuing through the summer. Fighting was particularly intense between the towns of Rovno and Kremianez-Dubno.

Ever since the winter of 1942–43, *SS-Obergruppenführer und General der Polizei* Hans Prützmann, leader of the *Höherer SS und Polizeiführer Ukraine und Russland Süd* command, had been using a mixed SS / police battlegroup that had not only been employed against the guerrillas, but against the Red Army as well. The composition of this *Kampfgruppe* varied over time. In addition, on 22 October 1943 he became the head of the *Höchster SS und Polizeiführer Ukraine.* This command was supposed to be the highest SS and police headquarters in the region of Ukraine.

Prützmann began January 1944 with the following units: *SS-Polizeiregiment 11* (only two battalions), and *SS-Polizeiregiment König.* The *SS-Polizeiregiment König* was in actuality *SS-Polizeiregiment 10,* whose commanding officer in January 1944 was *Major der Gendarmerie* Hellmuth König. One of König's battalions was depleted, having only 350 men. In addition to these two incomplete police regiments, Prützmann also had under his command *Fusilier Bataillon 217, II. Abteilung der Artillerie Regiment 219,* and *Reserve Artillerie Abteilung 257.*[8] This last reserve army artillery unit was lost a month later, in February.

The battlegroup fought north-east of Rovno from 26 January to 1 February 1944. Its neighbour to the south along the front lines was *454. Sicherungs-Division*.

Another police regiment that eventually joined Prützmann's battlegroup was *Polizei-Schützenregiment 35. Polizei-Schützenregiment 35* had been attached to *XIII. Armeekorps* in December 1943. In January 1944 it had been placed under *Kampfgruppe Messinger (Arko XIII)*,[9] but on 30 January tragedy befell the regiment when it was overrun by Soviet armoured forces between Cuman and Dubno, and virtually destroyed. Remnants of the regiment were absorbed by Prützmann's *SS Kampfgruppe* and in April 1944 it was officially dissolved. In February 1944 *Polizei-Schützenregiment 33* and *Schutzmannschaft Bataillon 202* were also attached to Prützmann's command. The fighting by Dubno and Kremianez (Kremenets) was so intense that by 25 March its *I. Bataillon* (German-manned) and *II. Bataillon* (Ukrainian-manned) had to be disbanded. The *III. Bataillon* (Ukrainian-manned) of this regiment was also disbanded but not until about a month later, on 14 April 1944. Between 2 and 8 March 1944, *Kampfgruppe Prützmann* lost 680 men (all ranks). Its combat strength on 8 March was only about 2,200 men.

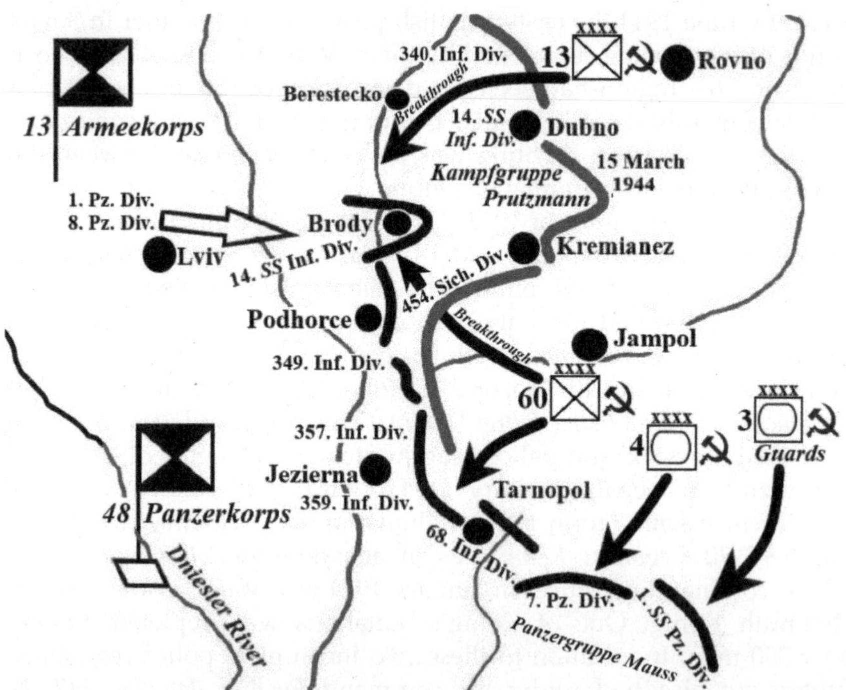

Figure 25. *Kampfgruppe Prützmann* by Kremianez, March–July 1944.

From 15 to 18 March 1944, Prützmann's force was in Kremianez (east of Brody) in fierce front-line fighting. Prützmann's SS battlegroup was then attached to the *36. Infanterie-Division (motorisiert)* and took part in the battle for Brody, where the *14. Waffen Grenadier Division der SS (Galizien Nr. 1)* was virtually destroyed. *Polizei-Schützenregiment 34* operated out of the city of Bialystok, north-east of Warsaw, while *Polizei-Schützenregiment 36* was stationed in Belarus, where it was also eventually destroyed. *Polizei-Schützenregiment 37* had begun forming in Rovno in November 1943. It was under the control of the *Kommandeur der Ordnungspolizei Rovno*, but never quite finished forming before it was committed to fighting under *454. Sicherungs-Division* in January 1944. It was destroyed two months later, in March, and disbanded in April. It should be noted that the size of *Kampfgruppe Prützmann* varied greatly from when it was formed to when it was finally disbanded. One author listed every single unit that served under this SS command, but the list is deceiving, given that not all of the units served at the same time. The following are the forces that at any one time served under this command:[10]

Polizeiregiment Gieseke (i.e. Polizeiregiment 17)[11]
SS-Polizeiregiment 4
Polizeiregiment 10/SS-Polizeiregiment 10
SS-Polizeiregiment 11
SS-Polizeiregiment 22
Polizei-Schützenregiment 33
Polizei-Schützenregiment 35
Polizei-Schützenregiment 37
Landesschützen-Bataillon Jehne
Landesschützen-Bataillon 268
Schutzmannschaft Bataillon 16
Schutzmannschaft Bataillon 202
Gendarmerie-Zug 1 (mot.)
Gendarmerie-Zug 3 (mot.)
Gendarmerie-Zug 4 (mot.)
Gendarmerie-Zug 5 (mot.)
Gendarmerie-Zug 15 (mot.)
Gendarmerie-Zug 16 (mot.)
Gendarmerie-Zug 41 (mot.)
Gendarmerie-Zug 45 (mot.)
Gendarmerie-Zug 51 (mot.)
Gendarmerie-Zug 55 (mot.)
Gendarmerie-Zug 57 (mot.)
Gendarmerie-Zug 60 (mot.)
Gendarmerie-Zug 61 (mot.)

Polizei-Nachrichten-Kompanie 81
Polizei-Nachrichten-Kompanie 83
Polizei-Nachrichten-Kompanie 121
Polizei-Reiter-Bataillon 1
Polizei-Reiter-Bataillon 2

Notice that *Polizeiregiment 10* is listed as both a regular police regiment and an SS police regiment. This is because the regiment served with this battlegroup prior to and after Heinrich Himmler's order of 24 February 1943, bestowing the police regiments with the honorary SS title. By the same token, if the other police regiments are only mentioned with the SS title, then most likely they served with the battlegroup sometime after 24 February 1943. Shortly after the end of *Unternehmen Wirbelwind* (Operation Whirlwind) on 21 July 1944, the AL Brigade *General Bern* moved to the Zichenau region north-west of Warsaw. On 2 August 1944, parts of the Brigade's 1st and 2nd Battalion fought against two motorised SS battalions near the town of Okalevko. They fought their way out of the encirclement. On 6 August 1944, a sub-unit of the 5th Battalion 'Narew' attacked a German platoon of a few dozen sappers near the town of Gaj, in the district of Nasielsk. This partisan battalion was under the command of Boleslaw Stepniewski. The attack had occurred with the aim of disrupting the construction of German fortifications. The partisans failed to surprise the Germans, who managed to repulse their first attack. After two hours of heavy fighting, it became clear that the Germans had superiority in both numbers and firepower, so the partisans withdrew.

A more important action was launched successfully on 1 September 1944, when an attempt by the Germans to blow up a vital bridge on the Narew River near the town of Karniewek was thwarted by the guerrillas. This thus allowed the Red Army to establish a very important bridgehead in the environs of the towns of Serock, Kacice, and Winnica. In January 1945 they would use this bridgehead as the springboard for the final conquest of the Third Reich. On 15 August in the vicinity of the town of Rogovo a platoon of thirty men from the 2nd Battalion of the veteran AL Brigade 'General Bern', whose commander was Lieutenant E. Kopka, fought against the German Gendarmerie, which was conducting an anti-partisan operation in this region. On 18 August sub-units of the 1st and 2nd Battalions, active in the operation in and around Mlawa in northern Mazowsze, conducted five armed drives during which station posts of the German Gendarmerie were destroyed. In addition, firearms were confiscated from the local German settlers, and a military protection unit of the Radzimowice Land Estate was destroyed. On 20 August the 1st and 2nd Battalions fought a full day of engagement at the town of Pokrytki, in the Ciechanow District, which had the following course:

> During a march into the area of the Jednorozec–Parciaki Forest where the partisans were to receive air drops with weapons, the two *AL* units stopped for a rest at Pokrytki. The *AL* grouping numbering around 100 partisans was commanded by Major Wladyslaw Marchol. On that very day two Waffen-SS battalions along with units of the German Army's Feldgendarmerie and of Vlasovites, encircled the partisans. The Germans attacked supported by armoured cars and artillery. Luftwaffe planes observed every move of the trapped troops and showered them with bombs. In order to break out of the encirclement, the battalions were ordered to split into three separate groups, which were supposed to pierce the ring in the direction of Budy Sulkowskie. The first group managed to fight their way out of the cauldron at 14:30 hours, while the second and third groups did not do so until 20:00 hours. The German operation ended in failure. The Germans suffered fifteen killed and twenty wounded, while we had seven killed and five wounded.[12]

There were six more anti-partisan drives launched in western and central Poland by the Germans in autumn 1944. During the period August–October 1944 and operating from the forests in the vicinity of the towns of Jednorozec and Parciaki in the Przasnysz District, the 3rd Battalion, along with Soviet airborne units of Major Orlov and Major Siergieyev, carried out twenty-five military actions. One of them was against a German regiment's headquarters protection platoon stationed at a manorial house in Romany. The German unit was destroyed during an engagement that lasted for over two hours, in the course of which seven German troops were killed, including one officer, and another seven were wounded. Many weapons were captured, along with two planes. In a forest near Parciaki, a platoon of German sappers guarding Polish forced labourers was dispersed. The Germans took casualties and the partisans were able to capture weapons. On the Chorzele–Wielbark railway line, a German military train was derailed. The Germans grew weary of the AL partisans and in October they decided to deal with them.

The first autumn offensive began on 11 September and lasted until 6 October. It was launched in the Kielce Region, about 100km south of Warsaw. This region was now the home of the AL 3rd 'General Bern' and 10th 'Zwyciestwo' Partisan Brigades. In addition, the 'Skala Battalion' of the AK 2nd Division was also operating in this area. In all, the partisans could count on around 1,400 men. The Germans had around 10,000 men under *Korück 532* and *Korück 585*. *Unternehmen Walkater* (Operation Forest Cat), was launched almost towards the end of the first autumn offensive. It was a two-day affair that centred on trying to destroy the Home Army's 25th and 72nd Regiments. The Germans employed units under *Korück 581*, as well as the *Gendarmerie-Bataillon 1 (motorisiert)* plus three regional defence battalions. The 3rd 'General Bern' AL Brigade would once again be the object of German attention when another drive to eliminate this communist guerrilla brigade was launched on 6 October 1944, this time in the Piotrkov–Tribunalski region. About 2,500 police and army troops were used. The last three major anti-partisan operations launched on Polish territory in 1944 lasted from 26 September to 17 November. One was called *Unternehmen Sternschnuppe* (Operation Shooting Star), and was launched in the Campinos Forest area just outside of Warsaw.

The Home Army was on the verge of surrendering in Warsaw when this German mopping up action took place. About 6,000 German troops belonging to *SS-Obergruppenführer* Erich von dem Bach-Zelewski, plus elements of the *23. Flak Division, IV. SS Panzerkorps,* and rear area troops under the command of *Korück 532,* all took part in this assault. Lasting from 26 to 30 September, the operation was a lopsided affair with the Polish guerrillas giving ground, but grudgingly. Two days later, General Bor surrendered in Warsaw. It is interesting to note that, according to the Poles, the Germans lost (captured or destroyed) the following during the fighting in the Campinos Forest area from 1 August to 2 October 1944: three planes, 310 tanks, assault guns, self-propelled artillery pieces, armoured cars, and half-tracks, four *Raketenwerfer* (rocket launchers), twenty-two towed artillery pieces (75mm calibre), and 340 trucks and other vehicles. Although these figures come from official Polish sources, they seem rather high. If they are accurate, then we can assume that the Germans lost the equivalent of two full-strength panzer divisions in this area alone. But again, this seems like a gross exaggeration, especially regarding the number of tanks claimed to have been destroyed or disabled by the Polish fighters.

The second German autumn offensive began on 18 October and lasted until 17 November. It was launched in the Starachowice–Vloszczova area. The Polish forces in question were the 2nd, 10th, and 11th AL Brigades, two battalions of the 1st AL Brigade, three BcH battalions, and the 25th AK Regiment. In this operation parts of a Waffen-SS division, the *3. SS Panzer-Division 'Totenkopf',* plus four Wehrmacht battalions, and *Gendarmerie Battalion 2 (motorisiert)* were employed. On 26 October 1944, the Germans surrounded the forest near the Parciaki Railway Station with troops from a 'Vlasovite' brigade.[13] All told, the forces amounted to some 2,500 troops. In addition, these units were supported by artillery and armoured units from the ground, and the Luftwaffe from the air. The encircled Polish–Soviet group numbered 170 fighters. They were members of the 3rd AL Battalion 'Myszyniecki' and the Soviet parachute 'Orlov', 'Siergieyev', and 'Captain Gregor' formations. During the full day of battle, the partisans repulsed several German attacks until the evening hours.

Under the cover of darkness, the Germans pierced the encirclement and moved to the forests near the town of Jednorozec. In the process they lost eleven killed and twenty wounded, while the Polish–Soviet group lost seven men. An AK detachment had been operating in the same area where the above Polish–Soviet group was fighting, but did not take part in the skirmish. On 1 November 1944, the Germans launched a second attempt to destroy the partisans in the forests near the towns of Parciaki and Jednorozec. Another final operation, launched simultaneously on 18 October and directed at Polish forces in the Starachowice area, was aimed at destroying the 10th AL Partisan Brigade. Lasting only two days, *Unternehmen Kriemhild* employed only the *Gendarmerie-Bataillon 1* (motorisiert) and four regional defence battalions. Guerrilla strikes behind the German lines in western Poland continued in autumn 1944, but the onset of winter reduced these significantly.

The Soviet winter offensive, launched on 11 January 1945, brought a final end to the German occupation of Poland and to anti-partisan operations there. The AL Brigade 'Synowie Ziemi Mazowieckiej,' which comprised five battalions, fought the *Kaminski Brigade*, plus a Gendarmerie battalion, in late 1944. The 1st, 3rd, and 4th Battalions continued their combat activities until January 1945, attacking German railway transports and fighting engagements against army and police units. One of the last engagements fought by the AL Brigade's elements was carried out by the Headquarters Company.

On 10 January 1945, a company led by Włodzimierz Ziemiecki, which happened to be accompanied by a unit of Soviet paratroopers under Major Siergieyev, made a daring attack on an artillery sub-unit of the Wehrmacht in the vicinity of the town of Gojsk, in the district of Sierpc. On that day the company was tasked with conducting reconnaissance of the forests in the area of Szczytowo, Okalewo, and Ruda, where the brigade intended to transfer its forces. During this mission the partisans encountered a German artillery sub-unit near

Gojsk. The partisans attacked it by surprise and after a few hours of fighting the Germans had suffered thirty-five killed and wounded and so withdrew in disarray. The AL partisans captured two artillery pieces along with numerous infantry weapons and plenty of other equipment and supplies. The AL Brigade 'Synowie Ziemi Mazowieckiej' was the last Polish partisan force to engage the Germans. This occurred on 20 January 1945.

Chapter 5

THE WARSAW UPRISING, 1944

> Burning down the houses is the most reliable means of liquidating the insurgents' hideouts.
>
> Governor General Hans Frank

Preparations for the uprising

The biggest event of the guerrilla and anti-partisan war in Poland between 1939 and 1944 was the Warsaw insurrection, perpetrated by the Polish Home Army (AK) in an attempt to wrest control of the Polish capital of Warsaw from the Germans. This action, part of Operation Tempest, was launched with the overly ambitious aim of capturing the entire city before the Red Army could do so. This capture was not only intended to be a symbol of Polish resistance, but the pro-Western AK also hoped to use it as a means of establishing the legitimacy of the Polish Government in exile (located in London). Stalin, however, had other plans. As early as 1942, the Polish government in exile in London had been planning a large-scale guerrilla uprising.

On 27 October 1943, that Polish government ordered General Tadeusz Bór-Komorowski, who at the time was the head of the Home Army, to launch Operation Burza (Operation Tempest). This was the code name for the large-scale diversionary operation against the Germans, while avoiding contact with the advancing Red Army. The Home Army wanted to remain hidden from the Soviets because AK units serving in eastern Poland had been disarmed and the bulk of their enlisted personnel forced to join General Zygmunt Berling's Polish (communist) forces. The AK officers fared worse, with many either being thrown in jail or disappearing, never to be heard from again.

General Bór had been ordered to avoid contact with the Red Army, but he ignored this order and instructed his AK units to show themselves to the Soviets in order to prove that they were the legal authority on Polish territory. Bór's de facto action was approved by the Polish government in London on 18 February 1944, but this course of action proved unwise and soon, any AK force that showed itself to the Red Army was treated as described above. The Poles watched with apprehension and fear, well aware that even though the advancing Russians would help get rid of one tyrant (Hitler), he would simply be replaced by another (Stalin). This dilemma, one that threatened the very existence and political direction of Poland, was difficult. A plan was devised that might resolve the problem. The Home Army was to launch an all-out offensive against the approximately 15,000 to 16,000 German troops in Warsaw, just as the Red Army neared the Polish capital.

That plan hinged on several things happening. First, it assumed that the Red Army would not dare attack a triumphant Home Army after it had expelled the Nazis from the Polish capital. They hoped that the Polish government in exile, which was currently based in London, might return to Warsaw. How that was to be achieved was another matter. This move, it was felt, would further strengthen their legitimacy as the rightful Polish government. Secondly, the military plan also called on the almost 40,000 troops of the Warsaw district's three AK divisions to be employed inside the Polish capital. This would give the Poles a better chance of overwhelming the German garrison stationed in the city. Thirdly, the plan counted heavily on the continuing advance of the Red Army which, it was hoped, would tie down German troops located east of the city. This was of critical importance because the Germans would surely call on reinforcements from outside the capital. If the Red Army continued its attack, surely that would draw some or all of the German relief troops away from the city. This last part of the plan would prove to be the decisive factor, one way or another.

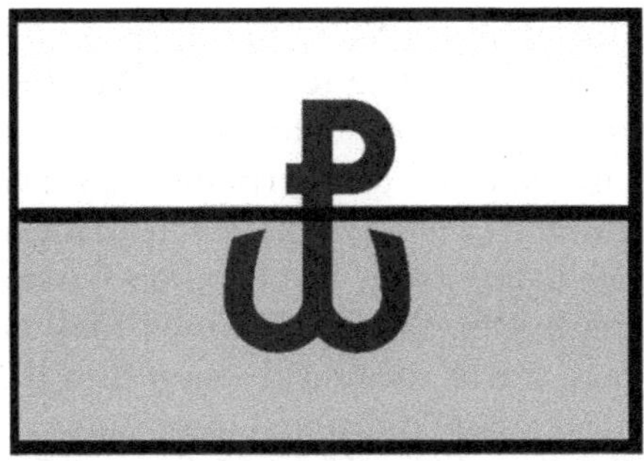

Figure 26. Flag of the Polish Home Army. A black Armia Krajowa symbol on a white and red rectangular background. For armbands worn on the sleeve of the field blouse, to identify Polish troops, the same symbol and colours were used. Some of the simpler armbands just sported the Polish colours, without the AK symbol. Because many Poles wore German attire and carried German weapons, the armbands were deemed necessary.

Unfortunately, this last part of the plan was to prove the undoing of the Polish Home Army in Warsaw. Stalin would prove too wily, for when the Poles rose up in Warsaw, he ordered that the Red Army's offensive be paused. This gave the Germans the respite and the time they needed to crush the Polish forces within the capital. It was inconceivable to believe that the Soviets, as antagonistic and as anti-Polish as they were, would stop their offensive simply to give their hated enemy, the Nazis, the necessary time to deal the Poles a devastating blow. But this is exactly what occurred, and it is one of the more tragic chapters in the history of the Polish nation. The Polish defenders of Warsaw were a varied, diversely organised and equipped army. They were also divided politically. The various political parties that existed in Poland had created their own fighting organisations.

An attempt had been made by the exiled Polish government in London to merge all of these numerous and politically diverse units into one unified command, but the success of this perfectly sound military goal had been met with resistance. The extreme right and left had been particularly entrenched. An example of this resistance was the right-wing and very anti-Semitic *Narodowe Sily Zbrojne* (NSZ, National Armed Forces), which had been an independent organisation until March 1944 when most of its members were made to come under the control of the AK. According to Polish records, the NSZ could count on around 35,000 men from all across the Polish nation. In the Warsaw district they numbered 5,300 men. Given that the NSZ organisation had been completely infiltrated by the Gestapo and SD, it was not trusted by the AK Command. When the uprising began, only about 800 NSZ men were thus available to take part in the uprising in the capital, simply because the NSZ leaders had not been warned of the upcoming uprising for fear that the Germans would be warned. *Polska Partia Robotnicza* (PPR, the Polish Workers' Party) had an armed militia known as the *Gwardia Ludowa* (GL, the People's Guard).

When the uprising began, the 800 GL men took part in the battle. The Socialist Workers' Party formed its men into their *Socjalistyczna Organisacja Bojowa* (Socialist Fighting Organisation), whose combat units they dubbed *Bataliony Chlopskie* (BcH, Peasant Battalions). In 1943 the BcH was made nominally subordinate to the AK. By late 1943 the BcH units numbered some 50,000 men, spread across the country. The BcH were especially strong in Lublin, Warsaw, Cracow, and Radom. The Polish Socialist Workers' Party militia, named the *Polska Armia Ludowa* (PAL, Polish People's Army) was commanded by Colonel Julian Skokowski. It could count on a total of only 1,000 men, 500 of whom took part in the uprising.

The communist *Armia Ludowa* (AL, People's Army) had 1,500–2,000 men in Warsaw. Estimates vary as to how many AL soldiers took part in the uprising, but one reliable source mentions that only 400 served under the AK command. The AK included three 'divisions' in the Warsaw district: the 8th Infantry Division under Colonel Mieczyslaw Niedzielski, 10th Infantry Division under Colonel Jozef Rokicki, and 28th Infantry Division under Colonel Edward Pfeiffer. These three AK divisions numbered between 25,000 and 28,000 men, if you included its reserves and units from the surrounding countryside.

The exact figures for the arms available to these three divisions has been listed by Polish writers as follows: 25,000 grenades, 2,000 pistols and revolvers, 1,000 rifles, sixty light machine guns, seven heavy machine guns, and thirty-five special rifles and bazookas. Another Polish source gave the following alternative figures: 43,971 grenades, 3,846 pistols and revolvers, 657 submachine guns, thirty flame-throwers, two anti-tank guns, 406 anti-tank grenades, 12,000 Molotov cocktails, 2,629 rifles, six mortars, and ten 'howitzers', although most of these so-called 'howitzers' were small, crudely made, and very unpredictable contraptions that could sometimes blow up in the faces of the Polish soldiers using them. As the table below indicates, the number of fighters tthat the Polish Home Army had available for the Warsaw Uprising was around 20,000. But half of these troops lay in the suburbs, and so were of minimal use. Given the Poles' lack of weapons and how outnumbered they were, it is truly amazing that the Poles in the city held out for more than two months.

Table 17. Organised AK units in and around Warsaw, 1 August 1944.

Area of the City	Unit Name	Officer in Charge	No. of Men
Old Town and Sródmieścic	three battalions	Lt. Col. Franciszek Edward Pfeiffer	1,500
City Centre	8th Krybar Regiment (ten battalions total)	Major Jerzy Kwiatkowski	5,000
Czerniakow-Sielce	Baszta Regiment (three battalions)	Lt. Col. Daniel Pająk	1,600
Soliborz, Marymont Bielany	Zywiciel Regiment	Major Stanisław Thun, then Major Mieczysław Niedzielski	1,300–2,000
Wola	Kedyw Regiment (three battalions plus one reserve battalion)	Lt. Col. Jan Tarnowski	1,650
Wola	Radoslaw Group (seven battalions)	Jan Mazurkiewicz	3,500
Ochota	three battalions plus the main medial unit of the AK	Lt. Col. Mieczyslaw Sokolowski	1,500 (plus 400 hospital personnel)
Praga	Krybar Group	Lt. Col. Szramka Gliszczyński	300
Mokotów	two battalions	Lt. Col. Aleksander Hrynkiewicz	500
Kampinos Forest	Four to five battalions	Col. Mieczyslaw Niedzielski	1,200
Surrounding Warsaw suburbs	Twenty to thirty battalions	Maj. Kazimierz Krzyżak ('Wigry' Battalion)	10,000
Note: Colonel Niedzielski was also the CO of the AK 8th Division.			19,950–20,065

Figure 27. Central Warsaw and the surrounding areas, 1944.

Polish armaments, saved up during the years of German occupation, were sometimes uncovered by the Nazis. For example, just prior to the Warsaw Uprising, the German Order Police discovered a cache of some 40,000 hand grenades, thus leaving the AK with only around 25,000 for the uprising. This modest supply was slightly augmented by a few more pistols and some explosives. In addition, 678 machine pistols along with around 60,000 rounds of ammunition were found after the war (in 1947), hidden in a bunker underneath Leszno Street. Apparently, the AK men in charge of this secret depot had either been killed or captured shortly before the uprising began, meaning that the arms remained hidden and were not used because no one knew of their presence. The 400 men of the AL who took part in the battle were as poorly armed as the AK units. A report from May 1944 listed the AL weapons as the following motley collection: one heavy machine gun, three machine pistols, six rifles, forty pistols, fifty-one hand grenades, and thirteen Molotov cocktails.

Also in the city were a number of other non-AK units that took part in the uprising. These included a 400-man AL battalion, which fought in the Wola district, and an 800-man NSZ battalion, which began the battle in the Old Town district. There was also a 500-man PAL battalion, as well as an 800-man GL battalion and three to four BcH battalions. In total the actual number of Polish fighters that would take part in the fight for the city itself was about 10,000, with the remainder being located in the outer suburbs and blocked from assisting the rest of the inner-city defenders. During the battle, several other AK battalions would be identified, including the 'Czata 49' Battalion commanded by Major Witold Kieżun. The men of this battalion became experts in street fighting and were used as the rearguard in every withdrawal. Although this battalion was not part of the original three battalions that made up the elite 'Kedyw' Regiment, it nevertheless became attached to this AK regiment (considered the best in the entire Warsaw district) during the battle.

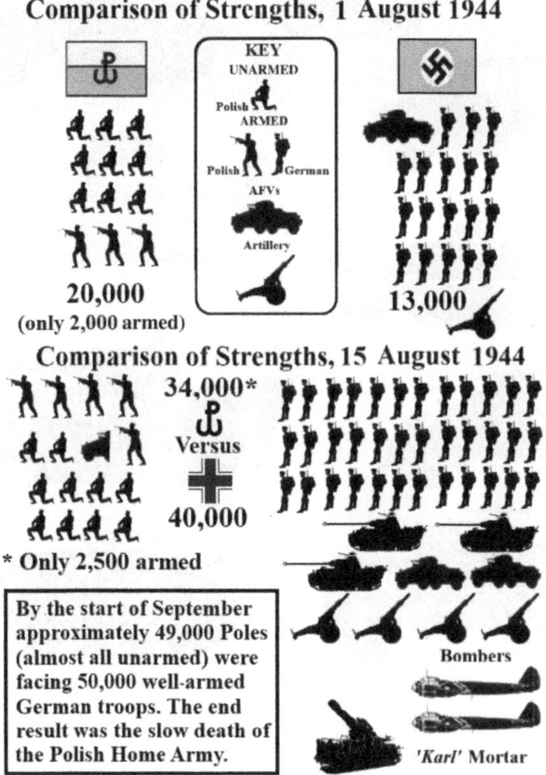

Figure 28. A comparison of Polish and German strengths on 1 August and 15 August 1944.

At the start of the uprising the estimated strength of the German garrison in Warsaw was somewhere between 16,000 to 18,000 men. The Polish Home Army had perhaps close to 20,000 men. Two weeks later, the strength of German forces fighting in the city was around 50,000 troops. The Poles increased the number of men but most were unarmed volunteers who had to wait for weapons to be made available for them. They did act as replacements for decimated AK units but, given that usually the weapons of AK soldiers who died fighting could not be recovered, most of these volunteers remained unarmed throughout the battle. The Polish Home Army armoured strength at the start of the battle included a few improvised armoured cars. However, during the battle, they managed to capture two Panther tanks, two armoured half-tracks, and a Hetzer tank destroyer.

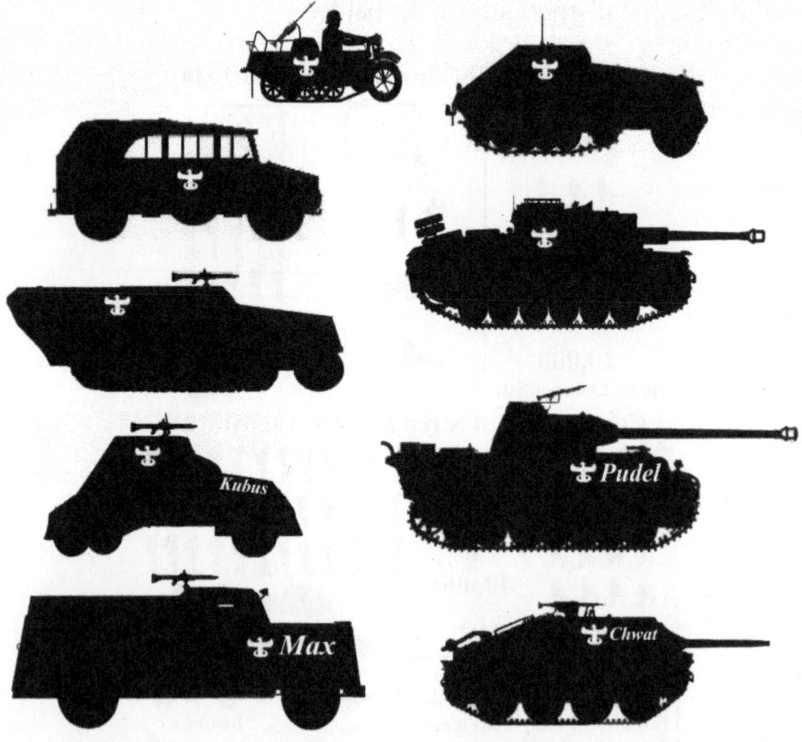

Figure 29. Some of the various types of vehicles employed by the Polish Home Army during the Warsaw uprising. A few were homemade, while most were captured from the Germans.

The 'Kedyw' Regiment began the uprising with three battalions named 'Zoska', 'Parasol', and 'Miotla'. The 'Baszta' Regiment also contained three battalions, although a 4th (Reserve) Battalion was attached and very quickly burned up due to heavy losses. The designations of these three battalions were Battalion 'O' (under Major Reda), Battalion 'B' (under Major Burza), and Battalion 'K' (under Major Majster). The 'Baszta' Regiment had the extremely difficult task of defending the southern city districts of Mokotow and Sielce. Various factors would make the fighting here especially difficult for the Home Army. First and foremost was the problem of the area's open terrain.

This district was composed mainly of private houses, with hardly any built-up areas such as large apartment buildings or factories. The few large plants or buildings that it did have were greatly spread out and were already occupied by German garrison troops. This brings us to the second problem facing the Home Army in this region: the large number of German forces there. There were 600–700 SS policemen (an entire full-strength battalion) stationed at the Sluzewiec Racetrack. The Luftwaffe base at Warsaw-Okecie Airfield had some fighters and bombers. The airfield was protected by a Luftwaffe infantry company. In addition, there was a 300-man Luftwaffe flak unit at the Dominican Monastery in Siuzew. Mokotow Fort was the home of a 450-strong Luftwaffe headquarters unit from Okecie Airfield. There was also the very heavily defended Gestapo headquarters located in this region, on Szucha Street.

The Gestapo headquarters in the city was defended by at least around 300–350 Sipo and SD men, all of whom equated to about a three-quarter-strength battalion. There was also the German horse artillery and light cavalry barracks, which housed a reserve and replacement unit of German SS cavalrymen: *SS-Kavallerie Ausbildungs und Ersatz Abteilung.*[1] The AK units in Mokotow were to take ten major objectives. Major Burza's 'B' Battalion had allocated two companies to take the Kazimierzowska School, while its remaining 3rd Company was to capture Narbuta Street, together with a few minor objectives. Major Reda's 'O' Battalion, considered the best led, trained, and armed of the entire *Baszta Regiment,* had been assigned the hardest job: its strongest and largest company, commanded by Lieutenant Zdich was to attack the 450-man Luftwaffe headquarters at Mokotow Fort. The 2nd Company of this battalion, commanded by Lt Zych, was to take the Woromcz School, while Lieutenant Ludwik Kiedrowski and the 3rd Company were ordered to attack the SS quarters located in a large, private mansion called Wedel's House, which was the home of a wealthy Polish confectionary manufacturer.

In addition, the 3rd Company was also required to eliminate and destroy two police precincts located in the Willowa and Dworkowa

Streets. Major Majster's 'K' Battalion was assigned the deadly task of clearing the Sluzewiec Racetrack of its 600–700 SS occupants, some distance away from the Willowa and Dworkowa Streets. An additional company of WSOP (Auxiliary Military Organisation for Guard Duty) men had been promised to the regiment, as well as two communication platoons. Nevertheless, the missions assigned by the Polish Home Army planners in this region of Warsaw were too demanding for the limited and under-armed AK units to carry out successfully. When the uprising began, this would be confirmed.

The Warsaw Uprising, 1 August 1944

'W' hour for the uprising in Warsaw had been set for 1700 hours on 1 August 1944. When it came, the soldiers who had spent the afternoon in hiding came out on to the streets to fight the Germans. Right from the beginning, it did not go as planned. The Germans had been on full alert since 1630, and the inexperienced Polish youths had to attack a fortified enemy in broad daylight. It came as no surprise then that many objectives were only partially (if at all) taken as intended. The most headway was made by Polish forces in the downtown area of the city. However, this wasn't enough to link up with the Polish fighters in the Starowka (the old part of the city, Powisle), or other parts of the capital. In some areas of Warsaw, like Zoliborz and Ochota, things went so poorly that the AK units in these areas were largely forced to retreat into the forests surrounding the city. The attacks on the Okecie and Bielany airports were repulsed, as was the attack on the Raszyn Radio Station.

The first stroke of the attack, on which so many things depended, was thus only partially successful. Large parts of the city were now controlled by the insurgents, but within those sections there were still many fortified pockets of German resistance. Both the Poles and the German garrison suffered heavy casualties that first day, despite both forces receiving reinforcements. The Germans were reinforced by the *Herman Goring Panzer-Division* and the *19. Panzer-Division*, both of which were passing through the city and its surrounding areas to join battle with the Soviets to the east. For the insurgents, reinforcements came in the form of mass support from the citizens of Warsaw. The insurgents thus got to benefit from all the supplies and experience that the populace had amassed in the five years of the German occupation. Volunteers now began to flood in, but arming them was another thing altogether. There just weren't enough weapons.

On 2 August the insurgents resumed the attack. By 4 August, Srodmiescie (downtown) was largely in Polish hands. Many of the Polish troops who had withdrawn to just outside of the city after the first day of the conflict, now had a chance to return, since the Germans were still confused and preoccupied with fighting the Soviets. The Home Army in Wola repulsed several German counter-attacks, shielding Srodmiescie. In other parts of the city the situation remained very fluid. Thus, by 4 August there were three large insurgent regions of the city. There was the Srodmiescie–Powisle–Starowka–Wola regions connected together. The other areas of Polish AK control were the Zyrardow region, and the Mokotow region, but they were not connected to each other or to the large Polish Home Army enclave. Overall, a large part of Warsaw had been liberated from the Germans. In those four crucial days, the partisan units acquired much combat experience and the support of the people. Yet by the end of those four days, the partisan units were lacking ammunition and other supplies.

It was also expected that by this time the Soviet troops would be crossing the river to help the insurgents. General Bór-Komorowski, the Home Army Commander-in-Chief, sent a message to London asking for supply airdrops and inquiring when the British-trained-and-formed 1st Polish (Independent) Parachute Brigade would arrive to reinforce the uprising. General Bór also asked the Polish government in exile in London to try and persuade Stalin to order the Red Army to cross the Vistula River and come to their aid. He also ordered all offensive operations to cease, so that ammunition might be conserved. The vain wait by the Polish patriots for Soviet and Western relief now began. All in all, the tasks assigned to the Baszta Regiment and many other AK units during the initial stages of the uprising were too great to accomplish. Some units attacked too soon, while others did not attack on time.

For example, the Baszta Regiment, faced with a superior enemy in well-placed and entrenched positions, soon faltered in its attack and was stopped dead in its tracks. So great was the German resistance that in the first day of the uprising the Baszta Regiment was almost destroyed, as most of its companies had been almost completely whittled down by losses. Only by the direct intervention of their commander, employing a reserve force, was the regiment finally able to rally and hold its position. Fighting in this district would last a total of fifty-seven days, but the weakness of the AK units here, coupled with the strong enemy presence that also included armoured support, certainly meant that for the rest of the uprising, the AK there was on the defensive.

The villas, with their unwalled gardens, provided hardly any cover at all for the beleaguered Polish forces. There were numerous other major objectives that the AK planned to take and hold. Some objectives were not taken, while others were. There was, for example, the Central Telephone Exchange, which was taken in the middle of August 1944 from the 100-plus Germans who were defending it. This large exchange was nicknamed the 'Big Pasta', while the Branch Telephone

Exchange, taken by the AK in the fourth week of the fighting, was called the 'Little Pasta'. The Branch Telephone Exchange was located in the City Centre South. It was defended by a very capable officer, *SS-Obersturmführer und Oberleutnant der Gendarmerie* Willi Jung. Jung's leadership would keep the Polish assault units at bay for close to four weeks. Later it would be learned that the combined German civil and military defenders there had totalled 500 men, the equivalent of one full-strength German battalion.

Other targets of major importance to the AK included the YMCA Building, which was captured during the first days of September, and Pawiak Prison, Fort Trauguta, the Citadel, Danzig Station, Pfeiffer Factory, Fiat Factory, the Mint, John Bosco Hospital, Mostowskich Palace, Krasinski Square, the Central Bank, Bruhl Palace, Police Headquarters, the Saxon Gardens, Józef Piłsudski University of Warsaw, the main Post Office, Napoleon Square, the Prudential Building, the electric works, the Central Station, the Polytechnic Institute, the Poniatowski Bridge, the New Railway Bridge, the Kierbedz Bridge, the Citadel Bridge, the Eastern Station, the gas works, and the freight depot. The Citadel, Kierbedz, New Railway, and Poniatowski Bridges all gave access from the western bank of the Vistula River to the eastern bank, where the city's Praga district was located.

The Eastern Station was located in Praga. The electric works and the Telephone Exchange were in the Powisle district. The Central Station, Police Barracks, Telephone Exchange, Napoleon Square, and Prudential Building were located in the city centre, while the Main Post Office, Saxon Gardens, Central Bank, Pilsudski Square, Bruhl Palace, Police Headquarters and theatre were all located between the Old Town and the city centre. The Old Town began with Danzig Station bordering the southern-most district of Soliborz,[2] followed by Fort Trauguta, the Fiat and Pfeiffer Factories, the Mint, John Bosco Hospital, Mostowskich Palace, and Krasinski Square. Pawiak Prison and the locomotive works were located north of the city centre and north-east of the Wola district. The prison itself was located in the middle of the Jewish ghetto. St Kinga Hospital was just across the cement walls of the ghetto's western border. It was surrounded by the Jewish and Christian cemeteries.

The gas works, freight depot, and Western Station were all located in the Ochota district, south of Wola and south-west of the city centre. As time would prove, most of these objectives would remain just out of reach for the Polish fighters. Although trapped at Bruhl Palace, the German city commander, Luftwaffe *Generalleutnant* Rainer Stahel, reported on 3 August that in the first three days of the uprising, German losses in the city were estimated to be between 500 and 600 men.[3]

Stahel and his headquarters staff would be relieved three days later on 6 August, just five days after the start of the insurrection. Although his headquarters was surrounded, on 1 August 1944, Stahel could count on the following forces at his disposal for the defence of Warsaw: *Grenadier Ersatz Regiment 4, Alarm Regiment Warsaw, Landesschützen-Bataillon 996, Landesschützen-Bataillon 997, Landesschützen-Bataillon 998, Kompanie der Oberfeldkommandantur 225, Feldgendarmerie Kompanie 146 (motorisiert), Panzer Zerstorer Kompanie 475,*[4] and *1. Kompanie der Panzerjäger Abteilung 743*, equipped with *Jagdpanzer 38t Hetzer* tank destroyers (Sd.Kfz. 138/2).[5]

Stahel's eventual liberators were not only German policemen from Posen (Poznan), but criminals from the *SS-Sonderregiment 'Dirlewanger'*.[6] Reports state that when Stahel's headquarters was relieved, most of its German defenders were completely drunk and the defences on the verge of collapse. Other German-held but surrounded strongpoints survived throughout the siege, like the Bank of National Recovery, which was well defended by its German troops and whose thick walls protected those inside. The major success of the Germans during the first week of the uprising was the cutting of the Polish defences in two, when *SS-Sonderregiment 'Dirlewanger'* reached the German troops at the Kierbedzia Bridge and Saxon Gardens on 7 August 1944. From the very beginning, the German SS and police forces entered into the fight against the insurgent forces with the intent to shoot any fighters and civilians they encountered. In fact, German atrocities committed by the *SS-Sonderregiment 'Dirlewanger'* and *Regiment 1* of the *Kaminski Brigade* proved to be so numerous and horrendous that it eventually stiffened the resolve of the Polish defenders. The level of the atrocities meant that the Germans later had difficulties in trying to get the Polish fighters to surrender.

The Warsaw Uprising: 5–12 August 1944

The initial air drop of supplies from the expected relief came, raising the hopes of the Home Army fighters. Polish bomber pilots flying from bases in Apula, Italy, started making nightly ammo drops over Warsaw. The pilots then had to fly back to Italy since the Soviets refused them permission to land in Soviet-controlled territory. Unfortunately, this wasn't enough and many of the airdrops literally fell into German hands. The deliveries were eventually called off because of the high risk and relatively low return. On 5 August came the first determined counter-attacks by the Germans. The thrust came from the Wola region. The Wola region was labelled as Defence District III by Colonel Antoni Chruściel, the officer in charge of all Polish forces in Warsaw. After three days of heavy fighting, the 5,000 army, SS, and police troops cracked part of the AK defences, which were fortified by about 1,650 men.

This then drove a wedge between Srodmiescie and Stare Miasto, splitting the largest insurgent enclave in two. At the same time, the other German thrust was bogged down in the Mokotow-Ochota region. The defence of those districts by the insurgents shielded Srodmiescie for more than a week, staving off a premature collapse of the armed effort. The Germans were able to make only limited headway, managing to recapture one of the main east–west thoroughfares across the Vistula. By 10 August, however, the AK leadership knew the result of the Soviet–German battle that had taken place, and realised that the Soviets would not be advancing to free Warsaw.

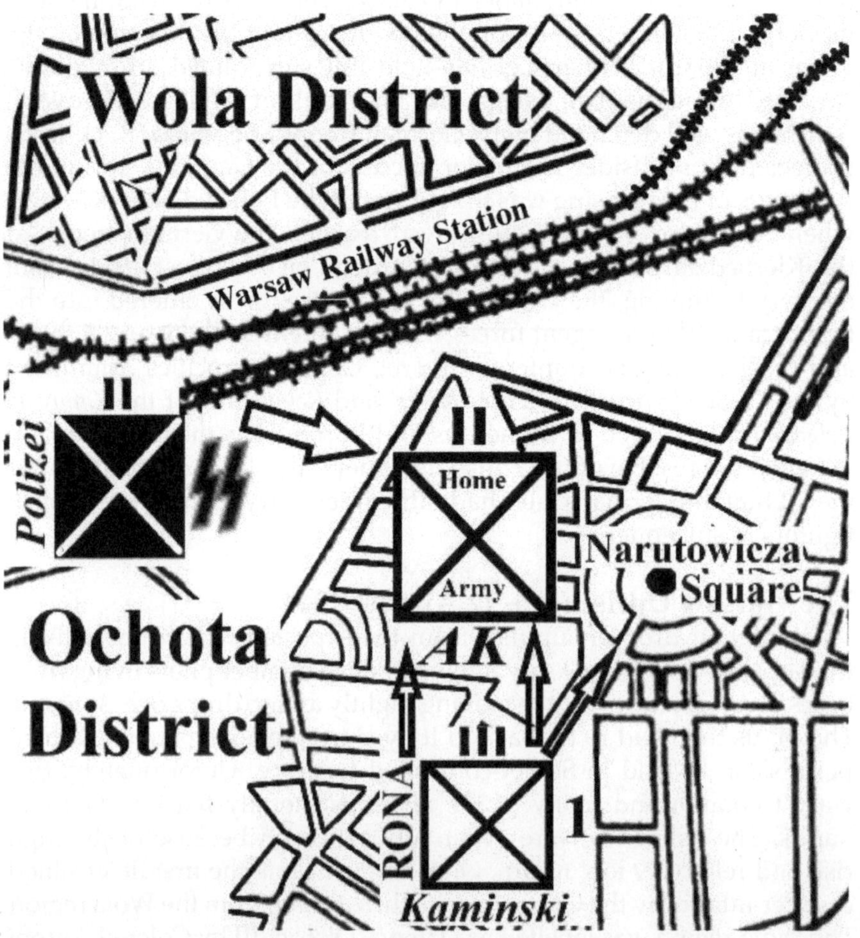

Figure 30. The march of *Regiment 1, Kaminski Brigade* through Ochota District, 7–9 August 1944.

A previous order that had stated insurgents should move out of the way of large German attacks was changed so that connectivity could once again be re-established between the various city regions. At that time, the Germans also began to vent their frustration and anger on the civilian population. At exactly 0800 on 5 August 1944, *SS-Gruppenführer und Generalleutnant der Waffen-SS* Heinz Reinfarth launched his assault on the Wola and Ochota districts of Warsaw. He employed 2,300 of his estimated 6,621 men against the Wola district, where the Home Army's replenished 'Kedyw' Regiment had 1,650 men positioned.

Figure 31. The Polish 'High-Water Mark', 5 August 1944.

Reinfarth left the Ochota district, which contained perhaps 300–400 poorly equipped AK volunteers, to Kaminski's 1,700-strong *Regiment 1*, although he made sure to employ a 500-man police battalion in the same sector in order to stiffen their attack.[7] When the attack was launched, Kaminski's unit *(Regiment 1)* was nowhere to be found. Only at 0930, or a full hour and a half after they were to advance, did the unit begin to move. A description of the German report dealing with the Kaminski regiment was eventually obtained and appeared in an English-language work:

> Kaminski's unit, which began its assault at a more leisurely 9:30 AM on August 5, only advanced 300 yards. One reason for the slow progress of its attack stemmed from stubborn Polish defenders who were hopelessly out-manned and under armed. Another reason, however, was the degeneration of the Kaminski counter-attack into an orgy of murdering, looting, and raping.[8]

Indeed, it now appeared that Kaminski's men were determined to outdo the degenerates of the *SS-Sonderregiment 'Dirlewanger'* in atrocities. The case seems to have been exactly as described in the above quote, as revealed by this *9. Armee* war diary entry for 5 August 1944: 'The 1st Regiment Kaminski has drunken its way through by way of the Reichstrasse up to the Machorka Factory.'[9] Another account describes their actions from 4–6 August:

> On 4 August fifty of Kaminski's mob surrounded some houses on Grojecka Street. Under the pretext of looking for arms, they looted homes and then took 160 unarmed men, including twelve-year-olds, led them into a cellar, and shot them in the backs of their heads. They poured gasoline over the corpses then threw grenades. The same morning on another street, Kaminski's men kicked 40 people into a cellar and machine gunned everyone. Only three survived. But the most hideous episode involving Kaminski's men began at 10:00 AM on 5 August at the Radium Institute. After invading the building, they robbed everyone – the nurses and the ninety patients. The Russians even stole hospital equipment, and what they could not cart off, they destroyed. A band of them tore apart the pharmacy and drank the rubbing alcohol until it ran out. Then they consumed ether. The orgy of plundering and drinking degenerated to raping not only the nurses but also the cancer patients, most of them elderly women. By Sunday, 6 August, the men shot inmates and began to burn the hospital room by room … thirty people died in the flaming rooms of the building or were shot that day. The others managed to save themselves by finding a place in the basement of

> the building and hiding there. The atrocities at the hospital did not end until the middle of the month.[10]

This behaviour on the part of Kaminski's troops continued until 10 August, sending *SS-Obergruppenführer* Erich von dem Bach-Zelewski into a rage:

> The attackers made slight progress here on the 9th and good progress on the 10th. All of the Axis troops pulled their weight, even the convicts of Dirlewanger showing great courage if little battle sense, except for Kaminski's men, who continued to spend more time looting and raping than fighting.[11]

In this way, by 8 August 1944, approximately 40,000 civilians: men, women, old folks, and little children of the Wola District, had been systematically murdered by the units under Hans Reinefarth's command. But it was *Reichsführer-SS* Heinrich Himmler, the head of the SS, who gave the order to raze the city and to eliminate any Pole that German forces encountered. In particular, *SS-Sonderregiment 'Dirlewanger'* did things that are still even today, so outrageous and monstrous that they beg the question as to whether the perpetrators had any shred of humanity. From their actions in Warsaw, it appears that they did not.

The manner in which Polish civilians were murdered was as disgusting as it was heinous. While most were shot or burned alive, even worse abominations were also perpetrated. There were numerous instances where young girls of varying age were raped before being killed. The commander of this SS penal unit, Oskar Dirlewanger, was himself a convicted paedophile from as far back as the 1920s. Other horrors also took place. Bayonets were thrust into women's private parts, and Polish men would be shot in the groin, which caused a slow and painful death as the victim would bleed to death while in agony. Thousands of civilians were executed, and many more died as they were driven before the German troops as those units moved towards the insurgent barricades.

On Saturday, 5 August, the Germans in the Wola district began to apprehend every civilian that they could find, and send them under armed guards to the Ursus factory, where agricultural machinery was produced. The Ursus factory was also located in the Wola district (at 15 Sienna Street). There, members of *SS-Sonderregiment 'Dirlewanger'* would bring a hundred civilians at a time into the building. They would then line them up against a wall and execute them using two machine guns. When space ran out inside the factory, the Nazis moved the executions to the back of the building. The massacre went on all day until a little over 6,000 Poles, men, women, old folks and even little children, were murdered.

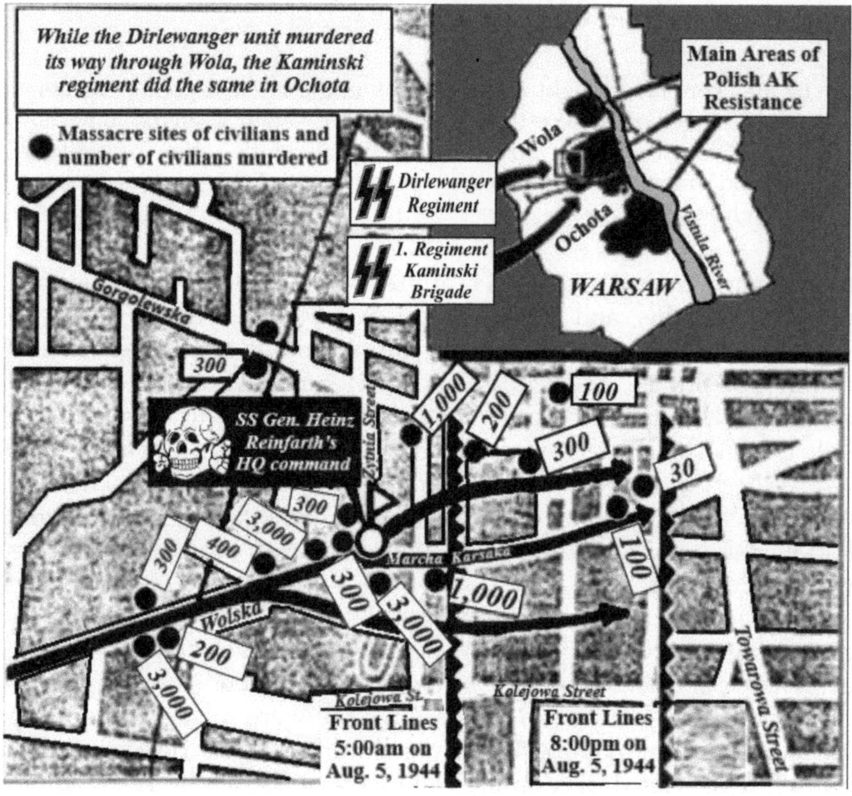

Figure 32. Murders perpetrated by the Kaminski and Dirlewanger SS formation in Wola and Ochota.

The executions at the Ursus factory would become known in Polish history as 'Black Saturday' (it is also referred to as the 'Wola Massacre'). Before it was all over, some 40,000–50,000 people would perish as a result of these killings, which were wilfully instigated against the Polish civilian population. As a result of these massacres, it had become clear to both sides that the rest of the fight would be a long and dirty struggle, which pitted supreme courage and determination from one side against a better-trained, better-armed, and numerically superior opponent.

The mission of the AK, beginning on 8 August, became more geared towards trying to shield the Polish population from further suffering rather than trying to take the city. Now it was no longer about capturing the city but about trying to save as many lives as possible. In addition, the Germans would encounter more and more AK soldiers who would refuse to surrender, knowing what awaited them if they gave themselves up to the Germans. This actually made the job of putting down the uprising all the harder for the Germans, given that the Polish resistance stiffened as a result. Therefore, one must point out the fact that the hardened Polish stance was mostly due to the heinous actions of Dirlewanger's men and other SS and police forces who, by 5 August 1944, had killed an estimated 12,000 men, women, and children in the Wola and Ochota districts. That gruesome tally sheet would only increase as the days passed.

Von dem Bach-Zelewski's efforts to quell the uprising were two-fold. One strategy being employed was the crushing of the insurrection by all military means. The second was a diplomatic one, egging the Home Army to surrender and give up their struggle. But when it became widely known to AK fighters about the massacres perpetrated on the civilian population, and the execution of Polish soldiers who had surrendered, their refusal to surrender only increased. It hardened the Polish resolve to fight to the bitter end. Von dem Bach-Zelewski therefore, began to put a stop to the wholesale slaughter of the Polish civilian population in the city. He also ordered a stop to the wholesale raping and looting that accompanied the massacres.

He wanted to withdraw the totally uncontrollable *Regiment 1* of the *Kaminski Brigade,* but in the beginning of the second week of August he lacked the necessary replacements to relieve even the ineffective and totally rowdy Kaminski formation. Nor was he then in complete control of the situation to order Kaminski's arrest. Kaminski had fallen out of favour and resentment against him had been brewing for some time. This was on account of the actions of Kaminski himself and his troops, which had been reported to Hitler's headquarters, a place where Kaminski had no friends. The behaviour of Kaminski's men was so debauched that even the Nazis thought he needed to go. By the time of the Warsaw Uprising, the unit had degenerated into a freebooter formation, the likes of which existed during the Thirty Years' War. He was proving an embarrassment to *Reichsführer-SS* Heinrich Himmler, who had enemies in Hitler's court. The same could be said of *SS-Sonderregiment 'Dirlewanger'*, but in Oskar Dirlewanger's case, *SS-Obergruppenführer and General of the Waffen-SS* Gottlob Berger, who was his friend, was protecting him. Kaminski had no such patron in Hitler's court. *Generalmajor* Günther Rohr, whom von dem Bach had appointed to lead the southern sector in Warsaw, was appalled at what Kaminski and his men were doing, but also agreed that for the present, the regiment could not be withdrawn.

The Germans react

When the Home Army began their attack on 1 August 1944, *SS-Obergruppenführer* Erich von dem Bach Zelewski reacted swiftly by sending all available forces of the *Höhere SS und Polizeiführer Ost* command, as well as army reserve, security, and replacement units to Warsaw. *SS-Gruppenführer und Generalleutnant der Waffen-SS und der Polizei* Heinz Reinfarth was placed in overall command of these forces. Reinfarth created two *Kampfgruppen* from the immediate forces given to him by von dem Bach. One battlegroup was code-named *Schmidt*, and was named after its commander, *Oberst* Wilhelm Schmidt, who led the *Sicherungs Regiment 608*. The other battlegroup was named after himself, *Reinfarth*. The following are initial strengths of both battlegroups:[12]

SS Kampfgruppe Reinfarth (2,581 men)

1. *Regiment 1* (two battalions) of the *Kaminski Brigade*, with 1,700 officers, NCOs, and men.
2. One battalion of *SS-Sonderregiment 'Dirlewanger'*, sixteen officers, and 865 NCOs and men.

Kampfgruppe Schmidt (4,040 men)

3. Elements of the *Polizeiregiment Posen*, with 45 officers and 2,695 NCOs and men.[13]
4. 25 officers and 1,275 NCOs and men of the *Heer*.

In addition to these reinforcements, other units eventually reached the Polish capital, including *SS Polizei Reiter Abteilung III* from Posen,[14] as well as *(litauische) Schutzmannschaft Bataillon 255*.[15] For most of its lifespan, *Schutzmannschaft Bataillon 255* had been stationed in Slutsk, just south of Minsk and halfway between Baranovichi and Bobruisk. When the uprising in Warsaw began, it was rushed to the Polish capital. The fighting in Warsaw would eventually cause the battalion to be disbanded in August because of heavy losses. The total German garrison strength in Warsaw at the beginning of the uprising was somewhere between 15,000 and 16,000 men.[16] The police and army forces identified as being stationed in the city at the time of the revolt included the following *Heer*, SS and police units:

1. *SS Polizei Wach-Bataillon Warschau* (four companies).
2. *SS-Polizeiregiment 17 (I., II., und III. Bataillone).*
3. *146. Feldgendarmerie Kompanie.*
4. *146. Bau Pionier Bataillon.*
5. *SS-Polizeiregiment 22 (I., II., und III. Bataillone).*[17]
6. *III. Kosaken Kavallerie Bataillon der Sicherungs-Regiment 57.*[18]
7. *II. (Aserbaidschanisches) Bataillon des Sonderverbandes Bergmann.*[19]
8. *Sicherheitspolizei und Sicherheitsdienst Warschau* (one reinforced SD company).
9. *SS und Polizeiführer Warschau* (one reinforced SS company).
10. Postal Police, Railway Police, and Fire-Fighting Police elements (in terms of numbers, two reinforced battalions).

Eventually, some of the units committed to crushing the Polish resistance in Warsaw would include the following additional forces:

Elements of the *Ostmuselmanische SS Regiment 1* (minus the *III. Bataillon*).[20]
One Cossack cavalry battalion of the *3. Kosaken Kavallerie Brigade.*
Sicherheitspolizei und Sicherheitsdienst Posen (one reinforced SD company).
Polizei-Schützen-Regiment 34 (arrived in the Campinos Forest on 30 September 1944).
Elements of the *25. Panzer-Division* (arrived between 14 and 16 September).
Elements of the *Panzer-Division 'Herman Göring'* (arrived in the first half of August).
5. SS Panzer-Division 'Wiking'
1. SS Flak Bataillon 'Reichsführer-SS'
2. SS Flak Bataillon 'Reichsführer-SS'
IV. Bataillon/Stellungs Werfer Regiment 102 (150 mm *Werfer-41*)

Other, minor, unidentified Army, SS, and police forces.
SS Kampfgruppe Reinfarth
Polizeiregiment Schallert [21] (*Oberst der Schutzpolizei* Hermann Schallert)[22]
SS-Sonderregiment 'Dirlewanger'
Regiment 1/Kaminski Brigade
Polizei-Schützen-Regiment 34
SS Polizei Nachrichten Kompanie 41
Polizei Kavallerie Schwadron Posen
SD Kompanie Posen
Kampfgruppe Schmidt
Sicherungs-Regiment 608 (CO: *Oberst* Wilhelm Schmidt)
Kosaken Schutzmannschaft Bataillon 209
Ost Reiter Abteilung 580
Kosaken Bataillon 572

Grenadier Bataillon z.b.V. 550 (a penal unit)
Aserbeidschan Bataillon I/111
II. (Aserbaidschanisch) Bataillon der Sonderverband Bergmann [23]

SS Polizei Nachrichten Kompanie 41 could count on 112 police officers, NCOs, and enlisted men. The *Polizei Kavallerie Schwadron Posen* had a force of some 150 men on horseback, drawn from the *Polizei Reiter Schule Posen* located in that same city (Poznan). Finally, the SD company was formed from security police forces led by *SS-Sturmbannführer* Hugo Krüger, who was the head of the Kripo *(Kriminalpolizei)* – the criminal police in Poznan. Krüger's subordinate and assistant company commander was Kriminal Rat Peterson, a career police inspector. Krüger's immediate superior was *SS-Obersturmbannführer* Rolff Hoeppner, who was the head of the Sipo and SD in Poznan.

SS-Obersturmbannführer Stossberg, who was Chief of the Poznan Gestapo, had requested to accompany the SD Company to Warsaw, but had been turned down by Hoeppner, who said he was needed at his post. His 'Ia' (second in command) at Gestapo headquarters in Poznan was *SS-Sturmbannführer* Klein, who was tasked with leading the SD company in Warsaw. Upon arrival at the capital, Reinfarth's battlegroup would have additional forces attached to it. *Oberst* Wilhelm Schmidt's *Sicherungs-Regiment 608* had a strength of twenty officers and 598 NCOs and men, so the regiment was understrength. The *Azerbaijani* battalion was a full-strength formation, having 677 officers, NCOs and men. Its primary deficiency was the fact that it only had five officers. The *Ostmuselmanische SS Regiment 1* had three battalions of volunteers, but for the battle of Warsaw only its *I. Bataillon* and *III. Bataillon* were available for combat employment. Both battlegroups reached the western outskirts of the Polish capital by 5 August 1944. The eastern part of Warsaw across the Vistula River was the Praga district. On 6 August this part of the city was still under German *9. Armee* control, since two German corps – the *XXXIX. Panzerkorps* and *III. (germanische) SS Panzerkorps* – were still on a bridgehead east of the Polish capital. At this time German forces on this bridgehead were as follows:

5. SS Panzer-Division 'Wiking'
3. SS Panzer-Division 'Totenkopf'
19. Panzer-Division
Fallschirm Panzer-Division 'Hermann Göring'
45. Infanterie-Division
1131. Grenadier Brigade

Between 6 August and the beginning of September, the Germans operating in this sector were able to slowly push back the Polish defenders. However, they were only able to achieve this by using withdrawn German units that had been fighting the Russians. A case in point was *19. Panzer-Division*, as well as some armoured elements of *3. SS Panzer-Division 'Totenkopf'* and *5. SS Panzer-Division 'Wiking'*. By 10 September 1944, the Russians (under political pressure from the British) made a concerted effort to take the Praga district. The last German unit east of the Vistula River, *73. Infanterie-Division*, withdrew in complete disarray. By 13 September the Red Army reached the banks of the Vistula by the Polish capital, but just as soon as the rearguard elements of *73. Infanterie-Division* crossed the bridges connecting Praga to the rest of the city, the Germans blew them up.

The only bridge that was not blown up was the northernmost one; it had been left intact for the *19. Panzer-Division* because that unit still had some elements east of the Vistula. On 14 September *19. Panzer-Division* was finally withdrawn but the Russians managed to establish a bridgehead across the Vistula in that area. This Russian jumping-off point west of the Vistula was named the Magnuszew bridgehead by the 8th Guards Army. It now seemed as though the Soviets were about to aid the Polish Home Army forces, but unlike all of the early Polish Home Army plans and expectations, the sight of Red Army soldiers coming to the aid of the Poles proved to be a chimera.

The Warsaw Uprising: 12 August–2 September 1944

After the fall of the Wola District, the German attack centred on the Stare Miasto area – the Old Town, which was defended by 9,807 AK men. This region was the largest insurgent enclave, and it was also the region with the bridges to the other side of the Vistula River. The attack came on 12 August and, after heavy fighting, the Poles were forced to retreat, leaving the area of the old Jewish ghetto. Yet at the same time that they were withdrawing from one position, the insurgents were carrying out a counter-attack to re-form a link between Srodmiescie and Stare Miasto. While this attempt was unsuccessful, it did force the Germans to divert some troops from the main thrust of their attack in order to deal with this new Polish action.

Seeing that re-establishing connections between the city districts was impossible, General Bor-Komorowski once again turned to the London government for aid. Another request was made for the deployment of the 1st Polish (Independent) Parachute Brigade, as well as for more supply drops. However, the brigade was earmarked for Field Marshal Montgomery's airborne operation in Holland, code-named Market Garden, which began well but ultimately ended in failure. In addition, given that the Western leaders had agreed with Stalin that Eastern Europe was to be the domain of Russian influence, the Churchill government was opposed to causing friction with the Soviet government by assisting the AK. As a result, the British turned down the request to use this Polish parachute brigade in Warsaw. An order was also sent out to all AK units in and around Warsaw to come to the aid of the insurgents. This was only partly successful, as only about 1,000 of the roughly 3,000-strong force outside of the city were able to make their way into the Polish capital.

This came in the form of 750 men led by Major Okon, who reached the Zoliborz (Soliborz) sector of Warsaw on 20 August. They had come from the Kampinos Forest. This large force had been preceded by a smaller, 200-man unit, which reached the Mokotow sector on 18 August. On 23 August Major Okon once again tried to move in more men from the Kampinos Forest area into the city. This time, however, he was blocked from bringing in the 2,368 men that he had with him. So strong was the German response that his large force lost 45 per cent of its effective strength on that very night and was eventually destroyed while trying to evade capture.

The Warsaw Uprising: 3–18 September 1944

On 2 September General Bor-Komorowski could still count on 4,800 fighters. Of this number, only 1,300 were well armed, though an additional 200 were lightly armed with pistols and revolvers. Fighters were constantly coming forward to volunteer for service, but as always the problem they faced was the lack of arms. On 4 September the Germans began their attack of the city centre and on 6 September they launched their assault on Powisle.[24] After the first four to five days of fighting, the areas controlled by both sides became stabilised. Barricades were built by both forces, but it was the Germans who had the clear advantage. Lack of weapons was a problem that the AK was never able to resolve.

The initial Polish attack had split up the German forces inside the city into a few isolated pockets, cut off from one another. One of the largest was in the Bruhl Palace in Plac Teatralny, where *Luftwaffe Generalleutnant* Rainer Stahel, the city's garrison commander, had his HQ. Fortunately for Stahel, his isolated garrison was one of the lucky ones to be relieved (and relieved early). When the men of *Grenadier Regiment 4* from the *562. Volksgrenadier Division* reached his besieged headquarters on 3 August, he reportedly told the officers and men to 'Kill all men encountered, remove women and children, and burn all of the homes'.[25] Although he showed some humanity by requesting that women and children were to be spared, his order was nevertheless a war crime, because it involved the murder of innocent civilians and the execution of all captured Polish Home Army fighters.

Besides a few fortified strongpoints inside the Polish AK lines, the Germans also controlled pieces of territory that darted deep into the heart of the city. Having taken the Old Town sector, the Germans commanded a wide stretch of Warsaw separating the city centre from Zoliborz in the north. Zoliborz was now a separate centre of fighting, Group North as such having ceased to exist and its commanding officer, Colonel Wachnowski, having become the deputy to Colonel Monter when he reached the city centre. Now the German attention was directed at eliminating the Home Army presence by the riverbank. German heavy artillery and specialised units by then included:

Sturm Morser Kompanie 218
Sturm Pionier Bataillon 500
Schwer Nebelwerfer Batterie 201[26]
Stellungswerfer-Regiment 102 (160mm & 320mm Nebelwerfer-Mörser)
Flamm Panzer Bataillon 'Krone'
Schwere Artillerie-Batterie 638–600mm Karl-Gerät Mörser (later replaced by *Schwere Artillerie-Batterie 428*)
Sturm Morser Kompanie 1000 (380mm mortars)[27]
23. Flak Division

Figure 33. The *Sturmmörserwagen 606/4* (380mm RW-61 howitzer). This German vehicle was known as the *Sturmtiger* (assault tiger). Its primary task was to provide heavy fire support for infantry units fighting in urban areas. Its speed was 25mph with a maximum operational range of 75 miles. The vehicle could only carry fourteen rounds given the large size of the shell. This is why these armoured vehicles were almost always accompanied by a truck or tracked prime mover that carried additional rounds. The shell of this vehicle was capable of levelling heavily defended buildings or fortified areas with a single strike. The explosive could penetrate up to 8.2ft of reinforced concrete. Sturm Morser Kompanie 1000 only possessed four of these armoured vehicles, divided into two platoons of two vehicles apiece. These armoured monsters were usually supported by a platoon of infantry. (*Author's line drawing*).

The German fear was that the Soviet-sponsored Polish communist units under General Berling would try and link up with General Bor-Komorowski's forces in the city. This fear was accentuated when the Soviet 47th Army attacked German forces in Praga. From 4 to 7 September the fight for the riverside raged on in the Old Town sector, and then the city centre on 11 September. The principal unit in this assault was the infamous *SS-Sonderregiment 'Dirlewanger'*. On 10 September, several Polish communist units serving in the Red Army launched an attack against the Germans defending Praga. The 7th and 8th Infantry Regiments of General Zygmunt Berling's 1st Polish Army launched attacks across the Vistula River.

These regiments were joined by Soviet forces and after five days of fighting, the Germans had been completely pushed out of the east bank of the Vistula River, opposite the Polish positions in Zoliborz, Solec, and Czerniakow. These positions were in the hands of the Red Army. In his attack across the Vistula River, General Berling had lost around 2,000 men. This loss did not go unnoticed by Moscow, who immediately recalled him. In effect, he was relieved of his command because he had apparently exercised 'poor leadership'. The reality was that Stalin had not wanted Berling to establish a bridgehead across the Vistula or to try and link up with the Polish Home Army. Berling's desire to come to the aid of these 'Western-supported' Polish patriots was based not on political conviction, but from a desire to help the Polish people of Warsaw against a common enemy. Stalin, of course, was vehemently opposed to any move that would aid the pro-Western leadership of the AK. This fact alone was likely the real reason why General Berling was dismissed from the position of commander of the Polish 1st Army. He was lucky that Stalin did not jail or execute him. He was relieved of his command and ordered to Moscow. There he was given a position at the War Academy. He was not allowed to return to Poland until 1947.

Figure 34. Areas still under Polish Home Army control, 3–18 September 1944.

By then, Stalin had established a communist government in the country without Berling's participation. Between 14 and 16 September, the newly arrived *25. Panzer-Division*, supported by Luftwaffe Ju 88 bombers, pushed AK units defending Zoliborz about a half mile from the riverbank, where the Polish defenders were able to establish a new defensive line. At the same time, in the southern part of the city what few areas of the river line remained in Polish hands were taken by another German drive. The Germans were still concerned about a possible bridgehead being established by the Red Army in the city itself.

The Warsaw Uprising: 19 September–2 October 1944

On 19 September 1944, after eight days and nights of bitter fighting in the city centre, the battle reached its zenith. The AK units, now surrounded in an area no larger than 500 square yards, were down to their last rounds of ammunition. Their supply of food and water had long been exhausted. Fighting here lasted until 23 September, when the last Polish positions by the riverside were overwhelmed. Most of the withdrawing Polish forces had to make their way through the sewer system to areas of the city still under AK control. The next area to be hit by a German assault was Mokotow. Having been reinforced by the *19. Panzer-Division,* the Germans launched their attack in this sector on 24 September. The attack of this Panzer-Division, an armoured unit that had been brought up to support what had been a mixture of German army reserve, police, and SS units, was preceded by two to three days of heavy bombardment. On the night of 26 September, the Polish defenders in Mokotow tried to make their way to an area of the city centre still in Home Army control by trying to navigate the sewer system, but the Germans were expecting this.

Of the 3,000+ Polish fighters in Mokotow, only 600 managed to reach the city centre, having got through the ingenious gas bombs that the Germans began to throw into the sewers to suffocate the withdrawing Polish soldiers. Around 2,000 Home Army men surrendered to German forces in Mokotow on 27 September. Further resistance there was no longer possible. Immediately after this the Germans moved their *19. Panzer-Division* north of the city and on the following day they unleashed this Panzer-Division against the Polish defenders in Zoliborz. After two more days of stiff resistance by the Polish defenders, and a rejection of surrender offered by the Germans to its commander, Lieutenant Colonel M. Niedzielski, General Komorowski's headquarters finally ordered him to lay down his arms.

On 30 September 1944, Colonel Niedzielski and his 1,500 defenders went into German captivity but defiant as ever. After consulting with the Polish civilian leaders, the Home Army accepted the fact that further resistance would not achieve the aims of the rising, but would simply cause more Polish deaths, especially of the city's civilian population. It was thus decided that the Home Army had to accept the German surrender terms. On 2 October 1944, a Polish AK delegation, headed by General Komorowski, signed the surrender terms at the German headquarters at Ozarow. The Warsaw Uprising had come to an end after sixty-three days of bitter fighting.

Polish and German losses

The Polish Home Army high-water mark occurred on 5 August 1944. By 2 September 1944, the Polish positions had been very much reduced and were basically split up into three pockets. These three areas of resistance within the city were supported by a fourth region. This fourth area was outside of Warsaw itself, in the Kampinos Forest, where General Bor-Komorowski's forces had 2,500 men split into two infantry regiments and two cavalry squadrons under the command of Major A. Kotowski. *SS-Obergruppenführer* Erich von dem Bach-Zelewski ordered this AK force to be destroyed. The assault against the Kampinos Forest began on 26 September 1944, by which time he knew that the Polish defenders in Warsaw were on the verge of surrendering. German and Polish losses during the uprising appear to have been more or less evenly split.

German losses appear to have been about 10,000 combatants killed, about 7,000 who were listed as MIA, 9,000 wounded, and perhaps 1,500 captured. [28] Polish military losses included 7,000 missing (most of them probably killed), and 15,900 taken prisoner (most of them when the AK in Warsaw surrendered, on 2 October 1944). The German occupation of Poland began on 1 September 1939 and did not end until the Wehrmacht was driven from its western-most regions in late January 1945. In total, the Polish nation suffered 6 million deaths in just over five years of occupation. That is an average of 1,200,000 people killed per year, or about 3,288 Polish citizens killed per day. The only other nation to suffer a greater loss is the Soviet Union, which endured almost four years of war and lost 25 million people.

The manner in which the occupation was carried out was quite brutal and left a lasting impression on the populace. When the tables were finally turned and the Germans began their retreat, many Poles and Russians vented their frustration and hatred against any German civilian or soldier that they could get their hands on. The Germans were reaping the 'fruits' of their bitter harvest. Regarding the 'efficacy' of the occupation, it must be said that Nazi brutality and oppression kept a lid on Polish resistance from 1939 until about late 1942. Thereafter, the Germans found it necessary to bring in more and more occupation troops. The requirements of properly garrisoning Poland necessitated the transfer of training, reserve, and replacement troops, which in normal circumstances would have remained inside the borders of the Reich, but were now transferred to Poland and elsewhere to help occupy Europe.

In addition, *Reichsführer-SS* Heinrich Himmler also found it increasingly essential to reinforce the existing SS and police forces already garrisoning Poland. The culmination of resistance to German rule has got to be the uprising by the Home Army on 1 August 1944, in the Polish capital. The defeat of the uprising was facilitated by Josef Stalin, who wanted to allow Germany to eliminate those Polish democratic forces who would wish to assume authority in Poland at the end of the war. Since the Soviet dictator wanted to install his own communist puppet government, the Home Army was an affront to those plans. The defeat of the Warsaw Uprising, then, extinguished the last breath of freedom that the Polish nation would experience for more than five decades after the end of the Second World War. Five years of Nazi oppression was followed by forty-four years of communist subjugation, until 1989 when communism fell in Poland. The legacy of the Nazi occupation, then, was the added 'gift' of forty-four years of additional misery for the Polish nation.

Chapter 6

CONCLUSIONS: WAS THE NAZI OCCUPATION OF POLAND A FAILURE?

A lasting order cannot be established by bayonets.

Ludwig von Mises

The nature of the Nazi occupation

German arrogance and ignorance of the eastern people, a sentiment that for the most part permeated from the highest echelons of the Wehrmacht and filtered down to the lowest ranks, was a major factor that contributed to the failure by the Nazis to create an empire in the East. When asked about why Germany failed in the East, many historians immediately point to the harshness of the Nazi occupation of Poland (and the USSR) and its policy of repression. But the overall contempt the Germans had for the Polish people guaranteed that Nazi Germany would never be able to pacify the population. The harder that the Germans bore down on the Polish nation, the greater the Polish resistance to that German rule. Of course, this arrogance and contempt was further heightened by Nazi ideology.

The Nazis made sure to imbue their soldiers and indeed, German society as a whole, with the idea that the Jews, Romani, and Eastern European people were inferior, and therefore by their twisted racist logic, they were *lebensunwertes leben* (life unworthy of life). They also tried to depict their genocidal war as a struggle between the so-called *herrenvolk* (master race) versus the *untermenschen* (subhumans). Once you are able to convince people that eliminating a targeted group is necessary, and you have effectively made them appear less than human, you have the conditions for a genocide to occur. The crux of this tactic is to paint those you are targeting as inferior and somehow damaging to your society, leading people to believe that those deemed 'life unworthy of life' should be expunged (in other words, eliminated). The strategy of demonising a group of people is not new.

The Turks in the First World War called the Armenians 'traitorous parasites', the Nazis called the Jewish people 'vermin', the Hutus of Rwanda called the Tutsis 'cockroaches'. Buddhist monks even to this day stir anti-Rohingya hatred in Myanmar by calling the Muslim minority there a 'plague on our land'.[1] Today the horrors heaped upon the Rohingya people are so appalling that they cannot be reconciled with the ideals of the Buddhist *metta* – cultivating kindness towards all human beings. Buddhist monks have thrown Rohingya children live into the flames of their own burning homes. This is a similar calibre of behaviour to the *SS-Sonderregiment 'Dirlewanger'* burning women and children alive in Warsaw, or that of *Generalkommissar für Weißruthenien*, Wilhelm Kube, who threw candy at Jewish children as they were being buried alive.[2]

These reprehensible acts of cruelty are not only an indicator of evil, but also of the effectiveness of indoctrination and propaganda on a society. Unfortunately, collective violence and genocide has had a long history in our world.[3] What made the Nazi mass murder so unique from previous genocides was the employment of advanced technology, which allowed a much greater number of deaths on an industrial level. Never before had mass murder been performed in an assembly line process; whether it was through mass shootings as occurred in the East, or through the employment of gas chambers and industrial-level crematoriums in the extermination camps, most of which were located in Poland. With these 'tools', the Nazis killed thousands of people per day.

Nazi propaganda, emphasizing the dehumanisation of Jewish, Romani, and Eastern European people, heightened and intensified the already existing representative biases that most Germans had during that epoch. The heady and seemingly quick German victories of 1939–41 added to the problem, since constant success tends to make one self-centred, overly confident, and arrogant. The German soldier went about conquering Eastern Europe believing in his own superiority, and by virtue of that thought the *Ostvölk* (eastern people) to be inferior. I believe that this social factor was a primary reason why the Germans were not able to successfully establish their eastern empire.

Did the harshness of the German occupation exacerbate the situation? Yes. Was the random execution of innocent people because of Polish resistance activities a contributing factor? Yes. Was the Nazi policy of collective punishment a factor? Yes. Were the economically harsh policies an aspect of the failure? Yes. Was the forced labour of the population a factor? Yes. Was the theft of Polish lands a factor? Yes. Was the fact that the Third Reich wanted to make sure that Poland would cease to exist as a nation another reason? Yes. Were the Nazi acts of genocide and democide also another factor? Most definitely. Did most German soldiers march into Poland, confident that they were better than the people they were about to conquer? The answer is also 'yes'.

German contempt of the very people they sought to rule was the seed of their defeat. Genocide, democide, repressive rules, collective executions, land theft, and economic exploitation were simply water and fodder to enable that 'seed' to germinate and grow. *Generalplan Ost*, which was written using the policy of *Lebensraum*, was a guidepost on how Germans were to behave in the East. One of the tenets laid out in *Generalplan Ost* was the employment of harsh policies, geared not only to cow and subjugate, but also to eliminate a good portion of the population living there. That, in turn, would make available land in the East that Germans could colonise.

The *SS Einsatzgruppen*, and the manner in which the Germans fought the anti-partisan war, was but a reflection of that harsh policy. Needless to say, the Nazi *Einsatzgruppen* in Poland, and elsewhere for that matter, was an echo of that hatred and contempt for human life that is now forever tied to Nazi Germany. The Nazis did not bring to Poland any hope for a better future for her people. Instead, they tore the country in half, robbed, pillaged, and murdered. In this Nazi 'New Order', Poles were scheduled to be a minority in their own land. Higher education was eliminated and the intelligentsia of the country was to be wiped out to assure that Poland would never rise again as a nation. The German occupation only brought murder, misery, and deprivations to the Polish people. With this Nazi mindset, there was never any room for compromise of accommodation with the occupying power.

For the Poles, resistance or accepting a slow death of their people were the only two options. Throughout the war, German treatment of the Polish people proved simply abysmal. The Nazis even mistreated those people who appeared to be friendly to them. One can only wonder and imagine how much different the outcome in the East might have been for the Germans had they adopted a more moderate policy in Poland and elsewhere. Of course, from the very narrow perspective of National Socialist ideology, this was not possible.

The noted German historian Hans Werner Neulen has described the reasons why Germany was not able to win the 'hearts and minds' of other peoples to their side:

> A 'European Carta' should have guaranteed the prosperity, sovereignty and freedom of all nations under Axis control, but the National Socialists, committed to the ways of terror and unforgiveness, turned down this project. National Socialist Germany, the leading power of the Axis, was totally unfit for the role of mediator. The daring exploits of the German tank divisions through Europe had not been followed by an inspiring or universal theory or doctrine. The propaganda of the superiority of the Germans might have attracted a minority in Europe, but was extremely useless for an ideology of integration into a European federation of states, because it denied the equality of nations and designed a racist hierarchy as the New Order of Europe. There was no place for Jews and Slavs in this vague 'New Order'. Not all Slavs were destined for extermination, but they could not expect a special place in 'New Europe'. [4]

A failed strategy: Nazi policies in practice in Poland

When Germany marched into Poland on 1 September 1939, she brought with her all of her bigotries and hatreds. The Germans were the *Herrenvolk* and the Eastern people, the Romani and the Jews were the *Untermenschen*. This racial policy, one that Adolf Hitler espoused in *Mein Kampf* and one of the base pillars of National Socialist ideology, was taken along into the Eastern territories. This would be the proverbial seed that would sow the destruction of the German *Tausendjähriges Reich* (thousand-year Reich). The very core of these racial policies was the idea of the inferiority of the Jewish, Romani, and Eastern Europeans. One perfect example of this arrogance in action were the so-called *Goldfasanen* or 'Golden Pheasants'. These Nazi officials who were to rule over 34,000,000 Poles, were sent to run the civilian administration in the GG with little or no training. These Nazi technocrats were called golden pheasants on account of their brown Nazi Party uniform and golden epaulettes. Almost all of them had no knowledge of the people and the land they were supposed to rule. They were not sent to the East to help improve the society there.

On the contrary, they came as imperial colonisers, ready to exploit the people and the resources of the land. They had no interest in improving the lives of the locals, nor did they come to offer them hope for a better future. These men had nothing but contempt for the Polish people. The population and the land itself were seen by the German occupiers like European imperial powers used to see the people and resources of the South American, African and Asian continents. They were to be completely exploited for the benefit of the Third Reich. In order to justify their actions, the Nazis declared that the Poles were not fit to rule themselves. Germany, they boasted, would step in and bring *Ordnung* (order) in the East. Because they were incapable of ruling themselves, went the argument, the land and its resources were the right of the German colonisers. Germany was also to have her *Lebensraum* (living space) at the expense of the Polish nation and people.

In order to make room for German settlers, many of these Poles needed to be eliminated or pushed off their land. Indeed, had not the Führer envisioned this in *Mein Kampf*? When Poland was invaded, the Germans attempted to carry out those goals, prearranged under *Generalplan Ost*. In 1941 these goals were expanded when the USSR was invaded. As previously stated, executing the policies of *Generalplan Ost* required the invader to be harsh and cruel, which in turn guaranteed the alienation and eventual loathing by the general population.

Again, Nazi policies and attitudes worked to create nothing but hatred and resentment on the part of the Polish people. Not only did the Nazis commit genocide in Poland (and elsewhere in the East) on a grand scale, they also committed democide, for they purposely targeted a percentage of the population in general for elimination. The justification for the criminal orders, which helped to create these policies of murder, were made by Nazi lawyers who framed the rationalisation for genocide and democide in legal arguments. Legal arguments that gave cover for mass murder. In that sense, these legal rationalisations formed, along with Nazi ideology, the scaffolding that tied this criminal behaviour together.

German rule in Poland and in the East in general, was harsher, crueller and more severe than German rule in the west European countries and in Scandinavia. In National Socialist ideology, the *Ostvölk* did not deserve any better. While technically speaking, the German occupation of Poland proved a workable success during the war, with acceptable losses, its eventual demise was a given fact by the manner in which the Nazis treated the Polish population. This begs the question as to why the Germans proved to be so wholly incapable of understanding just exactly how detrimental these *Ost* policies were. In the end, the Nazis proved to be their own worst enemy. If they intended to create a *Tausendjähriges Reich* by establishing a German empire in the East, they failed miserably. The way the Germans treated these people, coupled with their ill-advised policies, guaranteed the fall of Nazi rule. In retrospect we can say that the Nazis did not build their *Dritte Reich* on a solid foundation of fairness and equity, which would have likely won over the majority of the people they conquered. Instead, their arrogance and contempt for the very people they sought to rule, coupled with racist and exterminationist policies, served only to create a house of cards that eventually collapsed on them.

Appendix I

GLOSSARY OF GERMAN MILITARY AND POLITICAL TERMS

A

Abschnitt	Sector, district.
Abteilung	Battalion. It could also mean Section or Department.
Abwehr	The Intelligence and Clandestine Warfare Service of the German Armed Forces High Command.
Abzeichen	Insignia, badge of rank, appointment or distinction.
Adlerhorst	Eagle's nest. The name given by British intelligence to Hitler's mountaintop retreat located in Berchtesgaden, in the Bavarian Alps.
Afrika Korps	The German military force, led by Erwin Rommel, which fought in North Africa, 1941–43.
Amt	Office, Bureau, or Department.
Angriff	Attack.
Angriffspunkt	Attack point.
Anwärter	Cadet, or candidate.
AOK	*Armee-Oberkommando* – An army headquarters (HQ).
Arbeit	Work.

Arbeitsdienst	Literal translation is work service but was meant as labour service.
Arbeitskommando	Work commando or work group.
Arbeitslager	Work camp.
Armee	Army.
Armeegebiet	Army region or district.
Armeekorps	Army corps.
Artillerie	Artillery.
Aufklärung	Reconnaissance.
Ausbildung	Training.

B

Bahnlinie	Rail line.
Bahnschutzpolizei	Railway security police.
Bandengebiet	Bandit region (partisan-controlled region).
Banditen	Bandits. The Germans referred to the partisans behind the front lines as bandits.
Barbarossa	Coden ame for the German invasion of the USSR.
Bataillon	Battalion.
Bataillonsführer	Battalion commander.
Bataillonskommandeur	Battalion commander.
Batterie	Battery
Bau	Construction.
Baudienst	The national labour service of the Reich.
Baupionier	Construction engineer.
BdO	*Befehlshaber der Ordnungspolizei* (Supreme Commander of the Order Police).
BdS	*Befehlshaber der Sicherheitspolizei* (Supreme Commander of the Security Police).
Befehl	Command. The plural form of the word is *Befehle*.
Befehlshaber	Commander.
Begleit	Escort, usually denoting an elite unit.
Belarus	White Russia.
Beobachter	Artillery or air observer.

Beutepanzer	Captured tank or armoured vehicle.
Bewachungsmannschaft	The literal translation is security crew, but in Third Reich-era terminology, it referred to an SS guard detachment in a concentration camp.
Bezirk	A district or administrative unit of the German civilian government.
Brigade	A brigade of troops.
Brigadeführer	Generalmajor in either the SS or Police.
Brücke	Bridge.
Brücken	Bridging.
Bürgermeister	The mayor of a town or community.

C

Chef	Commander of a unit, or sub-unit.
Chef des Generalstabes	Chief of the General Staff.

D

der SS	Belonging to the SS. Usually a Germanic SS unit was prefixed with the title '*SS*' while the non-Germanic formations were referred to as '*der SS*' (of the SS).
Dienst	Service.
Dienstgrad	Rank.
Dienststelle	An administrative department, or administrative office.
Division	A division-sized military unit.
Dnjepr	German spelling for Dnieper, as in Dnieper River.
Dorpat	German spelling for the town of Tartu, in Estonia.
Drang nach Osten	Spread to the East, or Push to the East. It was the nineteenth-century German nationalist zeitgeist for a desire to expand German territory into Eastern European lands.

E

Eingeschlossen	Surrounded, trapped, encircled.
Eingreifgruppe	The literal translation is 'response group', but in military terms it meant 'assault group'.
Einheit	A detachment or a unit.
Einsatz	Mission, action.
Einsatzgruppen	An operational group made up of the *Sipo* (Security Police), *SD* (Security Service), and Order Police units used for special missions, initially for liquidation of the Jewish population, communist commissars etc., but later used to fight the partisans. One *Einsatzgruppe* could have as many as six *Einsatzkommandos*.
Einsatzkommando	A sub-group detachment of the *Einsatzgruppen*.
Ersatz	Replacement.
Ersatzheer	Replacement army.
Estland	Estonia
Estnische (est.)	Estonian, with the German abbreviation of the word in parenthesis.

F

Fallschirmjäger	Paratrooper.
Feind	Enemy.
Feldausbildungs	Field training.
Feldheer	Field Army.
Feldkommandantur	Field Command: A German Army military administration headquarters.
Feldwebel	Sergeant.
Feldzug	Military campaign.
Fellin	The German spelling for the Estonian town of Viljandi.
Festung	Fortress.
Feuerpolizei	Fire Police.
Finnische	Finnish.
Flak	Anti-aircraft.

Fluss	River
Frankreich	France
Freiwilliger	Volunteer. The plural form of the word is Freiwillige.
Front	Referring to the front line, or a front-line unit. Example: *(estnische) Front Bataillon 38.*
Frontkämpfer	Front-line soldier.
Führer	Leader; specifically, to the Second World War, as referring to Adolf Hitler.
Führungshauptamt	Leadership Head Office.

G

Gau	The main territorial division of the Nazi Party. Germany was divided into forty-two *Gau*. The conquered territories also had this system.
Gauleiter	The highest-ranking Nazi Party official in a *Gau*. The *Gauleiter* was responsible for all political and economic activity, mobilisation of labour and civil defence in his area.
Gefreiter	Enlisted rank. It was senior to the rank of private, but was not considered an NCO.
Geheimfeldpolizei	Secret Field Police of the *Heer* (Army).
Geheimstaatspolizei	State Secret Police. The abbreviation of the word was *Gestapo*. Was *Amt IV* (Department IV) of the *Reichssicherheitshauptamt* (*RSHA*); the Reich Main Security Office.
Gemeindepolizei	Municipal police.
Generalkommando	General command. Refers to a corps-sized unit in the military.
Gendarmerie	The rural police, including motorised units for traffic control.

Generalgouvernement	The General Government, i.e., German-occupied Poland administered by a German civilian governor with its headquarters in the city of Cracow. It was classed as an appended territory (*Nebenland*, meaning outlying) of the Reich.
Genesenden	Convalescent. Example: *Genesendenbataillon* (convalescent battalion).
Generalleutnant	Lieutenant general.
Goldfassanen	Golden Pheasants. It was basically the way the representatives of Alfred Rosenberg's Office for the Eastern Occupied Territories were referred to pejoratively. They wore the Nazi Party brown uniform with gold epaulets (shoulder insignia). The term was derogatory and it represented Nazi opportunists who sought their fortune by exploiting the captured Eastern territories, with no regard for the people they ruled.
Grenadier	Elite infantrymen of the seventeenth and eighteenth centuries. In 1943, Hitler redesignated most of his infantry units as 'Grenadier', thus elevating them to the status of elite troops, if only in name.
Grenzpolizei	Border police.
Grenzschutz	Frontier, or border.
Gruppenführer	The SS equivalent to *Generalleutnant* (lieutenant general).
Gulag	Soviet penal camp for political dissidents and others considered enemies of the state. The concentration camps were usually located in Siberia. Very few ever left these camps.[1]

H

Hauptamt	Main office.
Hauptmann	Captain.
Hauptmann der Polizei	Captain of the police.
Hauptsturmführer	The SS rank equivalent of captain.
Heer	Army.
Heeresgebiet	Army Region. It usually referred to an army rear area.
Heeresgruppe	Army group.
Heimat	Homeland.
Heimatwehr	The uncapitalised version of home guard.
Heimwehr	Home Guard (capitalised).
Hilfsdienst	Auxiliary service.
Hilfswilliger	Helper or assistant.
Höhere SS und Polizeiführer abbreviated to (HSSPF)	Higher SS and Police Commander. Also referred to as Senior SS and Police Commander. These staffs represented *Reichsführer SS* Heinrich Himmler's personal representatives in the Reich military districts, and in the occupied territories.
Hundertschaft	Century, equivalent to a company or more of men.

I

im Dienst	In service.
Infanterie	Infantry.
Inspekteur	Inspector.
Iwan	Ivan, the German slang term used to denote a Red Army soldier.

J

Jagdkommando	Hunting commando. In Second World War terms, a German anti-partisan unit of between a platoon and company in size.
Jagdpanzer	Tank destroyer.
Jäger	Hunter, but in military terms it meant light infantry.

K

Kaukasische	Caucasian. In the Second World War the Germans recruited Caucasian volunteers from the Caucasus mountains in southern Russia.
Kavallerie	Cavalry.
kollektive Gewaltmassnahmen	Collective violence, but meaning 'collective punishment'.
Kommandeur	Commander.
Kommandeur der Ordnungspolizei	Commander of the uniformed police. Abbreviated as *KdO*, it was a subordinate command to the *BdO*.
Kommandeur der Sicherheitspolizei	Commander of the security police. Abbreviated as *KdS*, it was a subordinate command to the *BdS*.
Kommissarbefehl	Commissar Order, the infamous command that ordered that all Red Army political officers were to be shot, even if they surrendered.
Kompanieführer	Company commander.
Konzentrationslager (KZL)	Concentration camp.
Korporal	Corporal.
Korps	Corps.
Korpsabteilung	Army detachment.
Korück	Abbreviation for *Kommandeur des Rückwartige Heeresgebiete* (Commander of the Army Rear Area)
Kriegsgefangener	PoW, prisoner of war. The plural of the word is *Kriegsgefangene*.
Kriegsmarine	The German Navy, as it was referred to between 1935 and 1945 (the Third Reich era).
Krim	Crimea.
Kriminalpolizei	Criminal police.
Krimtatar	Crimean Tartar. A Turkic people that live in the Crimea.

L

Landesschützen	The literal word is provincial shooters, but for the Nazi period it refers to older-age men who were members of regional defence battalions. Like the Army security forces, these battalions were employed behind the German lines. They guarded important geographical structures, such as bridges and rail lines, and physical structures vital to the war effort. They also took part in anti-partisan drives.
Landkreis	A rural administrative district.
Landrat	A district administrator.
Lebensraum	Living space. The Nazi belief that Germans needed land upon which to grow and expand.
Lebensunwertes Leben	Life unworthy of life. In Nazi thinking, a person who does not deserve to exist.
Leichte	Light.
Lettische (*lett.*)	Latvian. The abbreviation of the word is in parenthesis.
Leutnant	Lieutenant.
Litauische (*lit.*)	Lithuanian. The abbreviation of the word is in parenthesis.
Luftwaffe	The German Air Force, as it was referred to between 1935 and 1945 (the Third Reich) era).

M

Major	Major, a rank between captain and colonel.
Massenmörder	Mass murder.
Militär	Military.
Mitte	Centre, as in *Heeresgruppe Mitte* (Army Group Centre).
Mörser	Mortar.

N

Nachricht or Nachrichten	Communication, signals, or even intelligence.
Nachrichtendienst	Intelligence service.
Nachschub	Supply.
Nebelwerfer	Rocket artillery
Nord	North.
NSKK	The abbreviation for *Nationalsozialisten Kraftfahrkorps* (National Socialist Motor Corps).

O

Oberbaustab	The higher military construction staff. This headquarters usually controlled several construction regiments.
Oberbürgermeister	Lord mayor.
Oberführer	SS rank below *Brigadeführer*. There was no equivalent rank in the British or US Army.
Obergruppenführer	SS rank equivalent to Major-General.
Oberstleutnant	Lieutenant colonel. Example: *Oberstleutnant der Polizei* (lieutenant colonel of the Police).
Oberstgruppenführer	Like *Obergruppenführer,* the SS rank equivalent to Lieutenant-General.
Obersturmbannführer	SS rank equivalent to Lieutenant-Colonel.
OKH	Abbreviation for *Oberkommando des Heeres* (Army Hugh Command).
OKW	Abbreviation for *Oberkommando der Wehrmacht* (Armed Forces High Command).
Omakaitse	Estonian term meaning 'self-defence'.
Ordnungsdienst	The auxiliary service made up of foreign volunteers, that assisted the German police.
Ordnungspolizei	Order police.

Organisation Todt	This was a semi-military Nazi government agency established in 1933, and used mainly for the construction of strategic highways and military fortifications and installations.
Ortskommandantur	Local Command: they were local army headquarters below the *Feldkommandantur*.
Ost	East.
Ostbataillon	A battalion of foreign volunteers from Eastern Europe, including the USSR.
Ostfront	Eastern Front.
Ostheer	'Eastern Army'. It refers to the German Army fighting on the Eastern Front.
Ostland	A title given by the Germans to the Baltic region encompassing the Baltic countries of Lithuania, Latvia, and Estonia, and part of Belarus (White Russia).
Ostministerium	The (Nazi) Ministry for the Occupied Eastern Territories.
Osttruppen	Eastern troops that served in either the *Heer*, *SS*, or *Police* forces of the Third Reich.
Ostvolker	Eastern people.

P

Panzer	Armoured.
Panzerfaust	Literally 'armoured fist'. It was a disposable, hand-held, one-shot, anti-tank weapon.
Panzerschreck	German name for Bazooka, the hand-held, reusable anti-tank weapon.
Partisan	Partisan. The plural form of the word is *Partisanen*.
Partisanenjäger	Partisan hunter.
Partisanhelfer	Partisan helper.
Pferd	Horse.

Pionier	Engineer.
Pleskau	German spelling for the Russian city of Pskov.
Polizei	*Police.*
Prepjet-Sümpfe	German spelling for the Pinsk (Pripyat) Marshes. In English the spelling is Pripet.
Putsch	An internal uprising against an existing government, like a *coup d'etat.*

Q

Quartiėrmeister	Quartermaster.

R

RAD	Abbreviation for *Reichsarbeitsdienst*, the (Nazi) National Labour Service.
Radfahr	Bicycle.
Regiment	Regiment.
Reich	Nation.
Reichsführer SS	National Leader of the SS.
Reichskommissar	National Commissioner.
Reichskommissariat Ostland	The civilian occupation government in the Baltic states led by Hinrich Lohse.
Reichskommissariat Ukraine	The civilian occupation government in Ukraine headed by Erich Koch.
Reichsministerium für die besetzten Ostgebiete	Reich Ministry for the Occupied Eastern Territories.
Reiter	Horse, cavalryman.
Reserve	Reserve.
Reval	German spelling for the Estonian capital of Tallinn.
RSHA	Abbreviation for *Reichssicherheitshauptamt* (Reich Security Main Office).
Rückwärtig	Behind, as in the rear of the front lines.
Russische (russ.)	Russian. The abbreviation of the word is in parenthesis.

S

SA	*Sturmabteilung* (storm detachment). The militarised members of the Nazi Party.
Schlachtfliegerstaffel.	Attack squadron.
Schule	School.
Schutzmannschaft (Schuma)	Self Defence Guard. These men, organised into battalions, assisted the SS and Police. The abbreviation of the word is in parenthesis.
Selbstschutz	Self-defence. Referring to Eastern-raised militia units of volunteers from the USSR and other Eastern countries. It was originally to have consisted of ethnic Germans from these territories, but also included large numbers of non-ethnic German people.
Sicherheitsdienst	The SS Security Service.
Sicherung	Security.
Sipo	Abbreviation for the word *Sicherheitspolizei* (Security Police).
Sonder	Special. In Third Reich terminology, it could refer to a special detachment or even a penal formation.
Sonderdienst	Special Service. This organisation was a part of the German occupation force in Poland. It was made up of ethnic German poles serving as guards.
Sonderkommando	Sub-group detachment of the *Einsatzkommando.*
Sonderstab	Special staff.
SS *(Schutzstaffel)*	The SS originated as a small core of bodyguards for Adolf Hitler while he travelled the countryside giving speeches. This paramilitary branch of the Nazi Party expanded exponentially

	beginning in 1933, creating numerous sperate departments, in much the same way that an octopus has many tentacles. They included such branches as the *Allgemeine SS*, *Waffen SS*, and *SS Totenkopfverbände*.
SSPF	Abbreviation for *SS und Polizeiführer* (SS and Police Leader)
SS Waffengruppe	An armed group, usually or regimental or brigade size, serving in the *Waffen SS*.
Stabsoffizier	Staff officer.
Staffeln Flieger Gruppe	Squadron Air Group.
Stamm	Cadre.
Standarte	Basically another way to say regiment. The formation so named was equivalent to a regiment in size.
Standartenführer	SS colonel.
Strafe	Penal, referring to a penal (punishment) formation, such as *Strafbataillon* (penal battalion).
Sturmbannführer	SS major.
Sturmkompanie	Assault company.
Süd	South.

T

Technische Nothilfe	The Technical Emergency Corps, an auxiliary police force of the ORPO consisting of engineers, technicians and specialists concerned with communications, construction work, public utilities, salvage and recovery, etc. Each police regiment that entered the USSR in 1941 had one TN Company attached. Later on, these companies were detached and expanded into battalions.
Teilkommando	A sub-unit of a special force, such as a *Teilkommando* of an *SS Sonderkommando*.

Totenkopfstandarte	Any one of a series of SS Death's Head *(Totenkopfstandarte)* regiments.
Truppenübungslager	Troop Training Camp.
Truppenübungsplatz	Troop Training Ground.

U

Ukrainische (ukr.)	Ukrainian. The abbreviation of the word is in parenthesis.
Und (u.)	And. The abbreviation of the word is found in parenthesis.

V

Verband	Formation. Could also mean a military unit of brigade size.
Verbindungsoffizier	Liaison officer.
Vernichtungskrieg	War of extermination.
Vernichtungslager	Extermination camp.
V1/V2	These were designations for two types of flying bombs – the V1 pulse-jet powered and the V2 rocket powered – that the Nazis employed, mainly against the city of London.

W

Wach	Guard.
Wachbataillon	Guard battalion.
Waffen SS	Armed SS. The SS ground combat formations that fought in the field.
Wehrkreis	A German military district.
Wehrmachtbefehlshaber	The Armed Forces Commander for a military region or area. Example: *Wehrmachtbefehlshaber der Rückwärtig Heeresgebiet* (Armed Forces Commander of the Army Rear Area).
Weissruthenische	White Russian. Properly spelled using the *eszett: Weißruthenische.* It refers to Belarus.
Weltanschauungskrieg	Ideological war.
Wolga	Volga.

Z

Zug — Platoon.

Zugführer — Platoon leader.

z.b.V. — Abbreviation for *zur besondere Verwendung* (for special use, or special employment).

Appendix II

GERMAN REAR AREA ADMINISTRATIVE COMMANDS IN POLAND

Oberfeldkommandantur:
OK 393 - (12.12.1941) Warsaw (Kiev in 1942)

Feldkommandantur:
FK V-579 - (14.09.1939)

Ortskommandantur:
OK-401 - (20.05.1941) Poland
OK I-402 - (29.05.1941) Przemysl
OK I-403 - (29.05.1941) Rawa Ruska
OK I-404 - (29.05.1941) Poland
OK I-405 - (10.05.1941) Petrikau
OK I-406 - (10.05.1941) Poland
OK I-407 - (20.05.1941 Kolomea
OK I-408 - (16.05.1941) Biala-Podlaska
OK I-410 - (19.05.1941) Hrubieszow
OK I-408 - (01.06.1941) Poland
OK I-411 - (01.06.1941) Solokow
OK I-412 - (06.05.1941) Wolomia
OK II-421 - (21.05.1941) Poland
OK II-422 - (29.05.1941) Krynica
OK II-423 - (29.05.1941) Poland
OK II-424 - (29.05.1941) Poland
OK II-425 - (29.05.1941 Sarny, Poland MiG
OK II-426 - (29.05.1941 Poland MiG

OK II-427 - (10.05.1941 Ostrowicze, Poland MiG
OK II-428 - (01.06.1941 Chmielnik, Poland MiG
OK II-429 - (01.06.1941 Radomslo, Poland MiG
OK II-430 - (01.06.1941 Krassnystaw, Poland MiG
OK II-431 - (01.06.1941 Podwoloczyska, Poland MiG
OK II-432 - (01.06.1941 Wlodawa, Poland MiG
OK II-433 - (25.05.1941 Lubartow, Poland MiG
OK II-434 - (27.05.1941 Poland MiG
OK II-435 - (01.06.1941 Poland MiG
OK II-436 - (01.06.1941 Warsaw, Poland
OK II-437 - (28.05.1941 Poland MiG
OK II-438 - (21.05.1941 Otwock, Poland MiG
OK II-439 - (20.05.1941 Poland MiG
OK I-523 - (26.08.1939) Poland MiG
OK I-524 - (26.08.1939) Lublin, Poland MiG
OK II-525 - (02.08.1939) Sandomierz, Poland MiG
OK I-572 - (26.08.1939) Poland MiG
OK I-573 - (26.08.1939) Poland MiG
OK I-604 - (10.06.1940) Poland MiG
OK I-617 - (26.08.1939) Jaroslaw, Poland MiG
OK I-628 - (26.08.1939) Grojec, Poland MiG
OK I-640 - (26.08.1939) Reichshof, Poland MiG
OK II-646 - (26.08.1939) Ostwock, Poland MiG
OK I-648 - (26.08.1939 Krosno, Poland MiG
OK I-897 - (08.09.1940) Neu-Sandez, Poland MiG
OK I-898 - (10.09.1940) Krakau, Poland MiG
OK I-899 - (10.09.1940) Konskie, Poland MiG
OK I-901 - (05.09.1940) Tomasow, Poland MiG
OK I-902 - (10.09.1940) Krasnik, Poland MiG
OK I-903 - (10.09.1940) Zamosz, Poland MiG
OK I-904 - (10.09.1940) Cholm, Poland MiG
OK I-905 - (06.09.1940) Lowicz, Poland MiG
OK I-906 - (06.09.1940) Wolomin, Poland MiG
OK I-907 - (06.09.1940) Warsaw, Poland MiG
OK II-910 - (06.09.1940) Ostrow Mazowiecki, Poland MiG
OK I-923 - (25.10.1940) Kamiebba, Poland MiG
OK I-924 - (25.10.1940) Poland MiG
OK I-928 - (24.10.1940) Siedlce

Geheimfeldpolizei Gruppe:
GFP-13 (26.08.1939) Poland

Appendix III

GERMAN COMMANDERS OF MAJOR POLICE FORMATIONS

Gendarmerie-Bataillon 1 (motorisiert)
Commander: *Major der Gendarmerie* Erich Schwieger (1942–April 1943)
Major der Gendarmerie Kurt Sack (May 1943–1944)

Gendarmerie-Bataillon 2 (motorisiert)
Major der Gendarmerie Karl Axt (1943–18 December 1944)

Polizei-Kavallerie-Bataillon 1
Major der Schutzpolizei Ernst Aschrich (1941–1942)
Major der Schutzpolizei Adolf Hahn (1942–1 August 1944)
Major der Schutzpolizei Wilhelm Hofmann (2 August 1944–February 1945)

Polizei-Kavallerie-Bataillon 2
Major der Schutzpolizei Wilhelm Albrecht (July 1941–April 1942)
Major der Schutzpolizei Wilhelm Hoffmann (April 1942–February 1943)

Polizei-Kavallerie-Bataillon 3
Major der Schutzpolizei Alfred Eggert (1943–1944)

Polizeiregiment Galizien [existence as late as December 1941]
Oberst der Schutzpolizei Paul Worm
Oberstleutnant der Schutzpolizei Joachim Stach (9 August–11 November 1941)
Major der Schutzpolizei Franz Heitzinger (12–15 November 1941)
Oberstleutnant der Schutzpolizei Joachim Stach (16 November–12 December 1941)

Major der Schutzpolizei Franz Heitzinger (13 December 1941–8 January 1942)[1]
Oberstleutnant der Schutzpolizei Joachim Stach (9 January 1942–May 1942)

SS Polizei-Regiment 1
Oberstleutnant der Schutzpolziei Hermann Helwes
SS-Standartenführer und Oberst der Schutzpolizei Helmut Dörner (1944–1945)

SS Polizei-Regiment 2
Oberst der Schutzpolizei Paul Worm (1941–?)

SS Polizei-Regiment 3
SS-Standartenführer und Oberst der Polizei Karl Jakob Heinrich Brenner

SS Polizei-Regiment 4
Oberstleutnant der Schutzpolizei Bolko von Schweinichen (1942–April 1943)
Oberstleutnant der Schutzpolizei Erich Skowronnek (April 1943–15 July 1944)
Major der Schutzpolizei Walter Danz (16 July 1944–1945)

SS Polizei-Regiment 5
Generalmajor der Schutzpolizei Andreas May (July 1942–June 1944)
Oberstleutnant der Schutzpolizei Franz Lechthaler (15 July–?)

SS Polizei-Regiment 6
Oberstleutnant der Schutzpolizei Mailwald Barcs (June 1942–?)

SS Polizei-Regiment 7
Oberstleutnant der Schutzpolizei Schaber (1942–April 1943)
Oberstleutnant der Schutzpolizei Walter Giesecke (April 1943–6 July 1944)
SS-Obersturmbannführer und Oberst der Schutzpolziei Karl Schümer (7–22 July 1944)
SS-Obersturmbannführer und Oberst der Schutzpolziei Hans Traupe (23 July 1944–October 1944)
SS-Obersturmbannführer und Oberst der Schutzpolziei Otto Prager (October 1944–28 April 1945)

SS Polizei-Regiment 8
Oberstleutnant der Schutzpolizei Ernst Weis (June 1942–?)

SS Polizei-Regiment 9
Oberstleutnant der Gendarmerie Hans Köllner (29 January–8 May 1945)

SS Polizei-Regiment 10
Oberst der Schutzpolizei Rene Rosenbauer (? June 1941–9 July 1942)
SS-Standartenführer und Oberst der Schutzpolizei Hermann Kintrup (9 July 1942–15 December 1943)
? *Oberst der Gendarmerie* Hans Köllner (15 December 1943–15 July 1944)
? *Major der Gendarmerie* Hellmuth Köning (1943–14 July1944)
Oberst der Schutzpolizei Richard Stahn (15 July 1944–20 October 1944)
Oberstleutnant der Schutzpolizei Fritz Auscher (20 October–31 December 1944)
SS-Sturmbannführer und Major der Schutzpolizei Gustav Zuschneid (February–8 May 1945)

SS Polizei-Regiment 11
Oberst der Schutzpolizei Walter Griep (July 1942–?)

SS Polizei-Regiment 12
SS-Standartenfuhrer und Oberst der Schutzpolizei Wilhelm Machtan (July 1942–?)

SS Polizei-Regiment 13
SS-Obersturmbannführer und Oberstleutnant der Schutzpolizei Hans Fleckner (15 November 1943–20 October 1944)[2]

SS Polizei-Regiment 14
SS-Sturmbannführer und Oberst der Schutzpolizei Bernhard Griese (29 March 1943–6 March 1944)
SS-Standartenführer und Oberst der Schutzpolizei Willy Nickel (6 March 1944–January 1945)
SS-Sturmbannführer und Oberst der Schutzpolizei Bernhard Griese (January–April 1945)

SS Polizei-Regiment 15
Oberst der Schutzpolizei Leo von Braunschweig (15 March 1943–15 July 1943)
Oberstleutnant der Schutzpolizei Ludwig Buch (15 July 1943–20 October 1944)

SS Polizei-Regiment 16
Oberstleutnant der Schutzpolizei Karl Kemper (1942–February 1943)
Oberstleutnant der Schutzpolizei Emil Kursk (March 1943–June 1944)
Oberstleutnant der Schutzpolizei Walter Titel (July 1944–1944)
Oberstleutnant der Schutzpolizei Walter Gieseke (20 October 1944–1944)

SS Polizei-Regiment 17
Oberstleutnant der Schutzpolizei Erwin Gresser (?–20 April 1944 KIA)
Oberstleutnant der Schutzpolizei Franz Lechthaler (4 July 1944–?)

SS-Polizei-Gebirgsjäger-Regiment 18
Oberstleutnant der Schutzpolizei Hermann Franz (June 1942–August 1943)[3]
Oberstleutnant der Schutzpolizei Hans Hösl (August 1943–2 October 1944, wounded)
Major der Schutzpolizei Otto Mann (2–19 October 1944, KIA)
Major der Schutzpolizei Johann Poys (20 October 1944–8 May 1945)

SS Polizei-Regiment 19
SS-Standartenführer und Oberst der Schutzpolizei Bernhard Griese (9 July 1942–April 1943)
Oberstleutnant der Schutzpolizei Hubert Kolbinger (April 1943–15 July 1944)
Major der Schutzpolizei Alois Bartscht (15 July 1944–1945)

SS-Polizei-Regiment 22
Oberst der Schutzpolizei Rudolf Haring (June 1942–?)

***SS Polizei-Regiment 23* (Krakau)**
Oberst der Schutzpolizei Max Montua, (September 1939–February 1940)
Oberstleutnant der Schutzpolizei Werner Spitta, (February 1940)
Oberst der Schutzpolizei Hermann Keuper (March 1940–6 November 1941)
Oberstleutnant der Schutzpolizei Andreas May (7 November 1941–12 December 1941)
Oberstleutnant der Schutzpolizei Richard Gaβler (13 December 1941–30 July 1942 – died)
Oberstleutnant der Gendarmerie Werner Bardua (1 August 1942–17 April 1944)
Oberst der Gendarmerie Felix Bauer (April 1944–14 November 1944)
Oberstleutnant der Schutzpolizei Franz Heitsinger (15 November–1945)

***SS Polizei-Regiment 24* (Radom)**
Oberst der Schutzpolizei Ferdinand Heske (Nov 1939–Nov 1940)
Generalmajor der Polizei Paul Worm (Oct 1940–June 1942)
Oberstleutnant der Schutzpolizei Walter von Soosten (November 1942–20 April 1943)
Oberstleutnant der Schutzpolizei Russel (21 April 1943–9 April 1944)
Major der Gendarmerie Erich Schwieger (10 April–14 July 1944)
Oberst der Schutzpolizei Felix Bauer (15 July 1944–22 October 1944)
Oberstleutnant der Schutzpolizei Borgsen (23 Octoberr–2 December 1944)
Oberstleutnant der Schutzpolizei Paust (3 December 1944–January 1945)

SS Polizei-Regiment 25
Oberst der Schutzpolizei Walter Griphan (February–November 1941)
Oberstleutnant der Schutzpolizei Walther von Soosten (November 1941–May 1942)
Oberstleutnant der Schutzpolizei Hermann Kintrup (June 1942–1943)
Oberstleutnant der Schutzpolizei Josef Vogts (16 February–14 July 1944)
Oberstleutnant der Schutzpolizei Hermann Kintrup (June 1942–28 October 1943)
Oberstleutnant der Schutzpolizei Konrad Rheindorf (29 October 1943–October 1944)
Oberst der Schutzpolizei Rudolf Haring (October 1944–21 February 1945)

SS Polizei-Regiment 26
Oberstleutnant der Schutzpolizei Walter Strelow (July 1942–1944)
Oberstleutnant der Schutzpolizei Weissig (August 1944–November 1944)

SS Polizei-Regiment 27
SS-Standartenführer und Oberstleutnant der Schutzpolizei Walther Endler (July 1942–July 1944)
SS-Oberführer und Oberst der Schutzpolizei Hans Müller-Brunckhorst (July 1944–?)

SS Polizei-Regiment 28 'Todt'
Oberstleutnant der Schutzpolizei Fritz Helmut Kösterbeck (18 August 1942–20 October 1944)
Major der Schutzpolziei Johann Heinacker (20 October 1944–8 May 1945)

Polizei-Schützenregiment 31
Oberst der Schutzpolizei Heinrich Hannibal (21 April 1943–August 1944)
Major der Schutzpolizei Erich Vogt (August 1944–1945)
Included *Schutzmannschaft-Bataillone 51* and *54* as the *II.* and *III. Bataillone*

Polizei-Schützenregiment 32
Oberstleutnant der Schutzpolizei Franz Lechthaler (May–November 1943)

Polizei-Schützenregiment 33
Oberstleutnant der Gendarmerie Ernst Köllner (21 April 1943–May 1944)
Included *Schutzmannschaft-Bataillone 58* and *59* as the *II.* and *III. Bataillone*

Polizei-Schützenregiment 34
Oberstleutnant der Polizei Martin Dietz (1943–30 April 1944)
Oberstleutnant der Schutzpolizei Franz Wichmann (1 May 1944–1 September 1944)
Major der Schutzpolizei Nachtwey (2 September 1944–1945)

Polizei-Schützenregiment 35
Oberstleutnant der Schutzpolizei Friedrich Korff (30 April 1944–?)

Polizei-Schützenregiment 36
Oberstleutnant der Polizei Martin Valtin (May 1943–1944)

Polizei-Schützenregiment 37 (existed November 1943 to March 1944)
Oberstleutnant der Schutzpolizei Wilhelm Giesecke

Polizei-Schützenregiment 38
Oberstleutnant der Schutzpolizei Ernst Weiß
(Formed in August 1944 by the *Höheren-SS und Polizeiführer 'Schwarzes Meer'* in Galatz, Romania, and disbanded in November 1944).

Polizei-Regiment Ulrich (temporary affair)
Commander: *Major der Schutzpolizei* Ulrich
III. Bataillon der SS Polizei-Regiment 16
lettische Polizei-Bataillon 271
On 17 August 1944 *Polizei-Regiment Ulrich* was subordinated to *VI. SS-Freiwilligen-Armeekorps (lettisch).*[4]

Polizei Regiment Schulz (*Generalmajor der Polizei* Fritz Schulz)
– defending Königsberg in April 1945

SS Polizei-Kampfgruppe Schuberth (*Generalmajor der Ordnungspolizei* Schuberth)
– defending Königsberg in April 1945. Created from the remnants of three police regiments plus the SS and policemen command staff in Königsberg. This battlegroup contained two principal units:

Polizei-Schützenregiment 31 (*Major der Schutzpolizei* Erich Vogt)
I. Bataillon (only)
Although *Polizei-Schützenregiment 31* was officially disbanded in August 1944, one battalion *(I. Bataillon),* the German battalion (the *II.* and *III. Bataillon* were manned by Ukrainians) survived. It was led by *Major der Schutzpolizei* Voigt and continued to exist. It eventually joined *SS-Polizei-Kampfgruppe Hannibal* in East Prussia, before being assigned to battlegroup Schuberth.

Höhere-SS und Polizeiführer Nordost
One mixed battalion of SS/police troops

The following police regiments also defended Königsberg, but operated independently of ***Kampfgruppe Schuberth:***

SS-Regiment Böhme (*SS-Oberführer* Horst Böhme, former head of the BdS in Königsber).
I. Bataillon
II. Bataillon
III. Bataillon

SS-Polizei-Kampfgruppe Hannibal (*SS-Brigadeführer* und *Oberstleutnant der Schutzpolizei* Heinrich Hannibal). This battlegroup contained two principal units:

SS-Polizei-Regiment 4 (*Oberstleutnant der Schutzpolizei* Walter Danz)
I. Bataillon
II. Bataillon
III. Bataillon

Polizei-Geschütz-Abteilung I (three artillery batteries).

The following three police regiments were located in the Italian–Austrian theatre:

Polizeiregiment Brixen: *Oberst der Schutzpolizei* Josef Albert.
Polizeiregiment Bozen: *SS-Sturmbannführer und Oberstleutnant der Schutzpolizei* Ernst Korn.
SS-Polizeiregiment Alpenvorland: *Oberst der Gendarmerie* Hans Köllner (June 1944–1945).

SS-Polizeiregiment Schlanders: *Major der Schutzpolizei* Georg Hahn

SS-Polizei-Regiment z.b.V. a.k.a. *Polizeiregiment 11* (July 1942)
Oberst der Schutzpolizei Walter Griep (1941–July 1942)

SS-Polizei-Regiment 2 z.b.V. (becomes *SS-Polizei-Regiment 30*)
Oberstleutnant der Schutzpolizei Fritz Auscher (January–February 1945)

SS-Polizei-Regiment 29 a.k.a. *SS u. Polizei-Grenadier-Regiment 89 (35. SS-Polizei-Division)*
SS-Standartenführer Friedrich Wilhelm Korff (?–April 1945)
SS-Sturmbannführer Heinrich Spann (April–May 1945)

***SS-Polizei-Regiment* 30** a.k.a. *SS u. Polizei-Grenadier-Regiment 90 (35. SS-Polizei-Division)*
Oberstleutnant der Schutzpolizei Fritz Auscher (March–May 1945)

***SS-Polizei Regiment* 14** a.k.a. *SS u. Polizei-Grenadier-Regiment 91 (35. SS-Polizei-Division)*
SS-Standartenführer und Oberst der Schutzpolizei Willy Nickel (February–May 1945)

Brigade Wirth, a.k.a. *35. SS und Polizei-Grenadier-Division*
SS-Oberführer Johannes Wirth (January–28 February 1945)
SS-Standartenführer Rüdiger Pipkorn (1 March–27 April 1945, KIA)

BIBLIOGRAPHY

Primary Source Material

Belarus Central State Archives, Minsk, Records 1941–1949

Records Group RG-53.002M, Reels 3, 5, 11, and 13.

Belarusian State Minsk Archives, USHMM RG-53.002M (1993.A.0082), Folder 1262 and 1265.

Grodno Oblast Archive Records, 1940–1944. RG-53.004M. Reel No. 2, Fond 1, Section 100 – Grodno Amtskommissar correspondence.

Grodno Oblast Archive Records, 1940–1944. Records Group RG-53.004M, Reel 5.

Grodno Oblast Archive Records, 1940–1944. RG-53.004M. Reel No. 2, Fond 1, Section 100 – Grodno Amtskommissar correspondence.

Military Historical Institute (Prague), Records 1941–1944

Records Group RG-48.004M, Reels 1, 2, 3, 4, and 6.

RG-48.004M, (1993.A.0019), Reel No. 3 – *1. SS Infanterie-Brigade (mot.)– 29.11.42, 'Aufmarsch Glebokie'.*

Bundesarchiv, Koblenz

BAK-N756/214a, *SS Kampfgruppe von Gottberg: Band Zwei. Vgl. BArch Bestand RS 4 Brigaden, Legionen, Standarten sowie Kampfgruppen und Einheiten der Waffen-SS; Verschiedene Sperrverbände und Eingreifgruppen Fotografie von SS-Hauptsturmführer Robert Ancans.*

BAK-NS19-13, Reichsführer-SS Meldung an der Führer über Bandenbekämpfung. Feldkommandostelle, 8.10.1942. Neldung Nr. 23.

BAK-NS19-03, *Reichssicherheitshauptamt Nachrichten Uebermittlung,* NR 162/42 (G) AUS 160 ZWEI/42, pp.12–13.

BAK-NS19-11. 470

Bandenkampf Unternehmen – Folio: NS19/1, 1500, 1671, 1463, 2661, 2835, 3140, and 3695.

Meldung vom 06.06.1943 über die Personalstärke der landeseigenen Verbände (BA-MA, RH 21-2/509, Bl. 78 und 78r). Vgl. Tabelle im Anhang auf Seite 405f. Der Arbeit. Operations Abteilung, NO. 5645/42, Heeresgruppe Mitte. 15.07.42.

RH 22-229. Berück, Kriegstagebuch 07.04.42.

Bundesarchiv, Freiburg

1. *Reichssicherheitshauptamt. Höhere SS und Polizeiführer Ostland. 7.8.42. BAF, NS–19/1, 1500, 1671, 1463, 2661, 2835, 3140 and 3645.*
2. *Heeresgruppe Mitte, Ia. Nr.14550/43 g.Kdos.,8.XII.43., Anlage zur Kriegstagebuch, Heeresgruppe Mitte, Führungsabteilung, Akte XXIII, Heft 12, 1.X.-31.XII.43. 65002/24. Bundesarchiv, Frieburg. Chef der Sicherungstruppen – Rückwartigen Heeresgebiet 102, Operationsabteilung Nr.272/43, 25.1.43. 23).*
3. *Nachricht A.O.K. 9. Die im Fernschreiben B.d.O. i. G.G., Ia Tgb.-Nr. 3717/44 (G) vom 29.9.44 beantragte Herauslösung der SS. Pol. Reiter-Abt. III und des Schuma-Batl. (lit.) Nr. 252 konnte im Hinblick auf die Kämpfe im Raum Warschau und die dem Obergruppenführer von dem Bach vom Reichsführer-SS für den Einsatz der Kräfte verliehenen Sondervollmachten bisher nicht durchgeführt werden.*
4. Ortskommandantur I/524 to *Amt I*, Memorandum on the Conversation with Police Commanders at Army Headquarters XXXII on 8 December 1939 and 10 December 1939, file *Ortskommandantur I/524*, sygn. 31, pp.378–79, WAPL; Globocnik to Chief, District Lublin, 13 February 1940, file *Gouverneur, Distrikt Lublin*, sygn. 891, p.10, WAPL, and NARA RG-242 A3343/SSO, 0156B/242-243, formerly the Berlin Document Centre – now under the administration of the *Bundesarchiv*, Berlin. Documents of the Labour Office, Biała-Podlaska to Labour Department, Lublin, 18 July 1940, file Gouverneur, District Lublin, sygn. 746, pp.41–43, WAPL.
5. *Vorschlagsliste für die Verleihung von Kriegsverdienstkreuzen II. Klasse mit Schwertern vom 6.7.1941*, in BA D-HZM 1384 A 20.

Bundesarchiv/Militärarchiv Berlin-Lichterfelde

BA-MA WF 01/2151, Bl. 816.

BA-MA WF 03/15831, *Feldpolizeidirektor beim Befehlshaber Heeresgebiet 103.*

BA-MA RH–19 VII/2, Bl. 2.

BA-MA RH 19 XI/37, *Bericht des GFP-Angehörigen Georg Koch*, 37.

BA-MA RH 22/31, *Meldung Direktor GFP, Mai 1942.*

BA-MA RH 22/60, *Bericht GFP für Heeresgebiet B, August 1942.*

BA-MA RH 22/86, 27.

BA-MA RH 22/173, *Meldung Direktor GFP, Juli 1942.*

BA-MA RH 22/199 *Befehlshaber rückwärtiger Heeresgebiete Tätigkeitsberichte der Geheimen Feldpolizeigruppen* 1, 708, 719, 725, 730, 739, 721. – *Stärkemeldungen Laufzeit: Jan.–Aug. 1942.*

BA-MA RH 22/200 *Befehlshaber rückwärtiger Heeresgebiete Tätigkeitsberichte der Geheimen Feldpolizeigruppen 1, 708, 719, 725, 730, 739, 721. – Stärkemeldungen Laufzeit: Sept.–Dez. 1942.*

BA-MA: RH 23-25, *'Befehl Nr. 1 für Unternehmen 'Dreieck', 11 September 1942'.*

BA-MA: RH 23-25, 'Gefechtsbericht über Unternehmen "Dreieck" und "Viereck" vom 17.9–2.10.1942, 19 October 1942'.

BA/MA RH-24-22/21, folio 88–89.

BA-MA RH 24-22/23, *Jäger – Gen.Kdo.22 AK, 14 May 1944, Ic – Aussenstelle Korfu – Korpsgruppe Joannina/Ic, 25 April 1944.*

BA-MA RH-24, 23–24.

BA-MA RH-26 /117/16.

BA-MA RH-40, 10.

BA-MA RH-40, 11.

BA-MA RH 48.

Dienststellen und Einheiten der Ordnungstruppen, der Geheimen Feldpolizei, der Betreuungs und Streifendienste des Heeres. RW 40/170: Fester Platz Kreta, Sept. 1944 RW 40/172: Tätigkeitsbericht, Juli–Aug. 1944; Bundesarchiv.

Krüger to Gunst, 14 November 1939, W. Gunst SS Officer file (former BDC), RGp-242, A3343/SSO/043A/321, NARA; judgment in proceedings against Friedrich Paulus, May 26, 1977, p.6, file 4 Ks 1/74, State Prosecutor's Office in Frankfurt am Main.

Krüger to Gunst, 14 November 1939, W. Gunst SS Officer file (formerly Berlin Document Centre), RGp-242, A3343/SSO/043A/321, NARA; judgment in proceedings against Friedrich Paulus, May 26, 1977, p.6, file 4 Ks 1/74, State Prosecutor's Office in Frankfurt am Main.

National Archives, College Park, Maryland

NARA Microfilm T-78

Roll 413 and 645.

NARA Microfilm T-175

Roll 16, 111, 129, 140, 141, 174, 191, 225, 233.

NARS Microfilm T-315,

Roll 1665, 1687, 2213, 2214, 2215, 2216

NARS Microfilm T-580

Roll 88.

NARA RG-238 Working Conference on 23 April 1940, Service Diary of Governor General Hans Frank, Vol. 9.

National Archives, Kew, Richmond, Surrey, United Kingdom

CSDIC (UK) SIR (Special Interrogation Report) 730 (8 Aug 1944) 'Geheime Feldpolizei Gruppe 644'.

CSDIC (UK) SIR (Special Interrogation Report) 818 (20 Aug 1944) 'Geheime Feldpolizei in Greece 1942.'

CSDIC (UK) SIR (Special Interrogation Report) 1675 (24 May 1945) 'Notes on the GFP and Other Security Services in the Area of Army Group Nord (Later Kurland) – 1942–1 Jan 45'.

CSDIC (UK) SIR (Special Interrogation Report) 1676 (24 May 1945) 'Notes on the GFP and Other Security Services in the West – 1939–42'. CAB/129/28, *Kommandobefehl, den 18 Okt. 1942.*

CSDIC (UK) SIR (Special Interrogation Report) *G.G. 1203 (c) v. 6. Mai 1945, P.R.O. WO 208/4170 Generalleutnant SIRY171 (commander, 347 I.D.), captured Friedrichsroda 10. April 1945 Generalstabsintendant Pauer* (Formerly of the OKH), Captured Kleinrinderfeld, 7. April 1945.

German Armed Forces War Diary

Schramm, Percy. *Kriegstagebuch Des Oberkommandos Der Wehrmacht 1939–1945*, 8 Vols. Herrsching: Manfred Pawlak, 1982.

Diaries

NARA T-RG-238 Working Conference on 23 April 1940, Service Diary of Governor General Hans Frank, numerous volumes, Vol. 9.

Interviews

1. Interview of Roman Polanski by Catherine Bernstein for TV series *Grands Entretiens.*
2. *S.R. G. G. 1203 (c) v. 6. Mai 1945, P.R.O. WO 208/4170 Generalleutnant SIRY171 (commander, 347 Infantry Division), Captured Friedrichsroda 10. April 1945 Generalstabsintendant Pauer* (Formerly of the OKH). British military interview of *Generalstabsintendant Pauer.*
3. Personal testimony of retired Gendarme Heinz Houben, from Dortmund.

Internet

Jan Grabowski. *The Polish Police: Collaboration in the Holocaust.* United States Holocaust Memorial Museum: Washington, D.C. www.ushmm.org/m/pdfs/20170502-Grabowski_OP.pdf. 2017.

Supreme Headquarters Allied Expeditionary Force, Office of Assistant Chief of Staff G-2, Counterintelligence Sub-Division Evaluation, and Dissemination Section

E.D.S. Report No. 15 – *Geheime Feldpolizei* (Secret Field Police) 8 January 1945, Supreme Headquarters Allied Expeditionary Force, Office of Assistant Chief of Staff G-2, Counter-intelligence Sub-Division Evaluation and Dissemination Section.

Geheime Feldpolizei (GFP) Vol. I XE 019650 Par 43, SR 380-20-10. General Staff, U.S. Army G2 Central Records Facility, Fort Holabird, Baltimore 19, Maryland.

Geheime Feldpolizei – EI (GFP) G-2 Department of the Army, Volume II, XE 019650.

Office of Strategic Services Research and Analysis Branch, R and A N, 2500.15, 'German Military Government Over Europe: Economic Controls in Occupied Europe', Washington. D.C., 28 August 1945.

Box No. 4 – No. XE003923 German Police System in Occupied Czechoslovakia.

Box No. 5 – NND 881019, File No. XE019650 *Geheime Feldpolizei* (GFP) Volume I and Volume II.

Records of the Army Staff (Record Group 319) – CIC Collection – Declassified Files

Box No. 4 – No. XE003923 German Police System in Occupied Czechoslovakia,

Box No. 5 – NND 881019 File No. XE019650 *Geheime Feldpolizei* (GFP) (Secret Field Police) Vol. I and Vol. II.

Military Intelligence Service Centre/U.S. Forces European Theater CI

Final Interrogation Report No. 98 (14 Mar 1946) 'Reg.-u.Krim.Dir. Philipp GREINER, Leitender FP Direktor, Mil.Befh. Frankreich'.

The Seventh Army Interrogation Centre

Final Interrogation Report No. 20 (8 Aug 1945) 'Secret Military Police Unit 712'.

French Army Military Archive, Paris

Ordre De Bataille II - A - Etat-Major de la 30ěme Division d'Infanterie des Waffen-SS (Russe Nr. 2) (plustard): Stab Waffen Grenadier Brigade der SS (Weissruthenien).

Legal Court Cases

1. Innsbruck Court Case: GG Innsbruck 10 Nr. 415170-23 10 H 7170: 1–43.
2. Nuremberg Trial: NOKW 1382, Directive of the Quartermaster of the *Kommandant rückwärtiges Armeegebiet* 560 (Army Groups A, Twelfth Army, 560th Army Rear Area Security Command), 21 May 1941.
3. The Minister of Canadian Citizenship and Immigration vs. Vladimir Katriuk Court transcripts, Docket No.: T-2409-96. Date: 1999/01/29.
4. Court transcripts: *The Canadian Government vs. Vladimir Katriuk.* Docket No.: T-2409-96, Date: 1999.01.29. Nazi Conspiracy and Aggression (Washington, DC: Government Printing Office, 1946), 8:205–8. R-135.
5. Trials of War Criminals before the Nuremberg Military Tribunals under Control Council Law No. 10, October 1946–April 1949 (Washington, DC: Government Printing Office, 1949), 13:516-22. NO-3028.
6. *The Trial of the Major War Criminals Before the International Military Tribunal. Nuremberg 14 November 1945–1 October 1945.* Nuremberg: Secretary of the International Military Tribunal, Official text English edition. Volumes XXXVIII–XLI, 1949, and: National Archives Collection of World War II War Crimes Records (Record Groups 153, 238 and 549).

7. *Justiz und NS Verbrechen, Kriegsverbrechen, Andere Massenvernichtungsverbrechen,* Court Case No. 1017, the West German State vs. Kurt Melzer, Rudolf Hermann, and Arno-Ernst Schumann. This table was completely derived from hundreds of court proceedings and judgements in German trials of war criminals as listed in the multi-volume reference, *'Justiz und NS-Verbrechen'*, Volumes I–XXVIII.

Court Trial Testimonials

1. Testimony of Heinz Hermann Schubert, Office of Chief of Counsel for War Crimes. APO 696 A, U.S. Army, Document No. 4816, pp.3–4, 18).
2. Testimony of Private Albert Rodenbusch, Grenadier (Feldausbildungs) Regiment 635 given during court proceedings of the Minsk war crimes trials held in 1946 a, 1947. Belarusian SSR, 15–19 January 1946 (Minsk Trial), Minsk (1947), pp.262–63.
3. *Testimony of Erich von dem Bach-Zelewski at the Nuremberg War Crimes Trials: The Trial of German Major War Criminals.* Her Majesty's Stationary Office: London, 1946–1952. Twenty-four volumes.

Other Primary Sources

Meyer, Brünn. *Dienstalterliste der Waffen-SS: SS-Obergruppenführer bis SS-Hauptsturmführer; Stand vom 1 Juli 1944.* Osnabrück Biblio Verlag: 1987.

Telex: General Löhr to the *Befehlshaber Südost,* dated October 1, 1944-RH 19 VII/37, Part 1, Annex 12.

'Generalkommando LIV.A.K., Abt.Ic/A.O. vom 2.8.41, An den Führer des Sonderkommandos XIa Herrn SS-Sturmbannführer Zapp.', MAP, microfilm 56748, fr. 954; *'Geheime Feldpolizei 647, Koat II beim LIV.A.K., Tgb.-Nr. 77/41 vom 2.8.1941, An den Stab der Geheimen Feldpolizei 647 beim A.O.K. 11.'*, Ibid, fr. 945.

'Der Beauftragte des Chefs der Sicherheitspolizei und des SD beim Befehlshaber des rückwartigen Heeresgebiet Süd, Sonderkommando 11a, Tgb. 83/41 vom4.8.1941, Betrifft: Bericht über die Tätigkeit des Sonderkommandos in der Zeit vom 17. Juli bis 3. August und die Einsatzplanung für die erste Augusthalfte 1941'. On the concentration of Jews in labour camps in Bessarabia, see *'Die Gesandschaft in Bukarest an das Auswartige Amt'*, 6 August 1941, Nuremberg Doc. NO-2067, reproduced in ADAP, Series D, vol. XIII/1, 238–39.

Roosevelt, Franklin D. 'No Peace with Hitler: Eight Common Principles for a Better World', in *Vital Speeches of the Day.* Vol. 7 Issue 22 (1 September 1941).

'Central Registry of War Criminals and Security Suspects' (CROCASS Allied Control Authority, Part 1 and 2, U.S. Army, APO 742, 1947).

Publications Published by the Third Reich Printing Office, Berlin

Der Reichsführer-SS und Chef der Deutschen Polizei, Banden-bekämpfung. Berlin: Gedruckt im Reichssicherheitshauptamt, 1. Ausgabe, September 1942.

Dienstalterliste der Schutzstafel der NSDAP (SS-Obergruppenführer bis SS-Standartenführer) Stand vom 30. Januar 1942. Herausgegeben vom Personalhauptamt. Berlin: *Gedruckt in der Reichsdruckerei, 1942.*

Dienstalterliste der Schutzstafel der NSDAP (SS-Obersturmbannführer und SS-Sturmbannführer) Stand vom 1. Oktober 1944. Herausgegeben vom Personalhauptamt. Berlin: *Gedruckt in der Reichsdruckerei, 1944.*

Dienstalterliste der Schutzstafel der NSDAP (SS-Obergruppenführer bis SS-Standartenführer) Stand vom 1. Oktober 1944. Herausgegeben vom Personalhauptamt. Berlin: *Gedruckt in der Reichsdruckerei, 1944.*

Befehlsblatt des Chefs der Sicherheitspolizei und der SD, Nr. 14/44 Berlin, 1. April 1944. Herausgegeben vom Reichssicherheitshaupt-amt, Berlin: Gedruckt in der Reichsdruckerei, 1944.

Dienstalterliste der Schutzstaffel der NSDAP, Stand vom 1. Oktober 1934. Gedruckt in der Reichsdruckerei: Berlin, 1934.

Dienstalterliste der Schutzstafel der NSDAP, stand vom 30 Januar 1942. Gedruckt in der Reichsdruckerei: Berlin, 1942.

Dienstalterliste der Schutzstafel der NSDAP, stand vom Oktober/November 1944. Gedruckt in der Reichsdruckerei: Berlin, 1944. Wi. Kdo. Witebsk, 'Monatsbericht', 23 November 1942 (GMDS, Wi/ID 2.779).

Dienstalterliste der Schutzstafel der NSDAP, stand vom 1 Juli 1944. Gedruckt in der Reichsdruckerei: Berlin, 1944.

Secondary Source Material

Doctorate of Philosophy works cited

Birn, Ruth Bettina. *Die Höheren SS und Polizeiführer: Himmlers Vertreter im Reichs und in den besetzten Gebieten*. Droste Verlag, 1986.

Blood, Philip Warren. *Bandenbekämpfung: Nazi occupation security in Eastern Europe and Soviet Russia 1942–45*. A thesis submitted to fulfil the requirements for a Doctor of Philosophy degree. Cranfield University: Department of Defence Management and Security Analysis Security Studies Institute 2001.

Gordon, Gary Howard. *Soviet Partisan Warfare, 1941–1944. The German Perspective*. University Microfilms: Ann Arbor, 1972.

Porter, Jack Nusam. *Jewish Partisans: A Documentary of Jewish Resistance in the Soviet Union during World War II*. Volume II. University Press of America, Inc.: Washington D.C., 1982.

Pronin, Alexander. *Guerrilla Warfare in the German Occupied Soviet Territories 1941–1945*. Georgetown University Graduate School: Georgetown, 1965.

Sheppard, Ben. *German Army Security Units in Russia, 1941–1943: A Case Study*. A thesis submitted to the Faculty of Social Science and Commerce of The University of Birmingham for the degree of Doctor of Philosophy, Institute for German Studies Faculty of Social Science and Commerce: The University of Birmingham, June 2000.

Pamphlets, magazines and journals

Arad, Yitzhak. 'The Holocaust of Soviet Jewry in the Occupied Territories of the Soviet Union', *Yad Vashem Studies XXI*, No. 21 (1991).

Dreßen, Willi. 'The Role of the Wehrmacht and the Police in the Annihilation of the Jews, the Prosecution of Postwar Careers of Perpetrators in the Police Force of the Federal Republic of Germany', *Yad Vashem Studies XXIII* (1993).

German Anti-Guerrilla Operations in the Balkans, 1941–1944. DA Pamphlet 20-243, August 1954, Washington, DC: Center of Military History, U.S. Army.

Haberer, Eric. 'The German police and genocide in Belorussia, 1941–1944. Part I: Police deployment and Nazi genocidal directives', In *Journal of Genocide Research*, Part 3, 2001.

Kowalska, Magdalena. *A Polish heart in a feldgrau uniform – complicated journeys from the Wehrmacht to the Polish Army in Exile* in 'Polish Scientific Society Abroad in London', Poznań: Adam Mickiewicz University, Humanities Education No. 2 (33), 2015.

Krichbaum, Wilhelm. *The Secret Field Police*. MS # C-029. Edited by George Vanderstadt. Translated by M. Franke. Washington, DC: Center for Military History, U.S. Army Historical Division, 18 May 1947.

The Case Against General Heusinger. Documents Illustrating the Charges of the USSR Against Former Lieutenant-General Adolf Heusinger, Former Operations Chief of the Wehrmacht High Command. Soviet Government. New York: Translation World Publishers, 1961.

Published Works

Adair, Paul. *Hitler's Greatest Defeat. The Collapse of Army Group Center*. New York: Sterling Publishing, 1994.

Albrecht-Carrié, René. *A Diplomatic History of Europe Since the Congress of Vienna*. New York: Harper and Row, Publishers, 1958.

Anders, Wladyslaw. *Hitler's Defeat in Russia*. Chicago: Henry Regnery Company, 1953.

Anders, Wladyslaw. *Russian Volunteers in Hitler's Army, 1941–1945*. New York: Europa Books. 1997.

Andrew, Christopher. *Defend the Realm: The Authorized History of MI5*. New York: Knopf Doubleday, 2009.

Andreyev, Catherine. *Vlasov and the Russian Liberation Movement. Soviet Reality and Émigré Theories*. Cambridge: Cambridge University Press, 1987.

Angolia, Lieutenant Colonel John R. *Cloth Insignia of the SS*. San Jose: R. James Bender Publishing, 1983. 2nd (updated) edition.

Angrick, Andrej. *Besatzungspolitik und Massenmord: Die Einsatzgruppe D in der Sowjetunion 1941–1943*. Hamburg: Hamburger Edition, 2003.

Applebaum, Ann. *Red Famine: Stalin's War on Ukraine*. New York: Doubleday, 2018.

Arad, Yitzhak. 'The Holocaust of Soviet Jewry in the Occupied Territories of the Soviet Union', in Aharon Weiss (ed.). *Yad Vashem Studies XXI*, Jerusalem: The Holocaust Martyrs' and Heroes' Remembrance Authority, 1991.

Arico, Massimo. *Ordnungspolizei Volume 1: Encyclopedia of the German Police Battalions September 1939–July 1942*. Stockholm: Leandoer and Co. Forlag, 2016.

Armstrong, John A. Editor. *Soviet Partisans in World War II*. Madison: University of Wisconsin Press, 1964.

Armstrong, John A. *Ukrainian Nationalism*. Englewood: Ukrainian Academic Press, 1990.

Aschenauer, Rudolf. *Krieg Ohne Grenzen: Der Partisanenkampf gegen Deutschland 1939–1945*. Leoni am Starnberger. Druffel Verlag, 1982.

Axworthy, Mark W. A. *Axis Slovakia: Hitler's Slavic Wedge, 1938–1945*. New York: Europa Books, 2002.

Baker, Gabriel. *Spare No One: Mass Violence in Roman Warfare*. New York: Rowman & Littlefield, 2021.

Banach, Jens. *Heydrichs Elite: Das Führerkorps der Sicherheitspolizei und des SD 1936–1945*. Paderborn: Ferdinand Schöningh, 1998.

Bartov, Omer. *The Eastern Front 1941–1945: German Troops and the Barbarisation of Warfare*. New York: St Martin's Press, 1986.

Bartov, Omer. *The Eastern Front 1941–45: German Troops and the Barbarisation of Warfare*. New York: St Martin's Press, 1986.

Bartov, Omer, *Hitler's Army: Soldiers, Nazis, and War in the Third Reichs*. Oxford: Oxford University Press, 1992.

Bartov, Omer. *Mirrors of Destruction: War, Genocide, and Modern Identity*. Oxford: Oxford University Press, 2000.

Bartov, Omer. *Germany's War and the Holocaust: Disputed Histories*. Cornell: Cornell University Press, 2003.

Bauer, Eddy. *The History of World War II*. London: Galley Press, 1984.

Bayer, Hanns. *Die Kavallerie Der Waffen-SS*. Heidelberg: Selbstverlag der Truppenkameradenschaft der SS Kavallerie Divisionen, 1980.

Bayer, Hanns. *Kavallerie Divisionen der Waffen-SS im Bild*. Osnabrück: Munin Verlag, 1982.

Becker, Hans. *Devil on My Shoulder*. London: Jarrolds Publishers, 1955.

Beevor, Anthony. *Crete: The Battle and the Resistance*. New York: Penguin Books, 2014.

Bennett, Rab. *Under the Shadow of the Swastika: The Moral Dilemmas of Resistance and Collaboration in Hitler's Europe*. New York: New York University Press, 1999.

Bergen, Doris L. *War and Genocide: A Concise History of the Holocaust*. New York: Rowman and Littlefield Publishers, Inc., 2009.

Berthel, Hans Dieter. *Die Feldgendarmerie im Zweiten Weltkrieg und ihre Teilnahme an völkerrechtswidrigen Aktionen 1939–1945*. Norderstedt: Herstellung und Verlag, 2006.

Bethell, Nicholas. *The Last Secret. The Delivery to Stalin of Over Two Million Russians by Britain and the United States*. New York: Basic Books Inc., 1974.

Birn, Ruth Bettina. *Die Sicherheitspolizei in Estland, 1941–1944: Eine Studie zur Kollabouration im Osten*. Paderborn: Ferdinand Schöningh, 2006.

Bischof, Günther, Fritz Plasser, and Eva Maltschnig, editors. *Austrian Lives: Contemporary Austrian Studies Vol. 21*. New Orleans: University of New Orleans Press, 2012.

Blood, Philip W. *Hitler's Bandit Hunters: The SS and the Nazi Occupation of Europe*. Washington, D.C.: Potomak Books, Inc., 2006.

Bonn, Keith E., Editor. *Slaughterhouse: The Handbook of the Eastern Front*. Bedford: The Aberjona Press, 2005.

Boog, Horst, et al. *Germany and the Second World War. Volume IV, the Attack on the Soviet Union*. Oxford: Clarenden Press, 1998.

Borkiewicz, Adam, *Powstanie warszawskie 1944: zarys działań natury wojskowej*, Warszawa: PAX, 1962.

Boshyk, Yury, Editor. *Ukraine during World War II: History and its Aftermath*. Edmonton: Canadian Institute of Ukrainian Studies, 1986.

Brandon, Ray and Wendy Lower. *Shoah in Ukraine: History, Testimony, Memorialization*. Bloomington: Indiana University Press, 2008.

Browning, Christopher. *Ordinary Men: Reserve Police Battalion 101 and the Final Solution in Poland*. New York: Harper Collins Publishers, Inc., 1992.

Browning, Christopher. *The Origins of the Final Solution: The Evolution of Nazi Jewish Policy, September 1939–March 1942*. Lincoln: University of Nebraska Press, 2004.

Browning, Christopher R. *Project Muse. Nikolaev and Dnepropetrovsk Regions. The United States Holocaust Memorial Museum Encyclopedia of Camps and Ghettos, 1933–1945, Volume II: Ghettos in German-Occupied Eastern Europe*. Indiana University Press, 2012.

Bruns, Friedrich. *Die Brücke von Neuenburg: Eine Dokumentation über den Endkampf der 19 Armee in Elsaß 1945*. Celle: Self Published, 1990.

Buchanan, Patrick J. *Churchill, Hitler, and The Unnecessary War: How Britain Lost Its Empire and the West Lost the World*. New York: Crown Press, 2008.

Buchner, Alex. *Ostfront: The German Defensive Battles on the Russian Front 1944*. West Chester: Schiffer Military History, 1991.

Buhlan, Harald and Werner Jung. *Wessen Freund und Wessen Helfer? Die Kölner Polizei im Nationalsozialismus*. Köln: Emons Verlag, 2000.

Campbell, Bruce. *The SA Generals and the Rise of Nazism*. Lexington: The University Press of Kentucky, 1998.

Campbell, Stephen. *Police Battalions of the Third Reichs*. Atglen: Schiffer Publishers, 2007.

Carell, Paul. *Hitler Moves East, 1941–1943*. Boston: Little, Brown, and Company, 1964.

Carell, Paul. *Scorched Earth. The Russo-German War 1943–1944*. Boston: Little, Brown, and Company, 1970.

Carnier, Pier Arrigo. *L'Armata Cosaca in Italia 1944–1945*. Milan: Mursia Editoriale, 1990.

Caroe, Olaf. *Soviet Empire. The Turks of Central Asia and Stalinism*. New York: Macmillan and Co. Ltd, 1954.

Cesarani, David, ed. *The Final Solution. Origins and Implementation*, David Cesarani, ed., London: Routledge, 1994.

Chiari, Bernhard. *Alltag Hinter Der Front: Besatzung, Kollabouration und Widerstand in Weissrussland, 1941–1944*. Düsseldorf: Droste Verlag, 1998.

Cholawsky, Shalom. *The Jews of Belarusia during World War II*. Amsterdam: Harwood Academic Publishers, 1998.

Citino, Robert M. *The German Way of War: From the Thirty Years' War to the Third Reichs*. Lawrence: University Press of Kansas, 2005.

Clarke, Jeffrey J. and Robert Ross Smith. *United States Army in World War II. The European Theater of Operations: Riviera to the Rhine*. Washington, D.C.: Center of Military History, 1993.

Cooper, Matthew. *The Nazi War Against Soviet Partisans, 1941–1944*. New York: Stein and Day, 1979.

Conquest, Robert. *Harvest of Sorrow: Soviet Collectivization Methods and the Terror-Famine*. Oxford: New York, 1986.

Costantini, Colonel Aimé. *L'Union Soviétique En Guerre (1941–1945)*. Paris: Imprimerie Nationale, 1968, 3 volumes.

Coudry, Georges. *Les Camps Sovietiques Les Russes Livres a Stalin en 1945*. Paris: Albin Michel, 1997.

Crankshaw, Edward. *Gestapo: Instrument of Tyranny*. London: Greenhill Books, 1990.

Cüppers, Martin. *Wegbereiter der Shoah: Die Waffen-SS, der Kommandostab Reichsführer-SS und die Judenvernichtung 1939–1945*. Darmstadt: Wissenschaftliche Buchgesellschaft, 2005.

Curilla, Wolfgang. *Die deutsche Ordnungspolizei und der Holocaust im Baltikum und im Weißrußla, 1941–1944*. Paderborn: Verlag Ferdinand Schöningh GmbH, 2006.

Dallin, Alexander. *German Rule in Russia 1941–1945, A study of Occupation Policies*. London: Macmillan and Co Ltd, 1957.

Dasnoy, Philippe, and Jean Leon Charles. *Les dossiers secrets de la police allemande en Belgique. La Geheime Feldpolizei en Belgique et dans le Nord de la France, Vols. 1 and 2*. Brüssel: Arts et Voyages / Lucien De Meyer, 1972.

Davies, Edward and Ronald Smelser, *The Myth of the Eastern Front: The Nazi-Soviet War in American Popular Culture*. New York: Cambridge University Press, 2007.

Dawidowicz, Lucy S. *The War against the Jews 1933–1945*. New York: Holt, Reinhart and Winston, 1975.

Dean, Martin. *Collaboration in the Holocaust: Crimes of the Local Police in Belarusia and Ukraine, 1941–1944*. New York: St Martin's Press, 2000.

Dixon, Brigadier C. Aubrey and Otto Heilbrunn. *Communist Guerrilla Warfare*. New York: Frederick A. Praeger, 1954.

Dorril, Stephen. *M.I.6*. London: Fourth Estate Publishing Ltd, 2000.

Dreßen, Willi. 'The Role of the Wehrmacht and the Police in the Annihilation of the Jews; the Prosecution of Postwar Careers of Perpetrators in the Police Force of the Federal Republic of Germany', *Yad Vashem Studies XXIII*, 1993: 295–319.

Drum, D. Karl, et al. *Airpower in Russian Partisan Warfare*. USAF Historical Study No. 177. New York: Arno Press, 1968.

Dunnigan, James F., David C. Isby, E. C. McCarthy, Stephen Patrick, and Trevor N. Dupuy, Eds., *War in the East: The Russo-German Conflict, 1941–45*. New York: Simulations Publications Inc., 1977.

Eckmann, Lester, and Chaim Lazar. *The Jewish Resistance: The History of the Jewish Partisans in Lithuania and White Russia during the Nazi Occupation 1940–1945*. New York: Shengold Publishers, Inc., 1977.

Ehrenburg, Ilya, and Vasily Grossman. *The Black Book*. New York: Holocaust Library, 1981.

Erickson, John. *The Road to Berlin. Stalin's War with Germany*. London: Weidenfeld and Nicolson Ltd, 1983.

Evans, Richard J. *The Third Reich in Power*. New York: The Penguin Press, 2005.

Evans, Richard J. *The Third Reich at War*. London: Penguin Books Ltd, 2008.

Ezergailis, Andrew. *The Holocaust in Latvia 1941–1944*. Washington D.C.: The United States Holocaust Memorial Museum, 1996.

Faber, David. *Munich 1938: Appeasement and World War Two*. New York: Simon and Schuster, 2010.

Federov, Alexander. *partisans d'Ukraine – 2. operations contre la Wehrmacht*. Paris: Editions J'ai Lu, 1951.

Fischer, George. *Soviet Opposition to Stalin: A Case Study in World War II*. Cambridge: Harvard University Press, 1952.

Fontaine, Thomas. 'Chronology of Repression and Persecution in Occupied France, 1940–44', in *The Encyclopedia of Mass Violence* (Philadelphia: Running Press, 2004).

Förster, Jürgen. 'The German Army and the Ideological War against the Soviet Union' in *The Policies of Genocide: Jews and Soviet Prisoners of War in Nazi Germany*, 15–29. Gerhard Hirschfeld, editor (London: Allen and Unwin, 1986).

Franz, Hermann. *Gebirgsjäger der Polizei: Polizei-Gebirgsjäger-Regiment 18 und Polizei-GebirgsArtillerieabteilung 1942*. Bad Nauheim: Verlag Hans Henning, 1963.

Frei, Norbert. *Vergangenheitspolotik*. Einbeck: AHA-Buch GmbH, 1996.

Geldmacher, Thomas. *Wir als Wiener waren ja bei der Bevölkerung beliebt: Östtereichsische Schutzpolizisten und die Judenvernichtung in Ostgalizien 1941–1944*. Vienna: Mandelbaum Verlag, 2002.

Gellermann, Guenther W. *Moskau ruft Heeresgruppe Mitte. Was nicht im Wehrmachtbericht stand: Die Einsätze des geheimen Kampfgeschwaders 200 im Zweiten Weltkrieg*. Koblenz: Bernard and Graefe Verlag, 1988.

Gerlach, Christian. *Kalkulierte Morde: Die deutsche Wirtschafts- und Vernichtungspolitik in Weißrußland, 1941 bis 1944*. Hamburg: Hamburger Edition HIS, 2013.

Gerlach, Christian. 'Men of 20 July and the War in the Soviet Union', in *War of Extermination: The German Military in World War Two 1941–1944*, Hannes Heer and Klaus Naumann, eds. (New York: Berghahn Books, 2000).

Geβner, Klaus. *Geheime Feldpolizei*. Berlin: Militarverlag der Deutschen Demokratische Republik, 1986.

Geβner, Klaus. *Geheime Feldpolizei: Die Gestapo der Wehrmacht*. Berlin: Militärverlag, 2010.

Geyer, Michael, Charles S Maier and Andrew Gould, Eds. 'Traditional Elites and National Socialist Leadership,' 77–133, in *The Rise of the Nazi Regime: Historical Reassessments* (Boulder: Westview Press, 1986).

Gibson, Hugh, and Sumner Welles, editors. *Ciano Diaries 1939–1943, Complete, Unabridged Diaries of Count Galeazzo. Italian Minister for Foreign Affairs 1936–1943*. New York: Doubleday and Co., 1946.

Gilbert, Dr Martin. *Atlas of the Holocaust*. London: Lester Publishing, Ltd, 1988. Revised edition, 1993.

Gilbert, Dr Martin. *The Holocaust: A History of the Jews of Europe During the Second World War*. New York: Henry Holt And Company, 1985.

Gildea, Robert, Anette Warring and Olivier Wieviorka, eds. *Surviving Hitler and Mussolini: Daily Life in Occupied Europe*. New York: Bloomsbury Academic, 2006.

Glantz, David M. and Harold S. Orenstein. *Belarusia 1944: The Soviet General Staff Study*. London: Frank Cass, 2001.

Gogun, Alexander. *Stalin's Commandos. Ukrainian Partisan Forces on the Eastern Front*. London: I. B. Tauris, 2016.

Goldhagen, Daniel Jonah. *Hitler's Willing Executioners: Ordinary Germans and the Holocaust*. New York: Alfred A. Knopf, 1996.

Gooch, John. *Mussolini and His Generals: The Armed Forces and Fascist Foreign Policy, 1922–1940*. Cambridge: Cambridge University Press, 2007.

Görlitz, Walter, and David Irving, Eds. *In the Service of the Reich*. New York: Stein and Day, 1979.

Grenkevich, Leonid. *The Soviet Partisan Movement 1941–1944*. London: Frank Cass Ltd, 1999.

Gruenthal, Heide-Marie. *Nacht Über Europa: Die Faschistische Okkupationspolitik in Polen (1939–1945)*. Köln: Pahl-Rugenstein Verlag, 1989.

Grundmann, Siegfried. *Die V-Leute des Gestapo-Kommissars Sattler*. Berlin: Hentrich und Hentrich Verlag, 2010.

Hamburger Institut für Sozialforschung, ed. *Verbrechen der Wehrmacht: Dimensionen des Vernichtungskrieges 1941–1944*. Hamburg: Hamburger Edition HIS, 2002.

Hanusiak, Michael. *Lest We Forget*. Toronto: Progress Books, 1976.

Hartmann, Christian, Johannes Hürter, Peter Lieb and Dieter Pohl. *Der deutsche Krieg in Osten 1941–1944: Faceten einer Grenzüberschreitung*. Oldenbourg: Wissentschaftsverlag, 2009.

Hartmann, Christian, Johannes Hürter, and Ulrike Jureit. *Verbrechen der Wehrmacht: Bilanz einer Debatte*. Munich: Verlag C. H. Beck, 2005.

Haupt, Werner. *Army Group Center: The Wehrmacht in Russia 1941–1945*. Atglen: Schiffer Publishing, 1997.

Haupt, Werner. *Die 8. Panzer-Division im 2. Weltkrieg*. Friedberg: Podzun Pallas Verlag, 1987.

Haupt, Werner. *Die Schlachten Der Heeresgruppe Mitte 1941–1944*. Friedberg: Podzun Pallas Verlag, 1983.

Haupt, Werner. *Die Deutschen Infanterie-Divisionen*. Friedberg: Podzun Pallas Verlag, 1991. Three volumes.

Haupt, Werner. *Army Group North. The Wehrmacht in Russia 1941–1945*. Atglen: Schiffer Publishers, 1997.

Haupt, Werner. *Die Schlachten Der Heeresgruppe Süd. Aus der Sicht der Divisionen*. Friedberg: Podzun Pallas Verlag, 1985.

Haupt, Werner. *Army Group South. The Wehrmacht in Russia 1941–1945*. Atglen: Schiffer Publishers, 1997.

Haupt, Werner. *Leningrad: Die 900 Tage Schlacht 1941–1944*. Friedberg: Podzun Pallas Verlag, 1980.

Hausser, Paul. *Soldaten Wie Andere Auch. Der Weg der Waffen-SS*. Osnabrück: Munin Verlag GmbH, 1966.

Hechelhammer, Bodo, and Susanne Meinl. *Geheimobjekt Pullach: Von der NS-Mustersiedlung zur Zentrale des BND*. Berlin: Christoph Links Verlag, 2014.

Heer, Hannes, and Klaus Naumann. *Vernichtungskrieg: Verbrechen der Wehrmacht 1941–1944*. Hamburg: Hamburger Edition, 1995.

Heer, Hannes and Klaus Naumann, eds. *The German Army and Genocide: Crimes Against War Prisoners, Jews, and Other Civilians in the East, 1939–1944*. New York: The New Press, 1999.

Heer, Hannes, and Klaus Naumann, eds. *War of Extermination: the German Military in World War II–1944*. New York: Berghan Books, 2000.

Heer, Hannes and Klaus Naumann, eds. *Verbrechen der Wehrmacht: Dimensionen des Vernichtungskrieges 1941–1944*. Hamburg: Hamburger Institut für Sozialforschung, 2002.

Herbert, Ulrich, editor. *National Socialist Extermination Policies: Contemporary German Perspectives and Controversies*. New York: Berghan Books, 2000.

Herf, Jeffrey. *Reactionary Modernism: Technology, Culture, and Politics in the Third Reich*. New York: Cambridge University Press, 1984.

Hesse, Erich. *Der Sowietrussische Partisanenkrieg 1941 bis 1944*. Göttingen: Musterschmidt Verlag, 1969.

Hilberg, Raul. *Perpetrators, Victims, Bystanders: The Jewish Catastrophe 1933–1945*. New York: Harper Collins Publishers, 1992.

Hilberg, Raul. *The Destruction of the European Jews*. New Haven: Yale University Press, 2003, 3rd Edition.

Hill, Alexander. *The War Behind the Eastern Front: The Soviet Partisan Movement in North-West Russia, 1941–44*. New York: Frank Cass, 2005, Three volumes.

Hinsley, F. H. *British Intelligence in the Second World War*. London: His Majesty's Stationary Office, 1984. Volume 3, Part I.

Hinze, Rolf. *Der Zusammenbruch Der Heeresgruppe Mitte Im Osten 1944*. Stuttgart: Motorbuch Verlag, 1980.

Hinze, Rolf. *Rückzugskämpfe in der Ukraine 1943/44*. Meerbusch: Verlag Dr Rolf Hinze, 1991.

Hinze, Rolf. *Das Ostfront-Drama 1944*. Stuttgart: Motorbuch Verlag: 1988.

Hinze, Rolf. *East Front Drama 1944. The Withdrawal Battle of Army Group Center*. Winnipeg: J. J. Fedorowicz Publishing, 1996.

Hoffmann, Joachim. *Deutsche und Kalmyken 1942 bis 1945*. Friedberg: Verlag Rombach, 1986.

Hoffmann, Joachim. *Die Geschichte Der Wlassow-Armee*. Frieburg: Verlag Rombach, 1986.

Hoffmann, Joachim. *Kaukasien 1942/43. Das deutsche Heer und die Orientvölker der Sowjetunion*. Frieburg: Rombach Verlag, 1991.

Hoffmann, Joachim. *Deutsche und Kalmyken 1942 bis 1945*. Frieburg: Rombach Verlag, 1986.

Hoffmann, Joachim. *Die Ostlegionen 1941–1943*. Frieburg: Rombach Verlag, 1986.

Hogan, David J., Editor in Chief. *The Holocaust Chronicle: A History in Words and Pictures*. Lincolnwood: Publications International Ltd, 2002.

Höhne, Heinz. *The Order of the Death's Head. The Story of Hitler's SS*. New York: Coward McCann, Inc., 1970.

Höhne, Heinz. *Der Orden unter dem Totenkopf. Die Geschichte der SS*. Frankfurt am Main: Fischer Bücherei, 1969.

Höttl, Wilhelm. *The Secret Front: The Story of Nazi Political Espionage*. New York: Praeger Publishers, 1954.

Howell, Edgar M. et al. *The Soviet Partisan Movement 1941–1944*. Washington DC: Center of Military History, United States Army, 1956.

Hull, Isabel V. *Absolute Destruction: Military Culture and the Practices of War in Imperial Germany*. Ithaca: Cornell University Press, 2005.

Huxley-Blythe, Peter J. *The East Came West*. Caldwell: The Caxton Printers, Ltd, 1968.

Ignatov, P.K. *Partisans of the Kuban*. New York: Hutchinson and Co., 1944.

Ioanid, Radu. *The Holocaust in Romania: The Destruction of Jews and Gypsies under the Antonescu Regime, 1940–1944*. Chicago: Ivan R. Dee, 2008.

Jackson, Robert H. *Tyranny on Trial: The Evidence at Nuremberg*. Dallas: Southern Methodist University Press, 1954.

Jörgensen, Christer. *Hitler's Espionage Machine: The True Story Behind One of the World's Most Ruthless Spy Networks*. Guilford: The Lyons Press, 2004.

Juchniewicz, Mieczyslaw. *Poles in the European Resistance Movement 1939–1945*. Warsaw: Interpress Publishers, 1972.

Jurado, Carlos Caballero and Nigel Thomas. *Germany's Eastern Front Allies* (2) *Baltic Forces*. London: Osprey Men-at-Arms Series, Osprey Publishing, 2002.

Jurado, Carlos Caballero. *Breaking the Chains. 14. Waffen Grenadier Division der SS and Other Ukrainian Volunteer Formations, Eastern front, 1942–1945*. London: Shelf Books, 1998.

Jurado, Carlos Caballero. *Commandos En El Caucaso: La Unidad Especial Bergmann, Voluntarios Caucasianos En El Ejercito Aleman, 1941–45*. Granada: Garcia Hispan, 1995.

Jurado, Carlos Caballero. *Rompiendo Las Cadenas: La Division Ucraniana De Las Waffen-SS*. Granada: Garcia Hispan, 1992.

Jurs, August, editor. *Estonian Freedom Fighters in World War II*. Printed with a grant from the 'New Horizons Program.' Ontario: Vôitleja Relief Foundation, n.d.

Kamenetsky, Ihor. *Hitler's Occupation of Ukraine* (*1941–1944*). *A Study of Totalitarian Imperialism*. Milwaukee: The Marquette University Press, 1956.

Kampe, Norbert, Wolfgang Schleffler and Gerhard Schoenberger, eds., *Die Einsatzgruppen in der besetzten Sowjetunion 1941/42. Die Tätigkeits und Lageberichte des Chefs der Sicherheitspolizei und des SD*. Berlin: Edition Hentrich, 1997.

Karashuk, A., editor. *Russkiya Osvobodetelnya Armia 1939–1945* (Russian Liberation Army, 1939–1945). Moscow: Act Publishers, 1999.

Keegan, John. *The Second World War*. Toronto: Key Porter Books, 1989.

Keilig, Wolf. *Rangliste Des Deutschen Heeres 1944/45*. Friedberg: Podzun Pallas Verlag, n.d.

Kershaw, Ian. *Fateful Choices: Ten Decisions That Changed the World, 1940–1941*. New York: The Penguin Press, 2007.

Kirchubel, Robert. *Operation Barbarossa 1941: Army Group South*. Westport: Praeger Illustrated Military History Series, 2004.

Kirchubel, Robert. *Hitler's Panzer Armies on the Eastern Front*. London: Pen and Sword, 2009.

Klausch, Hans Peter. *Antifaschisten in SS-Uniform*. Bremen: Edition Temmen, 1993.

Klee, Ernst, Willi Dressen and Volker Riess. *The Good Old Days*. Old Saybrook: Konecky and Konecky, 1991.

Kleitmann, Dr K. G. *Die Waffen-SS: eine Dokumentation*. Osnabrück: Verlag 'Der Freiwillige' GmbH, 1965.

Kliment, Charles and Bretislav Nakladal. *Germany's First Ally: Armed Forces of the Slovak State 1939–1945*. Atglen: Schiffer Publishing Ltd: 1997.

Knopp, Guido. *Die Wehrmacht – Eine Bilanz*. Munich: Wilhelm Goldmann Verlag, 2009.

Kohl, Paul. *Der Krieg der deutschen Wehrmacht und der Polizei 1941–1944*. Frankfurt am Main: Fischer Taschenbuch Verlag, 1995.

Krannhals, Hans von. *Der Warschauer Aufstand, 1944*. Frankfurt am Main: Bernard and Gräfe Verlag, 1962.

Krätschmer, Ernst-Günther. *Die Ritterkreuzträger der Waffen-SS*. Preussich Oldendorf: Verlag K. W. Schütz KG, 1955.

Krausnick, Helmut. *Hitlers Einsatzgruppen. Die Truppen des Weltanschauungskrieges 1938–1942*. Frankfurt am Main: Fischer Taschenbuch Verlag, 1985.

Krausnick, Helmut, ed. *Anatomy of the SS State*. New York: Walker and Company, 1965.

Künrich, Heinz. *Der Partisanenkrieg in Europa 1939–1945*. Berlin: Dietz Verlag, 1968.

Kursietis, Andris J. *The Wehrmacht at War 1939–1945. The Units and Commanders of the German Ground Forces during World War II*. Soesterberg: Aspekt, 1999.

Kursietis, Andris J. *The Fallen Generals: The Destruction of the German Officer Corps in World War II and Its Aftermath*. Osceola: Ark Publications Co., 1994.

Kurowski, Franz. *Deadlock before Moscow: Army Group Center 1942–1943*. Atglen: Schiffer Publishers, 1992.

Kurowski, Franz. *The Brandenburgers – Global Mission*. Winnipeg: J.J. Fedorowicz Publishing, 1997.

Kurowski, Franz. *The Brandenburger Commandos: Germany's Elite Warrior Spies in WWII*. Mechanicsburg: Stackpole Books, 2005.

Laar, Mart. *War in the Woods: Estonia's Struggle for Survival, 1944–1956*. Washington DC: The Compass Press, 1992.

Landwehr, Richard. *Fighting for Freedom: The Ukrainian Volunteer Division of the Waffen-SS*. Silver Spring: Bibliophile Legion Books, 1985.

Laqueur, Walter. *The Holocaust Encyclopedia*. New Haven: Yale University Press, 2001.

Laub, Thomas J. *After the Fall: German Policy in Occupied France, 1940–1944*. New York: Oxford University Press, 2010.

Leide, Henry. *NS-Verbrecher und Staatssicherheit: Die geheime Vergangenheitspolitik der DDR*. Göttingen: Vandenhoeck and Ruprecht GmbH and Co., 2007.

Lemkin, Raphael. *Axis Rule in Occupied Europe: Laws of Occupation, Analysis of Government. Proposals for Redress*. Washington, D.C.: Carnegie Endowment for International Peace, 1944.

Lerski, George J. *Historical Dictionary of Poland, 966–1945*. Westport: Greenwood Press, 1996.

Leslie, R. F. *The History of Poland Since 1863*. Cambridge: Cambridge University Press, 1980.

Le Tissier, Tony. *Zhukov at the Oder: The Decisive Battle for Berlin*. Westport: Praeger Publishing, 1996.

Le Tissier, Tony. *The Battle of Berlin 1945*. New York: St Martin's Press, 1988.

Leumi, Vaad, ed. *The Black Book: The Nazi Crime Against the Jewish People*. New York: The Jewish Black Book Committee, 1946.

Lichtenstein, Heiner. *Himmlers grüne Helfer: Die Schutz-und-Ordnungspolizei im Dritten Reichs*. Bund Verlag: Berlin, 1996.

Lieb, Peter. *Konventioneller Krieg oder NS-Weltanschauungskrieg? Kriegfürung und Partisanenbekämpfung in FrankReichs 1943/44*. Munich: R. Oldenbourg Verlag, 2007.

Lieb Peter: 'Täter aus Überzeugung? Oberst Carl von Andrian und die Judenmorde der 707. Infanteriedivision 1941/42', in: Hartmann/Hürter/Lieb/Pohl, *Der deutsche Krieg im Osten 1941–1944* (Oldenbourg: De Gruyter, 2009).

Linck, Stephan. *Der Ordnung verpflichtet: Deutsche Polizei 1933–1949*. Paderborn: Ferdinand Schöningh Verlag, 2000.

Littlejohn, David. *The Patriotic Traitors: The History of Collaboration in German Occupied Europe, 1940–45*. Garden City: Doubleday and Company, 1972.

Littlejohn, David. *Foreign Legions of the Third Reichs, Volume IV – Poland, Ukraine, Bulgaria, Rumania, Free India, Estonia, Latvia, Lithuania, Finland and Russia*. San Jose: R. James Bender Publishing, 1987.

Littman, Sol. *Pure Soldiers or Sinister Legion: The Ukrainian 14th Waffen-SS Division*. Montreal: Black Rose Books, 2003.

Loftus, John. *The Belarus Secret*. New York: Alfred A. Knopf, 1982.

Logusz, Michael O. *Galicia Division: The Waffen-SS 14th Grenadier Division 1943–1945*. Atglen: Schiffer Publishing Ltd, 1997.

Longhardt-Söntgen, Rainer. *Partisanen, Spione und Banditen: Abwehrtätigkeit in Oberitalien 1943–1945*. Neckargemünd: Kurt Vowinckel Verlag, 1961.

Lower, Wendy. *Nazi Empire-Building and the Holocaust in Ukraine*. Chapel Hill: The University of North Carolina Press, 2005.

Lower, Wendy and Ray Brandon, eds. *The Shoah in Ukraine: History, Testimony, Memorialization*. Bloomington: Indiana University Press, 2008.

Lukas, Richard C. *The Forgotten Holocaust: The Poles under German Occupation 1939–1944*. Lexington: University Press of Kentucky, 1986.

Lumans, Valdis O. *Himmler's Auxiliaries: The Volksdeutsche Mittelstelle and the German National Minorities of Europe, 1933–1945*. Chapel Hill: The University of North Carolina Press, 1993.

MacLean, French L. *The Cruel Hunters. SS Sonderkommando Dirlewanger. Hitler's Most Notorious Anti-Partisan Unit*. Atglen: Schiffer Publishers, 1998.

MacLean, French L. *The Field Men. The SS Officers Who Led the Einsatzkommandos – the Nazi Mobile Killing Units*. Atglen: Schiffer Publishers, 1999.

MacLean, French L. *The Camp Men: The SS Officers Who Ran the Nazi Concentration Camp System*. Atglen: Schiffer Military History, 1999.

Maier, Charles S. and Andrew Gould, eds. *The Rise of the Nazi Regime: Historical Reassessments*. Boulder: Westview Press, 1986.

Mallmann, Klaus-Michael, Volker Rieβ, and Wolfram Pyta. *Deutscher Osten 1939–1945: Der Weltanschauungskrieg in Photos und Texten*. Darmstadt: Wissenschaftliche Buchgesellschaft, 2003.

Malthäus, Jürgen. *War, Pacification, and Mass Murder, 1939: The Einsatzgruppen in Poland*. Lanham: Rowman and Littlefield Publishers, 2014.

Manoschek, Walter. *Die Wehrmacht Im Rassenkrieg: Der Vernichtungskrieg Hinter der Front*. Vienna: Picus Verlag, 1996.

Mayer, Hermann Frank. *Blutiges Edelweiβ: die 1. Gebirgsdivision im Zweiten Weltkrieg*. Berlin: Christoph Links Verlag GmbH, 2008.

Megargee, Geoffrey P. *War of Annihilation: Combat and Genocide on the Eastern Front, 1941*. New York: Rowman and Littlefield Publishers Inc., 2006.

Mehner, Kurt. *Die Waffen-SS und Polizei 1939–1945*. Norderstedt: Militair-Verlag Klaus D. Patzwall, 1995.

Mehner, Kurt. *Die Geheimen Tagesberichte Der Deutschen Wehrmachtführung Im Zweiten Weltkrieg 1939–1945*. Biblio Verlag: Osnabrück, 12 volumes. 1989–1994.

Mendelsohn, John, ed. *Covert Warfare: Intelligence, Counterintelligence, and Military Deception during the World War II Era*, 18 volumes, Vol. 13: *The Final Solution of the Abwehr*. New York: Garland Publishing, Inc., 1988.

Mendelsohn, John, ed. *The Holocaust. Selected Documents in Eighteen Volumes*. New York: Garland Publishing, 1982, 18 volumes.

Messenger, David A. and Katrin Paehler, editors. *A Nazi Past: Recasting German Identity in Postwar Europe*. Lexington: University Press of Kentucky, 2015.

Messerschmidt, Manfred. *Die Wehrmachtjustiz 1933–1945*. Paderborn: Ferdinand Schöningh Verlag, 2005.

Michaelis, Rolf. *Die Russische Volksbefreiungsarmee 'RONA' 1941–1944*. Erlangen: Selbstspubliziert, 1992.

Michaelis, Rolf. *Ukrainer in der Waffen-SS: Die 14. Waffen Grenadier Division der SS (ukrainische Nr. 1)*. Berlin: Michaelis Verlag, 2000.

Michaelis, Rolf. *Die Kavallerie Divisionen der Waffen-SS*. Erlangen: Selbstpubliziert, 1993.

Michaelis, Rolf. *Der Weg zur 36. Waffen Grenadier Division der SS*. Rodgau: Verlag fuer Militaerhistorische Zeitgeschichte, 1991.

Michaelis, Rolf. *Russen in der Waffen-SS*. Berlin: Michaelis Verlag, 2002.

Miller, Norbert. *Deutsche Besatzungspolitik in der UdSSR 1941–1944*. Köln: Pahl-Rugenstein, 1980.

Milton, Sybil, transl. *The Stroop Report*. New York: Pantheon Books, 1979.

Mitcham, Samuel W. *Hitler's Legions: the German Army Order of Battle, World War II*. New York: Dorset Press, 1985.

Mitcham, Samuel W. *Crumbling Empire: The German Defeat in the East, 1944*. Westport: Praeger Publishers, 2001.

Mitcham, Samuel W. *German Order of Battle, Volume One: 1st – 290th Infantry Divisions in WWII*. Mechanicsburg: Stackpole Books, 2007.

Mitcham, Samuel W. *Hitler's Legions: The German Army Order of Battle, World War II*. New York: Dorset Press, 1985.

Mollo, Andrew. *Uniforms of the SS. Volume 5: Sicherheitsdienst und Sicherheitspolizei 1931–1945*. London: Windrow and Greene, 1992.

Müller, Rolf-Dieter and Gerd R. Ueberschaer. *Hitler's War in the East 1941–1945. A Critical Assessment*. Providence: Berghahn Books, 1997.

Müller, Rolf-Dieter, and Hans Erik Volkmann. *Die Wehrmacht: Mythos und Realität*. Oldenbourg: Wissenschaftsverlag, 1999.

Müller, Norbert. *Deutsche Besatzungspolitik in der UdSSR 1941–1944*. Köln: Pahl-Rugenstein Verlag, 1980.

Müller-Hillebrand, Dr Burkhart. *Das Heer 1933–1945. Band I*. Darmstadt: E. S. Mittler & Sohn GmbH, 1954.

Mulligan, Patrick Timothy. *The Politics of Illusion and Empire. German Occupation Policy in the Soviet Union, 1942–1943*. New York: Praeger Publishers, 1988.

Muñoz, Antonio, Editor. *The East Came West: Muslim, Hindu, and Buddhist Volunteers in the German Armed Forces, 1941–1945*. New York: Europa Books, 2002.

Muñoz, Antonio. *Göring's Grenadiers: The Luftwaffe Field Divisions 1942–1945*. New York: Europa Books, 2002.

Muñoz, Antonio. *Hitler's Eastern Legions, Volume I – The Baltic Schutzmannschaft 1941–1945*. New York: Europa Books, 1996.

Muñoz, Antonio. *The last Levy: Waffen-SS Officer Roster, March 1st 1945*. New York: Europa Books, 2000.

Muñoz, Antonio. *Hitler's Eastern Legions, Volume II – The Osttruppen*. New York: Europa Books, 1997.

Muñoz, Antonio. *The Druzhina SS Brigade: A History, 1941–1943*. New York: Europa Books, 2000.

Muñoz, Antonio. *The Kaminski Brigade: A History, 1941–1945*. New York: Europa Books, 1996.

Muñoz, Antonio. *The Kaminski Brigade: A History, 1941–1945*. New York: Europa Books, 2003, 2nd revised and expanded edition.

Muñoz, Antonio. *For Croatia and Christ: The Croatian Army in World War II, 1941–1945*. New York: Europa Books, 1996.

Muñoz, Antonio, ed. *The German Police*. Supreme Allied Headquarters, G-2 Section, prepared jointly with British MI-14(d). U.S. Army War Office: Washington, April 1945. Reprinted in revised and expanded format. New York: Europa Books, 1997.

Muñoz, Antonio. *Forgotten Legions: Obscure Combat Formations of the Waffen-SS, 1943–1945*. Boulder: Paladin Press, 1991.

Muñoz, Antonio. *Forgotten Legions Companion Booklet*. New York: Europa Books, 1995.

Nafziger, George F. *The German Order of Battle. Waffen-SS and Other Units in World War II*. Conshohocken: Combined Publishing, 2001.

Neufeldt, H.-J., J. Huck, and Georg Tessin. *Zur Geschichte der Ordnungspolizei: Die Stabe und Truppeneinheiten der Ordnungspolizei, 1936–1945*. Koblenz: Als Manuskript gedruckt. Bundesarchiv, 1957.

Neulen, Hans Werner. *An Deutscher Seite: Internationale Freiwillige von Wehrmacht und Waffen-SS*. München: Universitas Verlag, 1985.

Newland, Samuel J. *Cossacks in the German Army, 1941–1945*. London: Frank Cass and Co. Ltd, 1991.

Newton, Steven H. *Retreat from Leningrad. Army Group North, 1944/1945*. Atglen: Schiffer Publishing, 1995.

Newton, Steven H. *German Battle Tactics on the Russian Front*. Atglen: Schiffer Publishing, 1994.

Niehorster, Leo W. G. *The Royal Hungarian Army, 1920–1945*. New York: Europa Books, 1998.

Niepold, Gerd. *Battle for White Russia: The Destruction of Army Group Centre June 1944*. New York: Brassey's Defence Publishers, 1987.

Nirenstein, Albert. *A Tower from the Enemy: Contributions to a History of Jewish Resistance in Poland*. New York: The Orion Press, 1959.

Overmans, Rüdiger. *Deutsche militärische Verluste im Zweiten Weltkrieg*. München: R. Oldenbourg Verlag, 1999.

Overy, Richard. *Russia's War: A History of the Soviet War Effort, 1941–1945*. New York: Penguin Putnam, Inc., 1998.

Padfield, Peter. *Himmler*. New York: Henry Holt and Company, 1990.

Perro, Oskars. *Fortress Cholm*. Toronto: Kurland Publishing, 1981.

Person, Katarzyna. *Warsaw Ghetto Police: The Jewish Order Service during the Nazi Occupation*. Ithaca: Cornell University Press, 2021.

Piekalkiewicz, Janusz. *The Cavalry of World War II*. New York: Stein and Day, 1980.

Piotrowski, Tadeusz. *Poland's Holocaust: Ethnic Strife, Collaboration with Occupying Forces and Genocide in the Second Republic, 1918–1947*. Jefferson: MacFarland and Company, Inc., 1998.

Pohl, Dieter, et al, *Der deutsche Krieg im Osten 1941–1944*, Munich: De Gruytyer, 2009.

Pohl, Otto J. *Ethnic Cleansing in the USSR, 1937–1949*. Westport: Greenwood Press, 1999.

Poirier, Robert G. and Albert Z. Conner. *The Red Army Order of Battle in the Great Patriotic War*. Novato: Presidio Press, 1985.

Porter, Jack Nusan, ed. *Jewish Partisans: A Documentary of Jewish Resistance in the Soviet Union During World War II*. Washington DC: University Press of America, Inc, 1982.

Pottgiesser, Hermann. *Die Reichsbahn im Ostfeldzug*. Neckargemünd: Kurt Vowinckel Verlag, 1960.

Präg, Werner and Wolfgang Jacobson. *Das Dienstagebuch des deutschen Generalgouverneurs in Polen 1939–1945*. Stuttgart: Deutsche Verlag Anstalt, 1975.

Prechtl, G. M. *Unsere Ehre Heisst Treue: Kriegstagebuch des Kommandostabes Reichsführer-SS; Tätigkeitsberichte der 1. und 2. SS Infanterie-Brigade und von Sonderkommandos der SS*. Zürich: Europa Verlag, 1965.

Preradovich, Nikolaus von. *Die Generale der Waffen-SS*. Berg Am See: Kurt Vowinckel Verlag, 1985.

Ramme, Alwin. *Der Sicherheitsdienst Der SS*. Berlin: Deutscher Militärverlag der DDR, 1970.

Ready, J. Lee. *The Forgotten Axis: Germany's Partners and Foreign Volunteers in World War II*. Jefferson: MacFarland and Company, Inc., 1987.

Redcliffe, Alexander. *Lessons Learned from the Partisan War in Russia*. MS No. P055C, Washington D.C.: Office of the Chief of Military History, Department of the Army, 1947.

Redelis, Valdis. *Partisanenkrieg: Entstehung und Bekämpfung der Partisanen und Untergrundbewegung im Mittelabschnitt der Ostfront 1941 bis 1943*. Heidelberg: Scharnhorst Buchkameradenschaft, 1958.

Regenberg, Werner. *Panzerfahrzeuge und Panzereinheiten der Ordnungspolizei 1936–1945*. Friedberg: Podzun Pallas Verlag, 1996.

Regenberg, Werner. *Armoured Vehicles and Units of the German Order Police (Ordnungspolizei) 1936–1945*. Atglen: Schiffer Military History, 2002.

Reinicke, Adolf. *Die 5. Jäger-Division 1939–1945*. Friedberg: Podzun Pallas Verlag GmbH, n.d.

Reitlinger, Gerald. *The House Built on Sand: The Conflicts of German Policy in Russia, 1939–1945*. New York: The Viking Press, 1960.

Reitlinger, Gerald. *The SS, Alibi of a Nation, 1922–1945*. London: William Heinemann Ltd, 1956.

Reitlinger, Gerald. *The Final Solution. The Attempt to Exterminate the Jews of Europe 1939–1945*. South Brunswick: Thomas Yoseloff, 1961.

Richter, Hans. *Einsatz der Polizei bei den Polizei-Bataillonen im Ost, Nord, und West*. Berlin: Zentralverlag der NSDAP, 1943.

Romanko, Oleg and Antonio Muñoz. *Hitler's White Russians: Collaboration, Extermination and Anti-Partisan Warfare in White Russia, 1941–1944*. New York: Europa Books, 2002.

Rosch, Barry C. *Luftwaffe Codes, Markings and Units, 1939–1945*. Atglen: Schiffer Military / Aviation History, 1995.

Rossino, Alexander B. *Hitler Strikes Poland: Blitzkrieg, Ideology, and Atrocity* (Modern War Studies) Lawrence: University Press of Kansas, 2003.

Rürup, Dr Reinhard and Dr Peter Jahn, editors. *Der Krieg gegen die Sowjetunion 1941–1945*. Berlin: Berliner Festspiele GmbH, 1991.

Ryan, Cornelius. *The Last Battle*. New York: Simon and Schuster, 1966.

Scheibert, Horst. *Die Träger Der Ehrenblattspange Des Heeres Und Der Waffen-SS*. Friedberg: Podzun Pallas Verlag, 1986.

Scheibert, Horst. *Die Träger Der Deutschen Kreuzes In Gold: Kriegsmarine, Luftwaffe, Waffen-SS*. Friedberg: Podzun Pallas Verlag, n.d.

Schellenberg, Walter. *The Labyrinth. The Memoirs of Hitler's Secret Service Chief*. New York: Harper and Brothers, 1956.

Schmitz, Peter and Klaus-Jürgen Thies. *Die Truppenkennzeichen der Verbände und Einheiten der Deutschen Wehrmacht und Waffen-SS und ihre Einsätze im Zweiten Weltkrieg 1939–1945*. Osnabrück: Biblio Verlag, 1987–1994. Four volumes.

Schneider, Jost W. *Verleihung Genehmigt! Eine Bild und Dokumentargeschichte Der Ritterkreuzträger Der Waffen-SS und Polizei 1940–1945*. San Jose: R. James Bender Publishing, 1993.

Schülte, Theo. *The German Army and Nazi Policies In Occupied Russia 1941–1944*. New York: Berg Publishers, 1989.

Schumann, Wolfgang and Ludwig Nestler. *Nacht über Europa: Band II: Die faschistische Okkupationspolitik in Polen (1939–1945)*. Köln: Pahl-Rugenstein Verlag GmbH, 1989.

Schuster, Peter and Harald Tiede. *Die Uniformen und Abzeichen der Kosaken in der Deutschen Wehrmacht*. Norderstedt: Verlag Klaus D. Patzwall, 1999.

Seaton, Albert. *The Russo-German War 1941–45*. New York: Praeger Publishers, 1970.

Seewald, Dr Heinrich. *Das toenende Erz: Deutsche Propaganda gegen die Rote Armee im Zweiten Weltkrieg*. Stuttgart: Seewald Verlag, 1978.

Seidler, Franz W. *Die Kollabouration 1939–1945*. München: F.A. Herbig Verlagsbuchhandlung, 1995.

Seidler, Franz W. *Die Militaergerichtsbarfeit der Deutschen Wehrmacht 1939–1945*. Munich: Herbig Verlag, 1991.

Seidler, Franz W. *Deutscher Volkssturm: Das letzte Aufgebot, 1944–1945*. München: F. A. Herbig Verlag, 1989.

Shepperd, Ben. *War in the Wild East: The German Army and Partisans*. Cambridge: Harvard University Press, 2004.

Shkandrij, Myroslav. *In the Maelstrom: The Waffen-SS 'Galicia' Division and Its Legacy*. Montreal: McGill-Queen's University Press, 2023.

Silgailis, Arthur. *Latvian Legion*. San Jose: R. James Bender Publishing, 1986.

Snyder, Timothy. *Into the Bloodlands: Europe Between Hitler and Stalin*. New York: Basic Books, 2022.

Steenberg, Sven. *Vlasov*. New York: Alfred A. Knopf, 1970.

Stein, George H. *The Waffen-SS: Hitler's Elite Guard at War 1939–1945*. Ithaca: Cornell University Press, 1966.

Stöber, Hans. *Die Flugabwehrverbände der Waffen-SS*. Preussiche Oldendorf: Verlag K. W. Schütz KG, 1984. Stoves, Rolf. *Die Gepanzerten und Motorisierten Deutschen Grossverbände 1935–1945*. Friedberg: Podzun Pallas Verlag, 1986.

Stöber, Hans. *Die 22. Panzer-Division; 25. Panzer-Division; 27. Panzer-Division; und die 233. Reserve Panzer-Division*. Friedberg: Podzun Pallas Verlag, 1985.

Stockhorst, Erich. *5000 Köpfe: Wer War Was Im Dritten Reich*. Kiel: Arndt Verlag, 2000.

Strik-Strikfeldt, Wilfried. *Against Stalin and Hitler. Memoir of the Russian Liberation Movement 1941–1945*. New York: The John Day Company, 1973.

Tec, Nechama. *The Bielski Partisans*. Oxford: Oxford University Press, 1993.

Tessin, Georg, Norbert Kannapin and Brün Meyer. *Waffen-SS und Ordnungspolizei im Kriegseinsatz 1939–1945*. Biblio Verlag: OsnabrOck, 2000.

Tessin, Georg, with H. J. Neufeldt, and J. Huck. *Zur Geschichte der Ordnungspolizei, 1936–1945*. Koblenz: Bundesarchiv, 1956.

Tessin, Georg. *Verbände und Truppen der deutschen Wehrmacht und Waffen-SS 1939–1945*. Osnabrück: Biblio Verlag, 1975–2002. 18 volumes.

Thomas, Nigel and Carlos Caballero Jurado. *Wehrmacht Auxiliary Forces*. London: Osprey Publishing Ltd, 1992.

Thomas, Nigel, et al. *Partisan Warfare 1941–45*. London: Reed International Books Ltd, 1983.

Thorwald, Juergen. *The Illusion: Soviet Soldiers in Hitler's Armies*. Harcourt Brace Jovanovich, 1975.

Thurston, Robert W. and Bernd Bonwetsch, Editors. *The People's War: Responses to World War II in the Soviet Union*. New York: University of Illinois Press: Urbana, 2000.

Tieke, Wilhelm. *Das Ende Zwischen Oder Und Elbe: Der Kampf Um Berlin 1945*. Stuttgart: Motorbuch Verlag, 1994.

Tolstoy, Nikolai. *The Secret Betrayal 1944–1947*. New York: Charles Scribner's Sons, 1977.

Tys-Krokhmaliuk, Yuriy. *UPA Warfare in Ukraine: The Ukrainian Insurgent Army*. New York: Vantage Press, 1972.

Ullrich, Sebastian. *Der Weimar-Komplex. Das Scheitern der ersten deutschen Demokratie und die politische Kultur der frühen Bundesrepublik 1945–1959*. Göttingen: Wallstein Verlag, 2009.

Vakar, Nicholas P. *Belarusia: The Making of a Nation: A Case Study*. Cambridge: Harvard University Press, 1956.

Vizetelly, Frank H., Editor in Chief. *Funk and Wagnall's New Standard Encyclopedia of Universal Knowledge*. New York: Funk and Wagnall's Company, 1931. Volume 25.

Wegner, Bernd. *The Waffen-SS: Organisation, Ideology and Function*. Oxford: Basil Blackwell, 1990.

Werbizky, George G. *Ostarbeiters: Belarusian, Russian and Ukrainian Forced Labourers in Nazi Germany – World War II*. Endwell: Self Published, 2002.

Westermann, Edward B. *Hitler's Police Battalions: Enforcing Racial War in the East*. Lawrence: University Press of Kansas.

Westwood, David. *The Waffen-SS: Higher formations, Divisions, Brigades 1939–1945*. Derbyshire: Privately Published, n.d.

Wette, Wolfram. *The Wehrmacht: History, Myth, Reality*. Cambridge: Harvard University Press, 2007.

Wette, Wolfram. *Die Wehrmacht: Feindbilder, Vernichtungskrieg, Legenden*. Frankfurt am Main: S. Fischer Verlag, 2002.

Wicziok, Wilhelm. *Die Armee Der Gerichteten. Zur besonderen Verwendung – Bewaehrungsbataillon 500*. Essen: Heitz and Hoeffkes Verlag, 1992.

Wilhelm, Hans-Heinrich. *Die Einsatzgruppe A: der Sicherheitspolizei und des SD 1941/42*. P Frankfurt am Main: eter Lang Verlag GmbH, 1996.

Witte, Hans Joachim and Peter Offermann. *Die Boeselagerschen Reiter: Das Kavallerie-Regiment Mitte die aus ihm hervorgegangene 3. Kavallerie-Brigade/ Division*. München: Schild Verlag, 1998.

Witter, Robert E. *Chain Dogs: The German Army Military Police of World War II*. Missoula: Pictorial Histories Publishing Company, Inc., 1994.

Yelton, David K. *Hitler's Volkssturm: The Nazi Militia and the Fall of Germany, 1944–1945*. Lawrence: University Press of Kansas, 2002.

Yerger, Mark C. *Riding East. The SS Cavalry Brigade in Poland and Russia 1939–1942*. Atglen: Schiffer Publishers, 1996.

Yerger, Mark C. *Allgemeine-SS*. Atglen: Schiffer Military Publishing, 1997.

Yerger, Mark C. *Waffen-SS Commanders: Augsberger to Kreutz*. Atglen: Schiffer Military Publishing, 1997.

Yerger, Mark C. *Waffen-SS Commanders: Krüger to Zimmermann*. Atglen: Schiffer Military Publishing, 1999.

Zaloga, Steven. *Bagration 1944: The Destruction of Army Group Center*. Osprey Military: London, 1996.

Zawodny, J. K. *Nothing But Honour: The Story of the Warsaw Uprising, 1944*. Hoover Institution Press, 1978.

Ziemke, Earl F. and Magna E. Bauer. *Moscow to Stalingrad: Decision in the East*. Washington DC: Center of Military History, United States Army, 1987.

NOTES

Author's note

1 https://freedomhouse.org/report/freedom-world/2022/global-expansion-authoritarian-rule, accessed 13 June 2022.

2 Sebastian Ullrich. *Der Weimar-Komplex. Das Scheitern der ersten deutschen Demokratie und die politische Kultur der fruhen Bundesrepublik 1945–1959*. Göttingen: Wallstein Verlag, 2009, p.120.

3 In 1926, Marshal Józef Pilsudski established a dictatorship in Poland. Pilsudski claimed that he was doing this for the good of the nation. However, it is no coincidence that the political party he helped to create won all four of the next national elections (1928, 1930, 1935, and 1938). Most historians agree that the elections were rigged. Therefore, Czechoslovakia was the only nation in central Europe that remained a true democracy by 1938.

4 There were many instances between 1934 and September 1938 when Hitler broke the Treaty of Versailles and the democracies of the West did nothing.

5 Putin wanted this *Oblast*, which belonged to Georgia, because it has vast deposits of oil.

Introduction

1 The term literally translates to 'collective violence', but it was meant as collective punishment (*Kollektive Bestrafung*).

2 Christopher Browning, *Ordinary Men: Reserve Police Battalion 101 and the Final Solution in Poland*. New York: Harper Collins, 1992, p.182.

3 Christian Streit, 'Wehrmacht, Einsatzgruppen, Soviet PoWs and Anti-Bolshevism in the Emergence of the Final Solution', *The Final Solution. Origins and Implementation*, David Cesarani, ed., London: Routledge, 1994, p.110.

4 For our purposes, the term USSR refers to those lands that in 1941 encompassed the Baltic States, European Russia, Belarus (White Russia), and Ukraine. European Russia covers an area roughly 3,960,000km². Its Eastern border is defined by the Ural Mountains and (in the south) by the border with Kazakhstan. The Caucasus mountains and the region

bordering Turkey and Persia define the southernmost boundary, while the northern edge covers the border area with Finland and Norway.

5 *Ostheer*: 'Eastern Army', the German military forces fighting on the Russian Front.

6 International Military Tribunal, *Trial of the Major War Criminals before the International Military Tribunal*, 42 Vols. (Nuremberg: Secretary of the Tribunal), Vol. 7, p.59.

7 Matthew Cooper, *The Nazi War Against Soviet Partisans 1941–1944*. New York: Stein and Day, 1979, pp.171–172.

8 Ben Shepperd, *War in the Wild East: The German Army and Partisans*. Cambridge: Harvard University Press, 2004, p.130.

9 Shepperd, op. cit., p.233.

10 The American edition of this book was released a year later, in 1957.

11 Although a bit dated, the book is still considered a must-read for anyone interested in the topic of the German occupation of the East.

12 Alexander Dallin, *German Rule in Russia 1941–1945: A Study of Occupation Policies*. London: Macmillan and Co. Ltd, 1957, p.30.

13 Yitzhak Arad, 'The Holocaust of Soviet Jewry in the Occupied Territories of the Soviet Union', *Yad Vashem Studies XXI*, No. 21 (1991), p.6.

14 Gerald Reitlinger, *The House Built on Sand: The Conflicts of German Policy in Russia*. New York: The Viking Press, 1960, p.81.

15 Ibid.

16 *Landser* is the German equivalent of the American 'G.I.'.

17 Omer Bartov, *The Eastern Front 1941–45: German Troops and the Barbarisation of Warfare*. New York: St Martin's Press, 1986, p.68.

18 Theo J. Schulte, *The German Army and Nazi Policies in Occupied Russia*. Oxford: Berg Publishers, 1989, p.284.

19 Michael Geyer, 'Traditional Elites and National Socialist Leadership', *The Rise of the Nazi Regime: Historical Reassessments*, Charles S. Maier and Andrew Gould, eds. Boulder: Westview Press, 1986, p.71.

20 Edward Davies and Ronald Smelser, *The Myth of the Eastern Front: The Nazi-Soviet War in American Popular Culture*. New York: Cambridge University Press, 2007, pp.22–24.

21 Davies, et al, op. cit., p.24.

22 Paul Kohl, *Der Krieg der deutschen Wehrmacht und der Polizei 1941–1944*. Frankfurt am Main: Fischer Taschenbuch Verlag, 1995, p.333.

23 Walter Manoschek, *Die Wehrmacht Im Rassenkrieg: Der Vernichtungskrieg Hinter der Front*. Vienna: Picus Verlag, 1996, p.142.

24 Willi Dreßen, 'The Role of the Wehrmacht and the Police in the Annihilation of the Jews, the Prosecution of Postwar Careers of

Perpetrators in the Police Force of the Federal Republic of Germany', *Yad Vashem Studies XXIII*, (1993), pp.295–319.

25 Hannes Heer and Klaus Naumann, *Vernichtungskrieg: Verbrechen der Wehrmacht 1941 bis 1944*. Hamburg: Hamburger Edition, 1995, p.14.

26 Hannes Heer and Klaus Naumann, *War of Extermination: The German Military in World War II, 1941–1944*. New York: Berghahn Books, 2000, p.4.

27 Wolfram Wette. *The Wehrmacht: History, Myth, Reality*. Cambridge: Harvard University Press, 2006, p.296.

28 Wolfram Wette. *Die Wehrmacht: Feindbilder, Vernichtungskrieg, Legenden*. Frankfurt am Main: S. Fischer Verlag, 2002.

29 Wette, *The Wehrmacht*, op. cit., p.296.

30 Ibid., p.297.

31 Daniel J. Goldhagen, *Hitler's Willing Executioners: Ordinary Germans and the Holocaust*. New York: Alfred A. Knopf, 1996, pp.23–24.

32 Julius Schoeps, ed., *Ein Volk von Mordern? Die Dokumentation zur Goldhagen-Kontroverse um die Rolle der Deutschen im Holocaust*. Hamburg: Hoffmann und Campe, 1996, pp.1–5.

33 Dr. Fritz Stern, 'Book Review: *Hitler's Willing Executioners: Ordinary Germans and the Holocaust*', *Foreign Affairs*, Volume 75, No. 6 (November–December 1996), pp.640–44.

34 Geoffrey P. Megargee, *War of Annihilation: Combat and Genocide on the Eastern Front, 1941*. New York: Rowman and Littlefield Publishers, Inc., 2006, p.151.

35 *S.R. G. G. 1203 (c) v. 6. Mai 1945, P.R.O. WO 208/4170 Generalleutnant SIRY171 (Comd., 347ID), Captured Friedrichsroda 10. April 1945 Generalstabsintendant Pauer* (Formerly of the OKH), Captured Kleinrinderfeld, 7. April 1945.

36 Neitzel, op. cit., p.231.

37 Timothy Snyder. *Bloodlands: Europe Between Hitler and Stalin*. New York: Basic Books, 2010.

38 Mark Mazower. *Hitler's Empire: How the Nazis Ruled Europe*. New York: Penguin Books, 2008.

Chapter 1. German preparations for the invasion and occupation of Poland

1 Browning, *Ordinary Men*, op. cit., p.5.

2 Dr. Burkhart Müller-Hillebrand. *Das Heer 1933–1945. Band I.* Darmstadt: E. S. Mittler & Sohn GmbH, 1954, p.145.

3 Tessin, Georg. *Verbände und Truppen der deutschen Wehrmacht und Waffen SS 1939–1945.* Osnabrück: Biblio Verlag, 1976–1996, 14 Vols., Vol. 5, p.553.

4 Later redesignated as *SS-Polizeiregiment 20.*

5 Contained two bicycle companies and a motorised company.

6 *Höhere SS und Polizeiführer Süd.*

7 Contained two bicycle companies and a motorised company.

8 Later redesignated as *SS-Polizeiregiment 21.*

9 The regiment was later redesignated as *SS-Polizeiregiment 27.*

10 BdO – *Befehlshaber der Ordnungspolizei.*

11 Was later redesignated as *SS-Polizeiregiment 26.*

12 Later renamed as *SS-Polizeiregiment 22.*

13 This battalion contained four companies instead of three.

14 Contained two motorised and one bicycle company.

15 The regiment was later redesignated as *SS-Polizeiregiment 24.*

16 The regiment was later redesignated as *SS-Polizeiregiment 25.*

17 This battalion contained four, instead of the usual three companies. The battalion was completely motorised.

18 At the start of the Russian campaign, this battalion moved into Belarus as part of the occupation forces.

19 One motorised company and two bicycle companies.

20 One motorised company and two bicycle companies.

21 Stephan Linck. *Der Ordnung verpflichtet: Deutsche Polizei 1933–1949.* Paderborn: Ferdinand Schöningh Verlag, 2000, p.33.

22 During the war, the western parts of pre-war Poland were absorbed into the Reich.

23 Hans-Heinrich Wilhelm. *Die Einsatzgruppe A: der Sicherheitspolizei und des SD 1941/42.* Frankfurt am Main: Peter Lang Verlag GmbH, 1996, pp.157–59.

24 The *Befehlshaber der Ordnungspolizei* controlled not only the *Schutzpolizei, Gemeindepolizei,* and *Gendarmerie,* but also the *Verwaltungspolizei, Verkehrspolizei, Wasserschutzpolizei, Bahnschutzpolizei, Feuerschutzpolizei (Feuerwehr), Luftschutzpolizei, Technische Nothilfe, Funkschutz,* and *Werkschutzpolizei.*

25 This police group was under the control of Udo von Woyrsch's operational *Einsatzgruppe.* That group, in turn, was to advance behind *14. Armee.*

26 The police companies in this battalion were used to help augment Udo von Woyrsch's *Einsatzgruppe z.b.V. von Woyrsch.* As a result, this battalion operated outside of *Polizeigruppe 1.*

27 This police unit was employed behind the lines of *10. Armee.*

28 Operating behind the lines of *8. Armee.*

29 One reference says that *SS-Standartenführer und Oberst der Polizei* Karl Jakob Heinrich Brenner was in command of *Polizeiregiment 3* in September 1939. It also states that on 19 October 1939, he became the first commander of *Polizeiregiment Warschau.*

30 Not directly attached to *Polizeiregiment 4.*

31 '*z.b.V.*' stands for '*Zur besondere Verwendung*' (for Special Employment).

32 Poznan is spelled 'Posen' in German.

33 *Polizeigruppe 5* was operating behind the lines of *4. Armee.*

34 Mülverstedt would later be killed in battle near Luga, Russia, on 10 August 1941.

35 Preradovich, Nikolaus von. *Die Generale der Waffen-SS.* Kurt Vowinckel Verlag: Berg am See, 1985, p.94.

36 Two German sources state that this was not *Polizei-Bataillon 6,* but rather, *Polizei-Bataillon 1.* However, evidence exists that *Polizei-Bataillon 1* served alongside *Polizei-Bataillon 6,* which joined this police group on 5 September 1939, or four days after the start of the campaign.

37 In the case of *Polizeiregiment 2,* the cavalry platoon was replaced by a bicycle platoon. These two police regiments later became *Infanterie Regiment 243* and *Infanterie Regiment 244* of *60. Infanterie Division (motorisiert)* of the German Army (as of 18 October 1939).

38 This unit belonged to *Einsatzgruppe IV,* but was attached to *Einsatzgruppe V* for tactical employment.

39 Although Otto Rasch was in overall command of this *Einsatzkommando,* it was *SS Sturmbannführer und Major der Schutzpolizei* Ewald Träger who led the unit in the field.

40 SD: abbreviation for *Sicherheitsdienst* (the SS Security Service).

41 Counting all members from the Gestapo, Sipo, Kripo and SD, this *Einsatzgruppe* had about 350 men.

42 This *Einsatzkommando* contained fifty to eighty cadets from the *Führerschule der Sipo Berlin-Charlottenburg* (Security Police Officer's School at Berlin-Charlottenburg).

43 This *Einsatzkommando* contained forty to fifty cadets of the *Sipo Grenzpolizeischule Pretsch* (Security Police Border Guard School at Pretsch).

44 *III. Bataillon des 4. SS Totenkopf Regiment 4 'Östmark'.*

45 This unit eventually became a *gepanzert* (armoured) unit.

46 He has also been referred to as Lothar 'Beutel'.

47 Griep would later be promoted to *SS-Brigadeführer und Generalmajor der Polizei,* and was appointed *Befehlshaber der Ordnungspolizei Alpenland* on 1 October 1943. Prior to serving in Italy, Griep had been the commander of *Polizeiregiment z.b.V* (November 1941 to August 1942); then commander

of *Polizeiregiment 2* (October 1942 to August 1943), which was operating in Belarus.

48 Rossino, Alexander B. *Hitler Strikes Poland: Blitzkrieg, Ideology, and Atrocity*. University Press of Kansas: Lawrence, 2003, p.40.

49 MacLean, French L. *The Field Men: The SS Officers Who Led the Einsatzkommandos – the Nazi Mobile Killing Units*. Schiffer Military History: Atglen, 1999, p.121.

50 Schumann, Wolfgang and Ludwig Nestler. *Nacht über Europa: Band II – Die faschistische Okkupationspolitik in Polen (1939–1945)*. Pahl-Rugenstein Verlag GmbH: Köln, 1989, p.140.

51 Antonio Muñoz. *The Last Levy: Waffen SS Officer Roster, 1 March 1945*. New York: Europa Books, 2000, p.13.

52 The term Gestapo is an abbreviation of *Geheim Staatspolizei* ('State Secret Police'). The literal translation of the word *Sicherheitsdienst* is 'security service'. It represented the SS Secret Service that was run by Walter Schellenberg.

53 Schumann and Nestler, op. cit., pp.140–41.

54 The *Selbstschutz* were ethnic German Poles who supported the German invasion of Poland.

55 Schumann and Nestler, op. cit., p.193.

56 During the first half of the Polish occupation (1939–42), approximately 630,000 people were expelled from the annexed territories.

57 Tadeusz Piotrowski, *Poland's Holocaust: Ethnic Strife, Collaboration with Occupying Forces and Genocide in the Second Republic, 1918–1947*. Jefferson: McFarland and Company Inc., 1998, p.23.

58 Alexander B. Rossino, *Hitler Strikes Poland: Blitzkrieg, Ideology, and Atrocity*. Lawrence: University Press of Kansas, 2003, p.68.

59 Rudolf Aschenauer. *Krieg Ohne Grenzen: Der Partisanenkampf gegen Deutschland 1939–1945*. Leoni am Starnberger. Druffel Verlag, 1982, p.164.

60 Schumann and Nestler, op. cit., p.163.

61 Jürgen Malthäus, *War, Pacification, and Mass Murder, 1939: The Einsatzgruppen in Poland*. Lanham: Rowman and Littlefield Publishers, 2014, p.53.

62 The cataloguing of just exactly who was an ethnic German was divided into three groups by the Nazis: Category I, II, and II. Category I (Full Ethnic German): these individuals were considered to be full ethnic Germans by the Nazis. They were often directly recruited into the Wehrmacht or other military branches. Category II (Ethnic Germans with a mixed background): this category included individuals who had partial German ancestry or were considered to be 'racially' German but had integrated into Polish society. Category III (Ethnic Germans in occupied or border regions): these individuals had less direct German

ancestry or had been assimilated into the Polish population. However, many from these regions were still considered to be of 'German blood' by the Nazis, and some were recruited into the German Armed Forces, although this was a smaller proportion compared to Categories I and II.

63 Magdalena Kowalska. *A Polish heart in a feldgrau uniform – complicated journeys from the Wehrmacht to the Polish Army in Exile* in 'Polish Scientific Society Abroad in London', Poznań: Adam Mickiewicz University, Humanities Education No. 2 (33), 2015, p.103.

64 Piotrowski, op. cit., p.83.

65 Schumann and Nestler, op. cit., pp.200–01.

66 *Stapoleitstelle*: State Police Control Centre.

67 Bialystok region had been a part of Poland until the country was divided between the Germans and Russians.

68 R. F. Leslie. *The History of Poland Since 1863*. Cambridge: Cambridge University Press, 1980, p.216.

69 This area too was former Polish territory that had been annexed by the Soviet Union.

70 In spring 1942, the Germans established an entire SS recruit training regiment in this training ground.

Chapter 2. Garrisoning Poland and Polish resistance to Nazi rule, 1939–1944

1 The term *Wehrkreis* means 'Military District'. In this case, *Wehrkreis XXI* (21st Military District).

2 SS Death's Head regiments.

3 Yerger, Mark. *Allgemeine-SS: The Commands, Units and Leaders of the General SS*. Atglen: Schiffer Military History, 1997, p.212.

4 He was promoted to *Obersturmbannführer* on 20 April 1941.

5 NARA Microfilm T-175, Roll 129, Frame 504.

6 Exner was killed fighting Polish partisans on 8 August 1944.

7 NARA T-175, Rolls 111, 141 and T-580 Roll 88.

8 NARA T-175, R-111, Frames 0153-0167.

9 Ibid., Frames 0168-1074

10 Dr. K. G. Kleitmann, *Die Waffen SS – eine Dokumentation*. Osnabrück: Verlag 'Der Freiwillige' GmbH, 1965, p.442.

11 This regiment was raised in Cracow on 11 November 1939. Franz Breithaupt held this command until December 1939 when Leo von Jena assumed the post. He in turn was in command until 28 June 1940, when *SS-Standartenführer* Julian Scherner assumed control. Scherner remained in charge until 18 December 1940. Thereafter, *SS-Oberführer* Günther Claassen

took over until shortly before the start of the Russian campaign, when SS Standartenführer Hans Wilhelm Sacks was given control of the regiment.

12 The regiment was created in Radom on 11 November 1939, using personnel provided by *SS Totenkopf Standarte 4* and *SS Totenkopf Standarte 7* in three battalions. It was transferred on 22 May 1940 to the Netherlands for coastal defence duties. While stationed there, it raised a *13.* and *14. Kompanie*. It was outfitted with motorised equipment on 19 September 1940. An additional two companies (*15.* and *16. Kompanie*) were created before the invasion of the USSR. It eventually became a part of *2. SS Infanterie Division 'Das Reich' (motorisiert)*. Karl Diebitsch was the commander of this regiment until 1 December 1940, when *SS-Obersturmbannführer* Dr Wilhelm (Wim) Brandt assumed command. A side note on Brandt: he was an engineer by training who, during his spare time, developed camouflage patterns and camouflage equipment for the Wehrmacht during the war. By July 1941, *SS-Obersturmbannführer* Jürgen Wagner had become the new commanding officer of this regiment.

13 Sacks held this post until 28 July 1940.

14 Mark Yerger, *Riding East: The SS Cavalry Brigade in Poland and Russia 1939–1942*. Atglen: Schiffer Military History, 1996, p.71.

15 Harald Buhlan and Werner Jung. *Wessen Freund und Wessen Helfer? Die Kölner Polizei im Nationalsozialismus*. Köln: Emons Verlag, 2000, p.266.

16 *Deutsches Protektorat Böhmen und Mähren* (German Protectorate of Bohemia and Moravia).

17 Buhland, et al., op. cit., p.266.

18 '*Reichshof*' is German for 'Rzeszow'.

19 *Befehlshaber der Ordnungspolizei-Generalgouvernement* (Supreme Commander of the Order Police in the General Government).

20 Kurt Mehner, *Die Geheimen Tagesberichte der Deutschen Wehrmachtführung Im Zweiten Weltkrieg 1939–1945*. Osnabrück: Biblio Verlag GmbH, 1989, 12 Vols, Vol. 6, p.553.

21 Thomas Geldmacher, *Wir als Wiener waren ja bei der Bevölkerung beliebt. ÖsterReichsische Schutzpolizisten und die Judenvernichtung in Ostgalizien 1941–1944*. Vienna: Mandelbaum Verlag, 2002, p.16.

22 Georges Jerome, *Le Gouvernement General De Pologne: L'administration allemande dans les territories occupes de Pologne 1939–1945* (1) *L'administration, la police, le parti*. In *39/45 Magazine*. Editons Heindal: Bayeux, No. 183, October, 2001, p.32.

23 In March 1940, Brenner became the Chief of Staff to the BdO – GG in Cracow before being transferred to the *4. SS-Panzer-Grenadier-Division 'Polizei'*.

24 On several occasions, Stach took leave, at which point, his Ia, *Major der Schutzpolizei* Franz Heitzinger, assumed temporary command. *Oberstleutnant der Schutzpolizei* Joachim Stach was on holiday from

12 to 15 November 1941, and from 13 December 1941 to 8 January 1942. During this period *Major der Schutzpolizei* Franz Heitzinger took temporary control of the regiment. Heitzinger was also the *Kommandeur der Gendarmerie* in Distrikt Galizien.

25 BA-MA, *Befehl der Reichsführer-SS und Fuhrer der Deutschen Polizei vom 09.08.1941 BdO im Generalgouvernement, Tagesbefehl Nr. 39 v. 27.08.1941.*

26 BA-MA, *BdO im Generalgouvernement, Tagesbefehl Nr. 52 v. 13.11.1941 und Tagesbefehl Nr. 56 v. 05.12.1941.*

27 *BdO im Generalgouvernement, Tagesbefehl Nr. 52 v. 13.11.1941 und Tagesbefehl Nr. 56 v. 05.12.1941.*

28 Heitzinger had been the 'Ia' of *Polizeiregiment Galizien* under *Oberstleutnant der Schutzpolizei* Joachim Stach.

29 In issue No. 17 dated 23 April 1961 of the German-language magazine *Der Stern* an article appeared regarding Fritz Weise. The article claimed that, according to the statements of Oskar Mühlrad, a survivor of the Holocaust, the then commander of the *Schutzpolizei* in Lemberg (Lwów), *Major der Schutzpolizei* Fritz Weise, along with a few other members his command, had assisted Jews in fleeing the city. The article claimed that police vehicles were used to transport Jews fleeing the ghetto of Lemberg. Obviously if this story is indeed true then Weise and other German policemen risked their lives to help Jews escape. These acts apparently went unnoticed by Weise's superiors as well as the security police. Weise's post-war testimony apparently confirms as described in the article by Oskar Mühlrad.

30 Georg Tessin and Norbert Kannapin. *Waffen SS und Ordnungspolizei im Kriegseinsatz 1939–1945*. Osnabrück: Biblio Verlag, 2000, p.560.

31 Mehner, *Geheime Tagesberichte*, op. cit., Vol. 5, p.340.

32 Andreas Schulz and Günter Wegmann. *Die Generale der Waffen SS und der Polizei*. Biblio Verlag GmbH: Bissendorf, 2003, Vol. I, p.468.

33 Franz Anton Diermann had been an *Oberst der Gendarmerie* and commander of the *Gendarmerie* in Belarus in 1942. Before being posted as BdO of *Wehrkreis XX*, he had been assigned the command of *SS-Polizeiregiment 20* in Prague in September 1943.

34 This command was later renamed *Höhere SS und Polizeiführer Vistula* in January 1945.

35 Beginning in 1942, Karl Thier served in the *SS und Polizeiführer Kaukasus* command under Gerret Korsemann. He died fighting on the front lines, sometime in 1944.

36 Ludolf von Alvensleben was appointed commander of the *Höherer SS- und Polizeiführer Adriatisches Küstenland* in Friuli, Italy. The headquarters for this command was located in the city of Trieste. He held this post from 11 May 1944 until 10 April 1945. Thereafter he took over the post of *SS und Polizeiführer Adria-West* until the end of the war.

37 Buhlan, et al., op. cit., p.268.

38 Eric Haberer. 'The German police and genocide in Belorussia, 1941–1944. Part II: The 'second sweep': Gendarmerie killings of Jews and Gypsies on January 29, 1942', In *Journal of Genocide Research,* Part 2, 2001, p.23.

39 Eric Haberer. 'The German police and genocide in Belorussia, 1941–1944. Part I: Police deployment and Nazi genocidal directives', In *Journal of Genocide Research,* Part 3, 2001, p.17.

40 *Orpo* is the abbreviation of *Ordnungspolizei* (Order Police).

41 Wilhelm Koppe was injured in an assassination attempt by the Polish Home Army in Cracow on 11 July 1944.

42 Promoted to *Oberst der Schutzpolizei* on 9 November 1941.

43 BA MA *Vorschlagsliste für die Verleihung von Kriegsverdienstkreuzen II. Klasse mit Schwertern vom 6.7.1941,* in BA D-HZM 1384 A 20.

44 Apparently, Petsch held this post for only four weeks, while Mantua was on leave.

45 *SS-Brigadeführer* Franz Kutschera was assassinated on 1 February 1944 in Warsaw by the Polish Home Army.

46 Andreas Schulz and Günter Wegmann. *Die Generale der Waffen-SS und der Polizei.* Biblio Verlag: Bissendorf, 2003, p.362.

47 Beuthel was scheduled to be the first commander of the *Sicherheitspolizei* in Warsaw, but he was investigated for several crimes and demoted on 23 October 1939. He was demoted to private, fired from the SS and discharged from military service. His crimes included bribery and extortion, living and sleeping with a Jewish woman, and raping the daughter of a Polish woman who was a cook for the SS.

48 In April 1944, Hahn was promoted to the rank of *SS-Standartenführer und Oberst der Polizei.* Hahn left for Germany in November 1944.

49 Schulz, et al., op cit., p.228.

50 Promoted to *Oberst der Gendarmerie* on 1 November 1944.

51 Also had the title of *Generalinspekteur der SS Totenkopfstandarten.*

52 Former commander of *SS Totenkopf Standarte 8.*

53 Brünn Meyer. *Dienstalterliste der Waffen-SS. SS-Obergruppenführer bis SS-Hauptsturmführer, Stand vom 1. Juli 1944.* Biblio Verlag: Osnabrück, 1987, p.113.

54 This command ceased to exist when the city of Cracow was liberated by the Red Army on 20 January 1945.

55 His full rank was *SS-Brigadeführer und Generalmajor der Polizei.*

56 Subordinate to the *Kommandeur der Ordnungspolizei Distrikt Galizien* command.

57 Became the head of the *Gendarmerie* in Lemberg (Lviv) from 1943 to 25 October 1944.

58 Subordinate to the *Kommandeur der Ordnungspolizei Distrikt Galizien* command.

59 This SS and Police command was not a part of the *Höherer SS und Polizeiführer Ost*, but was nevertheless a part of pre-war Poland so was listed here for the sake of completeness.

60 This battalion was withdrawn from Poland in April 1941 and sent to reform in Münster. That same year it returned to occupation duty in Poland. Many police battalions experienced similar postings and tours of duty.

61 Sent to Belarus (White Russia) in May 1943 and returned to Poland in September 1944.

62 Returned to Hamburg in December 1939 for rest and refitting.

63 Sent to Belarus in May 1943. The unit returned to Poland in September 1944.

64 The *Polizei-Bataillone 301, 303, 304,* and *306* were used to help create the various regiments that were established in Poland as part of the occupation force.

65 Arrived in autumn 1939 to help form one of the police regiments in Poland. Was detached from *Polizeiregiment 'Warschau'* in the spring of 1941 to become a part of *Polizeiregiment 'Mitte'* for the upcoming invasion of the Soviet Union. Withdrawn from the USSR in spring 1942 to become the *I. Bataillon der Polizeiregiment 23 'Krakau'* in July 1942. Later redesignated as *III. Bataillon der Polizeiregiment 24 'Lemberg'*, but remained in Poland until 1945.

66 *Polizei-Bataillonen 308, 309, 310, 311, 313, 314,* and *321* arrived in autumn 1939 to help form the various police regiments that were established in Poland.

67 GB 1: *Gendarmerie Bataillon 1 (motorisiert)* – 1st (motorised) Rural Police Battalion.

68 GB 2: *Gendarmerie Bataillon 2 (motorisiert)* – 2nd (motorised) Rural Police Battalion.

69 PRB 3: *Polizei Reiter Bataillon 3* – 3rd Police Cavalry Battalion.

70 This number is an underestimation since it does not include the police guard battalions, and police militia battalions.

71 Wilhelm, op. cit., p.159.

72 Tessin, et al., op. cit., p.579. This regiment was stationed in Lemberg (Lviv/Lwów). It was disbanded in July 1942.

73 When Stach would be absent, his second in command, *Major der Schutzpolizei* Franz Heitzinger would assume command. Two examples were when Stach was absent from 12 to 15 November 1941, and 13 December 1941 to 8 January 1942.

74 In July 1942 it was redesignated as *II. Bataillon der Polizeiregiment 24.*

75 Sent to Norway in July 1942.

76 In July 1942 it was redesignated as the *II. Bataillon der Polizeiregiment 11.*

77 This battalion was led by *Major der Gendarmerie* Erich Schwieger.

78 Antonio Muñoz, *The Druzhina SS Brigade: A History, 1941–1943*. New York: Europa Books, 2000, p.30.

79 The officers who led *Gendarmerie-Bataillon 1 (motorisiert)* were as follows: *Major der Gendarmerie* Erich Schwieger (July 1942–8 January 1943). The Battalion Adjutant was *Major der Gendarmerie* Kurt Wuttke, who temporarily led the battalion between 8 January and 18 May 1943. Then *Oberst der Gendarmerie* Johannes Rogalski (4 May 1943–20 September 1943), *Major der Gendarmerie* Erich Schwieger (20 September 1943–March 1944), and *Major der Gendarmerie* Wilhelm Dörge (March 1944d1945).

80 Stefan Klemp, *'Nicht ermittelt'. Polizeibataillone und die Nachkriegsjustiz – Ein Handbuch.* Essen: Klartext-Verlag, 2005, p.303.

81 Werner Regenberg, *Armoured Vehicles and Units of the German Order Police (Ordnungspolizei) 1936–1945*. Atglen: Schiffer Publishing, 2002, p.179.

82 Tessin, vol. 13, p.271.

83 Werner Regenberg, *Panzerfahrzeuge und Panzereinheiten der Ordnungspolizei 1936–1945*. Friedberg: Podzun Pallas Verlag, 1995, p.34.

84 Formed in Warsaw, Poland from *Polizeiregiment 'Warschau'*. Sent to Belarus in July 1944 where it was destroyed.

85 A third battalion was formed by grouping together the individual police companies stationed in Zamosz, Lublin, and Cracow.

86 Formed and served in Cracow, Poland, from 1942 to 1944. This was simply a redesignation of *Polizeiregiment 'Krakau'*.

87 A second and third battalion was formed by grouping together the individual police companies stationed in Krakau (Cracow), Reichshof (Rzeszow), Lemberg (Lviv/Lwów), and Radom.

88 Formed in Lemberg (Lviv) in July 1942. This was simply a redesignation of *Polizeiregiment 'Radom'*. The 1st and 2nd Battalions were sent to Belarus in 1943, while the 3rd Battalion was sent to Krajina in Slovenia; then it was transferred once more, this time to France.

89 Formed in Lublin by simply redesignating *Polizeiregiment 'Lublin'*. The *I. Bataillon* was sent to Ljubljana, Slovenia in August 1944.

90 Myroslav Shkandrij. *In the Maelstrom: The Waffen SS 'Galicia' Division and Its Legacy*. Montreal: McGill-Queen's University Press, 2023, p.125.

91 Created in July 1943 from excess personnel not deemed fit to serve in *14. Waffen Grenadier Division der SS (Galizien Nr. 1)*. The *III. Bataillon* served in Holland in February 1944 but the entire regiment was disbanded on 9 June 1944 and its personnel were used as replacements to help reform the shattered *14. Waffen Grenadier Division der SS (Galizien Nr. 1)* in July 1944.

92 Created in July 1943 for service in Galicia and other parts of the GG. It took part in several anti-partisan drives in Lublin and Hrubieszow. It was disbanded on 9 June 1944, and its personnel were absorbed into the *14. Waffen Grenadier Division der SS (Galizien Nr. 1)*.

93 It was created on 6 August 1943 and disbanded 31 January 1944.

94 This regiment was disbanded and its police battalions were transferred over to the newly created *Galizien-SS Freiwilligen Regiment 5 (Polizei)* in July 1943.

95 It was created in March / April 1943 for service in the Bialystok District.

96 It was formed and employed in Poland on 24 June 1942. Was stationed in the Lublin region until August 1944, then in Petrikau.

97 It was formed in Lublin, Poland, in February 1943.

98 It was formed in and employed in Posen (Poznan), Poland.

99 It was formed in September 1944 for use in the region of Galicia.

100 It was formed in September 1944 for use in the region of Lublin.

101 It was formed in October 1944 for use in the region of Cracow.

102 This Cossack cavalry unit was the size of one platoon of about thirty to forty men.

103 Formed in August 1944.

104 It was formed in October 1944.

105 It was formed in October 1944.

106 It was formed in October 1944.

107 This formation was a company in size and consisted of rocket-propelled mortars.

108 It was formed in February 1944 in Poznan for operations in *Wehrkreis XX*. During the war about thirty-five *Polizei-Wachbataillone* were created and designated using Roman numerals. Most were employed in occupation duty outside of the Reich.

109 It was formed in June 1944 in Lodz for operations in *Wehrkreis XX*.

110 It was formed in December in the city of Poznan for defence of the city.

111 It was formed in August 1944 in the city of Warsaw from administrative police personnel for action in the Warsaw uprising.

112 It was formed in September 1944 for employment in the region of Cracow.

113 It was formed in October 1943 for operations in the Bialystok district. Around forty *Polizei-Landesschützen-Bataillone* were established during the war, employing men of older-age groups, as well as ethnic-Germans and even *Volkssturm* personnel.

114 It was formed on 5 September 1944, in the city of Poznan (Posen).

115 David K. Yelton, *Hitler's Volkssturm: The Nazi Militia and the Fall of Germany, 1944–1945*. Lawrence: University Press of Kansas, 2002, p.9.

116 It was formed in February 1944 and employed initially under the control of the German Order Police to fight Polish partisans. These were the so-called 'Grolmann Militia Battalions' made up of reliable, draft-exempt, or deferred Germans living in *Wehrkreis XXI* (Posen). They were so named after *General der Infanterie* Karl-Wilhelm von Grolmann, who in 1832 defended the city of Posen from Polish forces.

117 Franz W. Seidler, *Deutscher Volkssturm: Das letzte Aufgebot, 1944–1945*. Munich: F. A. Herbig Verlag, 1989, p.55.

118 Regenberg, op. cit., p.34.

119 Ibid.

120 The German police units involved in this operation included: *II/4 (**II. Bataillon**, Polizei-Regiment 4), I/16 (**I. Bataillon**, Polizei-Regiment 16), III/17 (**III. Bataillon**, Polizei-Regiment 17), II/22 (**II. Bataillon**, Polizei-Regiment 22), II/25 (**II. Bataillon**, Polizei-Regiment 25), **I/33** (**I. Bataillon**, formerly part of Polizei-Regiment 20), **I/34** (**I. Bataillon**, formerly part of Polizei-Regiment 21), and **Schutzmannschaft Bataillon 206**.*

121 Testimony of Heinz Houben, Dortmund.

122 https://encyclopedia.ushmm.org/content/en/article/killing-centers-an-overview, accessed 3 March 2022.

123 This figure includes the approximately 6 million Jews that were murdered during the war.

124 Hanusiak, op. cit., p.82.

125 Piotrowski, op. cit., p.85.

126 Jan Grabowski. *The Polish Police: Collaboration in the Holocaust*. United States Holocaust Memorial Museum: Washington, D.C., www.ushmm.org/m/pdfs/20170502-Grabowski_OP.pdf. 2017, p.2.

127 Antonio Muñoz, 'German SS, Police, and Auxiliary Forces in Poland, Part V – 1944 and the Warsaw Uprising', in *Europa Magazine*, Issue 15, Fall 1998, p.31.

128 Katarzyna Person, *Warsaw Ghetto Police: The Jewish Order Service during the Nazi Occupation*. Ithaca: Cornell University Press, 2021, p.90.

129 At peak strength, the Jewish Order Police in Warsaw reached about 2,500 men.

130 Albert Nirenstein, *A Tower from the Enemy. Contributions to a history of Jewish resistance in Poland*. New York: The Orion Press, 1959, p.16.

131 Piotrowski, op. cit., p.67.

132 NARA T-RG-238 Working Conference on 23 April 1940, Service Diary of Governor General Hans Frank, Vol. 9, pp.40–41.

133 Krüger to Gunst, 14 November 1939, W. Gunst SS Officer file (former BDC), RGp-242, A3343/SSO/043A/321, NARA; judgment in proceedings against Friedrich Paulus, 26 May 1977, p.6, file 4 Ks 1/74, State Prosecutor's Office in Frankfurt am Main.

134 *Ortskommandantur I/524* to *Amt I*, Memorandum on the Conversation with Police Commanders at Army Headquarters XXXII on 8 December 1939 and 10 December 1939, file *Ortskommandantur I/524*, sygn. 31, pp.378–79, WAPL; Globocnik to Chief, District Lublin, 13 February 1940, file *Gouverneur, Distrikt Lublin*, sygn. 891, p.10, WAPL, and NARA RG-242 A3343 / SSO, 0156B / 242-243, formerly the Berlin Document Centre – now under the administration of the *Bundesarchiv*, Berlin. Documents of the Labour Office, Biała-Podlaska to Labour Department, Lublin, 18 July 1940, file Gouverneur, District Lublin, sygn. 746, pp.41–43, WAPL.

135 David Littlejohn, *Foreign Legions of the Third Reichs, Vol. IV*. San Jose: R. James Bender, 1987, p.19.

136 Ray Brandon and Wendy Lower. *Shoah in Ukraine: History, Testimony, Memorialization*. Bloomington: Indiana University Press, 2008, p.140.

137 Koch would be promoted to *Major der Schutzpolizei* on 20 October 1942.

138 Tessin et al., *Waffen SS und Polizei*, op. cit., p.646.

139 The terms *Ortskommandantur*, *Feldkommandantur*, and *Oberfeldkommandantur* refer to different levels of military administrative commands for rear area forces. The three levels (from top to bottom) were:

1. *Oberfeldkommandantur* (Military Government Area Headquarters):
   - Role: These were senior-level field command authorities, overseeing larger operational areas or multiple field command zones. Scope: They had a higher rank and broader responsibilities compared to *Feldkommandanturen*, often encompassing multiple operational units or regions.
   - Hierarchy: *Oberfeldkommandanturen* held a higher command position, coordinating and supervising the activities of several *Feldkommandanturen*. In summary, the hierarchy from lowest to highest is *Ortskommandanturen* (local command), *Feldkommandanturen* (field command), and *Oberfeldkommandanturen* (senior field command).
2. *Feldkommandantur* (Field Command Military Government):
   - Role: These commandants were responsible for military operations in a specific field or combat area. Scope: They operated in operational theatres or zones of conflict, managing military units and operations on the ground.
   - Hierarchy: *Feldkommandanturen* were higher in the command structure than *Ortskommandanturen*, dealing with broader operational concerns and field command duties.
3. *Ortskommandantur* (Local Commandant Military Government):
   - Role: These were local military command authorities responsible for administrative and logistical oversight in

specific towns or districts. Scope: Typically in charge of small geographic areas, often at the level of a town or city. Their responsibilities included maintaining order, overseeing local military installations, and coordinating with other military and civilian authorities within their jurisdiction.

- Hierarchy: They operated at a lower level of command compared to *Feldkommandanturen* and *Oberfeldkommandanturen*.

In closing, each military administrative level had distinct responsibilities tailored to the scale of their command and operational needs.

140 This town lies about 312km (208 miles) south of Warsaw.

141 Arrived in Demba, Poland, in December 1942.

142 The battalion was relocated to Denmark on 1 July 1943.

143 This town lies about 67km north-east of Baranovichi, and 77km south-west of Minsk.

144 Arrived from Bohemia-Moravia in October 1942.

145 The division was disbanded on 19 February 1944 and its sub-units allocated to the *68. Infanterie Division.*

146 This town lies 17km east of Rzeszow. Rzeszow is approximately 177km south-west of Lublin.

147 Janow lies 29km north-west of Lublin.

148 This was simply an expansion of *Turkistanische Arbeits Ersatz Abteilung.* The brigade contained three battalions that supplied recruits for the *162. (turkistanische) Infanterie Division.*

149 This town is about 17km north-east of the city of Radom.

150 The town of Jedlnia was the base for the establishment of more than sixteen separate battalions of Caucasian, Volga Tartar, Azerbaijani, and Turkestani volunteers serving in the German Army. The following battalions were created there between 1942–1943: *Turkistanische Infanterie Bataillone 452* and *784, Kaukasicher Mohammedan Infanterie Bataillon 804, Aserbaidschanische Infanterie Bataillone 803, 806, 807, 817, 818,* and *819, Wolgatatar Infanterie Bataillone 825, 826, 827, 828, 829, 830,* and *831.*

151 This Legion training base was transferred to southern France in early 1944.

152 Trained the following volunteer battalions at Legionovo: *Turkistanische Infanterie Feldersatz Bataillone I./44, I./100, I./29, I./297, I./305, I./370, I./384, I./38, Turkistanische Infanterie Bataillone I./94, 452, 781, 782, 783, 785, 786, 787, 789, 790,* and *791.*

153 The town of Pulawy was the site where the Armenian Legion headquarters trained the following volunteer battalions: *Armenische Feldbataillone I./125,* and *I./198, Armenische Infanterie Bataillone 808, 809, 810, 812, 813,* and *814.*

154 Established in Rozan in June 1940 but left for Tilsit in August 1940. In September it was sent to Bohemia-Moravia, where it eventually became the *II. Bataillon der Infanterie Regiment 721.*

155 *Landesschützen-Bataillon 637* was created in Rozan in June 1941, but was quickly renamed as *Wach Bataillon 654.* It was earmarked for the Russian Campaign and assigned to *213. Sicherungs Division (Heeresgruppe Süd).*

156 This third battalion was established in Sanok in August 1942. It left for Norway in December 1942.

157 Arrived in October 1941. Modlin lies approximately 38km north-west of Warsaw.

158 *Grenadier Ersatz und Ausbildungs Bataillon 493.* This was simply a redesignation of *II. Bataillon/Infanterie Regiment 721.* It was withdrawn to Stablack, East Prussia, in 1945. Stablack (Stabławki) lies approximately 83km due south of Königsberg (present-day Kaliningrad).

159 Since March 1943. Originally titled as *I. Bataillon der Sicherungs Regiment 603.* It was renamed *Sicherungs-Bataillon 692* in October 1943. Strangely, the regimental headquarters *(Sicherungs Regiment 603)* was stationed in Minsk.

160 Employed in the front lines and destroyed along the Vistula River in January 1945.

161 Formed in August 1944 in Kielce, which lies about 190km west-south-west of Lublin. In January 1945 the battalion was fighting along the Vistula River bend, near Radom, where it was destroyed.

162 Arrived in Kielce, in the GG on 16 July 1941. This battalion was employed on PoW guard duty.

163 In 1943, it was transferred to Lublin.

164 This regiment was created in March 1943. Although it officially belonged to *Sicherungs Brigade 202* (at the time, deployed in Belarus), it nevertheless remained in the Kielce area with its two battalions and performed security duties there. From 6 February 1944, the regimental staff was deployed as part of the Polotsk Fortress. The town of Polotsk was part of north-eastern Poland before the war. It became a part of Belarus after the war, when Poland's borders were moved west. Polotsk lies about 237km north-east of Minsk. Sometime in 1944 the regiment was disbanded.

165 This unit was transferred from Lublin in December 1941. The three regimental staffs of the brigade (*603*, *608*, and *613*) were sent to Central Russia when the brigade was renamed as *Sicherungs Brigade 203* on 24 December 1941. However, six battalions from this brigade remained in the GG as security troops.

166 It was created in August 1944. The battalion was transferred to East Prussia at the beginning of 1945.

167 It was created in March 1943.

168 Arrived on 23 June 1941. In November 1942 it was relocated to Sarny in Ukraine.

169 Arrived from Posen (Poznan) in July 1941. It had served in Posen from 1939–1940. Contained the following transport security battalions: *Transport Sicherungs-Bataillonen 358, 384, 518, 567, 615, 616, 702, 882, 952.*

170 This was simply a redesignation of *Wach Bataillon 654*. In Sarny in January 1941, but was sent to Ukraine under *213. Sicherungs Division.*

171 Arrived December 1940. In July 1941 it was renamed *Landesschützen-Bataillon 998*. Left for central Russia in July 1941.

172 Stationed in Wieruschow (Wieruszów), a town that lies roughly between Lodz and Wroclaw. In November 1939 the battalion was shifted to Sieradsch (Sieradz), about 44km west of Lodz. There they were used to guard PoWs and as bridge guards on the Kalisch-Litzmannstadt railway line and the special coal railway line. In June 1940 it was transferred to Litzmannstadt. In 1941 the battalion was renamed *Landesschützen-Bataillon 476* and was sent to Warsaw.

173 Established in January 1942. It helped to create the following battalions: *Nordkaukasiche Infanterie Bataillone 800, 801, 803, 835, 836, 837, 842,* and *843.* In the spring of 1944, the legion was transferred to southern France.

174 This battalion arrived in Warsaw in January 1941.

175 Arrived in October 1944. Formed part of *Festungs Division 'Warschau'* (Fortress Division 'Warsaw').

176 Merely a redesignation of *Infanterie Ersatz Bataillon 484.* In March 1942 part of this battalion was used to build *Landesschützen-Bataillon 918.*

177 Created in Warsaw in March 1942.

178 Sent to Kovel in January 1944 and destroyed there in March.

179 Created using *Landesschützen-Bataillone 476* and *918.*

180 This regimental headquarters was sent to Cologne, Germany, in August 1943 with only *Landesschützen-Bataillon 476.*

181 Raised in Graudenz (Grudziądz), in *Wehrkreis XX,* in August 1944. Became the *IV. Bataillon der Festungs Infanterie Regiment 8* in January 1945.

182 Merely a redesignation of *Infanterie Regiment 88.*

183 It was formed in *Wehrkreis XX* in August 1944. Sent to become the *IV. Bataillon der Festungs Infanterie Regiment 88* in January 1945.

184 It was created in April 1940. It contained *Landesschützen-Bataillone 996, 997,* and *998.* It was destroyed in January 1945 during the battle by the Red Army to capture Warsaw.

185 It was created in Warsaw in March 1943. It was destroyed in heavy fighting along the Vistula River bend in late 1944/early 1945.

186 It was created in Warsaw in March 1943. It was disbanded in late August 1944 after taking heavy losses during the Warsaw Uprising.

187 It arrived in July 1941 and became the *I. Bataillon der Wach Regiment Warschau*. Disbanded in early September 1944 on account of heavy losses during the Warsaw Uprising.

188 It arrived in July 941 and became the *II. Bataillon der Wach Regiment Warschau.*

189 It was attached to 251. Infanterie Division in West Prussia in 1945.

190 It arrived in July 1941. Became the *III. Bataillon der Wach Regiment Warschau*. Sent to Modlin in October 1944, where it was committed to heavy fighting and took heavy losses. The battalion was disbanded at the end of 1944.

191 It arrived in March 1942. Left for southern Russia in June 1942.

192 It arrived in July 1940 as part of *Feldrekruten Infanterie Regiment 242* (established in *Wehrkreis XX* in June 1940). Left for Germany a month later.

193 This unit was merely an expansion of *Infanterie Ersatz Bataillon 500*. The regiment was relocated to Bohemia and Moravia in May 1944.

194 It arrived in December 1943. This was a penal unit composed of soldiers who had been in prison for various offences.

195 It arrived in May 1942. Later renamed *Transport Sicherungs-Bataillon 616* and transferred to Malkinia in June.

196 It arrived in December 1943 from Lyck (Ełk). Lyck lies approximately 112km north-north-west of Bialystok, in what was part of *Wehrkreis I* (Prussia). Disbanded in February 1944 so its men could be absorbed into *Schatten Division Wahn*. This division supplied replacement units for various depleted German divisions. This replacement division was formed on 17 January 1944 at *Truppenübungsplatz Wahn*, in *Wehrkreis VI*, as a shadow division of the 24th wave from the *182nd Reserve-Division*. On 28 February, the division was earmarked for employment under *Heeresgruppe A*, but by an order that was dated 16 March, the division was instead used to completely replenish the strength of *331. Infanterie Division*, which had been recently decimated. The staff for the division had come from the staff of *70. Infanterie Division.*

197 In January 1942, the battalion arrived in Lowitsch (Łowicz). In February it was assigned to *Heeresgruppe Mitte*. It was redesignated as *Sicherungs-Bataillon 909* in June 1942, and became a part of *201. Sicherungs Division* in the region of Polotsk-Nevel. It was then redesignated as *II. Bataillon der Sicherungs Regiment 601.*

198 It was established in the town in March 1943. In July 1944 the battalion was shifted to Yaroslav, but in November it was stationed in Przemysl. In 1945 the battalion was destroyed in Dukla Pass, in Slovakia.

199 It arrived in October 1942. On 2 November 1942 it was renamed *Reserve Grenadier Bataillon 414* November 2, 1942. Disbanded in March 1944.

200 It arrived in October 1942. On 2 November 1942 it was renamed *Grenadier Ersatz Bataillon 414*. This battalion was mobilised for front-line combat in April 1945.

201 Arrived in October 1942 and was disbanded in March 1944.

202 Since March 1943. Originally titled as *II. Bataillon der Sicherungs Regiment 603*. It was renamed *Sicherungs-Bataillon 693* in October 1943. The battalion was later moved to Warsaw in October 1943. Strangely, the regimental headquarters *(Sicherungs Regiment 603)* was stationed in Minsk. At the beginning of 1945 the battalion was in action in the Tarnow area. Later it was used in the Carpathian Mountains. The battalion was then deployed to Slovakia. There it was made subordinate to the *253. Infanterie Division.*

203 Arrived in Lemberg (Lviv) in September 1942.

204 Disbanded in March 1944. Used to help form *Infanterie Division 'Generalgouvernement'*.

205 Arrived in June 1941, but was transferred to Poltava in December of the same year.

206 Formed 13 February 1944 for *Infanterie Division 'Generalgouvernement'*.

207 Arrived from Breslau, Silesia. Was a part of *Transport Sicherungs Regiment Ukraine*, but remained in the Lemberg area.

208 It was established in March 1943. In October 1943 it was made *II. Bataillon der Sicherungs Regiment 603*. At the beginning of 1945, the battalion was employed in the Tarnow area, then the Carpathian Mountains.

209 It was formed in May from the remnants of *Sicherungs-Bataillon 857*, which was destroyed defending Vinnitsa in March 1944. By January 1945 this battalion was located in Slovakia.

210 Created from *Infanterie Ersatz Regiment 612* in September 1942. Absorbed *Landesschützen-Regiment 114*, which had arrived in July 1943. Became a part of *Infanterie Division 'Generalgouvernement'* in 1944.

211 Arrived in Lviv in September 1939. In November 1939 the battalion was shifted to Obornik, in *Wehrkreis XXI*, which had been created by the annexation of Polish territory.

212 On 25 July 1941 the battalion was shifted to Dobromysl, about 98km east of Posen (Poznan).

213 At the end of September 1942, the battalion was shifted to Lemberg (Lviv/Lwów).

214 In late May 1944 the battalion was transferred to Meppen, Germany.

215 When the battalion arrived in June 1941, it was posted to Cholm (Chelm), about 187km north of Lviv. Chelm lies closer to Lublin, about

70km east of Lublin. In November 1941 the battalion was once again shifted, this time to Drohobycz, about 80km south-west of Lviv. Then in April 1942 the battalion was transferred to Stanislaw (present-day Ivano Frankivsk), about 133km south-south-east of Lviv. It was not until 5 October 1942 that the battalion was finally quartered in Lviv. Beginning in August 1944, the battalion was involved in guard duty in a PoW camp (*Stalag XI*). In 1945 the battalion was still performing guard duty at a PoW camp in Germany.

216 Arrived in Lemberg in September 1941 and absorbed into *Landesschützen-Regiment 'Lemberg'*. In June 1944 the battalion was shifted to the Carpathian Mountains. By 1945 the battalion was a part of *8. Armee* in Slovakia.

217 The battalion arrived in September 1941 and absorbed into *Landesschützen-Regiment 'Lemberg'*. At the beginning of 1944, a special hunter company was raised from the battalion and posted to Horodenka, about 200km south-south-east of Lviv. In June 1944 the entire battalion was transferred to the Czech Protectorate.

218 Arrived on 5 July 1941 and made a part of *Landesschützen-Regiment 'Lemberg'*.

219 The unit took heavy losses while taking part in the defence of Lviv. In 1945, it withdrew under the overall command of *17. Armee.*

220 *Grenadier Ersatz und Ausbildungs Bataillon 385.*

221 Arrived in October 1942. The battalion was a part of *154. Reserve-Division.* In September 1942 it was shifted back to Germany.

222 Transferred to Lublin, in the GG in July 1941 from Potsdam. In December 1941 the headquarters of this brigade was relocated to Kielce.

223 Arrived in September 1942. It was absorbed by *26. Infanterie Division* in July 1944. The division contained the following units: *Reserve Grenadier Regiment 24, Reserve Grenadier Regiment 209, Reserve Grenadier Regiment 266, Reserve Artillerie Abteilung 14, Reserve Pionier Bataillon 14.*

224 Beginning August 1940. This battalion was also renamed from *Wach Bataillon 653* to *Landesschützen-Bataillon 636* in January 1941.

225 Simply a redesignation of *Wach Bataillon 653*. By 1 June 1941 this battalion had been posted to the region of *Heeresgruppe Nord,* under *207. Sicherungs Division.*

226 Created in Lublin in March 1940 from two battalions. In July 1940, a third battalion, *Wach Bataillon 653,* was created for the regiment. In January 1941 the regiment's first two battalions were redesignated as *Landesschützen-Bataillone 617* and *619*. The regimental headquarters was disbanded but the three battalions remained.

227 Moved to Bialystok in May 1941. Sent to Germany in August 1942.

228 Initially performing PoW guard duty in Kielce, but then sent to Lublin. It remained in Lublin until 1945 when it was sent to Pomerania.

229 In 1943 this battalion was moved to Lublin from Kielce. In 1945 this battalion was transferred to eastern Pomerania.

230 Created in Lublin in March 1940. In July 1940 the regiment returned to Germany, leaving behind *Wach Bataillon 655.*

231 Redesignated as *Landesschützen-Bataillon 623* in January 1941. In June 1941 the unit was redesignated as *Sicherungs-Bataillon 623* and sent to serve under the *Wehrmacht Befehlshaber Ukraine.*

232 Established in Lublin in January 1941. Redesignated as *Wach Bataillon 653* in June and sent to *Heeresgruppe Nord.*

233 Arrived in June 1941.

234 Remnants of the battalion were merged with *Landesschützen-Bataillon 992.*

235 Established in June 1941. Took heavy losses in front of Lublin. By 1945 it was stationed in Radom.

236 Established in November 1943 at *Truppenübungsplatz Radom* (Army Training Ground 'Radom'). Sent to the front lines near Tarnopol in March 1944. Contained the following units: *Grenadier Regiment 947, Grenadier Regiment 948, Grenadier Regiment 949, Divisions Füsilier Bataillon 359, Artillerie Regiment 359, Pionier Bataillon 359, Feldersatz Bataillon 359, Panzerjäger Abteilung 359, Divisions Nachrichten Abteilung 359, Divisions Nachschubführer 359.*

237 Created in Radom on 11 November 1939, using cadres furnished by *SS-Totenkopfstandarte 4* and *SS-Totenkopfstandarte 7* in three Sturmbann. The regiment was sent to the Netherlands on 22 May 1940 for coastal defence duties. While stationed there, the regiment raised the *13. Kompanie* and *14. Kompanie.* It was outfitted with all manner of vehicles in September 1940, making it a motorised regiment. The regiment established the *15. Kompanie* and *16. Kompanie* before the start of the Russian Campaign. *SS-Totenkopfstandarte 11* replaced *SS-Infanterie Regiment Germania* in the 2. *SS-Infanterie-Division 'Das Reich' (motorisiert).*

238 Arrived in Radom in February 1942. It was made a part of *Landesschützen-Regiment 65.* A month later, in March, the battalion was sent to Glebockie, in Belarus.

239 Sent to Radom in January 1942. Was attached to *Landesschützen-Regiment 65.* It remained in the Radom area into 1944. In July 1944 it became the *III. Bataillon der Sicherungs Regiment 603.*

240 Arrived in January 1942 and became a part of *Landesschützen-Regiment 65.* In April 1944 the battalion was deployed near Vitebsk, then was moved to Minsk in June, where it was destroyed that same month.

241 Arrived in Radom in January 1942 and became a part of *Landesschützen-Regiment 65.* In March 1942 it was sent to Belarus.

242 Arrived in December 1941 and placed under the control of *Oberfeldkommandantur 372.* At the beginning of 1945 the regiment was operating in upper Silesia.

243 Formed in October 1944. The division controlled the following units: *Festungs Regiments Stab z.b.V. 11, Sicherungs-Bataillon 1017, 1.–3. Kompanien der Sicherungs-Bataillon 1028, 4. Kompanie der Landesschützen-Bataillon 995, Landesschützen-Bataillon 528, Transport Sicherungs-Bataillon 595, Feldgendarmerie Trupp 938, 948, und 952, Oberfeldkommandantur I/927, Oberfeldkommandantur I/919, Oberfeldkommandantur I/600, Oberfeldkommandantur I/444, Oberfeldkommandantur I/325, 1. und 2. Nachrichten Kompanie der Nachrichten Abteilung 706, Sanitäts Kompanie 1601.* This division remained in January 1945. By February it had been moved to upper Silesia.

244 It arrived in March 1940.

245 It was transferred to *Heeresgruppe Mitte*, where it formed part of *Sicherungs Regiment 113 der 285. Sicherungs Division.*

246 It arrived in October 1939. Became the *II. Bataillon der Infanterie Regiment 644*. Later transferred to central Russia under this regiment.

247 It arrived in September 1939.

248 In March 1940 the battalion was incorporated under *Infanterie Regiment 645 der 358. Infanterie Division.*

249 It arrived in October 1939.

250 In March 1940 the battalion was incorporated under *Infanterie Regiment 645 der 358. Infanterie Division.*

251 It arrived in Cracow on 26 September 1939. From 10 October 1939, the battalion was deployed under *Oberfeldkommandantur Tarnow.*

252 From 10 March 1940, the battalion was redesignated as *I. Bataillon der Infanterie Regiment 647, 365. Infanterie Division.*

253 It was renamed in July from *Landesschützen-Bataillon 994.*

254 Beginning in July 1941.

255 It was destroyed in 1945 while defending Cracow.

256 It was renamed in July from *Landesschützen-Bataillon 995.*

257 Beginning in July 1941.

258 It was destroyed in 1945 while defending Cracow.

259 Arrived in October 1939. Contained the following units: *Feldrekruten Infanterie Regiment 210, Feldrekruten Infanterie Regiment 214, Artillerie Abteilung 95*, and *Pionier Bataillon 95.* Was transferred to Krasnik (about 240km north-east of Krakau) in March 1940 and renamed as *Kommandeur der Ersatztruppen 10.*

260 Raised in Cracow on 11 November 1939 from elements of *SS-Totenkopfstandarte 4* with three Sturmbann (three battalions). The unit became motorised in September 1940. It remained in Cracow until June 1941, when it was assigned anti-partisan duties under *1. SS Infanterie Brigade (motorisiert)* for Operation Barbarossa.

261 Arrived from Danzig (Gdansk) on 22 May 1940. Became motorised in September 1940. Assigned to anti-partisan warfare under *1. SS Infanterie Brigade (motorisiert)* for the invasion of the USSR. Left Cracow for Russia in June 1941.

262 Was stationed here from 15 September 1942 to 1 October 1944. Contained the following units: *Infanterie Ersatz Regiment 4, Infanterie Ersatz Regiment 223, Infanterie Ersatz Regiment 255, Infanterie Ersatz Regiment 256, Artillerie Ersatz Regiment 4, Beobachtungs Ersatz-Abteilung 4, Aufklärungs Ersatz Abteilung 10, Pionier Brücken Ersatz Bataillon 1, Pionier Ersatz Bataillon 24, Kraftfahr Ersatz Abteilung 4, and Fahr Ersatz Abteilung 24. Infanterie Ersatz Regiment 255* – all of which were located in Lviv (see Lviv in the table).

263 The training of these foreign volunteers provided the Germans with a sizeable garrison force that could be tapped in case the need was necessary. *The Turkistanische Legion*, which included Kazaks, Kirghiz, Uzbeks, Turkomans, Karakalpaks, and other minor tribes, was stationed near Legionowo; the *Georgische Legion* was stationed near Kruszyna; the *Nordkaukasische Legion*, with men from some thirty different tribes from the northern slopes of the range, was stationed near Wesola; the *Armenische Legion* was stationed near Pulawy; the *Wolgatatarische Legion* (aka. *Legion Idel-Ural*) was stationed near Jeldnia. The *Kaukasische-Mohammedanische Legion* – later split into the *Nordkaukasiche Legion* and *Aserbaidschanische Legion* – was stationed near Jeldnia.

264 Established in 1942 to train the Georgian volunteers for the German Army. A total of eight Georgian volunteer battalions were created: *Georgische Infanterie Bataillone 795, 796, 797, 798, 799, 822, 823,* and *824*.

265 Transferred from Poltava, Ukraine, in the summer of 1944. Was a part of *Division z.b.V. 601*.

266 At the beginning of 1945 the battalion was operating in Hungary, under the German *8. Armee*.

267 The battalion was redeployed to Lodenau, Germany, in May 1940. This town lay just across the border from Poland.

268 Arrived in June 1941. Moved to Drohobycz in November 1941. Moved to Stanislau in April 1942. Moved to Lemberg (Lviv/Lwów) in October 1942. In August 1944, the battalion was placed on guard duty in *Stalag XI*.

269 Rossino, op. cit., p.186.

270 Schumann et al., op. cit., p.362.

271 Piotrowski, op. cit., p.108.

272 Richard C. Lukas, *Forgotten Holocaust: The Poles under German Occupation 1939–1944*. Lexington: The University Press of Kentucky, 1986, p.93.

Chapter 3. Complicity in atrocities by the German Army, SS and Police forces in Poland, 1939–1944

1 Schumann et al., op. cit., p.356.

2 Browning, op. cit., pp.38–39.

3 Poprzeczny, op. cit., pp.180–81.

4 Ibid., p.233.

5 Lukas, op. cit., p.74.

6 Nineteen of whom were children.

7 They were locked inside a house and burned alive.

8 The *Sonderdienst* were auxiliary policemen who were ethnic German Poles.

9 Including forty-seven children.

10 Out of the thirty-four people killed, eleven of them were children.

11 The Wehrmacht units included tank and artillery formations.

12 Plus 100 sent to Maydanek concentration camp.

13 According to records, these twenty-seven people were burned to death.

14 Including sixty-six women and children.

15 This table was completely derived from hundreds of court proceedings and judgements in German trials of war criminals as listed in the multi-volume reference, *Justiz und NS-Verbrechen*, Volumes I–XXVIII.

16 Kobryn was located east of Brest-Litovsk, and was in an area designated as part of the Reichskommissariat Ukraine.

17 In July 1942 this police battalion became the *II. Bataillon der Polizeiregiment 2* in Tilsit.

18 In July 1942 *Polizei-Bataillon 41* was redesignated as *I. Bataillon der Polizeiregiment 22* in Warsaw.

19 At this time *Polizei-Bataillon 91* was acting as the *IV. Bataillon der Polizeiregiment 'Warschau'*.

20 In July 1942 this battalion had been redesignated as *III. Bataillon der Polizeiregiment 24*. In April 1943 *Reichsführer-SS* Heinrich Himmler decreed that all police regiments made up of Reich Germans were to be prefixed with the title 'SS' (i.e. *SS-Polizeiregiment 24*), and those made up primarily of foreigners were to be referred to as a '*Polizei-Schützen-Regiment*' (police rifle regiment).

21 Acting as *III. Bataillon der Polizeiregiment 25*.

22 *Justiz und NS Verbrechen, Kriegsverbrechen, Andere Massenvernichtungsverbrechen*, Court Case No. 1017, the West German State vs. Kurt Melzer, Rudolf Hermann, and Arno-Ernst Schumann. This table was completely derived from hundreds of court proceedings and judgements in German trials of war criminals as listed in the multi-volume reference '*Justiz und NS-Verbrechen*', Volumes I-XXVIII.

23 One defendant in the battalion was accused of killing his Ukrainian mistress.

24 This regiment was redesignated *Polizeiregiment 10* in July 1942.

25 For an example of one of these crimes, please go to the end of this table for a description of the actions of the *9. Kompanie, III. Bataillon der Polizeiregiment 15.*

26 *Major der Schutzpolizei* Otto Emil Wilke, then *Oberstleutnant der Schutzpolizei* Martin Valtin.

27 *The Trial of the Major War Criminals Before the International Military Tribunal. Nuremberg 14 November 1945–1 October 1945*. Nuremberg: Secretary of the International Military Tribunal, Official text English edition. Volumes XXXVIII–XLI, 1949, and: National Archives Collection of World War II War Crimes Records (Record Groups 153, 238 and 549).

28 Werner Präg and Wolfgang Jacobmeyer. *Das Diensttagebuch des deutschen Generalgouverneurs in Polen, 1939–1945*. Stuttgart: Verlags Anstalt, 1975, p.675.

29 Erich Stockhorst. *5000 Köpfe: Wer War Was Im Dritte Reich.* Kiel: Arndt Verlag, 2000, p.212.

30 Ludwig Fischer was the District Governor for Warsaw.

31 Antonio Muñoz and Oleg Romanko. *Hitler's White Russians: Collaboration, Extermination, and Anti-Partisan Warfare in Belorussia, 1941–1944*. New York: Europa Books, 2002, p.293.

32 Ibid., p.294.

33 The regiment was given the honorary title '*Todt*' because the unit contained men who had served previously in the '*Todt*' Labour Organization.

34 Massimo Arico, *Ordnungspolizei Volume 1: Encyclopedia of the German Police Battalions September 1939–July 1942*. Stockholm: Leandoer and Co Forlag, 2016, pp.457, 492.

35 Also sometimes spelled 'Kalmyks'.

36 Dr Frank H. Vizetelly, Editor. *Funk & Wagnalls New Standard Encyclopedia*. New York: Funk & Wagnalls Company, 1931. Vol. 17, pp.20–21.

37 Thomas Penson De Quincey (1785–1859) was an English writer and literary critic. He is best known for the book, 'Confessions of an English Opium-Eater' (published in 1821). His definitive study on the Kalmyk people was re-published in the United States in 1901 by Ginn & Company, Publishers (Boston). It was edited by Dr. William Edward Simonds.

38 Olaf Caroe. *Soviet Empire: The Turks of Central Asia and Stalinism*. London: Macmillan & Co. Ltd, 1954, p.71.

39 Paul Carell. *Hitler Moves East 1941–1943*. Little, Brown and Company: Boston, 1964, p.507.

40 Jürgen Thorwald. *The Illusion: Soviet Soldiers in Hitler's Army*. New York: Harcourt Brace Jovanovich, 1975, pp.70–71.

41 Sometimes also spelled as 'Vrba'. Werba was an ethnic German Russian who was born in pre-revolutionary Russia. During the First World War and during the Russian Civil War that followed, he had served as a Czarist officer. After the pro-Czarist White Army lost the civil war, he emigrated to the Sudetenland in Czechoslovakia. He began to work for the Abwehr (the intelligence department of the of the German Armed Forces) in 1938.

42 Janusz Piekalkiewicz. *The Cavalry of World War II*. New York: Stein and Day, 1980, p.218.

43 Muñoz, *German SS, Police, and Auxiliary Forces in Poland*, op. cit., p.33.

44 Hoffmann, op. cit., p.143.

45 *Generalleutnant* Hubert Lendle became the *Kommandierender General der Sicherheitstruppen und Befehlshaber* in *Heeresgruppe Mitte* from 5 July 1942 until 18 November 1944.

46 Dr. Leo W.G. Niehorster. *The Royal Hungarian Army, 1920–1945*. New York: Europa Books, 1998, p.167. Only parts of this division were employed, as the bulk of the unit was located in the city of Kobrin.

47 Muñoz, *German SS, Police, and Auxiliary Forces in Poland*, op. cit., p.33.

48 Heide-Marie Gruenthal. *Nacht Über Europa: Die Faschistische Okkupationspolitik in Polen (1939–1945)*. Köln: Pahl-Rugenstein Verlag, 1989, p.300.

49 Hoffmann, op. cit., p.144.

50 Of this number, 1,092 were German manufactured, 1,025 were Russian Negat rifles, and forty-three were Dutch. The forty-three Dutch rifles were all that remained of the approximately 1,000 Dutch rifles that were given to the men in the corps in early 1943. Perhaps they had been withdrawn because only 35,000 rounds of ammunition had been distributed for them.

51 Of this figure, thirty-three were German MP-40s and 135 were the popular Russian-made PPS.

52 Hoffmann, op. cit., p.153.

53 Ibid., p.136.

54 Ibid., p.152.

55 The Vlasov Army was led by Russian turncoat Andrei Vlasov and was composed of two divisions, a brigade and smaller elements made up of pro-German Russian volunteers. In a twist of fate, the men of the Vlasov Army never fought the Red Army (except for one episode along the Oder River front in 1945). Instead, as the war was coming to an end, its two principal divisions moved towards Prague, the Czech capital, and after some negotiations assisted Czech patriots in fighting the Germans

to free the city. The reason for this about-face was a last-minute attempt by Vlasov and his cohorts to persuade Western leaders in order to avoid being handed over to Stalin for punishment. The plan failed and Vlasov and his men were handed over to the NKVD who, after many show trials, exacted vengeance on the collaborators.

56 Pronin, op. cit., p.229.

57 Thorwald, op. cit., p.78.

58 Taras Borovets managed to evade capture by the Russians. He made his way to the American lines and asked for political asylum. Under a plan to recruit former Nazis because of their knowledge of the Soviet Union and its people, 'Operation Paperclip' brought thousands of Nazis and pro-Nazi individuals into the United States as 'refugees'. Borovets was one of them. He died peacefully in New York City in 1981.

59 Hanusiak, op. cit., p.230.

60 Between 1939–1842 this battalion had a total of four commanders: *Major der Schutzpolizei* Lüpke, Schneider, Walkhoff and Perling. As per Heinrich Himmler's decree of 9 July 1942, stipulating the creation of more police regiments, *Polizei-Bataillon 51* became the *I. Bataillon der Polizeiregiment 14.*

61 *SS-Totenkopf Reiterstandarte* only contained four cavalry squadrons, basically a battalion. In fact, its strength on 15 December 1939 was 587 officers, NCOs, and enlisted men. The unit was stationed in Radom.

62 Barry C. Rosch, *Luftwaffe Codes, Markings and Units, 1939–1945*. Atglen: Schiffer Military / Aviation History, 1995, p.168.

63 Ibid.

64 In 1943 *Polizei Reiter Abteilung 3* was led by *Major der Schutzpolizei* Hahn. This police cavalry battalion was stationed in Lublin, although it was organised and initially formed in Posen (Poznan) in May 1943, using three police cavalry squadrons. It was employed in helping to crush the Warsaw Uprising until withdrawn on 5 October 1944.

65 In June 1944 *SS-Polizeiregiment 17* would be attached to *SS Kampfgruppe von Gottberg.*

66 NARA Microfilm T-175, Roll 140, Frame 2667623.

67 This was in response to the so-called Zamosc Uprising.

68 The operation took place sometime in the third week of March.

69 A platoon of *Sicherheitspolizei und Sicherheitsdienst* men (from Radon) was employed under *SS-Untersturmführer* Flath.

70 *Polizei Reiter Abteilung* 3 translates to '3rd Police Cavalry Battalion'.

71 Mieczyslaw Juchniewicz, *Poles in the European Resistance Movement 1939–1945*. Warsaw: Interpress Publishers, 1972, p.123.

72 Muñoz, et al., *Hitler's White Russians*, op. cit., pp.359–61.

73 Ivan Kononov was the commander of the *5. Don-Kosaken-Kavallerie-Regiment*, which originated as *Kosaken Kavallerie Bataillon 102. Kosaken Kavallerie Bataillon 102* was, in actuality, a regiment in strength.

74 Leonid Grenkevitch, *The Soviet Partisan Movement 1941–1944*. Frank Cass: London, 1999, p.235.

75 Werner Regenberg, *Armoured Vehicles and Units of the German Order Police 1936–1945*. Schiffer Military History: Atglen, 2002, p.85.

76 Schumann et al., op. cit., p.386.

77 This Ukrainian *Schuma* battalion became a part of *Polizei-Schützenregiment 32* in September 1943. Therefore, we can assume that at least part of *Polizei-Schützenregiment 32* took part in this anti-partisan operation.

78 This force amounted to some 4,000 SS and police troops.

79 *SS-Polizeiregiment 14* had been reformed using the surviving *II. Bataillon*, creating two new *I.* and *III. Bataillone.* The unit was reformed in Marseille, France, in the spring of 1943, and was briefly sent to southern Poland in December 1943 before being transferred to Slovenia in February 1944.

80 The operation took place in the second week of March 1944.

81 German forces gathered for this sweep were grouped into *Kampfgruppe Gresser*, so named after *Oberstleutnant der Schutzpolizei* Erwin Gresser, the commander of *Polizei-Bataillon 307*, which eventually became the *III. Bataillon der SS-Polizeiregiment 24.*

82 The commander of this unit was *Major der Gendarmerie* Erich Schweiger.

83 This battalion was in reserve and was moved to Turbobin to cut off a possible access of retreat for the partisans.

84 About 30,000 troops took part in these two large-scale operations.

85 Muñoz, *German SS, Police, and Auxiliary Forces in Poland*, op cit., p.33.

86 This was still the old ex-*Schutzmannschaft Bataillon 203* acting as part of *Polizei-Schützenregiment 32.*

87 The composition of the *Korück* commands varied greatly from week to week and month to month. The commander of *Korück 532*, as of 7 September 1944, was *Generalleutnant* Friedrich-Gustav Bernhard. He led this *Korück* command from 13 April 1942 to 8 May 1945. On 11 September 1944), *Korück 532* was composed of the following forces: *Sicherungs-Bataillon 242, Landesschützen-Bataillone 238, 551,* and *981, Infanterie Ausbildungs Bataillon 500, Gepanzert Zug Nr. 30, Turkistanische Infanterie Bataillon 786, 1. und 4. Kompanie der Wolgatatar Baupionier Bataillon 830.* Verstärkunge (reinforcements): *Gepanzert Zug 'Polko' (Armoured Train 'Polko'), Landesschützen-Bataillon 234* and *Ost Bataillon 308.*

88 Sixteen officers and 850 men.

89 The reference is to auxiliary police recruited from Ukraine and the Baltic states.

90 Yad Vashem Archives, Jerusalem. Document No. PS-1061.

91 Sybil Milton, transl., *The Stroop Report*. New York: Pantheon Books, 1979.

92 This German division was formed on 24 September 1942 in Bialystok from *Divisionskommando z.b.V. Bialystok*. The division contained the following units: *Grenadier Ersatz und Ausbildungs Regiment 11, Grenadier Ersatz und Ausbildungs Regiment 491, Grenadier Ersatz Regiment 521, Pionier Ersatz und Ausbildungs Bataillon 311, Bau Pionier Ersatz und Ausbildungs Bataillon 1, Fahrzeug-Ersatz und Ausbildungs-Abteilung 1* and *Kraftfahr-Ersatz und Ausbildungs-Abteilung 1*. This division was relocated to the town of Osterode, in the Harz Mountains of Lower Saxony, in autumn 1944.

93 Eckman et al., op. cit., p.75.

94 Martin Gilbert, *Atlas of the Holocaust*. Toronto: Lester Publishing Limited, 1993, p.164.

95 Survivors of the Revolt – Sobibor Interviews, www.sobiborinterviews.nl.

96 Ibid.

Chapter 4. The guerrilla war in Poland in 1944

1 As a point of reference, the city of Kielce is 22km north of this town.

2 George J. Lerski. *Historical Dictionary of Poland, 966–1945*. Westport: Greenwood Press, 1996, p.251.

3 Interview of Roman Polanski by Catherine Bernstein for TV series *Grands Entretiens*.

4 Präg et al., op. cit., p.733.

5 Joachim Hoffmann, *Deutsche und Kalmyken 1942 bis 1945*. Friedberg: Verlag Rombach, 1986, p.144.

6 In 1942, *Oberfeldkommandantur 226* was renamed *Oberfeldkommandantur Krakau*.

7 Antonio Muñoz, ed., *The East Came West: Muslim, Hindu, and Buddhist Volunteers in the German Armed Forces 1941–1945*. New York: Europa Books, 2001, p.163.

8 On 2 November 1943 this battalion was renamed *Infanterie-Divisions-Nachrichten-Abteilung 349*.

9 *Arko XIII* is an abbreviation for '*Artillerie Kommando XIII*' (Artillery Commander 13).

10 Philip Warren Blood, *Bandenbekämpfung: Nazi occupation security in Eastern Europe and Soviet Russia 1942–45*. A thesis submitted to fulfil the requirements for a Doctor of Philosophy degree. Cranfield University: Department of Defense Management and Security Analysis Security Studies Institute 2001, p.261.

11 At this time, the regiment was led by *Oberstleutnant der Schutzpolizei* Otto Gieseke.

12 Piotrowski, op. cit., p.185.

13 Although the Polish source mentions 'Vlasovites', referring to anti-Stalinist and pro-German ROA (Russian Army of Liberation) troops, they more than likely encountered a unit of the *Kaminski Brigade*.

Chapter 5. The Warsaw Uprising, 1944

1 Tessin, *Verbände und Truppen*, op. cit., Vol. 16, p.196.

2 'Soliborz' can also be spelled 'Zoliborz'.

3 Präg, et al., op. cit., p.895.

4 Infantry company armed to the teeth with the *Panzerschreck* (German bazooka), including numerous *Panzerfaust* (single shot) anti-tank weapons.

5 This company contained the Jagdpanzer 38 tank destroyer, more commonly known as the Hetzer. The definition of the word 'Hetzer' is any of the following: 'baiter', 'chaser', or 'hunter'. The closest definition of the word is a hunter employing dogs. In any event, the term was meant to indicate that this small tank destroyer was designed to hunt tanks.

6 While the fighting was taking place, his regiment received 2,500 troops, of which 1,900 came from the SS prison camp at Matzkau near Danzig. At the end of the uprising his battalion at Warsaw had only 648 men left in its ranks.

7 At the time, the *Kaminski Brigade* was in the process of being absorbed into the Waffen SS. The 1st Regiment, which took part in the battle, was renamed *Waffen-Grenadier-Regiment der-SS Nr. 72* and was led by Colonel Ivan Frolov.

8 Lukas, op. cit., p.197.

9 Hans von Krannhals, *Der Warschauer Aufstand, 1944*. Frankfurt am Main: Bernard and Gräfe Verlag, 1962, p.123.

10 Lukas, op cit., pp.201–202.

11 Ready, op. cit., p.354.

12 Both battlegroups would later be reinforced with additional units.

13 This regiment was established as a blanket headquarters for *Polizei Wachbataillon I Posen,* and *Polizei Wachbataillon XX Posen.* These two police guard battalions were sent to help crush the Warsaw Uprising under the command of *Polizeiregiment Posen.*

14 *Nachricht A.O.K. 9. Die im Fernschreiben B.d.O. i. G.G., Ia Tgb.-Nr. 3717/44 (G) vom 29.9.44 beantragte Herauslösung der SS. Pol. Reiter-Abt. III und des Schuma-Batl. (lit.) Nr. 252 konnte im Hinblick auf die Kämpfe im Raum*

Warschau und die dem Obergruppenführer von dem Bach vom Reichsführer SS für den Einsatz der Kräfte verliehenen Sondervollmachten bisher nicht durchgeführt werden.

15 The commander of this Lithuanian battalion was *Oberstleutnant* Jonas Junkevičius, while the German liaison officer was *Hauptmann der Schutzpolizei* Schröder.

16 J. K. Zawodny, *Nothing but Honor: The Story of the Warsaw Uprising, 1944.* Stanford: Hoover Institution Press, 1979, p.57.

17 Neufeldt, et al., Part II, p.11.

18 This was *Kosaken Kavallerie Sicherungs Abteilung III. der Sicherungs Regiment 57,* which had operated from time to time in the Bryansk region alongside the *Kaminski Brigade* and other indigenous anti-guerrilla forces.

19 Neulen, op. cit., p.324.

20 Antonio Muñoz, *Forgotten Legions Booklet. Additional Data of Information.* Privately Published: New York, 1997, p.20.

21 Tessin, *Verbände und Truppen,* op. cit., p.108.

22 This police regiment was stationed in Posen (Poznan) and was composed of only one battalion: *Polizei Ersatz Bataillon Posen.*

23 Carlos Caballero Jurado, *Commandos en el Caucaso: La Unidad Especial Bergmann y Voluntarios Caucasianos en el Ejercito Aleman, 1941–45.* Granada: Garcia Hispan, Editor, 1995, p.202.

24 The Powisle region bordered the Vistula River, which crossed through the Polish capital and lay directly across from the Praga region, on the east bank.

25 Adam Borkiewicz, *Powstanie warszawskie 1944: zarys działań natury wojskowej,* Warszawa: PAX, 1962, p.108.

26 *Schwer-Nebelwerfer-Batterie 201* arrived in Warsaw on the evening of 6-7 August 1944. Another unit, *Stellungswerfer-Regiment 102,* arrived on the same four trains. Both units were unloaded at Pruszkow station.

27 This unit employed four *Sturmmörserwagen 606/4 mit 38 cm RW 61.* The large-calibre 380mm rocket-propelled mortar was mounted on to a Tiger I chassis. Only eighteen of these monster vehicles were ever built during the war. They were distributed to two units: *Sturm Morser Kompanie 1000,* which saw action in Warsaw and along the Vistula and Oder River, and *Sturm Morser Kompanie 1001,* which saw service during the Battle of the Bulge in December 1944).

28 Of this number, about half survived to be released when the Home Army surrendered on 2 October 1944. The Polish citizens of Warsaw suffered the most, with 200,000–250,000 men killed, most either from the 3,500–4,000 tons of artillery shells that landed on the city during the siege, or through massacres committed mainly by SS, SD, police units, and the Kaminski and Dirlewanger formations.

Chapter 6. Conclusions: Was the Nazi occupation of Poland a failure?

1 The Republic of Myanmar was formerly called Burma. Myanmar is currently run by a military junta.

2 The incident, which occurred in 1942 near Minsk, was witnessed and corroborated by Germans and non-Germans alike.

3 Gabriel Baker. *Spare No One: Mass Violence in Roman Warfare.* New York: Rowman & Littlefield, 2021, pp.1–10.

4 Antonio Muñoz, *For Croatia and Christ: The Croatian Army in World War II, 1941–1945.* New York: Privately published, 1996, p.12.

Appendix I. Glossary of German military and political terms

1 For example, when the German *6. Armee* surrendered at Stalingrad, the Red Army captured approximately 91,000 soldiers. They were force-marched to Siberian gulags. Many died along the way. From these camps, only about 3,000 survived to return to Germany between 1953 and 1956.

Appendix III. German commanders of major police formations

1 *BdO im Generalgouvernement, Tagesbefehl Nr. 52 v. 13.11.1941; BdO im Generalgouvernement, Tagesbefehl Nr. 56 v. 05.12.1941.*

2 When Fleckner and his regiment relocated to Carinthia, he and his unit came under the command of the *Höhere SS und Polizeiführer 'Alpenland'*, led by *SS-Obergruppemfuhrer und General der Polizei* Erwin Rösner. The *III. Bataillon/SS-Polizei-Regiment 13* was rebuilt. By May the *I. Bataillon/SS-Polizei-Regiment 13* and *II. Bataillon/SS-PolizeiRegiment 13* were stationed in Carinthia, while *III. Bataillon/SS-Polizei-Regiment 13* was located in Lower Styria.

3 Hermann Franz. *Gebirgsjäger der Polizei. Polizei-Gebirgsjäger-Regiment 18 und Polizei-Gebirgs-Artillerieabteilung 1942–1945.* Bad Nauheim: Mielke Verlag, 1963, p.180.

4 Silgalis, *Latvian Legion*, p.115.

UNIT INDEX

German Formations

Luftwaffe Air & Ground Units-

Rear Area Commands, Army Groups, Army Detachments, and Military Districts

Regiments

Reserve & Replacement Formations-

Fortress Units-

Special & Heavy Units-

Police Formations

Police Battalions-

Police Batteries, Squadrons & Companies-

Gendarmerie Platoons-

Battlegroups-

Schutzmannschaft Formations-

Eastern Volunteer Formations-

NAME INDEX